Advanced Data Science and Analytics with Python

The second edition of *Advanced Data Science and Analytics with Python* reflects the rapid transformation of artificial intelligence in recent years. While preserving its practical, modular structure, this edition significantly expands coverage of the techniques shaping modern AI practice.

The deep learning chapter has been substantially broadened to include reinforcement learning and generative adversarial networks, alongside a fully developed exploration of transformer architectures. Generative AI now takes centre stage, with dedicated coverage of self-attention, BERT, GPT, large language model evaluation and API-based interaction. Emerging agentic systems are introduced as part of the evolving AI landscape. Natural language processing has been enhanced with word embeddings, contextual representations and vector search, while network analysis now includes graph representation learning and embedding techniques. The chapter on data product deployment has been strengthened with modern Core ML workflows and new coverage of on-device Foundation Models, bridging experimentation and production.

Fully updated for the contemporary Python ecosystem, this edition equips practitioners with the tools and architectural understanding required to design, build and deploy intelligent systems in today's AI-driven world.

Jesús Rogel-Salazar is a lead data scientist, founder of RogueLoop, working for companies such as Ortus Technologies, Tympa Health Technologies, Barclays, AKQA, IBM Data Science Studio and Dow Jones. He is a visiting researcher at the Imperial College Business School, UK and a member of the School of Physics, Astronomy and Mathematics at the University of Hertfordshire, UK.

Chapman & Hall/CRC

Data Mining and Knowledge Discovery Series

Series Editor: Vipin Kumar

Data Mining
A Tutorial-Based Primer, Second Edition
Richard J. Roiger

Data Mining with R
Learning with Case Studies, Second Edition
Luís Torgo

Social Networks with Rich Edge Semantics
Quan Zheng and David Skillicorn

Large-Scale Machine Learning in the Earth Sciences
Ashok N. Srivastava, Ramakrishna Nemani, and Karsten Steinhaeuser

Data Science and Analytics with Python
Jesús Rogel-Salazar

Feature Engineering for Machine Learning and Data Analytics
Guozhu Dong and Huan Liu

Human Capital Systems, Analytics, and Data Mining
Robert C. Hughes

Industrial Applications of Machine Learning
Pedro Larrañaga et al

Automated Data Analysis Using Excel
Second Edition
Brian D. Bissett

Knowledge Guided Machine Learning: Accelerating Discovery using Scientific Knowledge and Data
Edited by Anuj Karpatne, Ramakrishnan Kannan, Vipin Kumar

Demystifying AI
Data Science and Machine Learning Using IBM SPSS Modeler
Dothang Truong

Exploratory Data Analysis Using R
Second Edition
Ronald K. Pearson

Advanced Data Science and Analytics with Python
Second Edition
Jesús Rogel-Salazar

For more information about this series please visit:

https://www.routledge.com/Chapman--HallCRC-Data-Mining-and-Knowledge-Discovery-Series/book-series/CHDAMINODIS

Advanced Data Science and Analytics with Python
Second Edition

Jesús Rogel-Salazar

CRC Press
Taylor & Francis Group
Boca Raton London New York

CRC Press is an imprint of the
Taylor & Francis Group, an **informa** business
A CHAPMAN & HALL BOOK

Designed cover image: Jesús Rogel-Salazar

Second edition published 2027
by CRC Press
2385 NW Executive Center Drive, Suite 320, Boca Raton FL 33431

and by CRC Press
4 Park Square, Milton Park, Abingdon, Oxon, OX14 4RN

CRC Press is an imprint of Taylor & Francis Group, LLC

First edition published by CRC Press 2020

Library of Congress Cataloging-in-Publication Data
Names: Rogel-Salazar, Jesús author
Title: Advanced data science and analytics with Python / Jesús
Rogel-Salazar.
Description: Second edition. | Boca Raton FL : CRC Press, 2026. | Series:
Chapman & Hall/CRC data mining & knowledge discovery series | Includes
bibliographical references.
Identifiers: LCCN 2026012305 (print) | LCCN 2026012306 (ebook) | ISBN
9781041103608 hardback | ISBN 9781041102854 paperback | ISBN
9781003654612 ebook
Subjects: LCSH: Data mining | Python (Computer program language) |
Databases | Artificial intelligence
Classification: LCC QA76.9.D343 R637 2026 (print) | LCC QA76.9.D343
(ebook)
LC record available at https://lccn.loc.gov/2026012305
LC ebook record available at https://lccn.loc.gov/2026012306

ISBN: 978-1-041-10360-8 (hbk)
ISBN: 978-1-041-10285-4 (pbk)
ISBN: 978-1-003-65461-2 (ebk)

DOI: 10.1201/9781003654612

Typeset in URW PalladioL-Roma Roman
by KnowledgeWorks Global Ltd.

Publisher's note: This book has been prepared from camera-ready copy provided by the authors.

To A. J. Johnson

Then. Now. Always.

Contents

List of Figures

List of Tables

Preface to the Second Edition

WRITING A SECOND EDITION IS an opportunity to revisit ideas, address loose threads, and expand a story that continues to unfold, particularly when that story involves a field as fast-moving as data science and artificial intelligence. This edition of *Advanced Data Science and Analytics with Python* follows hot on the heels of the revised second edition of the companion volume *Data Science and Analytics with Python*[1], and it seeks to complement it by delving deeper into the topics that have grown in importance in recent years, while maintaining the original ethos of the book.

[1] Rogel-Salazar, J. (2025). *Data Science and Analytics with Python*. Chapman & Hall/CRC Data Mining and Knowledge Discovery Series. CRC Press.

A lot has happened since the first edition of this book: Transformers are no longer just shape-shifting robots, they are modern AI architectures that have shifted the field. Similarly, generative AI (GenAI) has entered the mainstream capturing the imagination of millions of us, and reinforcement learning has gone from research to revenue. These shifts demanded a response. In this edition, we revisit the deep learning chapter and split it into two, substantially extend the coverage of advanced architectures including not only convolutional and recurrent neural networks, but also reinforcement learning, generative adversarial networks (GANs), and transformers and large language models.

At the same time, the foundations remain strong. Python is still our weapon of choice, and libraries like scikit-learn[2], pandas[3], Numpy[4], and their friends continue to serve us well. However, the ecosystem has evolved—and so too has the code in this book. All examples have been updated to reflect more recent versions of Python, and versions used are shown below.

[2] Pedregosa, F., G. Varoquaux, A. Gramfort, V. Michel, et al. (2011). Scikit-learn: Machine learning in Python. *Journal of Machine Learning Research 12*, 2825–2830.
[3] McKinney, W. (2012). *Python for Data Analysis: Data Wrangling with Pandas, NumPy, and IPython*. O'Reilly Media.
[4] Scientific Computing Tools for Python (2013). NumPy. `http://www.numpy.org`

Python - 3.12+	pandas - 2.2+
NumPy - 3.2+	Scikit-learn - 1.5.1 and 1.6+
SciPy - 1.15+	StatsModels - 0.14+
BeautifulSoup - 4.12+	NLTK - 3.9+
NetworkX - 3.4+	Keras - 3.9+
TensorFlow - 2.18+	

Like its predecessor, this book is written for technical readers, early-career data scientists, analysts, and developers, who already have some experience with machine learning and want to push further. You do not need to read Volume 1 to dive in here, but if you have, you will find familiar terrain peppered with new landmarks.

As ever, we keep the tone conversational (with the occasional SciFi and popular culture puns) and focus on practical understanding rather than academic formality. We are here to use machine learning and analytics to solve a problem—not to create theoretical monuments that no one visits. The examples were tested using Python 3.12. I continue to recommend the Anaconda distribution[5], although other distributions will work just as well.

[5] Anaconda (2025). Anaconda Distribution. `https://www.anaconda.com/download/`

The structure of the book remains modular. Each chapter is as self-contained as possible, and the topics range from time series to natural language processing (NLP), from network analysis to deploying models as full-fledged data products.

We still show code in boxes, margin notes abound, and the metaphor of the Jackalope—curious, inventive, perhaps a bit mythical—remains. This edition is still not a cookbook, nor a manual; it is a field guide for a practitioner in motion. As with the first edition, this work is indebted to many friends, collaborators, and Jackalopes who challenged assumptions, tested code, and helped shape the narrative. Any mistakes that remain are entirely mine, and the coffee's.

Thank you once again for joining me on this journey through data science, machine learning and artificial intelligence. May your models generalise well, your deployments go smoothly, and your curiosity remain unquenchable.

London, UK *Dr Jesús Rogel-Salazar*

May 2026

Preface

WRITING A BOOK IS AN exhilarating experience, if at times a bit hard and maddening. This companion to *Data Science and Analytics with Python*[6] is the result of arguments with myself about writing something to cover a few of the areas that were not included in that first volume, largely due to space/time constraints. Like the previous book, this one exists thanks to the discussions, stand-ups, brainstorms and eventual implementations of algorithms and data science projects carried out with many colleagues and friends. The satisfaction of seeing happy users/customers with products they can rely on is, and will continue to be, a motivation for me.

[6] Rogel-Salazar, J. (2017). *Data Science and Analytics with Python*. Chapman & Hall/CRC Data Mining and Knowledge Discovery Series. CRC Press.

The subjects discussed in this book are complementary and a follow-up to the ones covered in Volume 1. The intended audience for this book is still composed of data analysts and early-career data scientists with some experience in programming and with a background in statistical modelling. In this case, however, the expectation is that they have already covered some areas of machine learning and data analytics. Although I will refer to the previous book in

The book and its companion are a good reference for seasoned practitioners too.

parts where some knowledge is assumed, the book is written to be read independently from Volume 1. As the title suggests, this book continues to use Python[7] as a tool to train, test and implement machine learning models and algorithms. Nonetheless, Python does not live in isolation, and in the last chapter of this book we touch upon the usage of Swift[8] as a programming language to help us deploy our machine learning models.

[7] Python Software Foundation (1995). Python reference manual. `http://www.python.org`

[8] Apple Inc. (2014). Swift programming language. `https://swift.org`

Python continues to be, in my view, a very useful tool. The number of modules, packages and contributions that Pythonistas have made to the rest of the community make it a worthwhile programming language to learn. It is no surprise that the number of Python users continues to grow. Similarly, the ecosystem of the language is also evolving: From the efforts to bring Python 3.x to be the version of choice, through to the development of the computational environment that is the Jupyter Notebook and its evolution, the JupyterLab.

Visit `https://jupyterlab.readthedocs.io` for further information.

For those reasons, we will continue using some excellent libraries, such as scikit-learn[9], pandas[10], numpy[11] and others. After all, we have seen Nobel Prize-winning research being supported by Python, as have been a number of commercial enterprises, including consultancies, startups and established companies. The decision to use Python for this second volume is therefore not just one of convenience and continuity, but a conscious adoption that I hope will support you too.

[9] Pedregosa, F., G. Varoquaux, A. Gramfort, V. Michel, et al. (2011). Scikit-learn: Machine learning in Python. *Journal of Machine Learning Research 12*, 2825–2830.

[10] McKinney, W. (2012). *Python for Data Analysis: Data Wrangling with Pandas, NumPy, and IPython.* O'Reilly Media.

[11] Scientific Computing Tools for Python (2013). NumPy. `http://www.numpy.org`

As I mentioned above, the book covers aspects that were necessarily left out in the previous volume; however, the readers in mind are still technical people interested in moving into the data science and analytics world. I have tried to keep the same tone as in the first book, peppering the pages with some bits and bobs of popular culture, science fiction and indeed Monty Python puns. The aim is still to focus on showing the concepts and ideas behind popular algorithms and their use. As before, we are not delving, in general, into exhaustive implementations from scratch, and instead relying on existing modules.

I sincerely hope the most obscure ones do make you revisit their excellent work.

The examples contained here have been tested in Python 3.7 under MacOS, Linux and Windows 10. We do recommend that you move on from Python 2. For reference, the versions of some of the packages used in the book are as follows:

Maintenance for Python 2 has stopped as of January 2020.

Python - 3.5.2	pandas - 0.25
NumPy - 1.17.2	Scikit-learn - 0.21
SciPy - 1.3.1	StatsModels - 0.10
BeautifulSoup - 4.8.1	NLTK - 3.4.5
NetworkX - 2.4	Keras - 2.2.4
TensorFlow - 1.14.0	

As before, I am using the Anaconda Python distribution[12] provided by Anaconda (formerly known as Continuum Analytics). Remember that there are other ways of obtaining

[12] Anaconda (2025). Anaconda Distribution. `https://www.anaconda.com/download/`

Python as well as other versions of the software: For instance, directly from the Python Software Foundation or from package managers such as Homebrew. In Chapters 4 and 5 , we create conda environments to install and maintain software relevant to the discussions for those chapters, and you are more than welcome to use other virtual environment maintainers too.

Python Software Foundation `https://www.python.org`

Homebrew `http://brew.sh`

Note the chapter numbers have changed in this new edition, the old Chapter 5 is now 6.

We show computer code by enclosing it in a box as follows:

```
> 1 + 1 # Example of computer code


 2
```

We use a diple (>) to denote the command line terminal prompt shown in the Python shell. Keeping to the look and feel of the previous book, we use margin notes, such as the one that appears to the right of this paragraph, to highlight certain areas or commands, as well as to provide some useful comments and remarks.

This is an example of the margin notes used throughout this book.

As mentioned before, the book can be read independently from the previous volume, and indeed each chapter is as self-contained as possible. I would also like to remind you that writing code is not very dissimilar to writing poetry. If I asked that each of us write a poem about the beauty of a Jackalope, we would all come up with something. Some would write odes to Jackalopes that would be remembered by generations to come; some of us would complete the task with a couple of rhymes. In that way, the code presented here may not be award-winning poetry, but the aim, I hope,

I hope Sor Juana would forgive my comparison.

will be met. I would welcome to hear about your poems. Do get in touch!

We start in Chapter 1 with a discussion about time series data. We see how pandas has us covered to deal with the fiendish matter of date data types. We learn how to use time series data similar to that found in stock markets and see how pandas lets us carry out resampling, slicing and dicing, filtering, aggregating and plotting this kind of data. In terms of modelling, in this chapter we see how moving averages and exponential smoothing let us get a first approach at forecasting future values of the series based on previous observations. We look at autoregression and see how it can be used to model time series.

Time series data and analysis is covered in Chapter 1.

In Chapter 2, we take a look at processing text data containing natural language. We look at how we can obtain data from the web and scrape data that otherwise would be out of reach to us. We take a look at the use of regular expressions to capture specific patterns in a piece of text and learn how to deal with Unicode. Looking at text data in this way leads us to the analysis of language, culminating with topic modelling as an unsupervised learning task to identify the possible subjects or topics that are addressed in a set of documents.

Natural language processing is covered in Chapter 2.

In Chapter 3, we look into some fundamental concepts used in the analysis of networks, whether social or otherwise. We look at graph theory as a way to discover relationships encoded in networks such as small-world ones. We have a chance to talk about measures such as degree centrality,

Chapter 3 covers the use of graphs and network analysis, a topic that will inevitably make us more social.

closeness, betweenness, and others. We even do this with characters from a galaxy far, far away.

:)

Chapter 4 is probably the deepest chapter of all, pun definitely intended. It is here where we turn our attention to the "unreasonable effectiveness" of neural networks. We look at the general architecture of a neural network and build our own from scratch. Starting with feedforward networks, we move on to understand the famous backpropagation algorithm. We get a chance to look at the effect of the number of layers as well as the number of nodes in each of them. We then move on to the implementation of more complex, deeper architectures, such as convolutional and recurrent neural networks.

Chapter 4 looks at neural networks and deep learning.

Finally, in Chapter 5, we look at the perennial issue of bringing our models, predictions and solutions to our customers, users and stakeholders. Data products are the focus of our discussion, and we see how the availability, processing, meaning and understanding of data should be at the heart of our efforts. We then look at the possibility of bringing our models to the hands of our users via the implementation of a model inside a mobile device application in an Apple device such as an iPhone via Core ML.

Remember old Chapter 5 is now 6. It looks at the deployment of machine learning models.

Remember that *there is no such thing as a perfect model, only good enough ones.* The techniques presented in this book, and the companion volume, are not the end of the story, they are the beginning. The data that you have to deal with will guide your story. Do not let the anthropomorphic language of machine learning fool you. Models that *learn, see, understand* and *recognise* are as good as the data used to build them, and as blind as the human making decisions based on them. Use your Jackalope data science skills to inform your work.

As I said before, this book is the product of many interactions over many moons. I am indebted to many people who have directly and indirectly influenced the words you have before you. Any errors, omissions or simplifications are mine. As always, I am grateful to my family and friends for putting up with me when I excuse myself with the old phrase:*"I have to do some book... I am behind"*. Thank you for putting up with another *small* project from this crazy physicist!

You know who you are!

Do some work on the book of course...

London, UK *Dr Jesús Rogel-Salazar*

March 2020

Reader's Guide

THIS BOOK IS INTENDED TO be a companion to any Jackalope Data Scientist interested in extending their journey after exploring the foundations laid out in *Data Science and Analytics with Python*[13]. This second edition of the advanced volume builds upon that base, offering deeper explorations of modern AI topics, while remaining approachable and practical.

[13] Rogel-Salazar, J. (2025). *Data Science and Analytics with Python*. Chapman & Hall/CRC Data Mining and Knowledge Discovery Series. CRC Press.

The chapters are modular and self-contained, meaning you can dive in wherever your curiosity leads. If you are looking for guidance here is a suggested path through the material:

- Managers and readers curious about Data Science:
  - Chapter 6 discusses the deployment of machine learning models and the creation of data products, a must-read for understanding how these models go beyond the lab and into the hands of users.
  - Look into Chapters 1 and 3 of the companion volume to get a grasp of fundamental concepts like the data science process and basic visualisation.
  - A new addition to Chapter 6 is the use of Apple's

Foundation Models for the deployment of language models in apps. Take a look.

- Beginners (with some Python and ML background):
  - Chapters 2 and 3 of the companion book provide a gentle yet solid foundation.
  - Chapter 1 in this book is a great place to start exploring pandas and applied statistical modelling with time series data.
  - Chapter 2 introduces natural language processing, now enhanced with modern such as word embeddings, which make it powerful and exciting.
- Experienced readers and returning Jackalopes:
  - Navigate by subject or technology depending on what you are exploring:
  - **Time Series Analysis** (Chapter 1):
    * Time-aware data handling
    * Classical forecasting methods including the use of Prophet
    * Stationarity and seasonality
    * Introductory machine learning for temporal data and cross-validation
  - **Natural Language Processing** (Chapter 2):
    * Web scraping and text cleaning
    * Topic modelling and tokenisation
    * Word embeddings and contextual representations
    * Vector search

- **Network and Graph Analysis** (Chapter 3):
  * Graph theory foundations
  * Centrality, clustering, and visualisation
  * Case studies in social and fictional networks
  * Graph representation learning and embeddings
- **Deep Learning** (Chapter 4):
  * Neural networks from scratch
  * Convolutional neural networks
  * Reinforcement learning
  * Generative adversarial networks
- **Generative AI** (Chapter 5):
  * Recurrent neural networks
  * Long short-term memory networks
  * Transformers, attention, and generative models
  * Large language model evaluation
- **ML Deployment and Productisation** (Chapter 6):
  * Data products
  * Core ML and Python
  * Apple's Foundation Models

Whether you are building smarter products, exploring the latest AI tools, or brushing up on essential techniques, I hope this guide helps you plot your own path through the second edition. Happy exploring!

About the Author

Dr Jesús Rogel-Salazar is a Lead Data Scientist with experience in the field working for companies such as The Ortus Group, TympaHealth, Barclays Bank, AKQA, IBM Data Science Studio, Dow Jones and others. He is a visiting researcher at the Department of Physics, and the Business School at Imperial College London, UK and a member of the School of Physics, Astronomy and Mathematics at the University of Hertfordshire, UK. He obtained his doctorate in Physics at Imperial College London for work on quantum atom optics and ultra-cold matter.

He has held a position as senior lecturer in mathematics as well as a consultant and data scientist in the financial industry since 2006. He is the author of the book *Essential MATLAB and Octave* and the companion book to this volume *Advanced Data Science and Analytics with Python* and *Statistics and Data Visualisation with Python*, also published with CRC Press. His interests include mathematical modelling, data science and optimisation in a wide range of applications including optics, quantum mechanics, data journalism, telematics, fintech and healthtech.

Other Books by the Same Author

- **Data Science and Analytics with Python, 2nd Ed.**
  CRC Press, 2025, 9781032772523 (hardback), 9781032772493 (paperback), 9781003482062 (eBook).
  The second edition of *Data Science and Analytics with Python* builds on the widespread success of its predecessor, reflecting the rapid growth and transformation of the AI and machine learning landscape. Updated to incorporate the latest features in popular Python libraries such as scikit-learn, pandas, and numpy, the book introduces expanded content on generative AI, along with critical discussions on explainability, fairness, and transparency in AI systems. Widely adopted by both practitioners and universities, the book remains a practical, standalone resource for data analysts and aspiring data scientists, offering both foundational knowledge and insights into cutting-edge developments in the field.

- **Statistics and Data Visualisation with Python**
  CRC Press, 2023, 9780367749361 (hardback), 9780367744519 (paperback), 9781003160359 (eBook).
  This book is designed to bridge the gap for graduates and

business practitioners seeking to apply or refresh their statistical skills within the context of data science and analytics. Whether readers are revisiting statistics after some time or encountering it for the first time in a practical setting, *Statistics and Data Visualisation with Python* offers a clear, structured path into the subject. Beginning with the fundamentals of Python programming and data analysis, the book builds a solid foundation in statistical methods, enabling readers to understand core concepts in inferential statistics and hypothesis testing. These skills are essential for modern applications in business analytics, statistical modelling, and both traditional and applied machine learning.

- **Essential MATLAB® and Octave**
  CRC Press, 2014, ISBN 9781138413115 (hardback), 9781482234633 (paperback), 9780429170355 (eBook). Widely used by scientists and engineers, well-established MATLAB® and open-source Octave provide excellent capabilities for data analysis, visualisation, and more. By means of straightforward explanations and examples from different areas in mathematics, engineering, finance, and physics, the book explains how MATLAB® and Octave are powerful tools applicable to a variety of problems.

1

No Time to Lose: Time Series Analysis

Have you ever wondered what the weather, financial prices, home energy usage, and your weight all have in common? Well, apart from the obvious, the data to analyse these phenomena can be collected at regular intervals over time. Common sense, right? Well, there is no time to lose; let us take a deeper look into this exciting kind of data. Are you ready?

Not obvious? Oh... well, read on!

Or is it Toulouse, like "Toulouse" in France?

A time series is defined as a sequence of data read in successive order and can be taken on any variable that changes over time. So, if a time series is a set of data collected over time, then a lot of things, not just our weight or the weather, would be classed as time series, and perhaps that is true. There are, obviously and quite literally, millions of data points that can be collected over time. However, time series analysis is not necessarily immediately needed.

A lot of data is collected over time, but that does not make the dataset a time series.

Time series analysis encapsulates the methods used to understand the sequence of data points mentioned above and extract useful information from it. The main goal is that of forecasting successive future values of the series. In this chapter we will cover some of these methods. Let us take a look.

1.1 Time Series

KNOWING HOW TO MODEL TIME series is surely an important tool in our Jackalope data scientist toolbox. Jackalopes? Yes! Long story... You can get further information in Chapter 1 of *Data Science and Analytics with Python*[1]. But I digress, the key point about time series data is that the ordering of the data points in time matters. In many datasets the sequence in which the data are collected or presented is not particularly significant. One ordering is as good as any other, and although the arrangement might tell us something about the dataset, it is not an inherent attribute of the data itself.

[1] Rogel-Salazar, J. (2025). *Data Science and Analytics with Python*. Chapman & Hall/CRC Data Mining and Knowledge Discovery Series. CRC Press.

See for instance the datasets analysed in the book mentioned above.

However, for time series data the ordering is absolutely crucial. The order imposes a certain structure on the data, which in turn is of relevance to the underlying phenomenon studied. So, what is different about time series? Well, time! Furthermore, we will see later on in this chapter that in some cases there are situations where future observations are influenced by past data points. All in all, this is not a surprising statement; we are well acquainted with causality relationships.

What is different about time series? —Time!

Let us have a look at an example of a time series. In Figure 1.1 we can see a financial time series corresponding

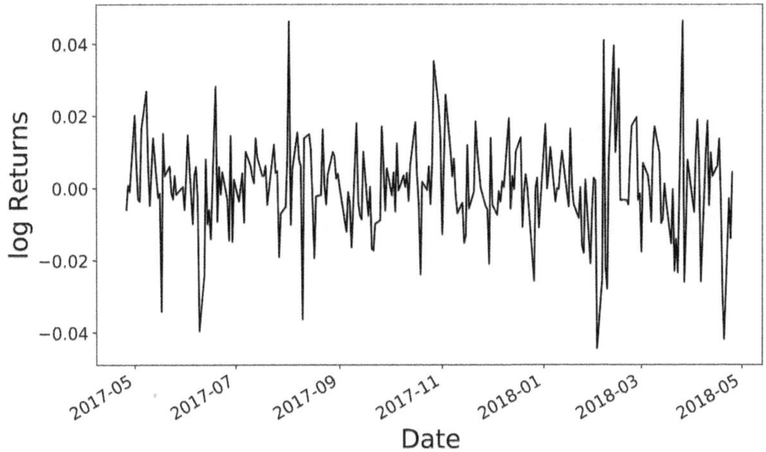

Figure 1.1: A time series of the log returns for Apple Inc. for a year since April 2017.

to the log returns of Apple for a year starting in April 2017. The log returns are used to determine the proportional amount you might get on a given day compared to the previous one. With that description in mind, we can see how we are relating the value on day n to the one on day $n-1$.

The log return is given by $\log\left(\frac{FV}{PV}\right)$, where FV is the future value and PV is the past value.

In that way, a Jackalope data scientist working in finance may be able to look at the sequence provided by the time series to determine a model that can predict the next value in the series. The same train of thought will be applicable to a variety of other human endeavours, from agriculture to climate change, and from geology to solar dynamics.

And hop all the way to the bank...

In contrast, in many other cases the implicit assumption we may be able to make is that our observations are not a sequence, and that the values are independent from each other. Let us consider a well-known dataset, the Iris dataset, which we have used in Chapter 3 of *Data Science and Analytics with Python*[2]. The dataset records measurements of three species of iris flowers in centimetres, including sepal length, sepal width, petal length and petal width. In collecting the information, there is no reason to believe that the fact the current iris specimen we measure has a petal length of, say, 6.1 cm tells us anything about the next specimen.

[2] Rogel-Salazar, J. (2025). *Data Science and Analytics with Python*. Chapman & Hall/CRC Data Mining and Knowledge Discovery Series. CRC Press.

In a time series the opposite is true, i.e., whatever happens at time t has information about what will happen at $t+1$. In that sense, our observations of the phenomenon at hand are at the same time both outcomes and predictors: Outcomes of the previous timestep, and predictors of the next one. I know what you are thinking—*cool!!*— and now how do we deal with that situation‽‽

t has information about what will happen at $t+1$.

Isn't it cool to be able to use interrobangs‽‽

You will be happy (although not surprised perhaps) that there is an answer: There are various ways to deal with this input/output duality and the appropriate methodology very much depends on what I call the *personality* of the data, i.e., the nature of the data itself, how it was obtained and what answers we require from it. In this chapter we shall see some of the ways we can analyse time series data. Let us start with a few examples.

I think data, like humans, has also some *personality*.

1.2 *One at a Time: Some Examples*

In the previous section we have seen a first example of a time series given by the log returns of Apple (shown in

Figure 1.1). We can clearly see a first maximum on August 2, 2017. This corresponds to the day Apple released their third-quarter results for 2017, beating earning and revenue estimates[3]. There are several other peaks and troughs during the year of data plotted. These are not uncommon in many financial time series, and not all may have a straightforward explanation like the one above.

[3] Archer, S. (2017). Apple hits a record high after crushing earnings (AAPL). http://markets.businessinsider.com/news/stocks/apple-stock-price-record-high-after-crushing-earnings-2017-8-100222647. Accessed: 2018-05-01.

Another interesting thing we can notice is that if we were to take the average of the values in the series, we can see that it is a fairly stable measure. Nonetheless, the variability of the data points changes as we move forwards in time. We shall see later on some models that will exploit these observations to analyse this type of data.

An average return of approximately zero!

Let us see another example from a very different area: Solar dynamics. In Figure 1.2 we can see the number of sunspots per month since 1749 through 2013. The earliest study of the periodicity of sunspots was the work by Schuster[4] in 1906. Schuster is actually credited with coining the concept of antimatter. However cool that fact is, in this case we would like to concentrate on the periodogram analysis he pioneered to establish an approximate 11-year cycle in the solar activity.

[4] Schuster, A. (1906). II. On the periodicities of sunspots. *Philosophical Transactions of the Royal Society of London A: Mathematical, Physical and Engineering Sciences* 206(402-412), 69–100.

Sunspots indicate intensive magnetic activity in the sun, and we can see in the figure the regular appearance of maximum and minimum activity. Understanding the behaviour of sunspots is important due to their link with solar activity and help us predict space weather that affects satellite communication and also provides us with awe-inspiring and spectacular auroras.

Sunspots are linked to solar activity, enabling us to carry out space weather predictions.

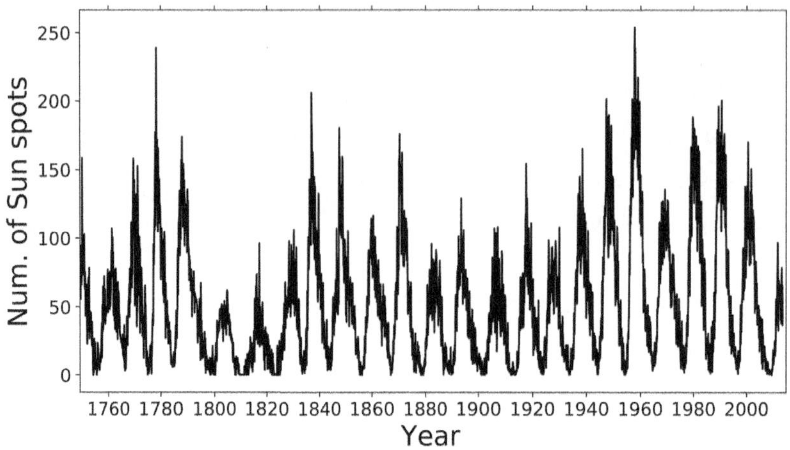

Figure 1.2: Solar activity from 1749 through 2013.

If our goal is indeed to generate predictions from the data in a time series, there are certain assumptions that can help in our quest. A typical assumption made is that there is some structure in the time series data. This structure may be somewhat obfuscated by random noise. One way to understand the structure of the time series is to think of the trend shown in the series together with any seasonal variation.

Structure = Trend + Seasonality

The trend in the Apple log returns discussed earlier may not be very obvious. Let us take a look at the closing price of the Apple stock during the same period. In Figure 1.3 we can see the behaviour of the closing price for a year since 2017. The plot shows that there is a tendency for the prices to increase overtime. Similarly, there seem to be some periodicity in the data.

Trend, it should be said!

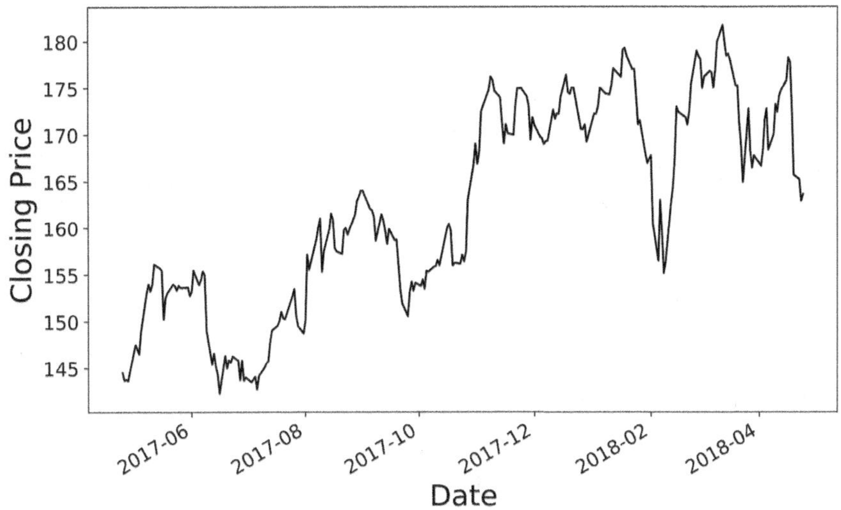

Figure 1.3: Closing prices for Apple Inc. for a year since April 2017.

This brings us to the seasonality in a time series. Seasonality is understood in this case to be the presence of variations observed at regular intervals in our dataset. These intervals may be daily, weekly, monthly, etc. Seasonal variation may be an important source of information in our quest for predictability, as it captures information that will clearly have an impact on the events we are measuring with our data. The seasonality in the sunspot activity shown in Figure 1.2 is undeniable.

Seasonality is the presence of variations at regular intervals.

1.3 *Bearing with Time: pandas Series*

Now that we have a better idea of what makes a time series dataset different from other types of data, let us consider how we can deal and manipulate them in a way that makes life easier for us Jackalope data scientists. I am sure that you have come across the great and useful Python module called pandas. Its original author, Wes McKinney, started developing the module to deal with **pan**el **da**ta, encountered in statistics and econometrics[5]. Indeed he started using Python to perform quantitative analysis on financial data at AQR Capital Management. Today, pandas is a well-established open-source piece of software with multiple uses and a large number of contributors.

[5] McKinney, W. (2011). pandas: a foundational python library for data analysis and statistics. Python for High Performance and Scientific Computing: O'Reilly Media, Inc.

Since time is an important part of a time series, let us take a look at some data that contains time as one of its columns. We can start by loading some useful modules including pandas and datetime:

A hint is in the name...

```
import numpy as np
import pandas as pd
from datetime import datetime
```

We can create a dictionary with some sample data:

```
data = {'date': ['2025-01-01', '2025-02-01',
    '2025-03-01', '2025-04-01',
    '2025-05-01', '2025-06-01',
    '2025-01-01', '2025-02-01',
    '2025-03-01', '2025-04-01',
    '2025-05-01', '2025-06-01'],
    'visitors': [35, 30, 82, 26,
    83, 46, 40, 57, 95, 57, 87, 42]}
```

We are creating a dataframe with two columns: Date and visitors. Each column is given as a list.

We have visitor monthly data for January through June 2025. The date is given in a format where the year comes first,

The date is given in the format `'YYYY-MM-DD'`.

followed by the month and the day. This dictionary can be readily converted into a pandas dataframe as follows:

```
df = pd.DataFrame(data,
    columns=['date', 'visitors'])
```

Let us take a look at the data:

```
> df.head()

   date          visitors
0 2025-01-01        35
1 2025-02-01        30
2 2025-03-01        82
3 2025-04-01        26
4 2025-05-01        83
```

As expected, we have a dataframe with two columns.

Notice that when looking at the dataset, the rows have been given a number (starting with 0). This is an index for the dataframe. Let us take a look at the types of the columns in this dataframe:

A very Pythonic way of counting.

```
> df.dtypes

date         object
visitors     int64
dtype: object
```

The type for `date` is object, whereas for `visitors` it is integer.

The `visitors` column is of integer type, but the `date` column is shown to be an object. We know that this is a date and it would be preferable to use a more relevant type. We can change the column with the to_datetime method in a pandas dataframe:

```
df['date'] = pd.to_datetime(df['date'])
```

We can use the to_datetime method to convert pandas columns into date objects.

Furthermore, since the date provides an order sequence for our data, we can do a couple of useful things. First, we can set the index to be given by the date column, and second, we can order the dataframe by this index:

```
df.set_index('date', inplace=True)
df.sort_index(inplace=True)
```

We set an index and sort the dataframe by that index.

We have used the inplace property for both commands above. This property lets us make changes to the dataframe *insitu;* otherwise, we would have to create a new dataframe object. Let us look at the head of our dataset:

```
> df.head()

            visitors
date
2025-01-01  35
2025-01-01  40
2025-02-01  30
2025-02-01  57
2025-03-01  82
```

The inplace property lets us make changes directly to the dataframe. Otherwise, we would need to make copies of it to apply the changes.

As we can see in the code above, the rows of the dataset have been ordered by the date index. We can now apply some slicing and dicing to our dataframe. For instance, we can look at the visitors for the year 2025:

```
df.loc['2025']
```

In this case this would correspond to all our data points.

The `loc` attribute accesses a group of rows and columns by label or a Boolean array. What about if we were interested in the visitors for May 2025? Well, that is easy:

```
> df.loc['2025-05']


              visitors
date
2025-05-01    83
2025-05-01    87
```

Here we are filtering for the visitors in May 2025.

Other slicing and dicing techniques used in collection objects are possible thanks to the use of the colon notation. For instance, we can request all the data from May 2025 onwards as follows:

```
> df[datetime(2025, 5, 1):]


                  visitors
date
2025-05-01          83
2025-05-01          87
2025-06-01          46
2025-06-01          42
```

The colon notation used in other collection objects in Python works for pandas time series too.

The `truncate` method can help us keep all the data points before or after a given date. In this case, let us ask for the data up to March 2025:

```
> df.truncate(after='2025-03-01')


            visitors
date
2025-01-01    35
2025-01-01    40
2025-02-01    30
2025-02-01    57
2025-03-01    82
2025-03-01    95
```

We can truncate the time series with the `truncate` method.

Had we used the `before` parameter instead, we could have truncated all the data points before March 2025 instead. We can use pandas to provide us with useful statistics for our dataset. For example, we can count the number of datapoints per entry in the index:

```
> df.groupby('date').count()


            visitors
date
2025-01-01    2
2025-02-01    2
2025-03-01    2
2025-04-01    2
2025-05-01    2
2025-06-01    2
```

We can calculate aggregations with the help of `groupby`. In this case we are interested in the count.

As expected, we have two entries for each date. We can also look at statistics such as the mean and the sum of entries. In this case, we are going to use the `resample` method for a series. In effect this enables us to change the time frequency in our dataset. Let us use the `'ME'` *offset alias* to tell pandas to create monthly (month-end) statistics. For the mean we have:

The `resample` method lets us change the time frequency in our dataset.

```
> df.resample('ME').mean()


              visitors
date
2025-01-31      37.5
2025-02-28      43.5
2025-03-31      88.5
2025-04-30      41.5
2025-05-31      85.0
2025-06-30      44.0
```

We can calculate the mean.

Similarly, for the sum we have:

```
> df.resample('ME').sum()
            visitors
date
2025-01-31        75
2025-02-28        87
2025-03-31       177
2025-04-30        83
2025-05-31       170
2025-06-30        88
```

And the sum too.

An offset alias, such as `'ME'` used in the code above is a string that represents a common time series frequency. In this case it refers to "Month End". We can see some of these aliases in Table 1.1.

Offset aliases are listed in Table 1.1.

We can even create a plot of the dataset. In this case, we show in Figure 1.4 the monthly sum of visitors for the dataset in question.

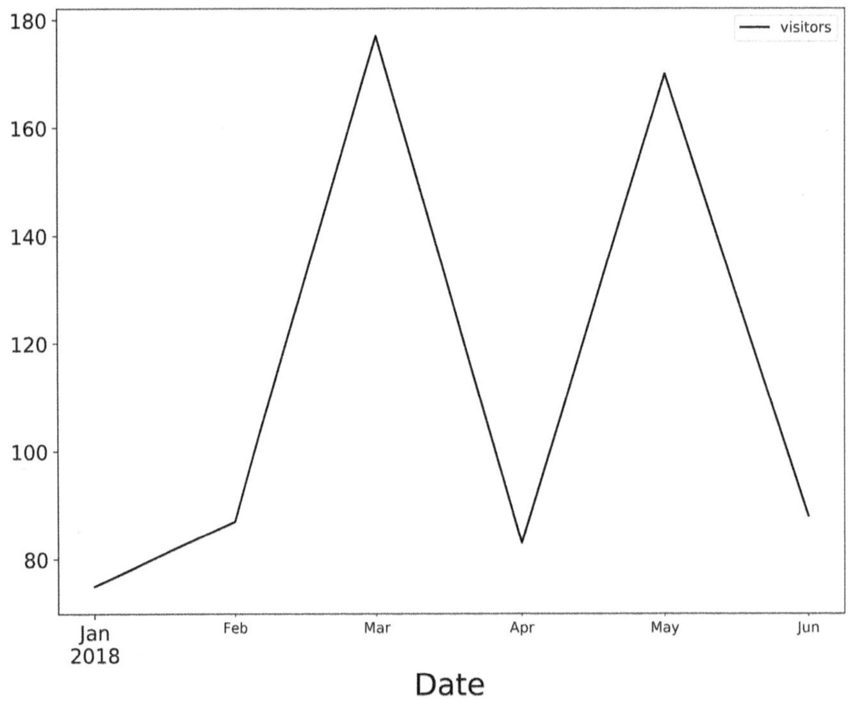

Figure 1.4: Total of monthly visitors for the data entered manually.

It is possible to obtain descriptive statistics with the use of the `describe` method, and we can do so per relevant group. For example, we can request the information for each date in the dataset:

Table 1.1: Offset aliases used by pandas to represent common time series frequencies.

Alias	Description
B	business day frequency
C	custom business day frequency
D	calendar day frequency
W	weekly frequency
ME	month-end frequency
SME	semi-month-end frequency (15th and end of month)
BME	business month-end frequency
CBME	custom business month-end frequency
MS	month-start frequency
SMS	semi-month-start frequency (1st and 15th)
BMS	business month-start frequency
CBMS	custom business month-start frequency
QE	quarter-end frequency
BQE	business quarter-end frequency
QS	quarter-start frequency
BQS	business quarter-start frequency
YE	year-end frequency
BYE	business year-end frequency
YS	year-start frequency
BYS	business year-start frequency
h	hourly frequency
bh	business hour frequency
cbh	custom business hour frequency
min	minutely frequency
s	secondly frequency
ms	milliseconds
us	microseconds
ns	nanoseconds

```
df.groupby('date').describe()
```

In Table 1.2 we see the descriptive statistics for the data entered manually earlier on. For brevity we have decided not to include the count column.

	Visitors						
	mean	std	min	25%	50%	75%	max
date							
2025-01-01	37.5	3.53	35.0	36.25	37.5	38.75	40.0
2025-03-01	88.5	9.19	82.0	85.25	88.5	91.75	95.0
2025-04-01	41.5	21.92	26.0	33.75	41.5	49.25	57.0
2025-05-01	85.0	2.82	83.0	84.00	85.0	86.00	87.0
2025-06-01	44.0	2.82	42.0	43.00	44.0	45.00	46.0

Table 1.2: Descriptive statistics for the data entered manually. We are not including the count in this table.

Given that date and time are important components of a time series, pandas has some neat tricks to help us deal with them. For example, it is possible to use date formats such as that shown above, i.e., `'YYYY-MM-DD'`. We can also provide a date in other formats, for instance, consider the following code:

We can provide a data in plain natural language and convert it to a date type.

```
> date = pd.to_datetime('5th of July, 2025'))
> print(date)


Timestamp('2025-07-05 00:00:00')
```

Table 1.3: Some format directives for the `strftime` method.

Directive	Meaning
`%a`	abbreviated weekday name
`%A`	full weekday name
`%b`	abbreviated month name
`%B`	full month name
`%c`	preferred date and time representation
`%d`	day of the month (1 to 31)
`%D`	same as %m/%d/%y
`%e`	day of the month (1 to 31)
`%m`	month (1 to 12)
`%M`	minute
`%S`	second
`%u`	weekday as a number (Mon=1 to 7)

We have successfully transformed a date given in natural language to a time stamp. We can also do the opposite; in other words, we can obtain a string of the time stamp to tell us the weekday, month, day, etc. We can do this thanks to the `strftime` method together with a format directive. Some format directives for `strftime` are listed in Table 1.3. Let us take a look at extracting the full weekday name (`%A`), the name of the month (`%B`) and the weekday number (`%u`).

How cool is that?

`strftime` lets us obtain a string out of the time stamp.

```
> date.strftime('%A')
'Saturday
> date.strftime('%B')
'July'
> date.strftime('%u')
'6'
```

1.3.1 *pandas Time Series in Action*

IN SOME CASES WE MAY need to create time series data from scratch. In this section we are going to explore some of the ways in which pandas enables us to create and manipulate time series data on top of the commands we have discussed up until this point.

The first thing to take care of is the time ranges required for our dataset. For example, we can ask pandas to create a series of dates with `date_range`:

We can determine a time range by specifying start and end times.

```
> pd.date_range('2025-05-30', '2025-06-02')


DatetimeIndex(['2025-05-30', '2025-05-31',
               '2025-06-01', '2025-06-02'],
               dtype='datetime64[ns]', freq='D')
```

Note that the output of the command above is an index covering the time range requested with a daily frequency, as shown in the output with `freq='D'`.

Recall the time offset aliases shown in Table 1.1.

An alternative to the above command is to provide a start date, but instead of giving an end date, we request a number of "periods" to cover with the time series:

Alternatively, we can provide a start time and a number of periods.

```
> pd.date_range('2025-05-30', periods=4)


DatetimeIndex(['2025-05-30', '2025-05-31',
               '2025-06-01', '2025-06-02'],
               dtype='datetime64[ns]', freq='D')
```

This hints to the fact that we can provide a number of periods to cover, as well as the frequency we require. For example, we can request four monthly periods:

```
> pd.date_range('2025-05-30', periods=4, freq='M')


DatetimeIndex(['2025-05-31', '2025-06-30',
               '2025-07-31', '2025-08-31'],
               dtype='datetime64[ns]', freq='ME')
```

Here we provide a start time, a number of periods and the frequency for those periods.

As you can see, all we had to do was specify the monthly frequency with `freq='ME'`.

Let us construct a more complicated dataset: For a period of four days starting on June 4, 2025, we take readings for four features called A, B, C and D. In this case we will generate the readings with a random number sampled from a standard normal distribution. Let us create some definitions:

The random number can be obtained with the method `random.randn` from `numpy`.

```
from numpy.random import randn
idx = pd.date_range('2025-06-04 00:00:00',
                    periods=4)
cols = ['A', 'B', 'C', 'D']
```

We will now create data for four rows and four columns with the help of `randn`:

randn(m, n) creates an array of `m` rows and `n` columns.

```
data = randn(len(idx), len(cols))
```

With this information, we now create our dataframe.

```
df = pd.DataFrame(data=data,
                  index=idx, columns=cols)
df.index.name='date'
> print(df)


                   A         B         C         D
date
2025-06-04 -0.328439 -0.156012 -1.274778  1.912496
2025-06-05  0.185948 -0.625127 -0.790185 -0.406829
2025-06-06  0.768787 -0.201153  0.321315  0.851157
2025-06-07  1.230974 -0.548803 -0.498133 -0.644061
```

Since we used random numbers to generate the data, the numbers shown here will differ from those you may obtain on your computer.

A table like the one above is useful to summarise data, and it is fit for "human consumption". However, in many applications, it is much better to have a "long format" or "melted" dataset, i.e., instead of arranging the data in a rectangular format as shown above, we would like all the data readings in a single column.

In other words, it is an arrangement that a human will find easy to read and understand.

In order to achieve this, we need to repeat the dates, and we also require a new column to hold the feature to which each reading corresponds. This can easily be done with pandas in a single command. The first thing we need to do is reset the index:

This is because we need the date to be part of the new formatted dataset.

```
df.reset_index(inplace=True)
```

In order to melt the dataframe, we will use the `melt` method that takes the following parameters: A column that will become the new identifier variable with `id_vars`, the columns to un-pivot are specified with value_vars and finally the names for the variable and value columns with var_name and value_name, respectively:

If no value_vars is provided, all columns are used.

```
> melted = pd.melt(df, id_vars='date',
                   var_name='feature',
                   value_name='reading')
> print(melted)
         date feature   reading
0  2025-06-04       A -0.328439
1  2025-06-05       A  0.185948
2  2025-06-06       A  0.768787
3  2025-06-07       A  1.230974
4  2025-06-04       B -0.156012
5  2025-06-05       B -0.625127
...
14 2025-06-06       D  0.851157
15 2025-06-07       D -0.644061
```

The original columns have become entries in the column called "features", and the values are in the column "reading".

We can now set the index and sort the melted dataset:

```
melted.set_index('date', inplace=True)
melted.sort_index(inplace=True)
> print(melted)
           feature   reading
date
2025-06-04       A -0.328439
2025-06-04       B -0.156012
2025-06-04       C -1.274778
2025-06-04       D  1.912496
...
```

1.3.2 *Time Series Data Manipulation*

LET US TAKE A LOOK at some of the manipulations we have described above used in a more real dataset. Remember the time series for Apple Inc. returns discussed in Section 1.2? Well, we will delve a bit more into that data. The dataset is available at[6] `https://doi.org/10.6084/m9.figshare.6339830.v1` as a comma-separated value file with the name "`APPL.CSV`". As usual, we need to load some libraries:

[6] Rogel-Salazar, J. (2018a, May). Apple Inc. Prices Apr 2017 - Apr 2018. https://doi.org/10.6084/m9.figshare.6339830.v1

```
import numpy as np
import pandas as pd
```

We need to load the dataset with the help of pandas; in this case, with the `read_csv` method:

```
appl = pd.read_csv('APPL.CSV')
appl.Date = pd.to_datetime(appl.Date,
    format='%Y-%m-%d')
```

Make sure that you pass on the correct path for the file!

In the first line of the code above, we have used the `read_csv` method in pandas to load our dataset. We know that the column called `Date` should be treated as datetime, and hence we use `to_datetime` to make that conversion. Please note that we are also giving pandas a helping hand by telling it the format in which the date is stored, in this case as year, followed by month and day.

We are using `to_datetime` to ensure that dates are appropriately typed.

The dataset contains open, high, low and close (i.e., OHLC) prices for Apple Inc. stock between April 2017 and April 2018. We are going to concentrate on the `Close` column, but before we do that, we need to ensure that the dataset is indexed by the time stamps provided by the `Date` column. We can easily do that with the `set_index` method as follows:

```
appl.set_index('Date', inplace=True)
```

We set up the index with `set_index()`.

We can take a look at the closing prices:

```
> appl['Close'].head(3)


Date
2017-04-25    144.529999
2017-04-26    143.679993
2017-04-27    143.789993
```

We centre our attention on the use of the closing prices.

Notice that although we only requested Python to give us a look at the `Close` column, the printout obtained added automatically the index given by the dates. The data provided is already ordered; however, in case we are dealing with data where the index is not in the correct order, we can use `sort_index`:

```
df.sort_index(inplace=True)
```

Sorting by the index is done with `sort_index()`.

The daily closing prices can be used to calculate the return at time t for example, this can be expressed as:

$$R_t = \frac{P_t - P_{t-1}}{P_{t-1}}, \tag{1.1}$$

Effectively a percentage change.

where P_t is the price at time t and P_{t-1} is the price at the previous time period. We can apply this calculation in a very easy step in pandas as follows:

```
appl['pct_change'] = appl.Close.pct_change()
```

We are using pct_change() to calculate the returns.

We can see the result of this calculation:

```
> appl['pct_change'].tail(3)


2018-04-23    -0.002896
2018-04-24    -0.013919
2018-04-25     0.004357
```

The percentage change from one day to the next is easily calculated.

Continuous compounding of returns leads to the use of log returns and they are calculated as follows:

$$r_t = \log(1 + R_t) = \log\left(\frac{P_t}{P_{t-1}}\right) = \log(P_t) - \log(P_{t-1}). \quad (1.2)$$

Continuous compounding of returns leads to the use of log returns.

We need to calculate the logarithm of the price at each time t and then take the difference between time periods. We can certainly do this in Python, and pandas gives us a helping hand with the `diff()` method:

```
appl['log_ret'] = np.log(appl.Close).diff()
```

The `diff` method calculates the difference from one time period to the next.

We can check the result of this operation by looking at the values in the new column we have created:

```
> appl['log_ret'].tail(3)


2018-04-23    -0.002901
2018-04-24    -0.014017
2018-04-25     0.004348
```

We are looking at the last three entries in our table.

This is the data that we show in Figure 1.1, and indeed this is the way we calculated that time series shown in the figure.

It is fairly common to have financial data series like the one we have used above, where the frequency is given by the end-of-day prices. However, the frequency can be different, for instance given by the minimum upward or downward price movement in the price of a security. This is known as a *tick*. Let us take a look at tick data for Bitcoin/USD exchange rate. The dataset is available at[7] `https://doi.org/10.6084/m9.figshare.6452831.v1` as a comma-separated value file with the name `bitcoin_usd.csv`, and it contains prices for covering tick data between March 31 and April 3, 2016.

A "tick" is a measure of the minimum upward or downward movement in the price of a security.

[7] Rogel-Salazar, J. (2018b, Jun). Bitcoin/USD exchange rate Mar 31-Apr 3, 2016. https://doi.org/10.6084/m9.figshare.6452831.v1

We can read the data in the usual way. However, if we were to inspect the data, we will notice that the date is stored in a column called `time_start`, and that the format is such that the day is placed first, followed by the month and the year; the time in hours and minutes is provided.

Pro tip: Inspect your data before importing it; it will save you a few headaches!

We can provide extra information to pandas to read the data and parse the dates at the same time:

```
fname = 'bitcoin_usd.csv'


bitcoin = pd.read_csv(fname,
          parse_dates=['time_start'],
          date_format="%d/%m/%Y %H:%M",
          index_col='time_start')
```

We specify the columns to be parsed and how they shall be parsed!

Notice that we are specifying what columns need to be parsed as dates with parse_dates and how the parsing should be performed with date_fortmat. We also load the dataset indicating which column is the index. Let us concentrate now on the closing price and the volume:

```
ticks = bitcoin[['close', 'volume']]
```

We are effectively creating a new dataframe called ticks.

The data is roughly on a minute-by-minute frequency. We can use pandas to resample the data at desired intervals. For instance, we can request for the data to be sampled every five minutes and take the first value in the interval:

```
> ticks.resample('5Min').first()

                      close     volume
time_start
2016-03-31 00:00:00  413.27   8.953746
2016-03-31 00:05:00  413.26   0.035157
2016-03-31 00:10:00  413.51  43.640052
...
```

We can resample our data with the help of resample().

We can also ask for the mean, for example,

```
> ticks.resample('5Min').mean()

                       close     volume
time_start
2016-03-31 00:00:00  413.270   2.735987
2016-03-31 00:05:00  413.264   2.211749
2016-03-31 00:10:00  414.660  37.919166
...
```

We can specify how the resampling will be performed.

In this way we could get the closing price for the day by resampling by day and requesting the last value:

```
> ticks.resample('D').last()

              close     volume
time_start
2016-03-31   416.02   0.200000
2016-04-01   417.90  52.099684
2016-04-02   420.30   0.850000
...
```

The closing for the new resampling interval can be obtained from the last value.

Now that we know how to resample the data, we can consider creating a new open, high, low and close set of prices for the resampled data. Let us do this for the five-minute bars:

```
> bars = ticks['close'].resample('5Min').ohlc()
> bars.head(3)

                       open    high     low   close
time_start
2016-03-31 00:00:00  413.27  413.27  413.27  413.27
2016-03-31 00:05:00  413.26  413.28  413.25  413.28
2016-03-31 00:10:00  413.51  414.98  413.51  414.98
```

The `ohlc()` method lets us find the OHLC prices for our new sampled data.

Notice that pandas will take the first and last values in the interval to be the open and close for the bar. Then it will take the max and min as the high and low, respectively. In this way, we start filtering the data. For example, imagine we are interested in the prices between 10 am and 4 pm each day:

```
> filtered = bars.between_time('10:00', '16:00')

                       open     high      low    close
time_start
2016-03-31 10:00:00  416.00   416.00   415.98   415.98
2016-03-31 10:05:00  415.98   415.98   415.97   415.97
...
2016-04-03 15:55:00  421.01   421.02   421.00   421.00
2016-04-03 16:00:00  421.01   421.01   421.01   421.01
```

Notice the use of between_time to filter the data.

We may be interested in looking at the price first thing in the morning — say 8 am:

```
> bars.open.at_time('8:00')


time_start
2016-03-31 08:00:00    416.11
2016-04-01 08:00:00    416.02
2016-04-02 08:00:00    420.69
2016-04-03 08:00:00    418.78
```

In this case we are using the at_time method.

Not only that, we can request the percentage change too by combining the methods we have already discussed:

```
> bars.open.at_time('8:00').pct_change()


time_start
2016-03-31 08:00:00         NaN
2016-04-01 08:00:00   -0.000216
2016-04-02 08:00:00    0.011225
2016-04-03 08:00:00   -0.004540
```

And the methods can be easily combined!

Please note that the first percentage change cannot be calculated, as we do not have a comparison data point from the previous interval. In this case, pandas indicates this by the use of `NaN`.

If we inspect the data with a bit more detail, we will see that for the last part of April 3rd, the frequency is such that we have some missing bars when sampling at five-minute intervals:

In many cases we may find that we have some missing data in our datasets...

```
> bars.tail()


                      open   high    low  close
time_start
2016-04-03 23:35:00  420.6  420.6  420.6  420.6
2016-04-03 23:40:00    NaN    NaN    NaN    NaN
2016-04-03 23:45:00    NaN    NaN    NaN    NaN
2016-04-03 23:50:00  420.6  420.6  420.6  420.6
2016-04-03 23:55:00  421.0  421.0  420.6  420.6
```

We can fill in missing data with the help of `fillna`, which takes a parameter called `method`. It can be either `'pad'` or `'ffill'` to propagate last valid observation forward; or instead either `'backfill'` or `'bfill'` to use the next valid observation to fill the gap. We can also limit the number of consecutive values that should be filled in with `limit`.

We can fill in missing data with the help of `fillna()`.

For instance, we can fill only one gap by propagating the last valid value forward:

```
> bars.fillna(method='ffill', limit=1)
...
2016-04-03 23:35:00  420.60  420.60  420.60  420.60
2016-04-03 23:40:00  420.60  420.60  420.60  420.60
2016-04-03 23:45:00     NaN     NaN     NaN     NaN
2016-04-03 23:50:00  420.60  420.60  420.60  420.60
2016-04-03 23:55:00  421.00  421.00  420.60  420.60
```

Here we have filled the missing data by bringing the last value forward and limitting the operation to one time period.

Let us fill both gaps and create a new dataframe:

```
filledbars = bars.ffill()
```

For the volume it would make sense to consider the sum of all the securities traded in the five-minute interval:

```
volume = ticks.volume.resample('5Min').sum()
vol = volume.fillna(0.)
```

A plot of the open, high, low and close prices for the five-minute bars, together with the corresponding volume for April 3rd between 9 am and 11.59 pm is shown in Figure 1.5 and can be created as follows:

```
filledbars.loc['2016-04-03'].between_time('9:00',\
    '23:59').plot(\
    color=['gray','gray','gray','k'],
    style=['-','--','-.','-+'])

vol.loc['2016-04-03'].between_time('9:30','23:59')\
    .plot(secondary_y=True, style='k-o')
```

The plotting commands that we know and love are available to the pandas series and dataframes too.

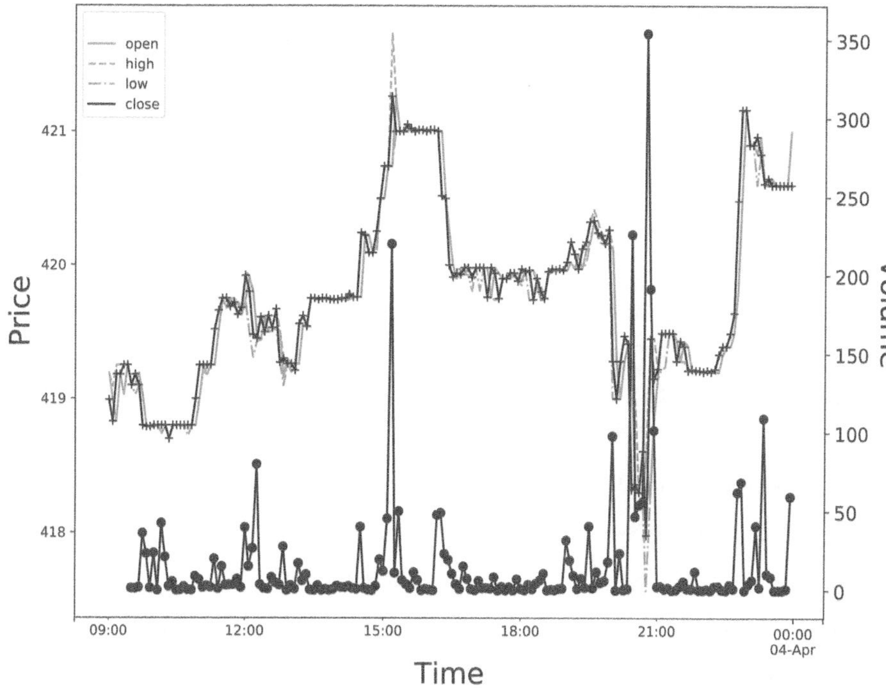

Figure 1.5: Open, high, low and close prices for the exchange rate of bitcoin/USD.

1.4 *Modelling Time Series Data*

We know that there is no such a thing as a perfect model, just good enough ones[8]. With that in mind, we can consider the assumptions we can make around data in a time series. We would like to start with a simple model, and perhaps one of the first assumptions we can make is that there is no structure in the time series. In other words, we have a situation where each and every observation is in effect an independent random variate.

[8] Rogel-Salazar, J. (2025). *Data Science and Analytics with Python*. Chapman & Hall/CRC Data Mining and Knowledge Discovery Series. CRC Press.

A good example of this would be white noise. In this case when facing this type of signal, the best we can do is simply predict the mean value of the dataset.

White noise intensity is the same at all frequencies within a given band.

Let us create some white noise in Python with the help of numpy:

```
import numpy as np
import pandas as pd


white = 2*np.random.random(size=2048)-1
white = pd.Series(white)
```

In the code above, we are using the `random` method in `numpy.random` to draw samples from a uniform distribution. We would like our samples to be drawn from Unif$[a, b)$ with $a = -1$ and $b = 1$ so that we have white noise with mean zero. A plot for one such time series is shown in Figure 1.6.

Hence the use of $(b - a)(sample) + a$.

Remember that we are assuming that each observation is independent from the other. If there is correlation among the values of a given variable, we say that the variable is *autocorrelated*. For a repeatable (random) process X, let X_t be the realisation of the process at time t; also let the process have mean μ_t and variance σ_t^2. The autocorrelation $R(s, t)$ between times t and s is given by:

We are keeping it simple.

$$R(s,t) = \frac{E[(X_t - \mu_t)(X_s - \mu_s)]}{\sigma_t \sigma_s}, \tag{1.3}$$

Autocorrelation.

where $E[\cdot]$ is the expectation value. Autocorrelation provides us with a measure of the degree of similarity between the values of a time series and a lagged or shifted

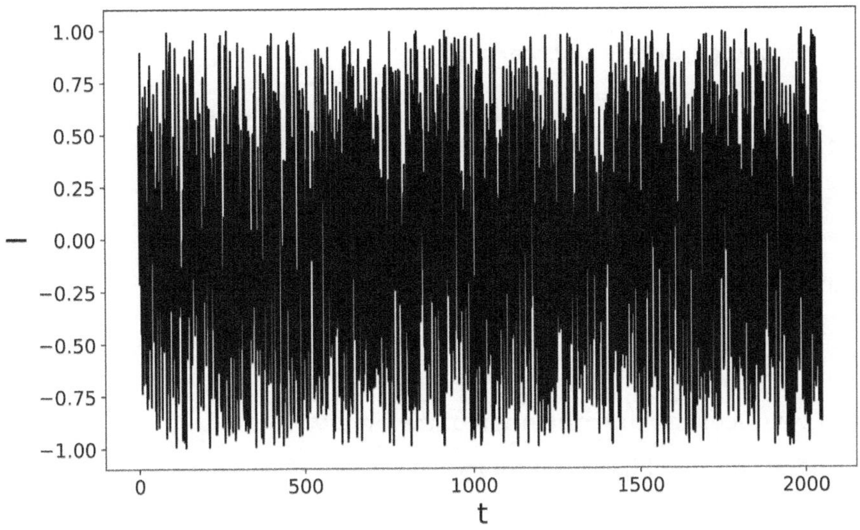

Figure 1.6: White noise with zero mean, constant variance, and zero correlation.

version of that same series. Notice that we can recover the usual correlation definition for the case where X_t and X_s are two random variables not drawn from the same process at lagged times.

Therefore, as with correlation, the values returned by an autocorrelation calculation lie between -1 and 1. It is also important to mention that autocorrelation gives us information about the existence of linear relationships. Even when the autocorrelation measure is close to zero, there may be a nonlinear relationship between the values of a variable and a lagged version of itself.

Autocorrelation values lie between -1 and 1.

Let us calculate the autocorrelation for our generated white noise:

```
> for lag in range(1,5):
    print("Autocorrelation at lag={0} is {1}".\
          format(lag,  white.autocorr(lag)))

Autocorrelation at lag=1 is 0.027756062237309434
Autocorrelation at lag=2 is 0.017698046805029784
Autocorrelation at lag=3 is -0.016764938190346888
Autocorrelation at lag=4 is -0.03636909301996918
```

Autocorrelation can be calculated with autocorr.

The values returned by autocorr are the same as those we would obtain if we calculated the correlation of the time series with a shifted version of itself. Take a look:

```
> print(white.corr(white.shift(1)))

0.027756062237309434
```

As we can see, the result is the same.

Here shift(n) translates the series by n periods, in this case 1, enabling us to calculate the autocorrelation value.

Finally, predicting (or calculating) the mean value can be readily done as follows:

```
> print(white.mean())

-0.019678911755368275
```

What we are seeing here is a foundational benchmark for modelling time series data: white noise, a process with no structure, no memory, and no predictable pattern. By generating and analysing white noise, we calibrate our expectations for what "no signal" looks like. This is essential because any meaningful model must outperform such a baseline; if it doesn't, it's no better than guessing. The near-zero autocorrelation values confirm the lack of temporal dependence, reinforcing our assumption of independence. Understanding and validating such assumptions early on is crucial. It helps us distinguish between randomness and structure, enabling us to build more nuanced models as we move toward time series with trend, seasonality, or autocorrelation. In short, before we model the storm, we must first recognise the calm.

After all, if your model cannot beat randomness, it's just elegantly guessing.

1.4.1 *Regression... (Not) a Good Idea?*

WE HAVE SEEN HOW TO deal with processes that have no inherent structure, and hence the predictions we can make are quite straightforward. Let us take a step forward and consider more interesting processes. If we were to compare the time series for the closing prices of the Apple stock shown in Figure 1.3 with the white noise we generated for Figure 1.6, we can clearly see that there is indeed more structure in the price data: There are peaks and troughs and we can even notice an upward trend.

And boring ones, for that matter.

We are familiar with some techniques such as multivariate regression, and it may be conceivable to apply these techniques to the data we have. At the very least, it may provide us with an idea of the trend in the time series. Ignoring seasonal variation and random noise, we can fit a polynomial model to the data as show in Figure 1.7. We can

Regression may provide us with an idea of the trend.

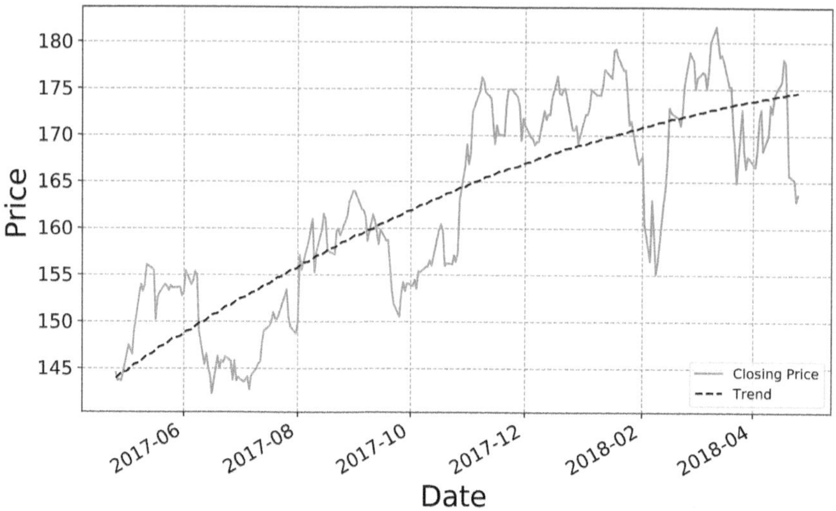

Figure 1.7: Closing prices for Apple Inc. for a year since April 2017 and a trend line provided by a multivariate regression.

see the general trend in the set. But is this really a suitable model?

It is hard to believe that the closing price of the Apple stock is simply a function of the calendar date!! It is more likely that the prices are a function of their own history, and therefore we require methods that are able to capture precisely this assumed dependency, and given the results decide whether the model is fit for purpose. We will tackle some models to achieve this in the rest of this chapter. Final word of advice, predicting prices is more of a dark art than science, not only are we trying to look at the structure of the time series, but we also contend with a myriad of external factors that affect price, e.g., market forces, product announcements, mergers, acquisitions, demand, social factors, social media, etc.

As well as market forces, product announcements, etc.

1.4.2 *Moving Averages and Exponential Smoothing*

WE ARE INTERESTED IN FINDING a model that is able to forecast the next value in our time series data. In the previous section, we have seen how we can make some assumptions about the data we have and use that to our advantage. In the example with the Apple Inc. prices, we have been able to fit a regression model to the data, but surely we can do better than that.

We are interested in creating a forecast.

What about if we are able to forecast the future value based on the past values of the time series? For example, we may be able to take the average of the last n observations as the forecast for the next time period. This methodology is known as *moving averages*. For example, in the case where $n = 3$, the smoothened value at time t, s_t, will be given by:

In moving averages, the forecast is provided by the simple mean over a period of time.

An alternative name for moving averages is rolling averages.

$$s_t = \frac{x_{t-2} + x_{t-1} + x_t}{3}. \tag{1.4}$$

We can also consider giving greater importance to more recent past values than older ones. It sounds plausible, right? Well, this is actually what *exponential smoothing* enables us to do. The weighting is performed via constant values called *smoothing constants*. The simplest method is appropriately called *simple exponential smoothing* (SES), and it uses one smoothing constant, α.

Exponential smoothing works by weighting past observations.

In SES, we start by setting s_0 to x_0 and subsequent periods at time t are given by:

$$s_t = \alpha x_t + (1 - \alpha)s_{t-1}, \tag{1.5}$$

The simple exponential smoothing method.

with $0 \leq \alpha \leq 1$. The smoothing is a function of α; we have a quick smoothing when α is close to 1, and a slow one when it is close to 0. We choose the value of α such that the mean squared error (MSE) is minimised.

We can calculate moving averages and exponential smoothing on a time series with pandas. For moving averages, we simply use the `rolling` method for pandas dataframes. In the case of the Apple Inc. closing prices we have been investigating, we can write the following:

We can use pandas to calculate moving averages and exponential smoothing.

```
appl['MA3']=appl['Close'].rolling(window=3).mean()
```

where we have provided the size of the moving window and indicated that the aggregation of the data will be the mean of the values.

EWM parameter	Definition
Centre of Mass (com)	$\alpha = \frac{1}{1+com}$, for $com \geq 0$
Span	$\alpha = \frac{2}{1+span}$, for $span \geq 1$
Half-life	$\alpha = 1 - \exp\left[\frac{\log(0.5)}{halflife}\right]$, for $halflife > 0$

Table 1.4: Parameters specifying the decay applied to an exponential smoothing calculation with `ewm`.

For exponential smoothing, pandas provides the `ewm` method. We simply pass the parameter α as follows:

EWM stands for Exponential Weighted Methods.

```
alpha=0.6
appl['EWMA']=appl['Close'].ewm(alpha=alpha).mean()
```

The method also accepts other definitions such as the centre of mass, the span or the half-life. In Table 1.4 we list the relationship between α and these alternative parameters.

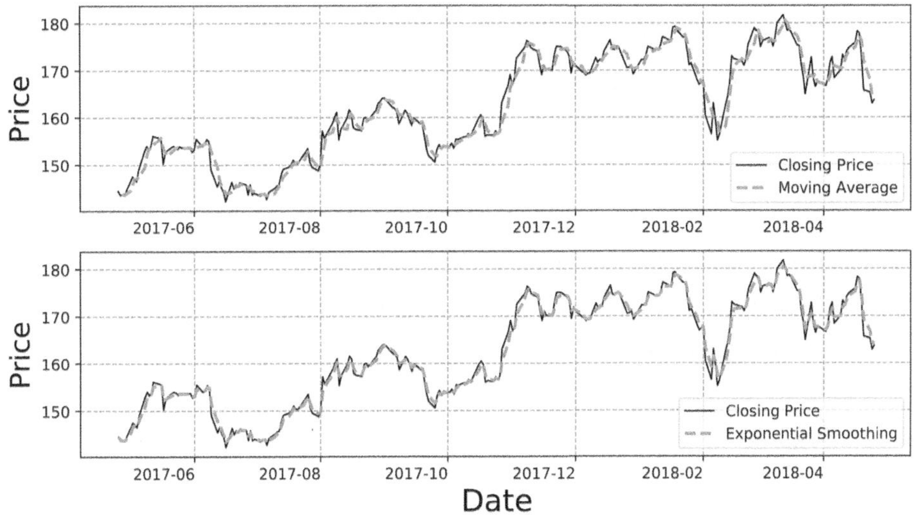

Figure 1.8: Moving averages (upper panel) and exponential smoothing (lower panel) applied to the closing prices for Apple Inc.

In Figure 1.8 we can see the result of using moving averages and exponential smoothing compared to the closing prices for Apple Inc. Not bad, eh?

1.4.3 *Stationarity and Seasonality*

We have been considering some of the assumptions we can make on our time series data in order to come up with models that enable us to understand the underlying phenomena and create predictions. One such common assumption is that our time series is stationary.

A stationary time series is one where its mean, variance and autocorrelation do not change over time.

In this context, we say that a process is stationary if its mean, variance and autocorrelation do not change over time. As you can imagine, stationarity can be defined in precise mathematical terms, but a practical way of remembering what we are talking about is effectively a flat-looking series. In other words, a series where there is no trend, has constant variance over time, and without periodic fluctuations, or seasonality.

Effectively a flat-looking series.

Before we continue our discussion about stationarity, let us take a look at seasonality. This can be understood as a cycle that repeats over time, such as monthly, or yearly, for example. This repeating cycle may interfere with the signal we intend to forecast, while at the same time it may provide some insights into what is happening in our data. After all, if there is a cycle, we would like to know about it.

Or any other time interval.

Understanding the seasonality in our data can improve our modelling as it enables us to create a clearer signal. In other words, if we are able to identify the seasonal component in our series, we may be able to extract it out leaving us with a component which we understand (the seasonal part) plus a clearer relationship between the variables at hand. When we remove the seasonal component from a time series, we end up with a so-called seasonal stationary series.

A time series with a clear seasonal component is said to be non-stationary.

There are many ways in which we can take a look at the seasonality in a time series. In this case, let us take a look at using the Fast Fourier Transform (FFT) to convert the time-dependent data into the *frequency domain*. This will enable us to analyse if any predominant frequencies exist. In other

Fourier transforms are awesome!

words, we can check if there is any periodicity on the data. We will not cover the intricate details of the mathematics behind the FFT, but a recommended reading is the excellent *Numerical Recipes*[9] book.

[9] Press, W., S. Teukolsky, W. Vetterling, and B. Flannery (2007). *Numerical Recipes 3rd Edition: The Art of Scientific Computing*. Cambridge University Press.

Let us take a look at the sunspot data we plotted in Figure 1.2. In that figure we have monthly observations for the sun activity. In the analysis below, we will resample the data into yearly observations. The data can be found[10] at `https://doi.org/10.6084/m9.figshare.6728255.v1` as a comma-separated value file with the name "`sunspots_month.CSV`". After loading the usual modules such as pandas, we can read the data as follows:

[10] Rogel-Salazar, J. (2018d, Jul). Sunspots - Monthly Activity since 1749. https://doi.org/10.6084/m9.figshare.6728255.v1

```
sun = pd.read_csv('sunspots_month.csv')
sun.Year = pd.to_datetime(sun.Year,
    format='%Y-%m-%d')
sun.set_index('Year', inplace=True)
```

While loading the data, we can specify the format for reading the date.

We are specifying the format in which the dates should be parsed. We also indicate which column is the index in our dataset.

As we mentioned before, we have monthly data and we would like to take a yearly view. The first thing we are going to do is obtain a yearly average:

```
sun_year = sun.resample('YE').mean()
```

We are resampling the data to a yearly frequency.

Let us now load the FFT pack from `scipy`:

```
from scipy import fftpack
```

Given the signal of the yearly sunspot activity, we can calculate its Fourier transform. We also calculate a normalisation constant n:

```
Y=fftpack.fft(sun_year['Value'].values)
n=int(len(Y)/2)
```

We calculate the FFT of the signal and a normalisation constant.

Note that `fft` expects a NumPy array, hence passing the values of our pandas series. We now can create an array to hold the frequencies in the signal, with the period being the inverse frequency:

```
freq=np.array(range(n))/(2*n)
period=1./freq[1:]
```

With this information we can obtain the period.

We can now calculate the power spectrum of the signal as follows:

```
power=abs(Y[1:n])**2
```

And finally the power spectrum of the signal.

A plot of the power spectrum versus the period is shown in Figure 1.9 where we can see that the sunspot activity data is periodic, and that the sunspots occur with a maximum in activity approximately every 11 years. Cool! Not quite tauspots—from Tau Ceti you see—but I am sure Dr Rayland Grace would approve[11].

[11] Weir, A. (2022). *Project Hail Mary: A Novel.* Random House Publishing Group.

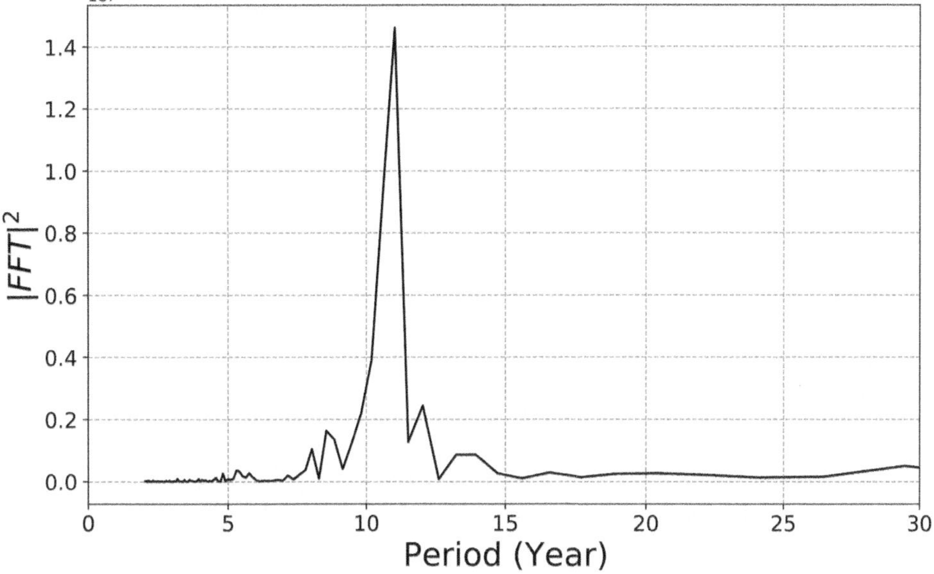

Figure 1.9: Analysis of the power spectrum of the sunspots data. We can see that a maximum in activity occurs approximately every 11 years.

1.4.4 *Determining Stationarity*

We have seen that there is seasonality in our sunspot data, and so, it is a non-stationary time series. In other cases we may need to check that the mean and variance are constant, and the autocorrelation is time-independent. We can do some of these checks by plotting rolling statistics to see if the moving average and/or moving variance vary with time.

Rolling statistics can help us determine stationarity.

Another method is to use statistics to test your hypothesis. You can learn more about hypothesis testing in *Statistics and Data Visualisation with Python*[12]. In this case, the Dickey-Fuller test lets us check for stationarity, and the null hypothesis is that the time series is non-stationary based on

[12] Rogel-Salazar, J. (2023). *Statistics and Data Visualisation with Python*. Chapman & Hall/CRC The Python Series. CRC Press

the results of a test statistic, and we have critical values for different confidence levels. If the test statistic is below the critical value, we can reject the null hypothesis and say that the series is stationary.

The Dickey-Fuller test enables us to check for stationarity too.

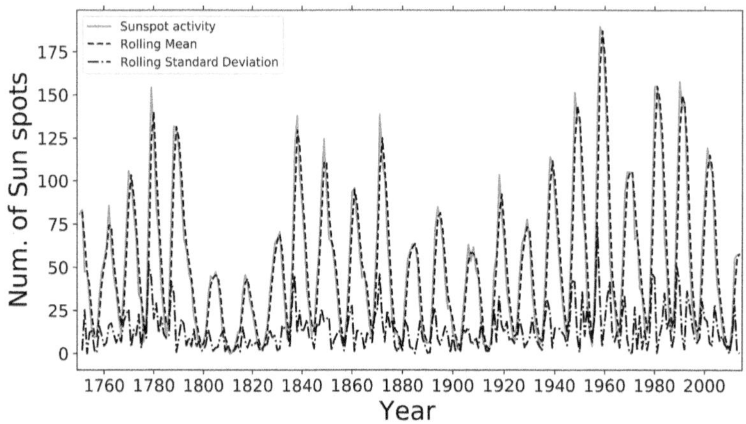

Figure 1.10: Sunspot activity and rolling statistics for the average and the standard deviation.

Let us see what this means for our monthly sunspot activity data. We can calculate rolling statistics for the mean and variance:

```
rolling_mean = sun_year['Value'].rolling(2).mean()
rolling_std = sun_year['Value'].rolling(2).std()
```

Rolling statistics for a window of 2 years.

In Figure 1.10 we can see the rolling statistics for the sunspot activity. The variation on the average is larger than that on the standard deviation, but it does not seem to be increasing or reducing with time.

Let us take a look at the Dickey-Fuller test. Technically speaking, the test checks that a unit root is present in a time series sample. A unit root is a characteristic found in certain stochastic processes—like random walks—that can complicate statistical analysis in time series modelling. A linear stochastic process is said to have a unit root when the number 1 is a solution to its characteristic equation. We can think of this as the current value of a series y_t being equal to the previous value y_{t-1} plus an error ϵ_t:

The Dickey-Fuller test checks for a unit root to be present in the series.

$$y_t = a y_{t-1} + \epsilon_t \tag{1.6}$$

with $|a| = 1$. While such processes are non-stationary, they do not necessarily exhibit a trend.

We are going to use the Augmented Dickey-Fuller (ADF) method[13], `adfuller`, in `statsmodels` time series analysis module `tsa.stattools`. The ADF test expands the Dickey-Fuller test to include high order regressive process in the model. ADF estimates the following equation:

[13] Said, S. E. and Dickey, D. A (1984). Testing for unit roots in autoregressive-moving average models of unknown order. *Biometrika 71(3)*, 599–607.

$$\Delta y_t = \mu + \beta t + (\theta - 1) y_{t-1} + \sum \delta_i \Delta y_{t-i} + \epsilon_t, \tag{1.7}$$

where θ is the variable of interest. The null hypothesis of the ADF test is that the series contains a unit root. If θ is significantly different from 1, this would indicate stationarity.

```
from statsmodels.tsa.stattools import adfuller
df_test = adfuller(sun_year['Value'],autolag='AIC')
```

The Dickey-Fuller test can be evaluated with the help of `adfuller` method in `statsmodels`.

The method has a parameter called `autolag` used to determine the lag length among the values $0, 1, \ldots,$ up to a maximum lag. We can determine the number of lags by minimising information criteria such as the Akaike Information Criterion (AIC). You can read more about information criteria in Appendix A.

Read more about information criteria in Appendix A.

Let us look at the results of the Dickey-Fuller test with the following function:

```
def isstationary(df_test):
  stationary=[]
  print('Test Statistic is {0}'.format(df_test[0]))
  print('p-value is {0}'.format(df_test[1]))
  print('No. lags used = {0}'.format(df_test[2]))
  print('No. observations used = {0}'.\
      format(df_test[3]))
  for key, value in df_test[4].items():
      print('Critical Value ({0}) = {1}'.\
          format(key, value))
      if df_test[0]<=value:
          stationary.append(True)
      else:
          stationary.append(False)
  return all(stationary)
```

The Dickey-Fuller test implementation returns 4 items including the test statistic, the p-value, the lags used and the critical values.

And here are the results:

```
> isstationary(df_test)


Test Statistic is -2.4708472868362916
p-value is 0.12272956184228762
No. lags used = 8
No. observations used = 256
```

In this case we see that the Dickey-Fuller test applied to the sunspots data supports the null hypothesis.

```
Critical Value (1%) = -3.4561550092339512
Critical Value (10%) = -2.5728222369384763
Critical Value (5%) = -2.8728972266578676
False
```

As we can see, we cannot reject the null hypothesis, and the yearly data for the sunspot activity can be assumed therefore to be non-stationary.

Extracting the trend and seasonality out of the time series data provides us with better ways to understand the process at hand. A useful technique for this is to decompose the time series into parts that are amenable to be described by a model. Given a time series Y_t, a naïve additive model decomposes the signal as follows:

Systematic components are those that can be modelled.

$$Y_t = T_t + S_t + e_t, \tag{1.8}$$

Additive decomposition.

where T_t is the trend, S_t is the seasonality and e_t corresponds to the residuals or random variation in the series. An alternative to this decomposition is the so-called multiplicative model:

$$Y_t = (T_t)(S_t)(e_t). \tag{1.9}$$

Multiplicative decomposition.

We can use `seasonal_decompose` from `statmodels` to decompose the signal using moving averages. In our sunsport data, we have seen that we have a seasonality of around 11 years; we will use this information to decompose our time series:

```
import statsmodels.api as sm
dec_sunspots = sm.tsa.seasonal_decompose(sun_year,\
    model='additive', period=11)
```

`seasonal_decompose` lets us decompose a time series into its systematic and non-systematic components.

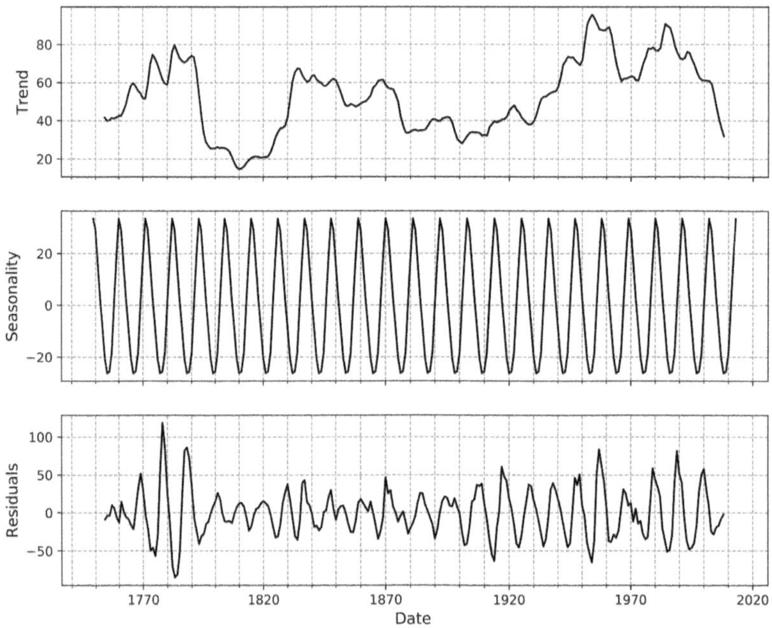

Figure 1.11: Trend, seasonality and residual components for the sunspot dataset.

We can use a multiplicative method by passing on the parameter `model='multiplicative'`. The result of the decomposition is an object that has a plotting method. We can look at the result of the decomposition by typing `dec_sunspots.plot()` and the output can be seen in Figure 1.11 where we have plots for the trend, seasonality and the residuals.

Let us apply the Dickey-Fuller test to the bitcoin tick data defined on page 26. Let us resample the data on 15-minute intervals and take the average:

```
closing_bitcoin=ticks['close'].\
    resample('15Min').mean()
df_test_bitcoin = adfuller(closing_bitcoin,\
    autolag='AIC')
```

The bitcoin data is non-stationary.

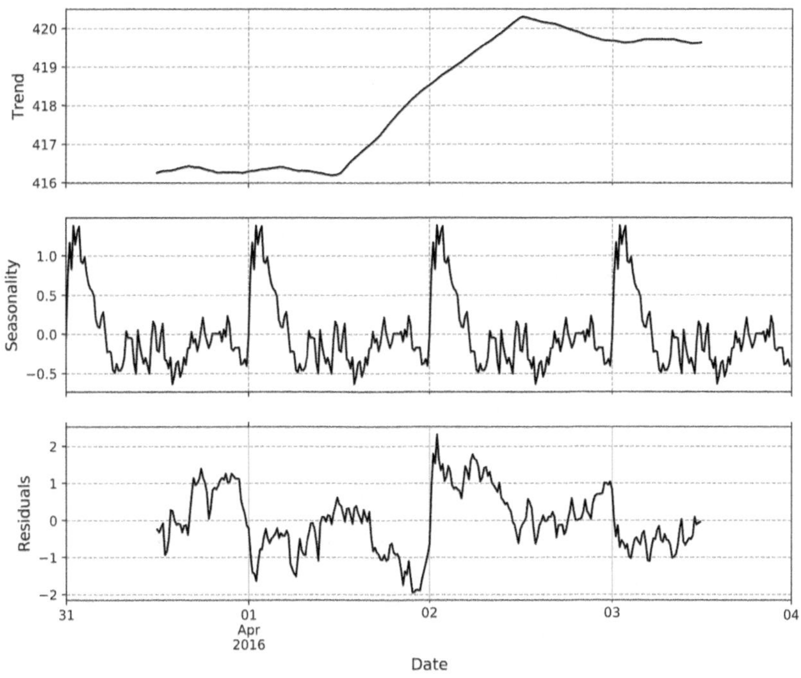

Figure 1.12: Trend, seasonality and residual components for the bitcoin dataset.

We can see the decomposition in Figure 1.12.

```
> isstationary(df_test_bitcoin)


Test Statistic is -1.4531293932585607
p-value is 0.5565571771135377
No. lags used = 10
No. observations used = 373
Critical Value (1%) = -3.448003816652923
Critical Value (5%) = -2.86931999731073
Critical Value (10%) = -2.5709145866785503
False
```

1.4.5 *Autoregression to the Rescue*

So far, we have been doing OK with the time series we have seen. However, we know that simply using a linear or polynomial fit to the data is not good enough. Furthermore, we cannot ignore the seasonal variation and the random noise that makes up the signal.

We have seen that using a linear or polynomial fit is not good for time series.

When we discussed the idea of moving averages, we considered that a better approach was to see if the next value in the series can be predicted as some function of its previous values. A way to achieve this is **autoregression**. We are therefore interested in building a regression model of the current value fitted on one, or more, previous values called *lagged values*. This sounds great, but how many lagged values do we need?

Autoregression is exactly what it sounds like: A regression on the dataset itself.

Well, we can take a look at the time series and check how much information there is in the previous values, helping us with our prediction. We can do this with the help of the autocorrelation function (ACF) we defined in Equation (1.3). Similarly, we can look at the partial autocorrelation function (PACF) which controls the values of the time series at all shorter lags, unlike the autocorrelation.

The correlation function will test whether adjacent observations are autocorrelated; in other words, it will help us determine if there are correlations between observations 1 and 2, 2 and 3, ... $n - 1$ and n. Similarly, it will test at other lags. For instance, the autocorrelation at lag 4 tests whether observations 1 and 5, 2 and 6,... are correlated.

This is known as "lag-one autocorrelation".

In general, we should test for autocorrelation at lags 1 to $n/4$, where n is the total number of observations in the analysis. Estimates at longer lags have been shown to be statistically unreliable[14].

[14] Box, G. and G. Jenkins (1976). *Time series analysis: forecasting and control*. Holden-Day series in time series analysis and digital processing. Holden-Day.

We can take a look at the autocorrelation and partial autocorrelation for the sunspot dataset with the following code:

```
sm.graphics.tsa.plot_acf(sun_year, lags=40)
sm.graphics.tsa.plot_pacf(sun_year, lags=40)
```

Figure 1.13 shows the result of the code above. We can see in the upper panel that the autocorrelation shows a periodic structure, reflecting the seasonality in the time series.

A similar computation can be carried out for the bitcoin dataset. The result can be seen in Figure 1.14. As we can see in the upper panel, the correlation fades slowly as we take longer and longer lagged values.

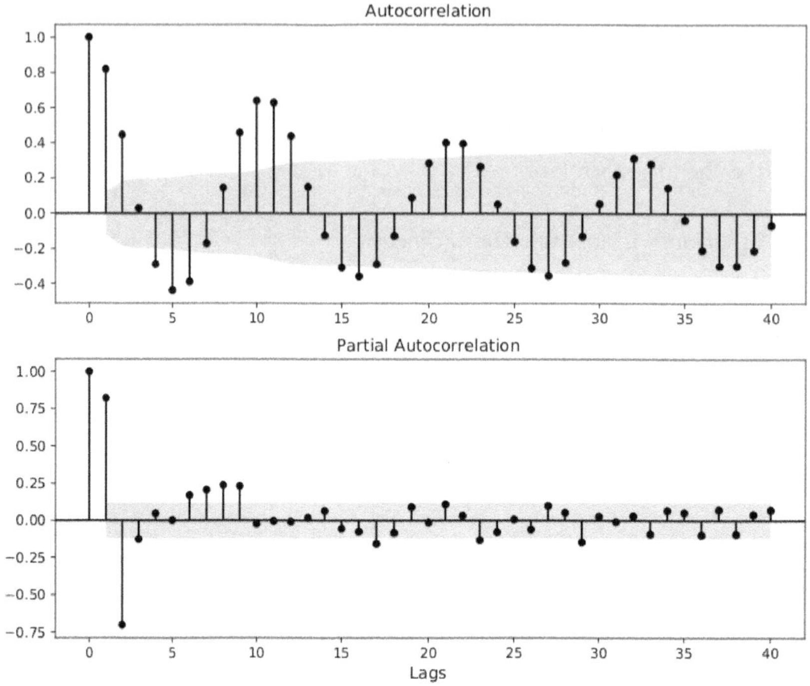

Figure 1.13: Autocorrelation and partial autocorrelation for the sunspot dataset.

It stands to reason that if value 0 is correlated with value 1, and value 1 is correlated with 2, it follows that 0 must be correlated with 2. This is why we need the partial autocorrelation, as it provides us with information about the relationship between an observation with observations at prior timesteps, but with the crucial difference that the intervening observations are removed.

Partial autocorrelation tells us about the relationship of observations with earlier ones, but without the intervening observations.

In the examples of the sunspot and bitcoin datasets, we can see from the lower panels of the correlograms in Figures 1.13 and 1.14 that only the most recent values are really useful in building an autoregression model.

A correlogram is a plot showing the correlation statistics.

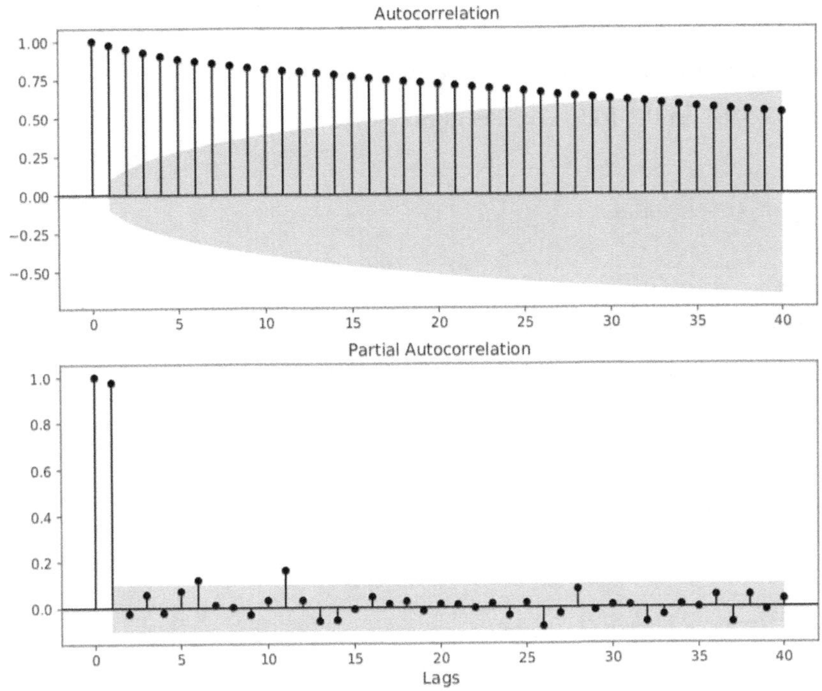

Figure 1.14: Autocorrelation and partial autocorrelation for the bitcoin dataset.

A PACF correlogram with a large spike at one lag that decreases after a few lags usually indicates that there is a moving average term in the series. In this case, the autocorrelation function will help us determine the order of the moving average term. If instead we have a large spike at one lag followed by a damped oscillating correlogram, then we have a higher-order moving average term. This is the picture we get from the lower panel of Figure 1.13 for the sunspot data.

A large spike followed by damped oscillations indicates a higher-order moving average term.

In the case of the correlogram shown in the lower panel of Figure 1.14, we have a few important correlations in the first few lags that die out quite quickly. In this case we can

A spike on the first lags followed by not very important ones suggests the presence of an autoregressive term.

interpret this as having a time series with an autoregressive term. We can determine the order of this autoregressive term from the spikes in the correlogram. We will discuss autoregressive models in the following section.

1.5 *Autoregressive Models*

AN AUTOREGRESSIVE (AR) MODEL IS a representation of a type of random process where the future values of the series are based on weighted combinations of past values. As such, an AR(1) is a first-order process in which the current value is based only on the immediately previous value:

$$Y_t = \beta_0 + \beta_1 Y_{t-1} + \epsilon_t. \tag{1.10}$$

AR(1) model.

An AR(2) process,

$$Y_t = \beta_0 + \beta_1 Y_{t-1} + \beta_2 Y_{t-2} + \epsilon_t, \tag{1.11}$$

AR(2) model.

determines the current value based on the previous two values, and so on.

It is possible to use autoregression and moving averages in combination to describe various time series. This methodology is usually called **autoregressive moving average** (ARMA) modelling. In ARMA modelling we use two expressions to describe the time series, one for the moving average and the other one for the autoregression. ARMA(p, q) denotes a model with autoregression of order p and moving average of order q.

ARMA - Autoregressive Moving Average.

A further generalisation of an ARMA model is the so-called **autoregressive integrated moving average** (ARIMA) model. The AR and MA parts of the acronym follow the discussion above. The integrated (or "I") part is perhaps less clear, but effectively it means that the time series has been rendered stationary by taking differences. In other words, instead of looking at the observation Y_1 we are interested in $Y_1 - Y_0$.

ARIMA - Autoregressive Integrated Moving Average.

An ARIMA(p, d, q) model puts together all the techniques we have discussed in this chapter and is specified by three parameters: $p, d,$ and q, where:

- p: Denotes the order of the autoregression
- d: Denotes the number of difference levels
- q: Denotes the order of moving average

The meaning of the parameters in an ARIMA(p, d, q) model.

We have some commonly used models, such as:

- ARIMA$(0, 0, 0)$ is simply predicting the mean of the overall time series. In other words, there is no structure!
- ARIMA$(0, 1, 0)$ works out the differences (not the raw values) and predicts the next one without autoregression or smoothing. This is effectively a random walk!

Some common ARIMA models.

Let us take a look at applying ARMA and ARIMA models to the sunspot dataset. For instance, we can apply an ARMA$(6, 0)$ model with an ARIMA$(6, 0, 0)$:

```
from statsmodels.tsa.arima.model import ARIMA
arma_sun = ARIMA(sun_year, order=(6, 0, 0)).fit()
print(arma_sun.params)
```

```
const       51.963469
ar.L1        1.290751
ar.L2       -0.473429
ar.L3       -0.177169
ar.L4        0.133995
ar.L5       -0.212000
ar.L6        0.158880
sigma2     278.734450
```

The results of applying an ARMA(6, 0) model to the sunspot dataset.

In the results above, `ar.L1` refers to the autoregressive term with the lag of 1, `ar.L2` represents the term with the lag of 2, etc. `sigma2` is the variance of the residuals, and it helps test the normality of residuals against the alternative of non-normality.

The best model can be found by changing the parameters p and q of the model such that we minimise any of the various information criteria such as the Akaike (AIC), the Bayesian (BIC) or the Hannan-Quinn (HQIC) information criterion.

See Appendix A for more details about these information criteria.

```
print("AIC: ", arma_sun.aic)
print("BIC: ", arma_sun.bic)
print("HQIC:", arma_sun.hqic)


AIC:  2262.5757141102913
BIC:  2291.2135527181813
HQIC: 2274.0819598213147
```

Evaluation of the AIC, BIC and HQIC information criteria.

We can also apply an ARIMA model, in this case an ARIMA$(3,1,1)$:

```
arima_mod= ARIMA(sun_year, order=(3,1,1)).fit()
> print(arima_mod.summary())

                    SARIMAX Results
=================================================
Dep. Variable:  Value   No. Observations:     265
Model:  ARIMA(3, 1, 1)   Log Likelihood  -1117.999
AIC             2245.997
BIC             2263.877
HQIC         2253.182

                coef    std err        z
-------------------------------------------------
ar.L1          1.1619      0.064     18.220
ar.L2         -0.3635      0.089     -4.102
ar.L3         -0.2542      0.062     -4.095
ma.L1         -0.8873      0.039    -22.893
sigma2       276.6309     20.759     13.326
```

An abridged version of the summary provided by the ARIMA$(3,1,1)$ model applied to the sunspot dataset.

The model above has a moving average component and hence apart from the autoregressive terms, we also have moving average terms, i.e., `ma.L1` being the moving average term with lag 1. In the abridged summary, we can also see results for `std err` which is an estimate of the error of the predictive value, and `z` is the standardised coefficient. We have omitted other columns such as the p-value coefficient and confidence intervals.

This model combines both AR (autoregressive) and MA (moving average) components.

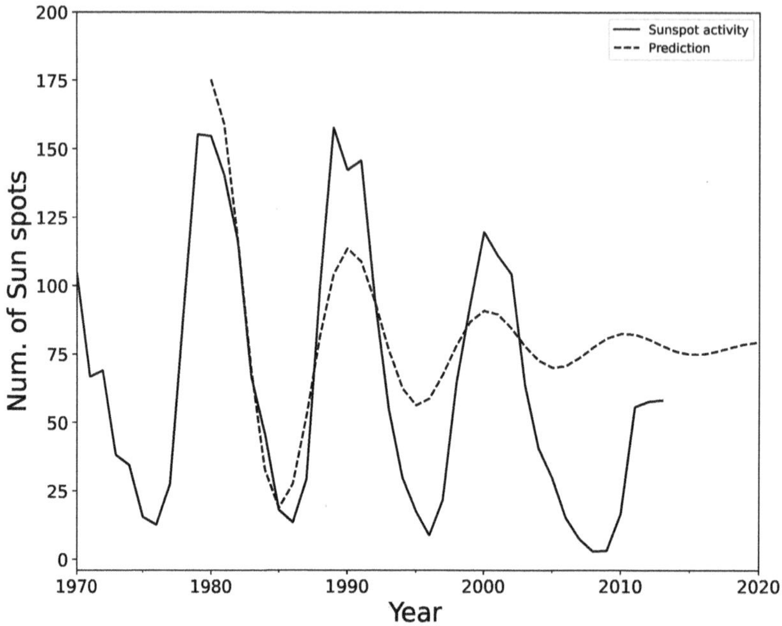

Figure 1.15: Prediction for the sunspot activity using an ARIMA(3, 1, 1) model.

Finally, it is important to note that in the ideal scenario we would carry out the analysis on a training dataset to develop a predictive model to be tested against a testing set. Nonetheless, let us take a look at the predictions we could draw, in this case for the autoregressive model ARIMA(3, 1, 1) applied to the sunspots dataset:

```
predict_sunspots = arima_mod.predict('1980',\
    '2050', dynamic=True)
```

We can run predictions from the models with the `predict` method for each of them.

The result can be seen in Figure 1.15 where we can compare the actual values of the sunspot activity against the predictions made by the model for the years 1980-2020. This is not bad for a model that has not been curated!!

1.6 *Forecasting with Prophet*

IMAGINE HAVING A CRYSTAL BALL—but instead of mystical symbols and cryptic incantations, it runs Python and outputs tidy dataframes. That is roughly the idea behind Prophet, a time series forecasting tool developed by the team at Meta. Prophet was built with the practical Jackalope Data Scientist in mind: It is fast, flexible, and handles all sorts of common forecasting quirks like missing data, seasonal trends, and sudden growth changes.

Also, you won't need to wear robes. Unless you want to. We won't judge.

Think of Prophet as that helpful friend who does not ask too many questions, works well with your pandas data, and knows what to do when the holidays roll around. It was specifically designed to handle business time series with strong seasonal effects and several seasons of historical data. We should not be fooled by its user-friendliness—under the hood, it packs a serious model based on additive regression with four main components: trend, seasonality, holidays, and error.

Seasonal holiday effects? Prophet's got you covered.

Let us roll up our sleeves and forecast some international air travel using the `AirPassengers` dataset. The dataset is available in GitHub[15], and it contains monthly figures for passenger numbers from 1949 to 1960. You will need to install Prophet before starting this section, and make sure you download a copy of the dataset too. Let us load the data:

[15] Brownlee, J (2018). Airline passengers. https://github.com/jbrownlee/Datasets/blob/master/airline-passengers.csv. Accessed: 2025-07-18.

```
import pandas as pd
from prophet import Prophet
airline = pd.read_csv('airline-passengers.csv'')
airline.head(3)

     Month  Passengers
0  1949-01         112
1  1949-02         118
2  1949-03         132
```

Let us predict international air travel.

We will consider the passenger numbers to be reported on a monthly basis at the beginning of each month. We can convert the column `Month` into a date format with pandas:

```
airline['Month'] = pd.to_datetime(airline['Month'])
airline.head(3)

       Month  Passengers
0 1949-01-01         112
1 1949-02-01         118
2 1949-03-01         132
```

We ensure we are using dates in our dataset with the help of pandas.

We keep it simple in this example: Just two columns—`Month` (datestamp) and `Passengers`. It is the latter dependent variable that we want to forecast. Now let us ask Prophet to see into the future. It does this by modelling a time series $y(t)$ as:

$$y(t) = g(t) + s(t) + h(t) + \epsilon_t, \tag{1.12}$$

We are modelling trend, seasonality and holidays with Prophet.

where $g(t)$ is the trend, $s(t)$ is the seasonality, $h(t)$ is a holidays component, finally ϵ_t is the normally-distributed error term. The trend component models changes either with a piece-wise linear or a logistic model. The seasonality component can be yearly, weekly or daily and is modelled using Fourier series. The holiday component aims to model irregular, but predictable, events with the use of delta functions.

The input for Prophet is always a dataframe with two columns: A datestamp (`ds`) and the dependent variable (`y`). We start by renaming our columns and instantiating the model:

Prophet expects two columns called `ds` and `y`.

```
airline.columns = ['ds', 'y']
model = Prophet(growth='linear',
  seasonality_mode='additive')
model.fit(df)
```

We instantiate a Prophet model with the `Prophet` function.

As you can see, we can specify parameters such as `growth='linear'` which uses a piece-wise linear function to model the trend. Other options are `'logistic'` or `'flat'` to specify a logistic or flat trend, respectively. The parameter `seasonality_mode` is `'additive'` by default, and the other option is `'multiplicative'`.

Let us ask Prophet to look into their crystal ball and predict the future. In this case we will create a dataframe to include 2 years' worth of predictions on a monthly basis:

We need a suitable dataframe to make our predictions.

```
future = model.make_future_dataframe(periods=24,
  freq='ME')
```

The predict method will assign each row in `future` a predicted value $\hat{y}$:

```
> forecast = model.predict(future)
> forecast.tail(3)

             ds       trend  ...       yhat
165  1962-09-30  552.327007  ...  529.942139
166  1962-10-31  555.461269  ...  501.251216
167  1962-11-30  558.494425  ...  530.792179
```

We can obtain predictions with the `predict` method.

We can look at the results of the prediction with a plot:

```
model.plot(forecast)
```

Figure 1.16 shows the result of the command above, and voilà! Just like that, you have forecasted 2 years into the future. The shaded area shows Prophet's uncertainty interval—after all, even algorithms have doubts.

Even algorithms have doubts.

1.6.1 *Peeking under the Hood: Components*

PROPHET MAKES IT EASY TO see what is driving your forecast. Is it a rising trend? A seasonal spike in July? If we are interested in seeing the forecast components of the model, you can use the `plot_components` method of Prophet. By default we will see the trend, yearly seasonality, and weekly seasonality of the time series. If we were to include holidays, we will see those too.

The `plot_components` method lets us visualise the trend, seasonality and holidays in our model.

```
model.plot_components(forecast)
```

We can see the components for our model in Figure 1.17, revealing the trend (i.e., long-term direction), the seasonal

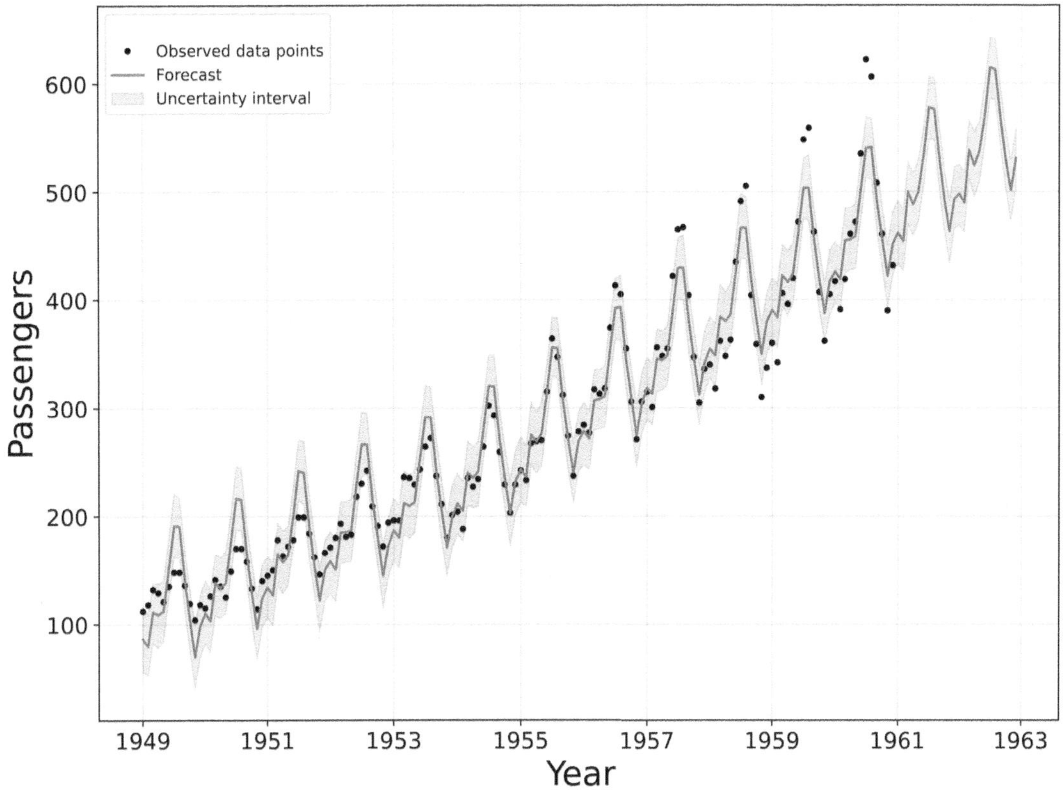

Figure 1.16: Prediction of monthly for airline passengers over 2 years between 1960 and 1961, obtained with Prophet.

pattern (those lovely humps and dips), and any holiday effects you may have added.

1.6.2 *Adding Holidays and Custom Seasonality*

SPEAKING OF HOLIDAYS, PROPHET ALLOWS us to include them explicitly—great for sales forecasts, public transport, or pumpkin spice latte demand. In order to include holidays, we must create a dataframe for them. The structure is as follows:

Yes, PSL sales are seasonal. I am sure you can check.

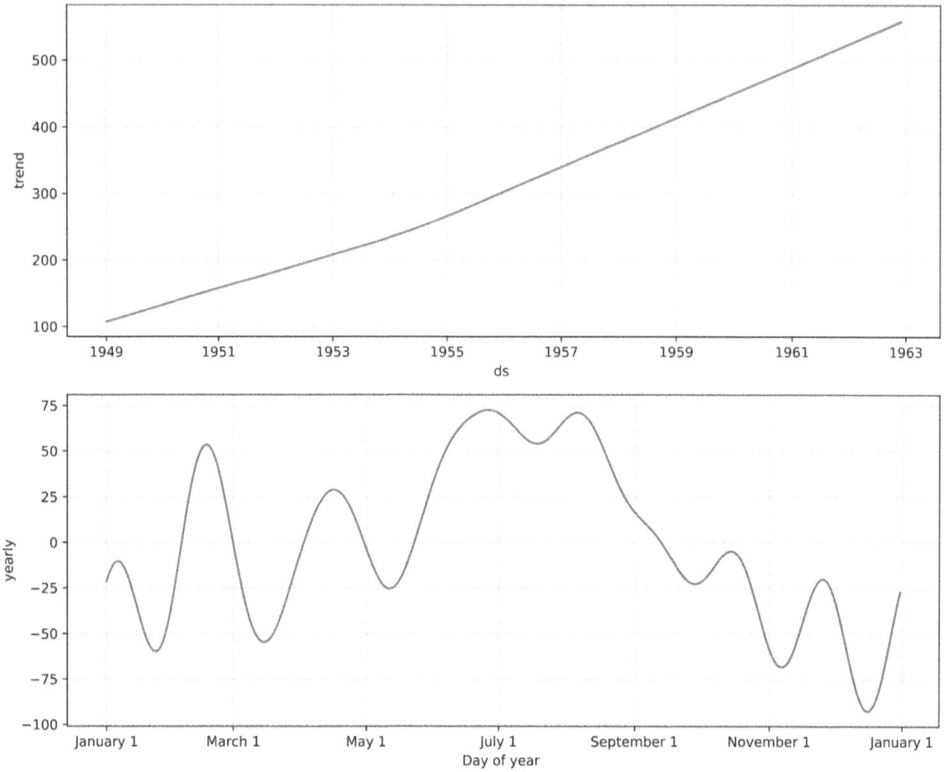

Figure 1.17: Trend and seasonality for our monthly airline passengers data.

- We need two columns: `holiday` and `ds` for the datastamp. We also need a row for each occurrence of the holiday.

- The dataframe must include all occurrences of the holiday, both in the past (back as far as the historical data go) and in the future (out as far as the forecast is being made). Note that if the holidays do not repeat, Prophet will model them and then not include them in the forecast.

These are the requirements for the holiday dataframe.

- We can can also include columns to extend the holiday using `lower_window` and `upper_window`, which extend the holiday out to `[lower_window, upper_window]` days around the date. In this way, if we want to include Christmas Eve and Boxing Day in addition to Christmas, we can add `'lower_window':-1` and `'upper_window':1`.

Let us create our dataframe using the information above:

```
from pandas.tseries.holiday import
  USFederalHolidayCalendar

holidays = pd.DataFrame(
  'holiday': 'USFederalHoliday',
  'ds': pd.to_datetime(
    USFederalHolidayCalendar().holidays(
      start='1949-01-01', end='1962-01-01')
  ),
  'lower_window': 0,
  'upper_window': 1,
)
```

Here we are using holiday information for the US.

Once the holidays dataframe is created, we can model holiday effects by passing them in with the holidays argument of the constructor:

```
model2 = Prophet(holidays=holidays)
model2.fit(df)

forecast2 = model.predict(future)
```

We can then simply pass the holiday dataframe as a parameter to the `Prophet` function.

We can see the holiday component included in Figure 1.18.

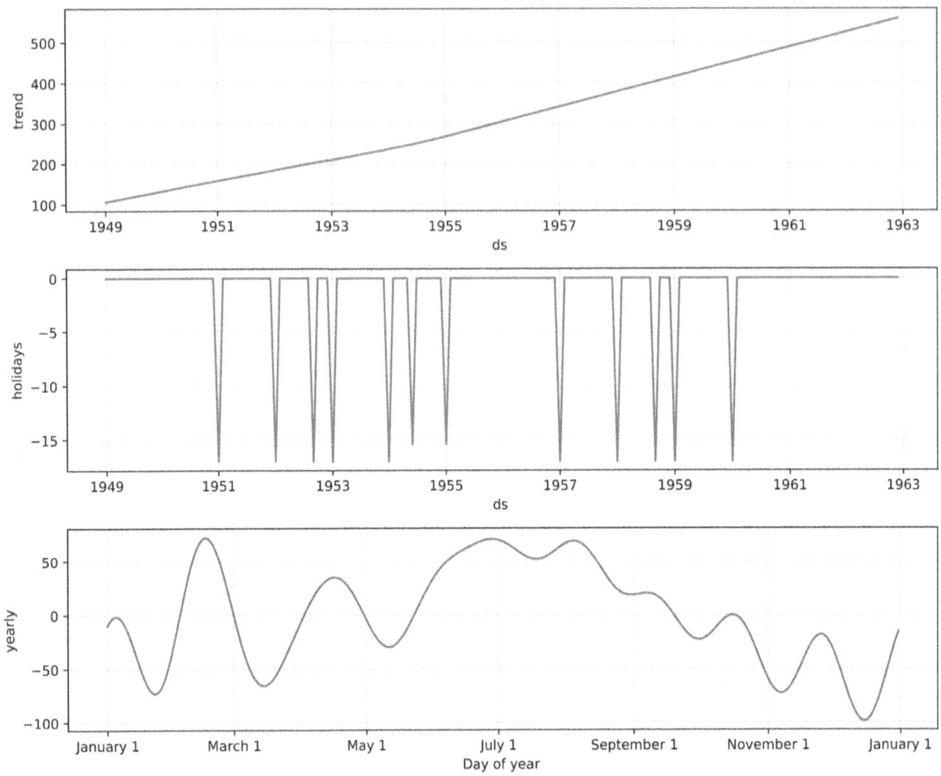

Figure 1.18: Trend, seasonality and holiday components for our monthly airline passengers data.

1.6.3 *Customising Growth and Changepoints*

PROPHET ASSUMES A PIECE-WISE LINEAR or logistic growth trend by default. If your data has a cap, such as a population limit, for example, we can use logistic growth. Let us imagine that we have a population limit of 580 passengers. We can include this in the model as follows:

If the data has a cap, we can use logistic growth.

```
df['cap'] = 580
model3 = Prophet(growth='logistic')
model3.fit(df)
```

All we need to do is specify the `growth` parameter as `'logistic'`.

Not only that, Prophet can also automatically detect changepoints where the time series trend shifts. If the model is overfitting trend changes (too much flexibility) or underfitting them (too little flexibility), you can control the behaviour using the `changepoint_prior_scale` parameter. This value determines the strength of the model's preference for fewer changepoints. By default, it is set to 0.05, but increasing it allows the trend to adapt more freely to shifts in the data.

We can adjust trend flexibility with `changepoint_prior_scale`.

```
model4 = Prophet(changepoint_prior_scale=0.05)
```

Prophet is fantastic for many practical forecasting problems, but it is not magic. It may underperform on highly noisy data, or datasets without enough history to establish seasonality. Also bear in mind that it is not designed for high-frequency data (like second-by-second price ticks). Still, for many applications—sales, web traffic, stock levels—it gives you a strong start, a quick prototype, and often a surprisingly good forecast.

Prophet is fantastic, but it is not magic!

So the next time someone asks you to forecast the future, you do not need a crystal ball, just Prophet, pandas, and a dash of Python charm.

And if that fails, tell them you'll get back to them in the future.

1.7 *Time Series Cross-Validation and Forecasting Evaluation*

YOU WOULD NOT GRADE A COOKING CONTEST BY RANDOMLY ASSIGNING DISHES TO JUDGES without caring who cooked what or when. So why would we evaluate a forecasting model by randomly splitting up our data? Time series data comes with an unbreakable law: Time moves forward. And that means our evaluation strategy needs to respect the arrow of time too.

You would not compare tomorrow's forecast to last year's storm. That's just weather-shaming.

As Jackalope Data Scientists, we know that when working with regular machine learning models, it is common to do a random train-test split or even k-fold cross-validation. But for time series, those approaches are strictly forbidden. Why? Because we cannot "peek" into the future to train our model—it wouldn't be fair.

Unless you're a time traveller, in which case, please invest in our retirement fund.

Time series cross-validation is an approach that simulates real forecasting scenarios by training the model on past data and testing it on future data, gradually expanding the window as we go. It is like going on a hike—you can only step forward, not teleport to the end of the trek. There are two main approaches:

This is also known as "walk-forward validation" or "rolling forecasting origin."

- **Expanding window**: The training set grows as time progresses.
- **Sliding (or rolling) window**: The training set size remains fixed, but it slides forward in time.

Let us put this into action using the same airline passenger dataset from earlier. We will import `cross_validation` and `performance_metrics` from `diagnostics` in Prophet, and we will use the first model we constructed in Section 1.6.

```
from prophet.diagnostics import cross_validation,
  performance_metrics
import pandas as pd

df_cv = cross_validation(model,
  initial='730 days', # First 2 years for training
  period='180 days',  # Predict every 6 months
  horizon='365 days') # Forecast up to 1 year ahead
```

Prophet has some cross-validation methods included. Use them!

We are asking our cross-validation to train for the first 2 years, then predict every 6 months and forecast up to 1 year ahead, and it repeats the process with each new chunk of data. We can now evaluate those forecasts using some common error metrics:

We can change our cross-validation window to fit our needs.

```
> df_perf = performance_metrics(df_cv)
>df_perf.head()
  horizon          mse       rmse  ...
0 40 days  1078.165434  32.835430  ...
1 42 days  1028.050051  32.063220  ...
2 46 days   919.989101  30.331322  ...
3 47 days  1060.787473  32.569732  ...
4 48 days  1049.895923  32.402098  ...

     mdape     smape  coverage
0    0.073982  0.079212  0.272727
1    0.081427  0.080811  0.227273
2    0.086248  0.081609  0.181818
3    0.087331  0.085655  0.181818
4    0.087331  0.083497  0.227273
```

A typical view of the performance metrics after cross-validation in a time series with Prophet.

The metrics we obtain include:

- **MAE** – Mean Absolute Error: How far off the forecast was on average.
- **RMSE** – Root Mean Squared Error: More sensitive to large errors.
- **MAPE** – Mean Absolute Percentage Error: Great for interpretable percentages.
- **Coverage** – The percentage of times the forecast captured the true value inside its uncertainty interval.
- **sMAPE** – Symmetric MAPE: Avoids the issue of large values in the denominator.
- **MASE** – Mean Absolute Scaled Error: Scales against a naïve forecast (e.g., "tomorrow equals today").

Metrics obtained with `performance_metrics`.

Depending on your domain, you may care more about under-forecasting than over-forecasting (e.g., stock-outs in supply chains), so always align metrics with context. Cross-validation of time series enables us to make fair comparisons between models. This also allows us to:

Walk-forward validation keeps everyone honest.

- Test how a model handles different levels of available history.
- Understand when our forecasts become unreliable.
- Optimise hyperparameters with realistic validation scores.

Forecasting is not just about building a clever model—it is about knowing how well it performs when the chips are down and the calendar pages turn. Cross-validation for time series might take a little more work, but it ensures your forecasts do not just look good on paper—they stand the test of time.

Prediction is hard, especially about the future. Said every statistician ever.

1.8 *Summary*

IN THIS CHAPTER WE ADDRESSED some important aspects of dealing with time series data and no Jackalope Data Scientist must be without this knowledge. We have seen that time series are different from other datasets due to the time component. We saw some relevant examples such as the prices of the Apple Ltd. stock, sunspot activity since the mid-1700s and even the exchange rate of bitcoins to US dollars.

We were able to deal with these various datasets thanks to Python modules such as pandas and statsmodels. We saw how pandas enables us to index our dataframes with time and looked at appropriate transformations that pandas enables us to carry out such as resampling, slicing and dicing, filtering, aggregating and plotting.

In terms of modelling time series, we covered how moving averages and exponential smoothing let us get a first approach at forecasting future values of the series based on previous observations. We discussed the concepts of seasonality and stationarity in a time series. We applied decomposition to our datasets, and finally we discussed how autoregression can be used to model time series, combining the topics discussed in this chapter.

We then explored the use of Prophet, a user-friendly forecasting tool developed by Meta that makes modelling seasonality, trend, and even holiday effects straightforward and powerful. Using Prophet, we generated forecasts, visualised their components, and even handled future uncertainty with confidence intervals. This practical approach allowed us to build robust models in just a few lines of code using real-world data.

Finally, we emphasised the importance of *time-aware* model evaluation. We saw that random train-test splits will not do for time series, and instead introduced rolling and expanding window cross-validation strategies. This ensures that our forecasting models not only look good in theory, but also they stand the test of time in practice.

2

Speaking Naturally: Text and Natural Language Processing

THERE ARE MANY KINDS OF language: We speak with our body language, need to "mind our language" in certain situations, we learn a foreign language to ask for a *pain au chocolat* or *una cerveza* and we need language to understand a French lecture on Sheep-Aircraft. Indeed we are also using the Python programming language to create workflows and train machine learning models. We speak the "language of love", and avoid being confusing by speaking in "plain language". What about *natural language*? Have you heard of it? What is it and when do we use it?

Lecture presented by *le célèbre* Jean-Brian Zatapathique of course (Baa-aa, baa-aa).

There are all kinds of languages, including natural language.

Let us take a step back: The common theme among the expressions we listed above is communication. In other words, the different expressions listed use the word *language* to emphasise the fact that we communicate with other humans in a variety of ways. Natural language is one of those forms of communication. The term refers to the use of

Natural language has evolved naturally in humans through continued use.

any language that has evolved naturally in humans through continued use, repetition and adaptation.

English, Spanish, Japanese and Nahuatl are some examples of natural languages. In contrast, languages like Python, C++, Scala or Java, as well as Esperanto, Klingon, Elvish or Dothraki are constructed languages. As you can imagine, natural language can take different forms such as speech, writing or even singing. In any case, communicating in a natural (or constructed) language is a useful, if complex, task. You may not notice it all the time, but imagine interviewing someone who speaks entirely in anagrams. The efforts to make sense of the conversation would bring things into focus.

These are some examples of natural languages.

Be ot or bot ne ot, tath is the nestquoi!

Now, imagine that in your intergalactic travels you encounter a rebel fleet where R2-D2 and C-3PO are on board and you have an important message for Princess Leia Organa. Naturally, you would like to communicate with them in natural language not in beep-bops. You tell them your message and they try to make sense of it, reacting rapidly with excited "Beep-bee-bee-boop-bee-doo-weep" and "You are quite clever you know... for a human being". Off they go to deliver the important information. Not bad... remember, 3PO alone is fluent in over six million forms of communication!

See what I did there!

The tasks achieved by the loyal androids to take natural language as input, and make sense out of it are referred to as *natural language processing*. Natural language processing (NLP) is an area of computer science and artificial

Natural language processing is concerned with the interactions between human language and computers.

intelligence concerned with the interactions between human (natural) languages and computers. In particular, the term refers to the programming of computers for processing and analysing large amounts of natural language data. Some typical challenges in the area go from natural language understanding to speech recognition and even language generation.

Language generation is related to GenAI, i.e., Generative Artificial Intelligence.

As you can imagine, in order for us to be able to parse, analyse and understand natural language with the aid of computers, we need to get hold of suitable data. A rich and readily available source of information—both for natural language and other data—is the web. In this chapter we will see how to extract data from the web using Beautiful Soup and cover some useful ways to process text data including the use of regular expressions and tokenisation. We will then use topic modelling, an unsupervised machine learning task, to start making sense of natural language. Finally we will talk about embeddings and vector search with large language models (LLMs).

Actually this is true not only for natural language processing.

2.1 *Pages and Pages: Accessing Data from the Web*

I AM SURE YOU HAVE heard the self-evident truism that *data is everywhere*. In the best of cases, it is indeed there, and it can be used immediately. Unfortunately, in more cases than not, the data that you want/need/desire is not in the appropriate format, let alone readily available to you.

Remember that seeing the information is not the same as accessing it...

A typical situation is for useful data to be displayed in webpages, but not be downloadable in a useful format. In other words, being able to see the data is not the same as accessing it. This is indeed a goal of many organisations interested in open data. Open data refers to data available to everyone and which can be freely used, reused and redistributed, subject only, at most, to the requirement to attribute and share alike. One of the tenets of open data is that the data must be available as a whole and at no more than a reasonable reproduction cost, preferably accessed via the web in a convenient and modifiable form.

Open data is data available to everyone.

In an ideal scenario, data can be obtained with appropriate *Application Programming Interfaces* (APIs) to make requests for example via the HTTP protocol. In these cases you can use the Requests module[1] in Python for example. While the efforts of the open data movement are slowly but surely making data accessible to all, it is often the case that we still need to obtain it in a more indirect way such as scraping the contents of a webpage: We could manually copy and paste the data but that is as interesting as watching paint dry. Instead, we automate the process to do this work programmatically. There are some great modules such as Scrapy[2] or Beautiful Soup[3] to do this work. In this case we will obtain some data with the help of Beautiful Soup.

[1] Reitz, K. Requests - http for humans. http://docs.python-requests.org/en/master/

Web scraping extracts or "scrapes" data from a webpage.

[2] Scrapy. https://scrapy.org

[3] Beautiful Soup. https://www.crummy.com/software/BeautifulSoup/

Given the semi-structured nature of the data encountered in the web, it is necessary for us to determine what information is relevant to be scraped and whether it requires multiple pages to be parsed. Typically, we will need to parse HTML code standard for creating webpages and web applications. The elements that describe the page are defined by *tags* using angle brackets, and they may look

HTML stands for Hypertext Markup Language.

like this: `<body>...</body>`. In this case we have a body tag and the text between `<body>` and `</body>` corresponds to the visible content of the page.

Each tag has opening and closing versions; the closing tag always precedes the element with a forward slash (/). There are many other tags such as those shown in Table 2.1.

Table 2.1: Common HTML tags.

Tag	Description
html	HTML document
head	Information used by search engines and browsers
title	Title of the document
body	Content of the webpage
h1, h2,...	Headers: h1 is the main header, then h2, etc.
p	Paragraph
div	Block of content
a	Link
ol	Ordered list
ul	Unordered list
li	List item inside an ol or ul tag
table	Table
tr	Table row
th	Table header
td	Table data cell

Once we have determined the data that we are looking for, we need to:

Beware old Jedis warning you that "These are not be the datasets you are looking for"...

1. Read the HTML page
2. Parse the raw HTML string into a nicer, more readable format

3. Extract the information we are interested in

Steps for web scraping the data we are interested in.

4. Process our data, i.e., clean it, make any appropriate transformations, etc.

5. Store, print, save, and take some actions with the data at hand

Let us take a look at a very small, simple HTML document:

```
<!DOCTYPE html>
  <html>
    <head>
      <title>Page Title</title>
    </head>

    <body>
      <h1>My First Heading</h1>
      <p>My first paragraph.</p>
    </body>
</html>
```

A very simple HTML document with a title, a headline and a paragraph marked with appropriate tags.

If you save that piece of code in a text file and open it in a browser, it will look similar to the screenshot shown in Figure 2.1. We can see at the top of the page the tab with the page title, and then the main header followed by a paragraph. It is not the most exciting website, but it provides us with a flavour of what is to follow.

The main thing we need to take into account when scraping the web for data is the terms and conditions of the site. In some cases website owners do not permit automated

Make sure you check the sites' terms and conditions.

Figure 2.1: A very simple webpage.

systems or software to extract data. The methods shown here are in no way an encouragement to abuse terms and conditions placed by websites. Please make sure that you:

- Respect the Terms of Service (ToS)
- Use an API if one is provided, instead of scraping data
- Respect the rules of `robots.txt`
- If ToS or `robots.txt` prevents you from crawling or scraping, ask using a written permission to the owner of the site, prior to doing anything else
- Do not republish your crawled or scraped data or any derivative dataset without verifying the license of the data, or without obtaining written permission from the copyright holder

`Robots.txt` is a text file that instructs web robots (such as search engines) how to crawl pages on a website.

The other thing that you need to consider when obtaining data from webpages is the fact that the sites you are getting the data from may change from time to time. The design may be different, the position of the data in the page will move, the tags may have different metadata, there may be pagination to consider, or simply the page may vanish into thin air. You will have to be prepared to change your code

And will definitely change!

accordingly if you are to obtain your data programmatically. Consider yourself forewarned.

2.1.1 *Beautiful Soup in Action*

NOW THAT WE HAVE A better understanding of the task we need to accomplish, let us take a look at obtaining some data from a website. In order to make the task reproducible, I have created a webpage with the Iris dataset. You can learn more about this dataset in *Data Science and Analytics with Python*[4], particularly chapter 6. The page looks similar to the screenshot in Figure 2.2.

[4] Rogel-Salazar, J. (2025). *Data Science and Analytics with Python*. Chapman & Hall/CRC Data Mining and Knowledge Discovery Series. CRC Press.

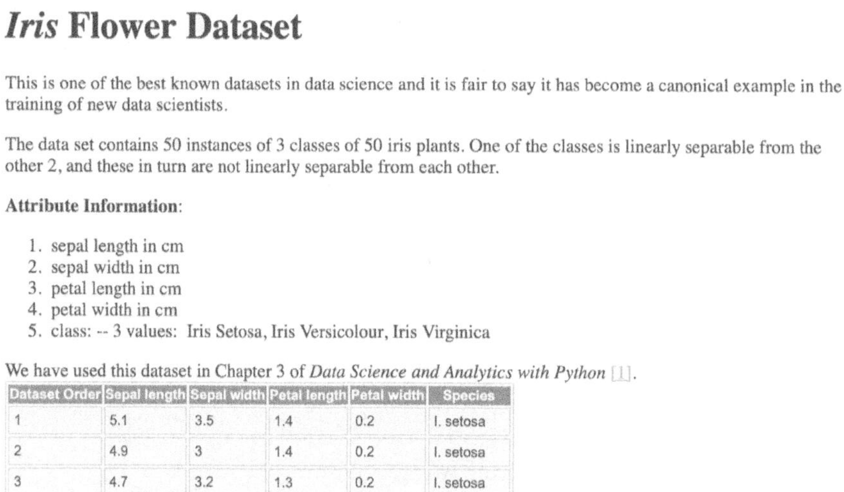

***Iris* Flower Dataset**

This is one of the best known datasets in data science and it is fair to say it has become a canonical example in the training of new data scientists.

The data set contains 50 instances of 3 classes of 50 iris plants. One of the classes is linearly separable from the other 2, and these in turn are not linearly separable from each other.

Attribute Information:

1. sepal length in cm
2. sepal width in cm
3. petal length in cm
4. petal width in cm
5. class: -- 3 values: Iris Setosa, Iris Versicolour, Iris Virginica

We have used this dataset in Chapter 3 of *Data Science and Analytics with Python* [1].

Dataset Order	Sepal length	Sepal width	Petal length	Petal width	Species
1	5.1	3.5	1.4	0.2	I. setosa
2	4.9	3	1.4	0.2	I. setosa
3	4.7	3.2	1.3	0.2	I. setosa

Figure 2.2: A preview of the Iris HTML webpage.

For the purposes of this book, we will work with a local copy of the page, but you can get content live from the web too. I will point out the way to do this as we go along. To work locally, you will need to download the page which can be found at[5] `https://doi.org/10.6084/m9.figshare.7053392.v4` as an HTML document.

[5] Rogel-Salazar, J. (2018c, Sep). Iris Webpage. https://doi.org/10.6084/m9.figshare.7053392.v4

Our task is to extract successfully the table in the page that contains the 50 data points in the set. In order to accomplish our task, we will need to look into the source code that generates the page. The first few lines look like this:

```
<!DOCTYPE html>
<html class="client-nojs" dir="ltr" lang="en">
  <head>
  <meta http-equiv="content-type" content=
      "text/html;
      charset=windows-1252">
    <title>Iris flower data set</title>
  </head>
  <body class="qt-body">
  <h1 id="firstHeading" class="firstHeading">
  <i>Iris</i> Flower Dataset
    </h1>
    <div id="bodyContent" class="mw-body-content">
    <p>This is one of the best known datasets in
    data science and it is fair to say it has
    become a canonical example in the training of
    new data scientists.</p>
      ...
```

The first few lines of the Iris HTML webpage. Notice the use of tags marking the different elements of the page.

We need to be able to read the source page and parse it so that we can make sense of its contents thanks to the tags provided. The first thing we will do is open the page. Here, I am assuming that the HTML file is saved locally in

We can now use Beautiful Soup to parse the HTML source code.

your machine with the name iris_page.html. We can ask Beautiful Soup to read and parse the HTML page as follows:

```
from bs4 import BeautifulSoup


fname = 'iris_page.html'
iris_soup = BeautifulSoup(open(fname), 'lxml')
```

Make sure you provide the appropriate path.

The third line above takes the HTML string to be parsed and the name of the HTML parser to use. In this case we are using lxml, and Beautiful Soup supports the parser included in Python's standard library, html.parser as well as others such as html5lib.

In this case the string to be parsed is the HTML file.

In a more realistic situation, you may not have a local version of the HTML page. Instead you would find the page directly in the web. In this case, first you will need to do a request to the URL of the page and parse the result, as follows:

```
from urllib.request import urlopen
from bs4 import BeautifulSoup
wp='http://wikipedia.org/wiki/Iris_flower_data_set'
pageSource = urlopen(wp).read()


IrisSoup = BeautifulSoup(pageSource, 'lxml')
```

We can parse HTML source code directly from live URLs in this way.

We are using urlopen to request the URL of the page we are interested in and pass the result as the HTML string that Beautiful Soup will parse. Neat!

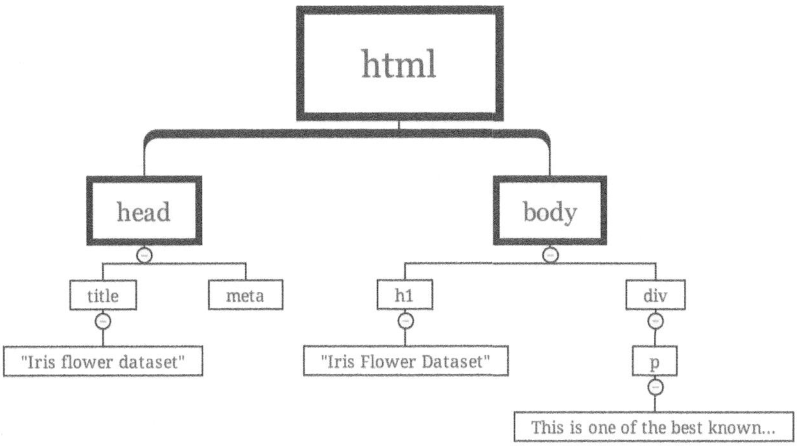

Figure 2.3: A schematic representation of HTML as a tree. We are only showing a few of the branches.

Beautiful Soup has parsed the HTML and has enabled us to make sense of the structure of the page. We can think of HTML as a tree (see Figure 2.3) with different types of objects. The objects that Beautiful Soup returns to us include:

- **Tags**: Beautiful Soup objects that correspond to the actual tags in the original HTML. Tags have attributes and methods.
- **Navigable strings**: Correspond to the text within a tag.
- **Comments**: A special type of navigable string to support comments in the original HTML.
- **Beautiful Soup**: Represents the document as a whole. It can be searched and navigated.

Beautiful Soup objects include tags, navigable strings, comments and a Beautiful Soup object.

Let us take a look at the Iris webpage soup we have in our hands. We can check the type of object in the usual manner:

Bowl?... May be better!

```
> type(iris_soup)

bs4.BeautifulSoup
```

We obtain a Beautiful Soup object when parsing our HTML file.

It is, as we can see, a Beautiful Soup object. It holds information about the original HTML document:

```
> print(iris_soup.name)

'[document]'

> print(iris_soup.title)

<title>Iris flower dataset</title>
```

The object has information about the tags in the HTML.

We can see that the name of the object is "document" and we can start looking at the different tags inside the Iris Beautiful Soup. In the code above, we are requesting the title of the website. Note that the output is a tag object:

```
> type(iris_soup.title)

bs4.element.Tag
```

We can refer to the tags directly by using their names.

In this case the tag is a "title" tag as we can easily verify directly in the HTML source. What about if we are interested in the actual title, i.e., the string inside the tag? Well, all we need to do is request the string of the tag as follows:

```
> print(iris_soup.title.string)

Iris flower dataset

> type(iris_soup.title.string)

bs4.element.NavigableString
```

It is possible to extract the strings inside a tag.

Et voilà! Notice the type of object that is returned by the `string` method for the tag: It is a navigable string. The string method returns a single string within a tag. In other words, if the tag has a single string child, then the returned value will be that string. However, if the tag has no children, or more than one child, the value returned will be `None`.

Remember the tree structure of the HTML code when we talk about parents and children!

In cases where the tag contains no children or more than one child, it is useful to know that you can use a `text` method which will return all the child strings concatenated. Let us look at an example: In our Iris dataset website, the first heading contains a string that reads "*Iris* **Flower Dataset**", with the first word in italics (see Figure 2.2). In HTML this is created with an `i` tag. Let us look at the contents of the heading with Beautiful Soup:

```
> iris_soup.h1.contents

[<i>Iris</i>, 'Flower\n Dataset\n ']
```

Notice that the result here is a list.

The object returned is a list with two elements. This means that the tag has effectively two children: The first one is a tag, and the second one is a string. If we were to ask for the string on this h1, we will get nothing. Instead we should be asking for the text as follows:

```
> iris_soup.h1.text


'Iris Flower \n Dataset\n'
```

The text method returns all the child strings concatenated.

Notice that the returned text has some white spaces including special characters such as the \n. We can clean these by replacing the spaces or using regular expressions, for example. Beautiful Soup offers the possibility of stripping leading and trailing whitespaces with the help of the stripped_strings generator:

See Section 2.2 for more information about regular expressions.

```
> for ss in iris_soup.h1.stripped_strings:
    print(repr(ss))


'Iris'
'Flower\n Dataset'
```

Think of a generator as a function that "generates" values on the fly.

We may still have to do some cleaning on the result. For example, in the example above we still have the line feed control character \n.

Let us now take a look at other parts of our soup. For example, let us look at the first div tag:

```
firstdiv = iris_soup.div
```

We are storing the content of the div in a variable we can later use:

```
> firstdiv

<div class="mw-body-content" id="bodyContent">
<p>This is one of the best known datasets in data
science and it is fair to say it has become a
canonical example in the training of
new data scientists.</p>
<p>The data set contains 50 instances of 3 classes
of 50 iris plants. One of the classes is linearly
separable from the other 2, and these in turn are
not linearly separable from each other.</p>
</div>
```

This particular `div` contains two paragraphs, denoted with `<p></p>` tags.

We can see that there are two paragraphs inside the div. We can search the contents of the different tags with the help of methods such as `find` and `find_all`. Let us get the string of the first paragraph:

```
> paragraph = firstdiv.find('p')
> paragraph.string

'This is one of the best known datasets in data
science and it is\n fair to say it has become
a canonical example in the training of\n new
data scientists.'
```

The `find` method locates the first instance of the tag searched.

The `find` method has enabled us to search for the first instance of the `p` tag. In contrast, we can use the `find_all` method to obtain all the instances inside a list. Notice that `find_all` lets us search for multiple tags. For instance, if we wanted all the paragraphs and list items in the document, we can type the following:

```
> iris_soup.find_all(['p', 'li'])


[<p>This is one of the best known datasets in data
science and it is fair to say it has become a
canonical example in the training of new
data scientists.</p>,
<p>The data set contains 50 instances of 3 classes
of 50 iris plants. One of the classes is linearly
separable from the other 2, and these in turn are
not linearly separable from each other.</p>,
 <li>sepal length in cm </li>,
 <li>sepal width in cm </li>,
 <li>petal length in cm </li>,
 <li>petal width in cm </li>,
 <li>class: -- 3 values:  Iris Setosa, Iris
 Versicolour, Iris Virginica </li>,
 <p id="rogel1">[1] <b>Rogel-Salazar, J</b>.
 (2017). <i>Data Science and Analytics with
 Python</i>. Chapman &amp; Hall/CRC
 Data Mining and Knowledge Discovery Series.
 CRC Press. <meta content="text/html;
charset=utf-8" http-equiv="Content-Type"/></p>]
```

The `find_all` method locates all the instances of the tag searched and returns a list.

It is possible to use the parameter `limit` in combination with the `find_all` method to limit the number of results returned. This is particularly useful when there is a large number of entries searched. We can thus limit our search to two results as follows:

```
iris_soup.find_all(['p', 'li'], limit=2)
```

Combining our search with filtering parameters is a great way to hone in on the information we are looking for. We can for example determine that we want all the paragraphs that have a particular identifier or id:

```
> bib  = iris_soup.find_all('p', id='rogel1')
> print(bib)

<p id="rogel1">[1] <b>Rogel-Salazar, J</b>.
 (2017). <i>Data Science and Analytics with
 Python</i>. Chapman &amp; Hall/CRC
 Data Mining and Knowledge Discovery Series.
 CRC Press. <meta content="text/html;
charset=utf-8" http-equiv="Content-Type"/></p>
```

We can use parameters to search for specific tags. In this case for instance we are searching for a particular `id`.

In this case, we are looking for all the paragraphs with the id `rogel1`, and we can see that the result is one single paragraph. Please note that the returned object is a list of tags. If we wanted to get the text of the first (and, in this case, only) element in the list, we can do this with:

```
> my_text = bib[0].text
```

The list elements are `tag` objects.

As we have seen, HTML organises the contents of our webpage. Sometimes, it is useful to define consistent style elements for different elements of the page under a single name. This is what a class attribute is used for in HTML. We know that Python is an object-oriented language, and as

Remember that `class` is a reserved word for both HTML and Python.

such it enables us to use "templates" to create objects. So what happens when we need to look for a class attribute in our Beautiful Soup with Python? Well, since `class` is a reserved word in Python, we simply append an underscore to the HTML attribute as such: `class_`.

We have enough information for the big finale of this section: Obtaining the table of data in the Iris website. Inspecting the source code for the page, we can see that the tag that holds the dataset is a `table` of class `tableizer-table`. We can use this information to find the table and parse it:

Note that we are using the parameter `class_` in the code below.

```
iris_table = iris_soup.find('table',
    class_='tableizer-table')
```

From Table 2.1 we know that a well-formed HTML table contains rows in `tr` tags, and the data cells in `td` tags. Let us locate all the table rows to start with:

Too many tables!! I can assure you there is no chance we may encounter Mr. Creosote in any of them.

```
tmp = iris_table.find_all('tr')
```

This returns a list with all the relevant tags. In particular the first element contains the header of the table, and the rest of the elements correspond to the rows of the dataset:

```
first = tmp[0]
allRows = tmp[1:]
```

Remember how we can slice and dice a list using the colon notation.

We can now extract the text inside each of the data cells. In the case of the header, the tag is actually a table header, i.e., `th`.

```
headers = [header.text for header in\
    first.find_all('th')]
> print(headers)

['Dataset Order',
 'Sepal length',
 'Sepal width',
 'Petal length',
 'Petal width',
 'Species']
```

We are using list comprehension to extract the relevant text from the th tags.

In the code above, we are using a Pythonic way to extract the relevant information: List comprehension. We traverse the list returned by find_all and extract the text as we go along, each entry is then stored as an element of a list.

As for the values, they are stored in td tags, and we can use a similar technique as in the code above:

```
values = [[data.text for data in\
    row.find_all('td')] for row in allRows]
> values[:2]

[['1', '5.1', '3.5', '1.4', '0.2', 'I.\xa0setosa'],
 ['2', '4.9', '3', '1.4', '0.2', 'I.\xa0setosa']]
```

We use the same technique as above for the actual table contents.

Note that the information extracted is actually of string type. This is important in those cases, such as here, where some of the data is numerical, and thus we may have to carry out appropriate manipulations; for example, cleaning the non-breakable space characters shown as \xa0.

Let us show some manipulations we can easily implement loading the data into a pandas dataframe:

```
import pandas as pd
df = pd.DataFrame(data=values, columns=headers)
```

Et voilà! We are now in a position to use our dataset for other purposes, such as in a classification algorithm as done in Chapter 3 of *Data Science and Analytics with Python*[6]. But before we do that, let us make some minor changes in our dataset. For example, we can convert the columns containing numbers as strings into actual numbers:

[6] Rogel-Salazar, J. (2017). *Data Science and Analytics with Python*. Chapman & Hall/CRC Data Mining and Knowledge Discovery Series. CRC Press.

```
cols = ['Dataset Order', 'Sepal length',
    'Sepal width', 'Petal length', 'Petal width']
df[cols] = df[cols].apply(pd.to_numeric,
    errors='coerce')
```

We can also clean the strings in the species' names. You may have noticed in the code shown on page 91 that there are some strange characters in the species' names. Namely, the non-breakable space encoded in Latin-1: `\xa0`. Let us clean up these spaces:

We will cover the use of regular expressions for this sort of task in Section 2.2.

```
df['Species'] = df['Species'].map(lambda x:
    x.replace('\xa0',' '))
df['Species'] = df['Species'].map(lambda x:
    x.replace('\n',''))
```

We are simply replacing the non-breakable spaces with blanks in the first line of the code above. In the second one, we are replacing the new line character with nothing.

2.2 *Make Mine a Regular: Regular Expressions*

HAVE YOU EVER HAD THE need to find a repeating design in words or numbers, and then either pull it out or get rid of it? Or perhaps you have had to spot a regular arrangement in text or a table of information, and then extract it, or make it disappear? Sometimes, it is possible to simply scan the document in question and manually find the expression of interest. In many cases, some applications enable the use of search and replace functions and they are all the rage. However, there are times when the expression we are seeking to process is more complex to be handled with a simple search.

I am sure you have! Particularly if, like Mr. Bounder, you need to replace the letter "C" with "K" to get the right pronunciation of some words.

Welcome to the world of regular expressions! As the name implies, a regular expression is an utterance (typically in text form) that appears in a *corpus* with certain frequency or regularity. Recognising those patterns in the corpus relies on determining the characters that make up the expression, including letters, digits, punctuation and any other symbol, including special characters and even in other scripts, such as the Japanese sentence in the margin, as well as many others like Chinese, Arabic or Devanagari for example.

A *corpus* is a large and structured set of texts upon which linguistic analysis can be performed.

このは日本語の文章です。

In Python, the `re` module enables us to use regular expressions. When working with Python strings which will be parsed with regular expressions, it is recommended to use raw strings. This is because, in raw strings, backslashes have no special meaning as an escape character. Anyway, we mentioned above that a simple search and replace function

A raw string in Python is preceded by an `r` as such `r'This is a raw string.'`

can be used to substitute a desired pattern, let us take a look at implementing this use case with re.

Imagine you are reading the following options from your local award-winning Viking Café:

Breakfast options:

1. Egg and baaacon - £10.0 ($12.83);
2. Egg, sausage and baaaaacon - £11.0 ($14.12);
3. Egg and beans - £12.0 ($15.40);
4. Egg, baaacon and beans - £13.0 ($16.68);
5. Beans, sausage, beans - £14.0 ($17.97);
6. Beans, baaaaacon, beans, tomato and beans - £15.0 ($19.25);

The famous Viking Café menu, *sans* Spam...

That new Commis Chef is at it again! Do they not know that our speciality is wonderful Spam? We need to take action immediately and change the menu before the Vikings come in. Let us fire our Python engines and read each of the lines in the corpus above. We will then use the sub method to substitute the word "beans" for "spam". We will deal with the extra bacon — the surplus letter "a" — later.

We need to replace the word "beans" with "spam".

```
import re


corpus =  r"""Breakfast options:
1. Egg and baaacon - £10.0 ($12.83);
2. Egg, sausage and baaaaacon - £11.0 ($12.83);
3. Egg and beans - £12.0 ($15.40);
4. Egg, baaacon and beans - £13.0 ($16.68);
5. Beans, sausage, beans - £14.0 ($17.97);
```

The string could be stored in a file. In this case we are defining a raw string: Notice the r at the start.

```
6. Beans, baaaaacon, beans, tomato and beans -
    £15.0 ($19.25); """
```

```
for line in corpus.splitlines():
    line = re.sub('beans','spam', line.rstrip())
    print(line)
```

The sub method enables us to make substitutions in the string.

As you would expect, after running the code, the printed new lines will have changed the word "beans" for "spam":

```
Breakfast options:
1. Egg and baaacon - £10.0 ($12.83);
2. Egg, sausage and baaaaacon - £11.0 ($12.83);
3. Egg, and spam - £12.0 ($15.40);
4. Egg, baaacon and spam - £13.0 ($16.68);
5. Beans, sausage, spam - £14.0 ($17.97);
6. Beans, baaaaacon, spam, tomato and spam - £15.0
    ($19.25)
```

The famous Viking Café menu, with wonderful Spam...

But , wait a minute, what about lines 5 and 6 above where the word "Beans" has not been changed? Well, the reason is that in those cases the capital "B" does not match the lower case "b". We shall address how to deal with this issue in the next subsection.

As well as with the misspelling of the word "bacon".

Also, note that we have not changed the text in the `corpus` variable; we simply took the text and made on-the-fly modifications. If we need to keep the changes, we need to make sure that the new lines are stored somewhere.

This is a nice task for you to complete now, new Commis Chef!

2.2.1 *Regular Expression Patterns*

As YOU CAN SEE, LOOKING for sequences of characters is pretty straightforward, as most characters match themselves. Sounds obvious, right? However, there are some exceptions: `+ ? . * ^ { } $ () [ ] | \`. These characters are used to define expression patterns as we shall see. If we need to match them, we do so by "escaping" them by prefixing them with a backslash (\). You see, to match the backslash we need to "escape" it with a backslash. In Table 2.2 we are listing the use of these characters to match patterns in a string.

Exceptions include control characters such as `+ ? . * ^ { } $ () [ ] | \`.

For example, suppose we want to match a literal full stop (.) in a string. In regular expressions (or regex for short), as seen in Table 2.2, a dot means "any character", so to match an actual dot, we must escape it using a backslash:

```
pattern = r'\.'
```

The `re` module we encountered previously supports two different ways to find patterns using regular expressions: `match` and `search`. The first one matches only at the beginning of a string, whereas the second one searches for a match anywhere in the string. If you are interested in using a single regular expression multiple times, you may want to use the `compile` method in conjunction with `match` and `search`.

We can use `match` or `search` with the `re` module.

We can use `compile` in cases where we need to use an expression multiple times.

OK, so we are ready to start matching some patterns in our Viking Café menu. We can match lines beginning with a

Table 2.2: Regular expression patterns. We use ellipses (...) to denote sequences of characters.

Pattern	Description
`^...$`	Starts and ends
`*`	Zero or more repetitions
`+`	One or more repetitions
`?`	Optional character
`.`	Any character
`abc...`	Letters
`123...`	Digits
`\d`	Any digit
`\D`	Any non-digit character
`[abc]`	Only `a`, `b`, or `c`
`[^abc]`	Not `a`, `b`, nor `c`
`[a-z]`	Characters `a` to `z`
`[0-9]`	Numbers 0 to 9
`\w`	Any alphanumeric character
`\W`	Any non-alphanumeric character
`{m}`	`m` repetitions
`{m,n}`	`m` to `n` repetitions
`\s`	Any whitespace
`\S`	Any non-whitespace character
`[...]`	Character sets
`(...)`	Capture group
`(:?...)`	Non-capture group
`(a(bc))`	Capture sub-group
`(.*)`	Capture all
`(123|abc)`	Matches 123 or `abc`

number using an expression such as:

```
'^1',  '^2', ..., '^6'
```

The caret symbol (^) matches a pattern at the beginning of a string.

What about if we are interested in a more general expression that captures a line starting with any number? From Table 2.2 we can see that the pattern \d matches any digit!

```
'^\d'
```

\d matches any single digit.

So, we can actually write the following to print all the lines that start with a number:

```
numlines = re.compile(r'^\d')
for line in corpus.splitlines():
    result = numlines.search(line)
    if result:
        print(line)
```

This piece of code prints lines in the corpus that begin with a number.

Try it out and convince yourself that the outcome is as expected. Note that this only works for strings that begin with the pattern provided.

We can also search for lines ending in a particular pattern. In this case, we need to use the dollar sign ($). For example, if we wanted to print only the lines that finish with a closing parenthesis, we will have to write the following regular expression:

```
endparenthesis = re.compile(r'\)$')
```

The dollar sign ($) matches a pattern at the end of a string.

Note that we need to "escape" the closing parenthesis, i.e., `\)`, to match expressions containing that character. The same behaviour applies to any of the other control characters we have described above.

Remember the task we were trying to accomplish in the last section? We were interested in replacing all the "beans" for "spam", but capitalised words were not replaced. One way (among many) to deal with this is the use of character sets such that we search for the word "bean" spelled either with "B" or with "b". We can do that with the following expression `'[Bb]eans'`

The square brackets represent character sets, the pattern `[123]` matches a single 1, 2 or 3 and nothing else. It is possible to match sequential characters: `[0-9]` will match a single digit between 0 and 9.

```
> for line in corpus.splitlines():
    line = re.sub('[Bb]eans','spam', line.rstrip())
    print(line)

Breakfast options:
1. Egg and baaacon - £10.0 ($12.83);
2. Egg, sausage and baaaaacon - £11.0 ($12.83);
3. Egg and spam - £12.0 ($15.40);
4. Egg, baaacon and spam - £13.0 ($16.68);
5. spam, sausage, spam - £14.0 ($17.97);
6. spam, baaaaacon, spam, tomato and spam - £15.0
    ($19.25)
```

In this case we are using `[Bb]eans` to match the words "beans" or "Beans".

What if we wanted to match all the words that started with the letter "b", either upper- or lowercase? We can achieve this with the help of \w which matches any alphanumeric character. In order to ensure that we capture words of any length, we can use the + character that will match one or more repetitions. This leaves us with the following expression:

The pattern \w matches any alphanumeric character.

Whereas the + matches one or more repetitions of a character.

```
bwords = re.compile(r'[Bb]\w+')
```

Let us use this compile regular expression with another great method in the re module: findall which will return a list with all the matches for the pattern provided:

```
> bwords.findall(corpus)

['Breakfast', 'baaacon', 'baaaaacon',
'beans', 'baaacon', 'beans',
'Beans', 'beans', 'Beans',
'baaaaacon', 'beans', 'beans']
```

We find all the matches for words starting with "B" or "b" .

Not bad, eh? We can use the repetition to capture all those misspelled "bacons":

```
> re.findall(r'ba+\w+', corpus)

['baaacon', 'baaaaacon', 'baaacon', 'baaaaacon']
```

Here we look for all the words that have a "b" followed by any number of letters "a".

In this case we are searching for all the words that have the letter "b" followed by any number of letters "a", and any number of other characters. We can also specify the number of repetitions as follows:

```
re.findall(r'ba{3,5}con', corpus)
```

In the code above we are looking for repetitions of the letter "a" between 3 and 5 times followed by the letters "con".

For the next pattern, let us get the prices in sterling from the menu. We are interested in the figures after the pound sterling symbol (£), so we will use the parentheses to capture the group (see Table 2.2).

The use of parentheses lets us specify a group in the pattern that we are interested in extracting.

```
> re.findall(r'£(\d+\.0)', corpus)


['10.0', '11.0', '12.0', '13.0', '14.0', '15.0']
```

Here we are looking for any number of digits (\d+) followed by a dot (\.) and a zero. Notice that we enclose the expression in parentheses to capture only the information required, leaving out the pound symbol. For the prices in dollars, we need to make sure to escape the dollar sign and the parentheses:

We use `\.` to specify a dot in the pattern. On its own, a dot is a wildcard that represents any character.

```
> re.findall(r'\(\$(\d+\.\d+)\)', corpus)


['12.83', '12.83', '15.40', '16.68', '17.97',
'19.25']
```

We need to escape both the dollar sign ($) and the parentheses.

Finally, let us use the capture sub-group to get both prices at the same time:

```
prices=re.compile(r'(£(\d+\.0) \(\$(\d+\.\d+)\))')
captures = prices.findall(corpus)
```

The result will be a list with tuples containing a match for the entire expression (e.g., '£10.0 ($12.83)'), a match for the first sub-group (e.g., '10.0') and a match for the second sub-group (e.g., '12.83'). We can then use the resulting list for our own purposes, for example:

We can use the sub-group pattern (a(bc)) to capture multiple groups of interest.

```
> for capture in captures:
    print('{0} in pounds and {1} in dollars'.
          format(capture[1], capture[2]))


10.0 in pounds and 12.83 in dollars
11.0 in pounds and 12.83 in dollars
12.0 in pounds and 15.40 in dollars
13.0 in pounds and 16.68 in dollars
14.0 in pounds and 17.97 in dollars
15.0 in pounds and 19.25 in dollars
```

The Commis Chef can now use their newly acquired knowledge of regular expressions to fix the menu:

```
fix_bacon = re.compile(r'ba+con')
fix_spam = re.compile(r'[Bb]eans')
new_corpus = ''
for line in corpus.splitlines():
    line = fix_bacon.sub('bacon', line)
    line = fix_spam.sub('spam', line)
    new_corpus += line+'\n'
```

This is one way the Commis Chef can fix the menu!

First we create regular expressions to find the misspelled words with multiple letters "a", then one to find the words "beans" and "Beans". We then parse each line making appropriate replacements and saving the new fixed lines in a new corpus.

```
> print(new_corpus)


Breakfast options:
1. Egg and bacon - £10.0 ($12.83);
2. Egg, sausage and bacon - £11.0 ($12.83);
3. Egg and spam - £12.0 ($15.40);
4. Egg, bacon and spam - £13.0 ($16.68);
5. spam, sausage, spam - £14.0 ($17.97);
6. spam, bacon, spam, tomato and spam - £15.0
    ($19.25)
```

Et voilà!

It is not quite perfect yet, as we have some instances of "spam" that should really be capitalised, but getting there.

Check out re's documentation for further information[7], as there are many more things you can do with regular expressions. Python also has other tricks up its sleeve. For example, there are some flags that you can set:

[7] re - Regular expression operations. https://docs.python.org/3.6/library/re.html

- `re.IGNORECASE`: case insensitive pattern matching
- `re.DOTALL`: Make the special character `.` match any character including newline (`\n`)
- `re.MULTILINE`: make `^` and `$` match at the beginning/end of the string and of each line

Some flags can be set to be used with your regular expressions.

Do not be discouraged by how cryptic some of the regular expressions seem to be. The vast majority of us will probably not become master regex ninja Jackalopes, but with the help of a cheat sheet like Table 2.2 and an online tester such as https://pythex.org or https://regex101.com, we can all find the perfect match.

There are some interesting attempts to make readable and maintainable regular expressions such as `cursive_re` for Python 3.6 and up[8]. For instance, matching the prices in sterling from our Viking Café menu can be achieved as follows with `cursive_re`:

[8] Cursive Re. https://github.com/Bogdanp/cursive_re

```
import cursive_re as cre
pound = cre.text('£')
pndnum = pound + cre.group(cre.one_or_more(
    cre.any_of(cre.in_range('0','9'))) +
    cre.text('.0'))
```

In the second line above, `text` matches the given string exactly, escaping any special characters. The `any_of` function matches any of the given characters, and in this case they are characters in the range from 0 to 9. Since we want one or more of these digits, we use the `one_or_more` function. Finally, the `group` function lets us define the group whose contents we want to retrieve. We can see the result of these commands by casting the result as a string:

Cursive Re provides a number of functions that attempt to make regular expressions easier to read and maintain.

```
> str(pndnum)


'\\£([0-9]+\\.0)'
```

We can compile the expression into a real regular expression and use it as normal:

```
> testing = cre.compile(pndnum)
> testing.findall(corpus)

['10.0', '11.0', '12.0', '13.0', '14.0', '15.0']
```

2.3 *Processing Text with Unicode*

WHEN DEALING WITH TEXT DATA, it is unavoidable to consider the characters that we use to represent words. We rarely think about this, but ever since we start learning how to read and write, we are encoding information particular to the natural language we use in our everyday lives. You are able to read these lines of text because you are familiar with the Latin alphabet with 26 characters that is used in English, but that is not the whole story. *Si leyeras estas líneas en Español, necesitarías 27 caracteres, más vocales acentuadas como: á, é, í, ó, ú, & ü.* Other languages have their own letters, and they all need to be encoded so that they can be represented by your computer.

If you were reading these lines in Spanish, you would need 27 characters plus accented vowels.

For many decades, computers were able to represent characters based on the American Standard Code for Information Interchange, better known as ASCII, first proposed in the early 1960s[9]. ASCII defines 256 characters using 8 bits to encode characters including the usual printable ones in a Latin alphabet including accented vowels and other characters such as ç, ß and ñ (among others), plus some control characters such as carriage return, line feed, etc.

[9] Russell, A. (2014). *Open Standards and the Digital Age*. Cambridge Studies in the Emerg. Cambridge University Press.

All this is well and good, but what happens with languages that do not use the Latin alphabet such as Japanese, Chinese, or Greek? ASCII would not be able to accommodate these scripts, and thus we need a new character set. Welcome to Unicode!

Languages with non-Latin scripts are not supported in ASCII.

Unicode does not have every imaginable character in it, but at least in version 16.0 there is a total of 292,531 characters including 168 different scripts and even emojis[10]. This all makes sense and you would think that this is the end of the story, right? Well, you will be surprised to see the *"It's... not"*. There are different ways to implement Unicode such as the Unicode Transformation Format (UTF), and the Universal Coded Character Set (UCS).

[10] Unicode 16.0. http://www.unicode.org/versions/Unicode16.0.0/

No need to run in from the sea to tell you this.

Let us take for instance UTF encoding. If we chose to use 8 bits to do the encoding we would end up with UTF-8, which offers great compatibility with ASCII. Alternatively, we can use 16 bits and end up with UTF-16. There are other mappings out there, including UTF-32, UTF-7, etc. As you can imagine, dealing with encodings can be a bit tricky.

Some common encodings include UTF-8 and UTF-16.

In Python 3, all text is Unicode[11], but it is important to remember that encoded Unicode is represented by binary data. This is one of the main differences with Python 2.7. Python 3 has one text type, i.e., `str` which holds Unicode data, and there are two byte types `bytes` and `bytearray`. Let us take a look at some of this. For example, let us define a string in Python and look at its type:

[11] van Rossum, G. (2009). Text Vs. Data Instead of Unicode Vs. 8-bit. https://docs.python.org/release/3.0.1/whatsnew/3.0.html

```
> type('Hello world!')

str
```

A string is indeed a string.

It is indeed an object of `str` type, or a string. What about if we want to define a `bytes` literal? Well, we can simply prefix the string with a `b`:

```
> type(b'Hello world!')

bytes
```

We can define a `bytes` literal with the `b` prefix.

Let us try to define a byte object containing non-ASCII characters:

```
> type(b'こんにちは世界！')

SyntaxError: bytes can only contain ASCII literal
characters.
```

In this case, we are printing "Hello world!" in Japanese!

This error tells us that we will need to transform our string with non-ASCII characters into a bytes object first, and we will need to provide an encoding to do this:

```
> sekai = 'こんにちは世界！'

> bytes(sekai, 'utf-8')

b'\x81\x93\xe3\x82\x93\xe3\x81\xab\xe3\x81\xa1\xe3
\x81\xaf\xe4\xb8\x96\xe7\x95\x8c\xef\xbc\x81'
```

When casting as a `bytes` literal, we need to specify the desired encoding.

There is no easy way to determine what type of encoding is used in byte strings. In Section 2.1.1 we learnt how to scrape a website, and in reality we need to check what encoding is used for the strings we are getting from the web. That is true of any other processing we need to carry out with strings.

It is best practice to specify the encoding when reading files, but it may not be that easy to tell what encoding has been used.

After the operation above is executed, we have a `bytes` object encoded in UTF-8. Another, and probably better, way to do this is to use the `encode` method for strings:

```
> sekai.encode()

b'\x81\x93\xe3\x82\x93\xe3\x81\xab\xe3\x81\xa1\xe3
\x81\xaf\xe4\xb8\x96\xe7\x95\x8c\xef\xbc\x81'
```

A better way to deal with the encoding is to use the `encode` method.

As you can see, we have obtained the same result as before, please note that by default Python 3 uses UTF-8 for encoding. Should we need to use a different encoding, we simply pass it to the method. For example, we can encode our string in UTF-16 as follows:

```
> sekai.encode('utf-16')

 b'\xff\xfeS0\x930k0a0o0\x16NLu\x01\xff'
```

You can specify other encodings too.

As you can imagine, it is possible to do the reverse operation and `decode` bytes objects too:

```

> japan = b'\xe6\x97\xa5\xe6\x9c\xac'
> japan.decode()

'日本'
```

We can also decode a `bytes` literal, i.e., a literal whose type us `bytes`.

Please remember that you will need to provide the correct encoding (UTF-8, UTF-16, etc.) to the decoding method; otherwise, you will get a Unicode error at best or a misencoding at worst!

Providing the correct encoding is important.

Since we are dealing with characters, and all text in Python 3 is Unicode, it makes sense that the regular expression patterns that we discussed in Section 2.2 also hold for non-Latin characters:

The use of regular expressions patterns can be applied to Unicode too.

```
> thirtyseven='さんじゅなだ''
> re.sub('だ'', 'な'', thirtyseven)

'さんじゅなな'
```

It is also possible to use the `\uFFFF` Unicode notation, enabling us to use character ranges and all the fun that comes with regular expressions:

This is a hexadecimal representation for the Unicode character.

```
> re.sub('\u3060', '\u306a', thirtyseven)

'さんじゅなな'
```

You can check the Unicode code points in sites such as www.utf8-chartable.de or www.key-shortcut.com for example.

Check Unicode tables in sites such as www.key-shortcut.com.

In Section 2.1.1 we read an HTML page, and we encountered some interesting non-breakable spaces shown as `\xa0`. It turns out that these are non-breakable spaces encoded in Latin1 or ISO-8859-1. We dealt with this issue with a replacement in pandas. An alternative may be to use a regular expression to remove all non-US-ASCII characters, i.e., characters outside the `\u0000-\u007f`.

```
> test_text='abc\xa0\u3060\u306a\u3060\xa0de!'
> print(test_text)

abc だなだ de!

> only_ascii = re.compile(r'[^\u0000-\u007f]')
> only_ascii.sub('', test_text)

'abcde!'
```

Here we are removing characters outside the range of US-ASCII characters.

Notice that when printing the string there are some blank spaces between the Latin and Japanese characters. In this case, we are using an exclusion in a character set to remove all non-US-ASCII characters. It is a drastic measure, but I am sure you get the point.

Remember that `[^abc]` means not a, b nor c.

As you can imagine, it is not unusual to come across encoding problems when opening files in Python 3, and there are some modules that may help with these issues. Say you are interested in opening a CSV file to be loaded into a pandas dataframe. If the stars align and the creator of your CSV is magnanimous, they may have saved the file using UTF-8. If so, you may get away with reading the file as follows:

Python 3 uses UTF-8 as default. You may need to specify the file encoding to ensure appropriate handling for other encodings.

```
import pandas as pd
df = pd.read_csv('myfile.csv')
```

As we mentioned before, it is not easy to tell what encoding was used to create a file, and in principle you should pass a parameter to pandas telling it what encoding the file has been saved with; so a more complete version of the snippet above would be:

In pandas you can provide an encoding parameter.

```
import pandas as pd


df = pd.read_csv('myfile.csv', encoding='utf-8')
```

What happens when you do not know what encoding was used to save the file? Well, you can ask, but it is very unlikely that the file creator would know or tell you... In those cases, modules such as `chardet`[12] can help you detect the character encoding in your file. The `detect` function in the module returns a dictionary containing the auto-detected character encoding and a confidence level from 0 to 1.

[12] Chardet. https://chardet.readthedocs.io

```
> import chardet
> chardet.detect(b'I.\xa0setosa')


{'encoding': 'ISO-8859-1', 'confidence': 0.73',
'language': ''}
```

In this case, the string is detected to be encoded in ISO-8859-1.

The example above tells us that the likely encoding for the string passed to the `detect` function is ISO-8859-1 (with a confidence level of 0.73). Let us take a look at an example implementation for a file:

```
import chardet
import pandas as pd



def find_encoding(fname):
    r_file = open(fname, 'rb').read()
    result = chardet.detect(r_file)
    charenc = result['encoding']
    return charenc



my_encoding = find_encoding('myfile.csv')
df=pd.read_csv('myfile.csv', encoding=my_encoding)
```

Use this snippet to detect file encodings with chardet.

Finally, what about writing a file with the correct encoding? Well, if you are using pandas, it is quite straightforward as you simply pass a parameter with the desired encoding as follows:

Or nothing, as the default is UTF-8.

```
> df.to_csv('newfile.csv', encoding='utf-8')
```

Otherwise, you need to ensure the encoding of the strings as you write them down:

```
sekai = 'こんにちは世界！'

with open('sekai.txt', 'wb') as f:
    f.write(sekai.encode())
```

Do not forget to encode your strings when writing to a file, and tell your users!

2.4 *Tokenising Text*

WE HAVE BEEN DEALING WITH text in full, and most of our discussion has been about obtaining and preprocessing it. We started this chapter by talking about the importance of natural language and how to make sense of it with the aid of computers. One of the first tasks that will enable us to do this is to split up our text into meaningful units, or tokens. This is called *tokenisation*, and it is a typical first step in natural language processing.

In this context, a token is a meaningful unit of text.

In languages like English or Spanish, simple tokenisation can be used by separating the tokens by whitespaces. Unfortunately, for languages such as Chinese or Japanese, where whitespaces are not used between words, the tokenisation tasks become more involved. The tokenisation process may also require us to discard some tokens such as punctuation, numbers, or some common words. We will cover more of this later on in this section.

A common tokenisation technique involves separating tokens by whitespaces.

We can readily split a string of text as follows:

```
> sentences = 'I know, I know! Nobody expects the
    Spanish Inquisition. In fact, those who do
    expect -'
> sentences.split()

['I', 'know,', 'I', 'know!', 'Nobody', 'expects',
'the', 'Spanish', 'Inquisition.', 'In', 'fact,',
'those', 'who', 'do', 'expect', '-']
```

We can separate tokens with the `split` method for strings.

We could in principle also define a string of characters on which to split the sentence. For example, if we wanted to split on the comma, we can do the following:

```
> sentences.split(',')


['I know',
' I know! Nobody expects the Spanish Inquisition.
  In fact',
' those who do expect -']
```

We can also specify other separators for splitting.

You may notice that in the first example, the punctuation marks are joined to the words, and in the second one there are some whitespaces at the beginning of the second and third elements in the list. We can use regular expressions to split on the desired marks, in this case for instance on comma, exclamation mark, dot, hyphen and whitespaces:

See Section 2.2 for more on regex.

```
> import re
> re.split(r'[,!\.\-\s]+',sentences)


['I', 'know', 'I', 'know', 'Nobody', 'expects',
'the', 'Spanish', 'Inquisition', 'In', 'fact',
'those', 'who', 'do', 'expect', '']
```

We can even use a regular expression to specify the separator!

There are other ways to start our processing of natural language and a package that comes to mind in this context is the Natural Language Toolkit, or NLTK for short. Word tokenisation can be done with the `word_tokenize` function:

Do check out what NLTK has to offer!

```
> import nltk
> nltk.download('punkt_tab')
> nltk.word_tokenize(sentences)

['I', 'know', ',', 'I', 'know', '!', 'Nobody',
'expects', 'the', 'Spanish', 'Inquisition', '.',
'In', 'fact', ',', 'those', 'who', 'do', 'expect',
'-']
```

You only need to download the tokeniser model the first time you use it.

Word tokenisation can be easily done with NLTK's `word_tokenize`.

Furthermore, we can use NLTK to tokenise at a sentence level:

```
> nltk.sent_tokenize(sentences)

['I know, I know!',
 'Nobody expects the Spanish Inquisition.',
 'In fact, those who do expect -']
```

Whereas sentence tokenisation is handled with `sent_tokenize`.

As we can see, in this case we end up with a list with three sentences. Not bad!

We can now start to normalise the text so that we can match tokens despite some differences such as the use of capital letters (cat, Cat and CAT can be assumed to refer to the same friendly Über-being) or inflections (cat, cat's, cats and cats' all come from the same common base *cat*). It is possible to use the `lower` method to deal with the use of capital letters:

We can normalise the text so that we can match tokens that may be different in form but not in meaning

```
> words = nltk.word_tokenize(sentences.lower())
```

We can take a look at the result of the tokenisation:

```
> print(words)

['i', 'know', ',', 'i', 'know', '!', 'nobody',
'expects', 'the', 'spanish', 'inquisition', '.',
'in', 'fact', ',', 'those', 'who', 'do', 'expect',
'-']
```

In this case, we have changed all the text into lowercase.

To deal with inflections, we can use *stemming* or *lemmatisation*. The former refers to the process of severing word endings, whereas the latter relies on a more systematic analysis to obtain the so-called *lemma*, or dictionary form, of a word. NLTK comes with a couple of stemmers, such as the Porter stemmer:

Lemmatisation and stemming can help us normalise the text too.

```
> porter = nltk.PorterStemmer()
> [porter.stem(word) for word in words]

['i', 'know', ',', 'i', 'know', '!', 'nobodi',
'expect', 'the', 'spanish', 'inquisit','.', 'in',
'fact', ',', 'those', 'who', 'do', 'expect', '-']
```

An example of stemming text with `PorterStemmer`.

Lemmatisation can be done with `WordNetLemmatizer` which is part of WordNet. WordNet is a lexical database for the English language, which was created by Princeton and is part of the NLTK corpus. Let us first download WordNet:

```
nltk.download('wordnet')
```

We can now instantiate our lemmatiser:

```
> lemmatiser = nltk.WordNetLemmatizer()
> [lemmatiser.lemmatize(word) for word in words]

['i', 'know', ',', 'i', 'know', '!', 'nobody',
'expects', 'the', 'spanish', 'inquisition', '.',
'in', 'fact', ',', 'those', 'who', 'do', 'expect',
'-']
```

Lemmatising can be done with `WordNetLemmatizer`.

Another useful thing that comes with NLTK is the `regexp_tokenize` function with similar functionality to `re.findall`, but efficient for the tokenisation task. It becomes particularly useful in the tokenisation of utterances in social media such as so-called tweets. For example, lets take the following made-up tweet:

Tokenisation can also be done with the help of regular expression.

> @norwegian_blue This parrot is no more!!! :(#sad
> https://rogueloop.com

If we use the tokeniser straight out of the box, we end up with some tokenisations that are no longer meaningful in the context of a tweet:

Should we call it an "ex" now? "X-eet"? Anyway...

```
> tweet='@norwegian_blue This parrot is no more!!!
    :( #sad... https://rogueloop.com'
> nltk.word_tokenize(tweet)

['@', 'norwegian_blue', 'This', 'parrot', 'is',
'no', 'more', '!', '!', '!', ':', '(', '#', 'sad',
'...', 'https', ':', '//rogueloop.com']
```

Using the tokeniser straight out of the box results in a bad tokenisation.

It may be preferable to parse the text so as to render a meaningful tokenisation. We can use regular expressions to do this, and in particular, we can use the `regexp_tokenize` function that comes with NLTK offering consistency with other NLTK functions. Also it may provide some efficiencies when parsing for the desired pattern. It is important to note that the order of the arguments in the `regexp_tokenize` function is as follows: First the string to be parsed and then the regular expression. We shall put together a sequence of regular expressions that break our strings in the chosen manner.

re functions take their arguments in the reverse order.

Let us then define a regular expression pattern that enables a more meaningful tokenisation for our example tweet above:

```
pattern = r'''(?x) # A verbose regex
     [\$£]?\d+[\.:%]?\d*%?
     |(?:[A-Z]\.)+
     |(?:https?://)?(?:\w+\.)(?:\w{2,})+(?:[\w/]+)?
     |[@\#]?\w+(?:[-']\w+)*
     |\.\.\.
     |[!?]+
     |:[()]'''
```

Looks complex, but we shall unravel the regexp line-by-line below.

The first line in our regular expression starts with `(?x)` which lets the parser know that we are defining a verbose regular expression. This lets us create a more readable pattern and even include comments with #. The next line, `[\$£]?\d+[\.:%]?\d*%?` captures decimal numbers, percentages and currency figures (in this case dollars $, or

A lot of useful information here. Make sure you check out the regular expression patterns in Table 2.2.

pounds £). We then use `(?:[A-Z]\.)+` to obtain abbreviations where characters are separated by dots. The fourth line captures URLs, and the next one deals with @ mentions and hashtags (#). We capture ellipses with `\.\.\.` and multiple exclamation and question marks with `[!?]+`. Finally, we capture a couple of ASCII emoticons such as `:)` and `:(` with `:[()]`.

We can now try our new shiny pattern on the example tweet we have used before:

```
> nltk.regexp_tokenize(tweet, pattern)

['@norwegian_blue', 'This', 'parrot', 'is', 'no',
'more', '!!', ':(', '#sad', '...',
'https://rogueloop.com']
```

This is a much better tokenisation of the sample Tweet!!

This has broken down the tweet in a more meaningful way, where we can distinguish hashtags (`#sad`) , user mentions (`@norwegian_blue`), and even emoticons. This sort of task is so common that NLTK inlcudes a tweet tokeniser:

```
> from nltk.tokenize.casual import TweetTokenizer
> TweetTokenizer().tokenize(tweet)

['@norwegian_blue', 'This', 'parrot', 'is', 'no',
'more', '!', '!', ':(', '#sad', '...',
'https://rogueloop.com']
```

Check out the `TweetTokenizer` that comes with NLTK.

You can see some differences in the results compared to those from our own pattern. The flexibility offered by using either pattern depends on our particular use case.

2.5 *Word Tagging*

Now that we are able to tokenize a corpus and break it down into its (meaningful) components, we can turn our attention to the categorisation of those units. For instance, we can try to distinguish between verbs, adjectives and nouns and start making sense of the utterances in the corpus.

Categorising the words into the parts they play in the speech is imaginatively called *Part-Of-Speech tagging*, or POS tagging. NLTK lets us carry out POS tagging with the `post_tag` function. You may need to download some models from NLTK before doing this:

Part-Of-Speech tagging categorised the words into the parts they play in a sentence.

```
nltk.download('averaged_perceptron_tagger_eng')
nltk.download('maxent_ne_chunker_tab')
```

Let us take a look using the corpus `sentences` we defined in page 113. For the purposes of this example, we will concentrate on the second sentence, i.e., *"Nobody expects the Spanish Inquisition"*:

```
s = nltk.sent_tokenize(sentences)
s1 = nltk.word_tokenize(s[1])
> nltk.pos_tag(s1)

[('Nobody', 'NN'),
 ('expects', 'VBZ'),
 ('the', 'DT'),
```

A POS tagged sentence with NLTK.

```
('Spanish', 'JJ'),
('Inquisition', 'NNP'),
('.', '.')]
```

We can see that "Nobody" is a noun (`NN`), "expects" is a verb in the present tense (`VBZ`), "the" is a determiner (`DT`), "Spanish" is an adjective (`JJ`) and "Inquisition" is a proper noun (`NNP`).

You can look at the definitions of the tags using `nltk.help.upenn_tagset()` and pass the tag as an argument.

We can put all this together and analyse a larger corpus than the ones we have been dealing with so far. Let us take a look at one of the first speeches made by Barack Obama back in 2009. We will carry out the following steps:

1. Visit The American Presidency Project website
2. Scrape the speech from the "Address Before a Joint Session of the Congress" from February 24, 2009[13]
3. Save the speech to a local plain text file
4. Parse the sentences of the speech
5. Run some POS and determine the top named entities in the speech

https://www.presidency.ucsb.edu

[13] Address Before a Joint Session of the Congress. Barack Obama. 44th President of the United States: 2009-2017. https://www.presidency.ucsb.edu/node/286218

It sounds like something we can definitely do. So let us get started by reading the speech page and loading it into Beautiful Soup:

Yes, we can!

```
wp='https://www.presidency.ucsb.edu/node/286218'
pageSource = urlopen(wp).read()
pa2009 = BeautifulSoup(pageSource, 'lxml')
```

We can now find the place where the actual speech is located. In this case, it is in a `div` with class `field-docs-content` inside another `div` with class `main-container container`, yes... two containers... We are interested in all the paragraphs, and therefore we use the `find_all` method to obtain them:

Remember that if the page source changes, this code will need to be adapted accordingly.

```
maincontainer = pa2009.find('div',
    class_='main-container container')
content = maincontainer.find('div',
    class_='field-docs-content')
content_p = content.find_all('p')
```

Refer to Section 2.1 for the use of Beautiful Soup.

Now that we have the paragraphs, we can get the text and start cleaning it. For example, we need to get rid of heading and trailing spaces:

```
> paragraphs = [p.get_text().strip() for p in
    content_p]
> paragraphs[0][:120]


''Madam Speaker, Mr. Vice President, Members of
Congress, the First Lady of the United
States--she's around here somewhere''
```

We are looking at the first 120 characters of the first paragraph in the speech. A good shout-out to the First Lady there! We can now look at joining the paragraphs in a single string:

```
    speech = ' \n'.join(paragraphs)
```

We are concatenating all the paragraphs, leaving a new line in between them.

We can now use this string to write the text to a file:

```
with open('obama2009.txt', 'wb') as f:
    f.write(speech.encode())
```

It is possible now to separate each of the sentences in the speech:

We use sentence tokenisation to separate each of the sentences in the speech.

```
sentences = nltk.sent_tokenize(speech)
```

and to obtain the word tokens that can be POS tagged:

```
tokenized_sentences = [nltk.word_tokenize(sentence)
    for sentence in sentences]
tagged_sentences = [nltk.pos_tag(sentence) for
    sentence in tokenized_sentences]
```

Finally we tokenise each of the sentences and POS tag the tokens we have obtained.

So far, so good! We now have tagged sentences, and we could take a look at those to obtain the nouns mentioned in the speech. However, we are interested in more than simply getting all the nouns. We would like to get those named entities that are the subject of the sentences, in other words the protagonists of the speech. To that end, we will use a technique called *chunking*, which is a process to extract phrases from unstructured text. In this way, a phrase such as "United States" becomes a single entity instead of ending up with two separate words "United" and "States".

Chunking lets us extract phrases from unstructured text, and in this case obtain named entities.

A it is the case with POS tagging, there are standard chunk tags that can be obtained, such as Noun Phrases (NP),

Verb Phrases (VP) and Named Entities (NE) for example. In NLTK we can use the `ne_chunk_sents` which uses a maximum entropy (MaxEnt) classifier using data from the ACE (Automatic Content Extraction)[14] corpus. The ACE corpus has been manually annotated for named entities. The named entity chunker uses the following features to predict NEs, among others:

[14] ACE 2004 Multilingual Training Corpus. https://catalog.ldc.upenn.edu/LDC2005T09

- Capital letters, no numbers in the word
- Word length
- First and last three letters of the word
- POS tag
- Dictionary words
- POS tags of the preceding and following words

These are some of the features that determine a named entity in NLTK.

Let us determine the named entities in the tagged sentences from Obama's speech:

```
chunked_sentences = nltk.ne_chunk_sents(
    tagged_sentences, binary=True)
```

We are using NLTK's `ne_chunk_sents` to chunk the sentences.

In this case, `binary=True` lets NLTK know that we want to use the binary named entity chunker. The result is a generator with `Tree` objects. In this context, a tree is a hierarchical grouping of syntactical elements that make up a natural language utterance.

A `Tree` consists of a node value which is typically a string label and a Python iterable object comprising the node's children which in turn can also be Tree objects themselves. Let us look at an example with the sentence shown in Figure 2.4.

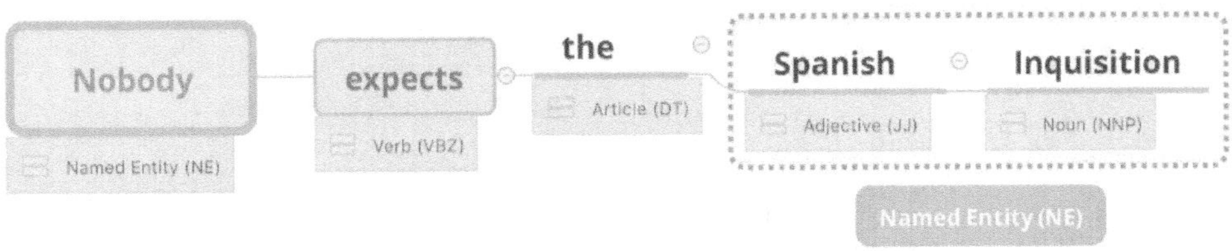

Figure 2.4: A chunked sentence with two named entities.

The sentence has two named entities, i.e., "Nobody" and "Spanish Inquisition", one verb in the present tense ("expects") and a definite article ("the"). We can recreate that Tree in NLTK as follows:

```
from nltk.tree import Tree
ne1 = Tree('NE', [('Nobody', 'NN')])
ne2 = Tree('NE', [('Spanish', 'JJ'),
    ('Inquisition', 'NNP')])
s = Tree('S', [ne1, ('expects', 'VBZ'),
    ('the', 'DT'), ne2])
```

The Tree structure of the chunked sentence shown in Figure 2.4.

In this case, we can see that the first named entity is a tree labelled NE and the token is appropriately tagged as a noun (NN). With this knowledge, let us write a function that parses the Tree recurrently and gets the entity names in a chunked sentence:

```
def get_entity_names(tree):
    entity_names = []
    if hasattr(tree, 'label') and tree.label:
        if tree.label() == 'NE':
            entity_names.append(' '.join([child[0]
                for child in tree]))
        else:
            for child in tree:
                entity_names.extend(
                    get_entity_names(child))
    return entity_names
```

A function to extract named entities from a given Tree.

We can finally apply our function to the speech we are analysing:

```
entity_names = []
for tree in chunked_sentences:
    entity_names.extend(get_entity_names(tree))

> entity_names[-5:]

['South Carolina', 'American', 'God',
'United States', 'America']
```

We extract the named entities from the speech using the function above.

Let us finish this section by creating a dataframe with the data obtained and determine the top 10 named entities by frequency of mentions in the speech made by Obama in 2009 before a Joint Session of the Congress:

```
from collections import Counter
import pandas as pd

data_names = Counter(entity_names)
df = pd.DataFrame(list(data_names.items()),
    columns=['Entity Name', 'Freq'])
df.set_index('Entity Name', inplace=True)
```

The named entities can be loaded into a pandas dataframe and can be analysed.

We can see the top 10 named entities in the speech in Figure 2.5.

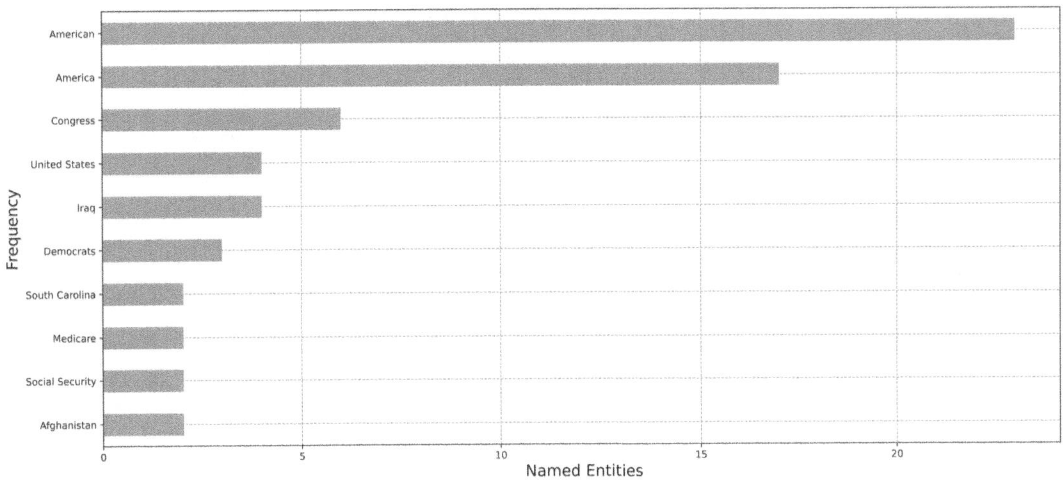

Figure 2.5: Top 10 named entities in the 2009 speech made by Barack Obama before a Joint Session of the Congress.

2.6 *What Are You Talking About? Topic Modelling*

Understanding the different themes or topics that a piece of text is about constitutes another important and useful application of natural language processing. The identification of topics from the word patterns present in a

The identification of topics from word patterns is the main task in topic modelling.

corpus is known as topic modelling and is an unsupervised task. In contrast to topic modelling, we have rule-based text mining approaches based on the use of keyword searching.

But, what is a topic? In this context, we are interested in looking for repeating patterns of terms that co-occur in a given corpus. This means that the end result of topic modelling is a set of words that can be used to describe the theme or themes in the corpus. Please note that the algorithm does not provide a closed, definitive topic. Instead, we require a human to provide the label. Also, since topic modelling is an unsupervised task, the other important task in the process requires the identification of the likely number of topics in the corpus.

Since topic modelling is an unsupervised task, no labels are provided. Our task is to find them!

2.6.1 *Latent Dirichlet Allocation*

One of the most popular algorithms employed in topic modelling is the Latent Dirichlet Allocation algorithm (LDA). It enables us to explain existing observations based on latent, or unobserved, groups of variables that account for similarities in the original data.

LDA stands for Latent Dirichlet Allocation.

One of the first descriptions and uses of LDA was in the area of population genetics by Pritchard, Stephens and Donnelly[15]. In their paper, the authors address the problem of assigning individuals to K populations (with K potentially being unknown). In this case, instead of different pieces of text, we have individual genotypes, and instead of looking at the frequency of words in each text, we are interested in the allele frequencies in the populations. The

[15] Pritchard, J. K., Stephens, M., and Donnelly, P. (2000). Inference of population structure using multilocus genotype data. *Genetics* 155(2), 945–956.

distribution on these frequencies is assumed to have a Dirichlet distribution which has the property that the frequencies add up to 1.

In short, the Latent Dirichlet Allocation algorithm takes information from latent variables taking samples over a probability simplex representing probabilities over K distinct categories, and the aim is to allocate each observation to one of the categories.

Think of a simplex as a set of numbers that add up to 1.

A more formal description of the LDA algorithm was done by Blei, Ng and Jordan[16] in 2003. In that paper, LDA is presented in the context of topic modelling where each piece of text is seen as a mixture over an underlying set of topics. Here, we will provide an intuitive explanation of the main concepts behind the algorithm.

[16] Blei, D. M., Ng, A. Y., and Jordan, M. I. (2003). Latent Dirichlet Allocation. *Journal of Machine Learning Research 3*, 993–1022.

Let us start by considering a collection of documents we are interested in analysing. Each individual document talks about particular subjects and we can safely assume that each document contains a mixture of different topics. One topic may contain the words "quantum", "atom", "energy" and "tunnelling", whereas another may have words such as "data", "statistics", "python" and "analytics".

Any given document is thought of containing a mixture of different topics.

Topics are therefore abstract entities that we cannot directly see. Nonetheless, the appearance of the words mentioned in our example lets us infer that documents that contain the first set of words are about "*quantum physics*", whereas those containing the second are about "*data science*", for example.

Nonetheless, we can try to identify a dominant topic in each document.

This all sounds very encouraging; however, it is not possible to infer the topics exactly. There may be some documents about doing research in quantum physics using Python to analyse data! In any event, we may be able to work backwards and still be able to say something about the latent topics in our corpora.

We can, for instance, assume that we know which topic created each and every word in the collection, and then we see a word w_n in document $\mathbf{w}$ whose topic of origin is unknown to us. Furthermore, we have a corpus made out of M documents denoted $D = \{\mathbf{w}_1, \mathbf{w}_2, \ldots, \mathbf{w}_M\}$. Our task is to decide if word w_n comes from topic z_n.

A document here is a sequence of N words denoted by $\mathbf{w} = (w_1, w_2, \ldots, w_N)$.

Some avenues we may be able to pursue to answer the question include the frequency with which word w_n appears in documents about topic z_n. Also, we may want to consider if topic z_n is prevalent in the rest of document $\mathbf{w}$. At this point, it may be convenient to remind ourselves of the powerful Bayes' theorem:

The powerful Bayes' theorem strikes again!

$$P(A|B) = \frac{P(A)P(B|A)}{P(B)}, \tag{2.1}$$

where $P(A|B)$ is the conditional probability of event A taking place given B. We provided a derivation of this expression in chapter 6 of *Data Science and Analytics with Python*[17].

[17] Rogel-Salazar, J. (2025). *Data Science and Analytics with Python.* Chapman & Hall/CRC Data Mining and Knowledge Discovery Series. CRC Press.

In this case, we know the frequency of the word w_n in topic z_n as well as the total number of words in that topic. Also we have a prior of the number of words in document $\mathbf{w}$ that come from topic z_n. We can use Bayes' theorem to determine the probability of having topic z_n given the word w_n in document $\mathbf{w}$.

In LDA for each document **w** in corpus D, we require the following constructs:

- The sequence of N words that make up a document follows a Poisson distribution, and
- The topic distribution θ follows a Dirichlet distribution denoted $\mathrm{Dir}(\alpha)$.

This requirement on N can be relaxed.

α will become one of our parameters.

For each of the N words, we choose a topic z_n that follows a multinomial distribution with parameter θ, and then we choose a word w_n from the multinomial probability conditions on the topic z_n, i.e., $p(w_n|z_n, \beta)$.

Another parameter in our model is β.

What does this all mean? Well, remember that we started up assuming that the words in a document come from a specific topic, and vice versa. Let us then get all the words and allocate them to random topics to test if our initial assumption holds. Effectively, we use the words in the documents to assess the words in the topics, and then we use the words in the topics to assess the words in the documents. If the words fit in the topic distribution, then we can go home. However, if they do not, then we change the topic the word is in. This is done iteratively until not many words need to be changed.

This is in effect the iterative work we require in the algorithm to determine the topic distribution in our corpus.

In the expressions above, you may have noticed two hyperparameters in our model, namely α and β. The first one is related to the document-topic density, in other words the number of topics per document; whereas the second one tells us something about the topic-word density. That is the number of words per topic. The other parameter that needs to be given as an input is the number of topics!

The higher the value of α, the higher the number of topics in a document. The higher the value of β, the higher the number of words per topic.

As stated by Blei et al[18], the inferential problem in LDA is computing the posterior distribution of the latent variables given a document:

[18] Blei, D. M., Ng, A. Y., and Jordan, M. I. (2003). Latent Dirichlet Allocation. *Journal of Machine Learning Research* 3, 993–1022.

$$p(\theta, \mathbf{z} | \mathbf{w}, \alpha, \beta) = \frac{p(\theta, \mathbf{z}, \mathbf{w} | \alpha, \beta)}{p(\mathbf{w} | \alpha, \beta)}. \qquad (2.2)$$

It is possible to represent the LDA model as a probabilistic graphical model as shown in Figure 2.6. The parameters α and β are sampled once and are defined at a corpus level. The variables θ are sampled once per document, whereas w and z are sampled once for each word in each document.

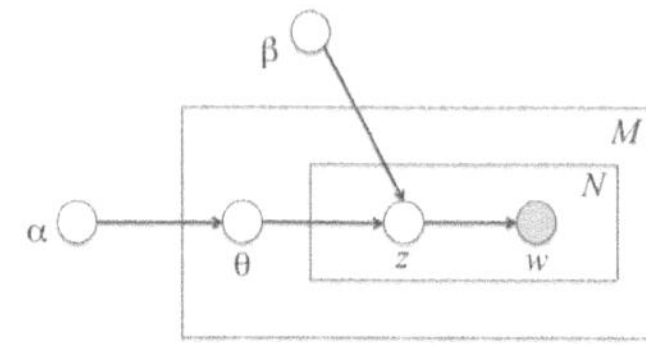

Figure 2.6: Graphical model representation of LDA.

From the discussion above, it is clear that we need to break down our documents into the constituent words, and the information presented earlier on in this chapter is therefore quite useful. In particular, we will need to create a vocabulary of all the known words and measure their presence in our corpus. This is usually referred to as a *bag of words*, where information about the word order or even the sentence structure is disregarded, and we are only concerned with whether individual words are present or not in a document. If we look at individual words, we have a *unigram* analysis; in case we are interested in pairs of words appearing together we are analysing *bigrams*, and as you can imagine this can be extended to *n-grams*.

We need to determine the vocabulary in our corpus, and we do this with a bag of words approach.

For probabilistic models, it is common to use the log-likelihood of a held-out test for evaluation. We should be familiar with the idea of partitioning our dataset into training and testing sets, and in this case we would have $\mathbf{w}_d$ unseen documents, and for our purposes of evaluation we

The likelihood function measures how well a statistical model explains observed data.

can ignore the topic-distributions as they correspond to the training set. The *perplexity* measure is defined in terms of the log-likelihood as:

$$\text{Perplexity}(\mathbf{w}_d) = \exp\left(- \frac{\sum_d \log p(\mathbf{w}_d | \mathbf{z}, \alpha)}{\text{count of tokens}} \right). \quad (2.3)$$

The perplexity measure can help us determine the performance of our model.

The perplexity is a decreasing function of the log-likelihood of the unseen documents, and the lower the perplexity, the better the model. We will cover other aspects of perplexity in Section 5.6 in the context of Large Language Model benchmarking.

See more about perplexity in Section 5.6, page 438.

2.6.2 *LDA in Action*

IT IS NOW TIME TO take a look at LDA in action. There are several options we have with Python including the excellent gensim[19] package, or spaCy[20]. In this case we are going to concentrate on our good old friend scikit-learn.

In chapter 6 of *Data Science and Analytics with Python*[21], we encountered a dataset containing a number of tweets used in the context of explaining the naïve Bayes classifier algorithm. We will be using the same corpus here. The data contains two sets: A training dataset with labelled tweets, and a testing dataset without labels. For the purposes of the discussions in this chapter, we will not be using the given labels in the training dataset. Remember that topic modelling is an unsupervised task!

[19] Řehůřek, R. and P. Sojka (2010, May). Software Framework for Topic Modelling with Large Corpora. In *Proceedings of the LREC 2010 Workshop on New Challenges for NLP Frameworks*, Valletta, Malta, pp. 45–50. ELRA. http://is.muni.cz/publication/884893/en

[20] spaCy. https://spacy.io

[21] Rogel-Salazar, J. (2025). *Data Science and Analytics with Python*. Chapman & Hall/CRC Data Mining and Knowledge Discovery Series. CRC Press.

The data can be obtained at `https://doi.org/10.6084/m9.figshare.2062551.v1`[22]. Let us first read the data into Python:

[22] Rogel-Salazar, J. (2016, Jan). Data Science Tweets. https://doi.org/10.6084/m9.figshare.2062551.v1

```
import pandas as pd


tweets = 'Train_QuantumTunnel_Tweets.csv'
tweets = pd.read_csv(tweets, encoding='utf-8')
```

The location of your file may be different!

As we are interested in the words that appear in our tweets, we are bound to lose some information such as URLs and even @-mentions and hashtags. We will process our data to capture this information with the following function:

```
def mentions_hashtags_urls(tw):
    mnt = re.compile(r''@\w+(?:[-']\w+)*|'')
    hash = re.compile(r'#\w+(?:[-]\w+)*')
    urls = re.compile(r'http\S+')
    mention = ' '.join(mnt.findall(tw))
    hashtag = ' '.join(hash.findall(tw))
    link = ' '.join(urls.findall(tw))

    return mention, hashtag, link
```

This function lets us capture @-mentions, hashtags and URLs.

This compiles a regular expression to capture @-mentions, hashtags and URLs and returns a concatenated version of each of these items. We can now map this function from the "Tweets" column in our dataset to three new columns as follows:

Remember that `findall` returns a list.

```
tweets['Mentions'], tweets['Hashtags'],\
    tweets['URLs'] = zip(*tweets['Tweet'].\
        map(mentions_hashtags_urls))
```

Here we use the power of `zip` to populate three columns in our dataframe! Cool, right?

We are not going to do much else here with this information, but you can take a look at the results and perhaps use them to improve the vocabulary in our bag of words. Here is some of that information though:

```
tweets[['Mentions', 'URLs', 'Hashtags']].tail(3)


Mentions      URLs                       Hashtags
@R_Trotta
              https://t.co/no4Usx6djV    #maths
              http://t.co/fW7pSgTWGj
```

These three columns can help inform our topics. We will not use them in the rest of our analysis though.

We are ready to start the tokenisation of our corpus, and for that we need to bring up some useful packages and functions. First we will be using the `TweetTokenizer` we encountered in Section 2.4. We can also decide to use a lemmatiser or a stemmer for the preprocessing part. In this case, we will use a stemmer which we hope will help with some differences in spelling for example between American and British English:

You write *tokenize*, I write *tokenise*. Let's call the whole thing off.

```
import nltk
from nltk.tokenize.casual import TweetTokenizer


porter = nltk.PorterStemmer()
```

We may also want to get rid of the most common words in our bag, either in the language of the corpus such as "a", "the" "this", "that", ..., or words that we specifically would like to remove. For that we will use `stopwords` from NLTK:

In this case, the language is English.

```
from nltk.corpus import stopwords
import string


stop_words = stopwords.words('english')
stop_words.extend([''i've''])
```

Notice that we can even extend the list of words adding those which are of no interest to us. NLTK supports other languages including Spanish, German, Italian, etc. Another thing we will need to take care of is punctuation. For that matter, we will use the `punctuation` method of `string` when processing our documents.

Stop words for other languages are available. We will also eliminate punctuation in our documents.

In a bag of words analysis we need to consider that for a computer, upper- and lowercase letters are not the same. So "President" and "president" would count as two different words in their eyes. We can deal with this issue by transforming all uppercase letters into lowercase as part of the preprocessing we need to carry out.

I know... anthropomorphising computers is not very useful but then again...

Here are the steps we will be taking:

- Transform the text into lowercase characters
- Remove @-mentions
- Remove character sequences that contain numbers

- Remove URLs
- Tokenise each document with TweetTokenizer
- Remove stop words (English)
- Stem the tokens
- Remove punctuation
- Finally we join back the tokens in a processed string

Let us take a look:

```
def tw_preprocess(tw):
    tw = tw.lower()
    tw = re.sub(r'@\w+(?:[-']\w+)*', '', tw)
    tw = re.sub(r'\S*\d\S'', '', tw)
    tw = re.sub(r'http\S+'', '', tw)
    tw = re.sub(r''[#|']'', '', tw)
    tokens = TweetTokenizer().tokenize(tw)
    tokens = [t for t in tokens if t not in
              stop_words]
    tokens = [porter.stem(t) for t in tokens]
    tokens = [t for t in tokens if t not in
              string.punctuation]
    tokens = ' '.join(tokens)
    return tokens
```

We will use this function to process our corpus. It will later be employed on unseen tweets too.

OK, it is now time to process our corpus:

```
tweets['Processed_Tweet'] = tweets['Tweet'].\
    apply(tw_preprocess)
```

We need to process our corpus.

Let us preview the result:

```
> tweets['Processed_Tweet'].tail(6)


 go ausvarg much would love argentina final sup...
                              perhap peopl level
 yay connect automat eduroam univers michigan g...
 true mean would cinema arriv late also paid en...
             report card famou mathematician math
      princeton guid linear model logist regress r
```

Remember that we have stemmed our words.

We are in a position to vectorise our documents; in other words, we would like to create a (sparse) matrix containing the words that make up each of the documents in our corpus. We can do this in scikit-learn with the help of `CountVectorizer`:

```
from sklearn.feature_extraction.text import \
    CountVectorizer

no_features = 1000
vectoriser = CountVectorizer(min_df=2,
    max_features=no_features)
```

`CountVectorizer` creates a matrix of token counts from the words contained in our corpus.

We are defining a matrix of token counts where we require at least 2 occurrences of the token (`mid_df=2`) and consider a vocabulary of 1000 features ordered by term frequency across the corpus (`max_features`). We can define other parameters such as the use of `stop_words` to remove stop words, or define regular expressions to extract tokens with `token_pattern`.

We have already taken care of stop words above.

Now that we have instantiated our vectoriser, let us learn the vocabulary and return the term-document matrix for our corpus:

```
tw_vectorised = vectoriser.\
    fit_transform(tweets['Processed_Tweet'])
tw_vectorised_names = vectoriser.\
    get_feature_names_out()
```

We use `get_feature_names_out` to obtain a human-readable version of the tokens used in our model.

We can get the actual tokens that have been used in the construction of the matrix with the help of the `get_feature_names_out` method. Let us look at the first few entries:

```
> print(tw_vectorised_names[:5])


['actual', 'ai', 'algorithm', 'alien', 'amaz']
```

See the result of `get_feature_names_out` here.

The term-document matrix we have now obtained can be used to feed to the Latent Dirichlet Allocation algorithm. Scikit-learn has an implementation of the LDA algorithm in `sklearn.decomposition`. We will now instantiate an object to be used in our modelling:

Scikit-learn provides `LatentDirichletAllocation` to implement LDA.

```
from sklearn.decomposition import\
    LatentDirichletAllocation
```

Remember that the number of topics is an input parameter. However, we do not know a priori how many topics there are. So, we are going to carry out a grid search on the number of topics. The implementation offers two learning methods: A batch variational Bayes method, and an online one. The latter uses a mini-batch of training data to update the topics incrementally. The learning rate for the online method is controlled by the learning decay and learning offset parameters.

Number of components in the language of scikit-learn.

Our grid search will be done over both the number of topics and the learning decay. We will look at having between 3 and 7 topics in the corpus and learning decay equal to 0.6, 0.8 and 1.0.

We will carry out a grid search over two parameters: The number of topics and the learning decay.

```
n_components = range(3, 8)
search_params = {''n_components'': n_components,
    ''learning_decay'': [0.6,  0.8, 1.0]}
```

Let us instantiate our LDA model:

```
lda = LatentDirichletAllocation(
    max_iter=10,
    learning_method=''online'',
    random_state=0,
    evaluate_every=-1,
    learning_offset=50.0)
```

Our model needs to be instantiated before we are able to use it. This is true for other scikit-learn models too.

We have a model with 10 as the maximum number of iterations, using the online Bayesian method with a random number generator seeded with 0. We can evaluate the perplexity at a number of iterations. If the `evaluate_every` parameter is 0 or negative, we do not evaluate the perplexity in training at all. Finally, a positive learning offset down-weights early iterations of the online learning method.

Let us search the parameters; in this case, we are requesting a 15-fold cross-validation.

```
from sklearn.model_selection import GridSearchCV


model = GridSearchCV(lda, param_grid=search_params,
    cv=15)
```

In this case we are performing a grid search with a 15-fold cross-validation.

Training the model may take some time, and in the end we are interested in the best estimator found:

```
model.fit(tw_vectorised)
best_lda_model = model.best_estimator_
```

The best model out of the grid search is returned with the `best_estimator_` method.

The best model obtained has the following parameters:

```
> print(''Best Model's Params: '',
    model.best_params_)


Best Model's Params: {'learning_decay': 1.0,
    'n_components': 3}
```

The chosen parameters for the best estimator can easily be obtained.

As you can see, we seem to have 3 topics in the corpus. The model's score is:

```
> print(''Best Log Likelihood Score: '',
    model.best_score_)


Best Log Likelihood Score:  -937.1175972870192
```

Note that the process involves some randomisation, so your scores and results may vary slightly.

And its perplexity is:

```
> print(''Model Perplexity: '',
    best_lda_model.perplexity(tw_vectorised))

Model Perplexity:  733.9819454674919
```

The same note above applies here.

With the model trained, we can now create our document-topic matrix and extract the dominant topic for each document:

Once we have the model, we can create our document-topic matrix.

```
lda_output=best_lda_model.transform(tw_vectorised)
```

The output of the LDA model can be added to our original dataframe:

```
topicnames = ['Topic' + str(i) for i in
    range(best_lda_model.n_components)]

tweets = pd.concat([tweets,
    pd.DataFrame(
        np.round(lda_output, 2),
        columns=topicnames)], axis=1)
```

The output of the model can be added to our original dataframe.

Finally, we can obtain the dominant topic for each of the documents:

```
dominant_topic = np.argmax(
    df_document_topic[topicnames].values, axis=1)

tweets['Dominant_Topic'] = dominant_topic
```

The dominant topic is the one with the highest score.

We can take a look at some of the results obtained:

```
> tweets[['Tweet', 'Dominant_Topic']].head()

Tweet                                    Dominant_Topic
Oh... It is even worse... They ...              0
RStudio OS X Mavericks Issues ...               2
A Hubble glitch has produced ...                0
@kwbroman Good question. I've ...               1
Data and visualization year in ...              1
```

And the results are in!

The first and second tweets correspond to topic 0, the second one to topic 2 and the fourth and fifth ones to topic 1. We can take a look at the distribution of the tweets among the three topics:

```
df_topic_distribution = (
    tweets['Dominant_Topic'].\
        value_counts().reset_index(
            name="Num Documents"))
df_topic_distribution.columns = ['Topic Num',
    'Num Documents']
```

We can take a look at the distribution of topics.

This leaves us with the following distribution:

```
> print(df_topic_distribution)

  Topic Num  Num Documents
        2             123
        0             109
        1              92
```

Once again, your results may be different from these ones.

Topic modelling tells us the most likely dominant topic for each of the documents in our corpus. Nonetheless, we must remember that the method is an unsupervised task, and therefore it cannot provide us with a label for each of the topics. That falls to the human in the middle. In other words, we may take a look at the words that are contained in each of the topics, and we can try to make sense out of them. With that in mind, let us create a function that is able to extract the top n_words from each of the topics:

We can take a look at the words that make up each topic to provide a label.

```
def topic_words(model, feature_names, n_words=10):
    for idx, topic in enumerate(model.components_):
        print('Topic '.format(idx))
        print(' '.join([feature_names[i]
            for i in topic.\
                argsort()[: -n_words - 1: -1]]))
```

This function extracts the top n_words in each topic for us to assess.

The function above will provide by default the top 10 words in each of the topics found in the training of our algorithm. For our purposes, let us take a look at the top 5 words in our topics:

```
> topic_words(best_lda_model, tw_vectorised_names,
    n_words=5)


Topic 0
rugbi via xma think us
Topic 1
new physic statist time star
Topic 2
data great xkcd use scienc
```

Et voilà!

From the information above, we can see that Topic 0 is a general topic including tweets about rugby, Topic 1 can be safely labelled as physics and science, and Topic 2 as data science and machine learning.

I can say it is a general topic given the familiarity with the documents. It may not be that obvious in other corpora!

Our last step is to use these new labels on unseen tweets. Fortunately in this case we have a testing dataset. Let us take a look:

```
testtweets = 'Test_QuantumTunnel_Tweets.csv'
testtweets = pd.read_csv(testtweets,
    encoding='utf-8')
```

We need to perform the same processing done to our documents, and this can easily be carried out by applying the `tw_preprocess` function defined above to our test tweets:

We need to apply the same processing to unseen documents for scoring.

```
testtweets['Processed_Tweet'] = \
    testtweets['Tweet'].apply(tw_preprocess)
```

We will need to apply the vectoriser transformation to our new documents and then the model itself so that we can get the dominant topic. All this can be done with the following function:

```
def determine_topic(x, vec, model):
    mytext = [x]
    vec_transf = vec.transform(mytext)
    topic_prob_scores = model.transform(vec_transf)
    topic = np.argmax(topic_prob_scores)
    return topic
```

This function lets us score unseen documents with the trained model obtained.

All that is left to do is to apply this function to our dataset:

```
testtweets['Topic']=testtweets['Processed_Tweet'].\
    apply(determine_topic, vec=vectoriser,
        model=best_lda_model)
```

Together with the processed tweets, the results can easily be saved if we wanted to. For now, we can take a look at some of the predictions made:

```
> testtweets[['Tweet', 'Topic']].tail()


                               Tweet  Topic
Halfpenny ruled out of World Cup ...      0
159  CRAN now has 5000 R packages...      0
knitr in a knutshell tutorial htt...      2
Up all night to get data, a music...      0
A survival guide to Data Science ...      2
```

And there we have it, topic modelling completed!

And there you have it; LDA is served!

2.7 *What's in a Word? Embeddings and Vector Search*

IMAGINE YOU'RE AT A DINNER PARTY, and someone remarks that, "The hors d'oeuvre were immaculate". You smile and nod, but what does that even mean? As humans, we learn from context. Words like "immaculate" shift meaning depending on the sentence, the speaker, and whether it is said with an arched eyebrow or a social media filter.

It could well have been Margo Leadbetter to Jerry!

Computers, alas, do not do nuance naturally — unless we teach them.

That is where *embeddings* come in. These are like your brain's gut feeling packaged into numbers: A way to represent words, phrases, or even whole documents as vectors in a multi-dimensional space, where distance captures meaning. With embeddings, words like `cat` and `kitten` sit close together, while `kitten` and `carburetor` are socially distanced. Before we delve more into the innings of this immaculate party, let us take a historical detour.

Embeddings are a way to represent natural language as vectors in a multi-dimensional space.

2.7.1 *From Bag-of-Words to Word Embeddings*

IN THE BEGINNING, *text* WAS just a big "bag of words". In the 1970s, Gerard Salton introduced the idea of representing a document as a vector of word counts, the so-called **vector space model**[23]. In a nutshell, a scenario where stored items (like documents) are compared with each other or with a query (like a search request), it is useful to represent each item in a multi-dimensional space where each dimension corresponds to a keyword or feature. In this space, documents are treated as vectors. The goal is to position these document vectors so that they are as far apart from one another as possible, making them easier to be distinguished.

[23] Salton, G., A. Wong, and Yang, C.S. (1975). A vector space model for automatic indexing. *Communications of the ACM 18*(11), 613–620.

The effectiveness of such an indexing system can be thought of in terms of how densely packed the vectors are in this space. If the space is too dense (i.e., the vectors are too close to one another), it is harder to tell documents apart, and

The performance of document retrieval to the "density" of the vector space.

retrieval performance suffers. Conversely, if documents are well separated in this space, retrieval is more accurate. This idea is used to guide the selection of an optimal set of indexing terms (vocabulary).

Soon after, Karen Spärck Jones[24] added *inverse document frequency* to weight down common words, yielding the famous TF-IDF formula. TF-IDF is a numerical statistic used to measure how important a word is to a document in a collection (or corpus). It combines two ideas:

[24] Spärck Jones K (1972). A statistical interpretation of term specificity and its application in retrieval. *Journal of Documentation 28*, 11–21.

- Term Frequency (TF) — how often a word appears in a document.
- Inverse Document Frequency (IDF) — how unique or rare that word is across the whole collection.

The key idea is that words that appear often in a document are important (high TF). However, words that appear in many documents are less useful for distinguishing content (low IDF). So TF-IDF gives a high score to terms that are frequent in a document but rare in the collection.

TF-IDF boosts terms frequent in a document but rare across documents, making them good content discriminators.

Consider that you have a term t, a document d, and a collection of documents D, then TF , measures how often t appears in d:

$$\text{TF}(t,d) = \frac{\text{Times } t \text{ appears in } d}{\text{Total number of terms in } d}, \qquad (2.4)$$

whereas the IDF measures how rare t is across the corpus, i.e.,

$$\text{IDF}(t,D) = \frac{\ln(\text{Total number of documents in } D)}{1 + \text{Number of documents containing } t}. \qquad (2.5)$$

In that way, TF-IDF is given by:

$$\text{TF-IDF} = \text{TF}(t, d) \times \text{IDF}(t, D), \tag{2.6}$$

and it helps us dentify keywords in a document. Furthermore, with it we can build vector representations of documents for comparison (e.g., using cosine similarity[25]) and thus improve search engines, ranking, and topic extraction. For example, in a document about "quantum physics", the word "quantum" might have a high TF-IDF because it is common in that document but rare in others. On the other hand, words like "the" or "and" have low TF-IDF, as they appear everywhere. Let us see a sketch example:

[25] Rogel-Salazar, J. (2025). *Data Science and Analytics with Python*. Chapman & Hall/CRC Data Mining and Knowledge Discovery Series. CRC Press.

Imagine you have three documents in your corpus:

- Doc1: "AI is the future"
- Doc2: "AI and machine learning"
- Doc3: "The future is bright"

A simple example to understand how TF-IDF works.

Let us say that you have the task of searching for the term "AI". It is easy to see that the term in question is common to Doc1 and Doc2, but not present in Doc3. In other words, the TF for the term is high in the first two documents, but its IDF is lower because it is not rare across documents. Now, compare this with the term "machine": It only appears in Doc2, giving it a higher IDF, and potentially a higher TF-IDF score in Doc2.

These Bag-of-Words and TF-IDF methods are simple and useful, i.e., staples of early information retrieval, but they had a glaring limitation: They completely ignored context and meaning. In a TF-IDF vector, synonyms like *car* and *automobile* are as unrelated as *car* and *potato*. That is not good!

Linguists knew something was amiss and J.R. Firth famously quipped:

> You shall know a word by the company it keeps.[26]

[26] Firth, J.R. (1957). A synopsis of linguistic theory 1930–1955. In *Studies in Linguistic Analysis*. Philological Society.

The above highlights that context defines meaning. This insight birthed the so-called *distributional semantics*: The idea that words occurring in similar contexts have similar meanings. The 1990s saw methods like **Latent Semantic Analysis**[27] (LSA) that tried to capture this by taking giant sparse term-by-document matrices and factorised them with Singular-Value Decomposition[28] (SVD) and linear algebra techniques to uncover latent semantic dimensions. In essence, it gave each word a vector based on co-occurrence patterns, a big step towards meaning-based representations.

[27] Deerwester, S. and Dumais, S.T. and Furnas, G.W. and Landauer, T.K. and Harshman, R. (1990). Indexing by latent semantic analysis. *Journal of the American Society for Information Science 41*(6), 391–407.

[28] Rogel-Salazar, J. (2025). *Data Science and Analytics with Python*. Chapman & Hall/CRC Data Mining and Knowledge Discovery Series. CRC Press.

We will cover neural networks in Chapter 4 of this book.

The next leap came from the world of neural networks. One of the first neural language models was trained by Yoshua Bengio and colleagues[29]. The model simultaneously learned a probability model for word sequences, and a distributed vector representation for each word. In this model, every word is embedded as a point in a continuous vector space, such that "nearby" words (in meaning) end up with similar vectors. For example, if *dog* and *cat* often appear in similar contexts, the model's training process will nudge their vectors closer together. Bengio's pioneering work effectively invented modern **word embeddings**, proving that we

[29] Bengio, Y. and Ducharme, R. and Vincent, P. and Jauvin, C. (2003). A neural probabilistic language model. *Journal of Machine Learning Research* 3, 1137–1155.

could fight the "curse of dimensionality"[30] by giving words some shared underlying features. It was a slow, heavy model by more modern standards, but it was conceptually groundbreaking.

[30] Rogel-Salazar, J. (2025). *Data Science and Analytics with Python*. Chapman & Hall/CRC Data Mining and Knowledge Discovery Series. CRC Press.

A real turning point came in 2013, when Tomas Mikolov and team unleashed Word2Vec and kicked word embeddings into high gear[31]. Word2Vec introduced two lightweight models: Continuous Bag-of-Words (CBOW) and Continuous Skip-gram. The models aimed to learn word vectors by predicting words from their context (and vice versa). Critically, it was fast — training on billions of words in mere hours — and the vectors it produced captured startling linguistic patterns, giving us the now-famous example:

[31] Mikolov, T., K. Chen, G. Corrado, and J. Dean (2013). Efficient estimation of word representations in vector space. *CoRR abs/1301.3781*.

$$\mathbf{V}(Queen) \simeq \mathbf{V}(Woman) + \mathbf{V}(King) - \mathbf{V}(Man). \quad (2.7)$$

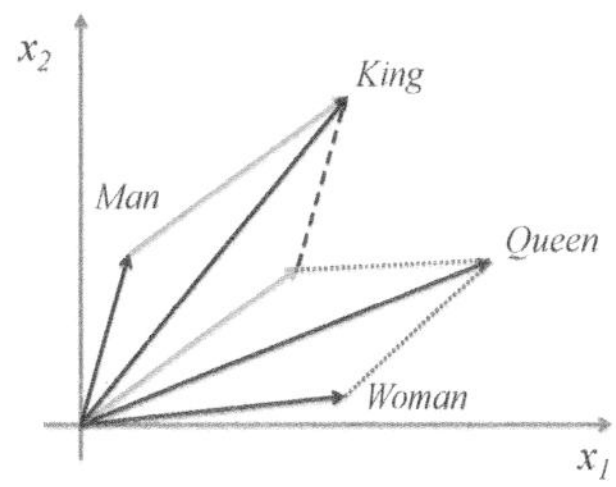

Figure 2.7: Illustration of word vector relationships, showing how *Man* relates to *King* in the same way *Woman* relates to *Queen* in embedding space.

We can see a simplified diagram representing Equation (2.7) in Figure 2.7. It illustrates how vector embeddings can capture semantic relationships between words in a geometric space.

Each word—*Man*, *King*, *Woman*, and *Queen*—is represented as a point (a vector) in the embedding space. The (simplified) features x_1 and x_2 show that the transformation from *Man* to *King* is nearly identical to the transformation from *Woman* to *Queen*, indicating that the model has learned a consistent *royalty* relationship. In mathematical terms, the vector difference between *King* and *Man* is approximately equal to the difference between *Queen* and *Woman*, a

See Section 5.2 for more on Word2Vec within the context of neural networks.

property that allows embedding models to solve analogy problems such as that represented by Equation (2.7), demonstrating how embeddings preserve both similarity and relational structure in a way that supports reasoning over meaning. In other words, Word2Vec showed that a simple neural network could learn analogies and word relationships that made linguists smile. Suddenly, word embeddings went from a curiosity to a mainstream NLP tool, as they allowed computers to measure word similarity and even solve analogy puzzles with uncanny accuracy.

See Section 3.5.1 for the usage of Word2Vec.

Or at least do a double-take.

While Word2Vec learned from local context windows in the text, we have other approaches such as that of **GloVe**[32] taking a more global approach. GloVe stands for Global Vectors and it trained on aggregated word–word co-occurrence counts. This is done essentially by factorising a huge matrix of word co-occurrences with a weighted least squares objective function. The result was another set of powerful embeddings, with GloVe achieving about 75% accuracy on a word analogy benchmark, matching Word2Vec's prowess.

[32] Pennington, J., R. Socher, and C. Manning (2014, October). GloVe: Global vectors for word representation. In A. Moschitti, B. Pang, and W. Daelemans (Eds.), *Proceedings of the 2014 Conference on Empirical Methods in Natural Language Processing (EMNLP)*, Doha, Qatar, pp. 1532–1543. Association for Computational Linguistics.

In plain English, GloVe demonstrated that you can teach an old matrix new tricks, combining the statistical strength of methods like LSA with the efficiency of neural networks. Together, Word2Vec and GloVe firmly cemented the field's shift from sparse *bag-of-words* representations to dense, trainable *word vectors* as the new standard for representing meaning. And they gave NLP researchers two new favourite buzzwords in the process.

In plain natural language even!

2.7.2 *Embeddings in Python: No Crystals Required*

HOW CAN WE IMPLEMENT EMBEDDINGS? Luckily for us, we do not need a quantum computer for this. Instead what we need are *Transformers*, which have revolutionised natural language processing, laying the foundation for a wide range of advanced machine learning models known as large language models (LLM). One of the most influential of these is **BERT**, which is built from multiple stacked transformer encoders. BERT stands for Bidirectional Encoder Representations from Transformers, and it has been widely adopted for tasks such as sentiment analysis, question answering, and increasingly, for generating word embeddings.

We will cover transformers in more details in Section 5.4.

In many real-world applications, we often need to generate embeddings not just for individual words, but for entire sentences. The original BERT model was not designed with this in mind. This limitation led to the development of several BERT-based extensions that aim to create high-quality sentence embeddings. One example is Sentence-BERT, or SBERT, a state-of-the-art model specifically designed for producing effective sentence-level representations. This model is the one we will employ in this section. As usual, Python has just the thing: We will use `sentence-transformers`[33], a rather handy library that wraps powerful SBERT models in a simple API. Make sure you install it. Sentence Transformers can be used for working with cutting-edge embedding and reranking models. It provides simple interfaces for:

BERT produces embeddings at the word level.

[33] Reimers, Nils and Gurevych, Iryna (2019, 11). Sentence-BERT: Sentence Embeddings using Siamese BERT-Networks. In *Proceedings of the 2019 Conference on Empirical Methods in Natural Language Processing*. Association for Computational Linguistics.

- Computing sentence embeddings using pre-trained Sentence Transformer models
- Measuring similarity with Cross-Encoder models (also called rerankers)
- Generating sparse embeddings using Sparse Encoder models

Some of the things you can do with `sentence-transformers`.

If you need more tailored solutions, the library also makes it easy to train or fine-tune your own embedding, reranking, or sparse encoding models — perfect for adapting to domain-specific tasks.

Then, let us get our hands dirty and import `SentenceTransformer` so we can load a pre-trained model:

Here, we will use a MiniLM model.

```
from sentence_transformers \
  import SentenceTransformer

model = SentenceTransformer('all-MiniLM-L6-v2')
```

In the code above we are loading the `all-MiniLM-L6-v2` model, which is a MiniLM model fine-tuned on a large dataset of over 1 billion training pairs[34]. It maps sentences and paragraphs to a 384-dimensional dense vector space and can be used for tasks like clustering or semantic search.

[34] Hugging Face. (2019). Sentence-transformer all-MiniLM-L6-V2. https://huggingface.co/sentence-transformers/all-MiniLM-L6-v2. Accessed: 2025-08-07.

Let us now create some sentences to play with:

```
sentences = [
    'The cat sat on the mat.',
    'A feline reclined atop a rug.',
    'Quantum gravity bends reality.',
    'Cats love warm spots.',
    'Schroedinger has a cat.'
]
```

We are now able to convert our sentences into embeddings, in other words, into dense vector representations of the text. These embeddings capture the semantic meaning of the sentences, allowing for various applications such as similarity comparison, clustering, and semantic search. We do this with the `model.encode` function:

Embeddings capture the semantic meaning of the sentences.

```
> embeddings = model.encode(sentences)
> print(embeddings.shape)

(5, 384)
```

Each of the five sentences has become a 384-dimensional vector — not visible to the naked eye, but ready for mathematical matchmaking.

Once we have embeddings, we can start measuring similarities. A common technique is *cosine similarity*[35]. Think of it as the angular distance between two points: If the angle is small, the meanings are close.

[35] Rogel-Salazar, J. (2025). *Data Science and Analytics with Python*. Chapman & Hall/CRC Data Mining and Knowledge Discovery Series. CRC Press.

```
> from sklearn.metrics.pairwise \
  import cosine_similarity
> similarities = cosine_similarity([
    embeddings[0]], embeddings)
```

In this case we are only looking at a comparison of the first sentence against the others. Let us look at the results:

```
> print(similarities[0])


[[ 1.0000   0.4892   -0.0385   0.4108   0.418 ]]
```

The first sentence is identical to itself, i.e., we have a cosine similarity of 1. We can see that it has a score of 0.4892 when compared to the second sentence. This is easy to explain when we look directly at the small corpus in this example. The first sentence ("A cat sat on a mat") is close in meaning to "A feline reclined atop a rug". On the other hand, it is least similar to the third sentence, which is all about quantum physics, but no cats!

No cats were harmed in the making of this example.

The library has its own implementation fo cosine similarity in the `similarity` method:

```
> sim = model.similarity(embeddings, embeddings)
> print(sim)


tensor([
   [ 1.0000,  0.4892, -0.0385,  0.4108,  0.4187],
   [ 0.4892,  1.0000, -0.0221,  0.3376,  0.3047],
   [-0.0385, -0.0221,  1.0000, -0.1021,  0.2935],
```

We can obtain an array of cosine similarity scores with the `similarity` method.

```
[ 0.4108,  0.3376, -0.1021,  1.0000,  0.3179],
[ 0.4187,  0.3047,  0.2935,  0.3179,  1.0000]])
```

From the array above, we can see that the third sentence, i.e., "Quantum gravity bends reality", has the greatest similarity (0.2935) to the last sentence "Schrödinger has a cat". This makes sense, after all Schrödinger proposed[36] his famous quantum mechanics thought-experiment with the help of a curious feline.

[36] Schrödinger, E. (1935). Die gegenwärtige Situation in der Quantenmechanik. *Naturwissenschaften* 23(48), 807–812.

2.7.3 *In Your FAISS: Vector Search*

Now that we can embed and compare, we can turn this into something far more useful: Search. In this way we can build memory palaces for machines by using a vector search engine.. Think of it as a search bar that understands meaning, not just keywords.

This is search that understands meaning, not just keywords.

To that end, we will `faiss`, a library developed by Facebook AI Research that does fast similarity search over dense vectors. As machine learning systems increasingly rely on embeddings—high-dimensional vectors that capture the meaning of text, images, or other data—efficient similarity search has become a fundamental building block of modern AI applications. FAISS is designed specifically to solve this problem at scale, providing both exact and approximate nearest neighbour (ANN) search in a highly optimised package. Whether these embeddings describe images, documents, or sentence meanings, we often want to search these vectors by asking questions such as, "Which of these items is most similar to this query?".

FAISS stands for "Facebook AI Similarity Search".

At its core, FAISS allows us to index and search through collections of vectors in a way that is much faster and more scalable than traditional methods. Unlike naive pairwise comparisons using NumPy or scikit-learn, FAISS is written in C++ with Python bindings and leverages low-level optimisations. It also supports GPU acceleration, enabling real-time performance even on billions of vectors.

FAISS enables fast, scalable vector search.

FAISS offers a variety of indexing structures tailored to different use cases. For small datasets, the `IndexFlatL2` and `IndexFlatIP` types provide exact brute-force search using Euclidean or inner product distance, respectively. For larger datasets, FAISS shines with its approximate algorithms such as `IndexIVFFlat`, which uses a clustering-based inverted file structure to drastically reduce the number of comparisons. Other variants, like `IndexIVFPQ`, add compression through product quantisation, making it possible to store millions of vectors in memory-efficient formats. FAISS also supports graph-based indexes like `IndexHNSW`, which use small-world graphs to provide fast and accurate ANN search with excellent recall rates.

FAISS provides exact indexes for small data and approximate, memory-efficient structures for fast large-scale vector search.

Let us see an example based on the sentences we used in Section 2.7.2. Let us start by importing `faiss`:

```
import faiss
import numpy as np
```

FAISS expects the input data to be in `float32` format and stored as a NumPy array. Here, a list of embedding vectors is converted to a 2D NumPy array of shape given by the number of sentences and embedding dimensions.

We need to ensure our vectors have the correct format.

```
embedding_matrix = np.array(embeddings).\
  astype('float32')
```

We now need to create a flat (brute-force) index that uses L2 (Euclidean) distance to compare vectors:

```
index=faiss.IndexFlatL2(embedding_matrix.shape[1])
```

The argument `embedding_matrix.shape[1]` specifies the dimensionality of the vectors. `IndexFlatL2` is exact (not approximate), making it suitable for small-to-medium datasets. Other FAISS index types (like `IndexIVFFlat`, `IndexHNSW`) support scalable ANN search for large corpora.

Here we are using a MiniLM with 384 dimensions.

We can now add the entire embedding matrix to the index. Each row becomes an item that can be searched later.

We index our embedding matrix in this way.

```
index.add(embedding_matrix)
```

We are now able to do our search: A new query sentence is encoded using the same embedding model as the dataset. It is converted to `float32` to match FAISS requirements:

```
q = 'Where do cats sit?'
query = model.encode([question]).astype('float32')
```

Here is where the magic happens.

And finally, we can do our search.

```
distances, indices = index.search(query, k=2)
```

FAISS performs a vector search:

- `query`: a 2D array with one row (our query vector)
- `k=2`: return the top 2 nearest neighbours
- `distances`: an array of shape $(1, 2)$ with the L2 distances
- `indices`: an array of shape $(1, 2)$ with the indices of the most similar items in the dataset

Finally, we can print out the top matching sentences from the original corpus by indexing into the sentences list using the returned indices.

Here is the result of our search. Not bad!

```
> print('Top matches for query: {}'.format(q))
  for i in indices[0]:
      print(sentences[i])


Top matches for query: Where do cats sit?
The cat sat on the mat.
Cats love warm spots.
```

As we can see, the results speak for themselves. FAISS can be used for speed; even brute-force search is faster with FAISS than NumPy + loops. Furthermore, it is scalable, as we are able to switch to ANN indexes when scaling to millions of vectors. It is flexible, supporting L2, cosine (via normalisation), inner product, and quantisation. Finally, it is production ready, as it is used in real-world systems like Facebook Search and semantic retrieval systems.

FAISS has several advantages going for it.

FAISS is a high-performance library for searching through large collections of vectors efficiently. This code sets up a simple search engine that finds the closest sentence(s) to a given query using Euclidean distance between sentence embeddings — all in just a few lines of Python. The result? A way for your program to answer questions like "What's this about?" with flair. Instead of brittle keyword matching, we have meaning matching — quite the upgrade. In the age of large language models and endless information, embeddings let us cut through the noise and find the signal. And this is all in a few lines of Python—not bad for something that does not require a quantum computer, divine inspiration or a linguistics *je ne sais quoi*.

FAISS enables quick nearest-neighbour searches on embeddings, letting Python code find similar sentences efficiently.

Now, if only we could embed that dinner party vibe...

2.8 Summary

THIS CHAPTER HAS A LOT of very useful information to deal with unstructured data such as text. We started our discussion by defining what natural language is, and how natural language processing is concerned with programming computers to process and analyse large amounts of natural language data. That sounds like something a good Jackalope data scientist should master, right?

We saw how to use Python to access data directly from the web, and in particular we saw the use of Beautiful Soup to scrape data from webpages. This required an understanding of HTML and the way information is organised in terms of tags. Beautiful Soup enabled us to scrape data from a page containing the Iris Dataset, and we got to grips with using tags, navigable strings, comments and Beautiful Soup objects in general.

We also covered the use of regular expressions to capture specific patterns in a piece of text that is of interest to us. We discussed some regular expression patterns and familiarised ourselves with the `re` module in Python. This led our discussions to the processing of text in Unicode, and we addressed some of the ways in which Python deals with encoding issues. We even played with writing in Japanese and processed the characters appropriately.

As part of the process of understanding text, we discussed tokenisation and used NLTK as a way to extract meaningful tokens out of our text. We did this with the help of available methods as well as creating our own, based for example on regular expressions. NLTK was also used in the context of stemming and lemmatising our tokens.

We saw how it is possible to use part-of-speech (POS) tagging on our tokens so as to be able to distinguish between important elements in a natural language, e.g., verbs, adjectives, nouns, clauses, etc. We used POS tagging in a US presidential speech to extract named entities mentioned.

We discussed topic modelling as an unsupervised learning task to identify the possible themes or topics that are addressed in a set of documents. The Latent Dirichlet Allocation algorithm (LDA) was our main discussion point, and we applied it to a corpus of tweets we had used in the context of the naïve Bayes classifier. C-3PO watch your step, here we come!

From there, we stepped into the world of *embeddings*, a powerful way to represent language where meaning is captured in dense numerical vectors. We traced the path from early bag-of-words and TF-IDF approaches, through distributional semantics and Latent Semantic Analysis, to modern neural methods such as Word2Vec, GloVe, and transformer-based models like BERT and SBERT.

To make these embeddings truly useful, we then turned to FAISS, a high-performance library for similarity search. By indexing our vectors and querying them for the nearest neighbours, we created a semantic search system that retrieves related sentences based on meaning rather than mere word overlap. Together, embeddings and FAISS form a modern NLP toolkit that lets us build systems capable of understanding and navigating meaning—a fitting finale for a chapter all about making sense of unstructured text.

3

Getting Social: Graph Theory and Social Network Analysis

Network analysis encompasses the study of relations between interconnected entities. It is based on the use of graphs to represent those entities (called nodes or vertices) and their connections (called edges, arcs or lines). These graphs can be layered with attributes and can also be rendered as diagrams.

Graph in the mathematical sense; not to be confused with a plot or a chart.

Network analysis has a large number of applications, from statistical physics to biology and from communications to finance. In particular, their application to undestanding social structures has gained prominence in behavioural organisational settings as well as psychology, political science and sociology.

Applications of network analysis can be quite wide.

As you can imagine, networks can be varied, and the field tends to be rather multidisciplinary. In this chapter we will introduce network analysis for social relationships.

However, the tools and methods we will cover can readily be applied to a variety of other areas. Once you start looking through the lens of a graph analysis, you may start seeing networks everywhere.

3.1 *Socialising Among Friends and Foes*

AN INTEGRAL PART OF BEING human is our ability to identify a variety of structures and patterns. That is also certainly true when it comes down to social relationships between individuals, organisations, teams, countries, etc. Think about your own social relationships; there are people with whom you have a strong social bond such as your close family and friends. You may even have met friends of friends, some of whom have become closer to you over time. Others may not, and in some situations they may even have become your nemeses.

You may want to hug your friends (please do!), and through the Holy Hand Grenade of Antioch towards thy foe! (please don't!).

The purpose of social network analysis (SNA) is to understand the relationships between actors with a tie. The actors in the network are referred to as nodes or vertices, and the ties are usually called edges (undirected), arcs (directed) or lines. In a social network, the nodes are usually people, and the edges represent a social connection between them. The focus of analysis is not necessarily at the individual level; instead we are interested in the connections that are embedded in the network. In other words, we would like to understand what information passes through the network.

Here, we will refer to *nodes* and *edges*.

It is easy to see that relationship between actors in the network carries some meaning. Going back to thinking about your own social relationships, the meaning may represent the level of affection, membership, or communication, etc. These ties can have a direction. Consider for example the relationship "love" where the feeling may sadly not be reciprocated. In those cases, we have a *directed* graph. However, in a situation where the tie means "shared interests" the relationship is directionless, and we therefore have an *undirected* graph.

Directed graphs have edges with direction, represented with an arrow.

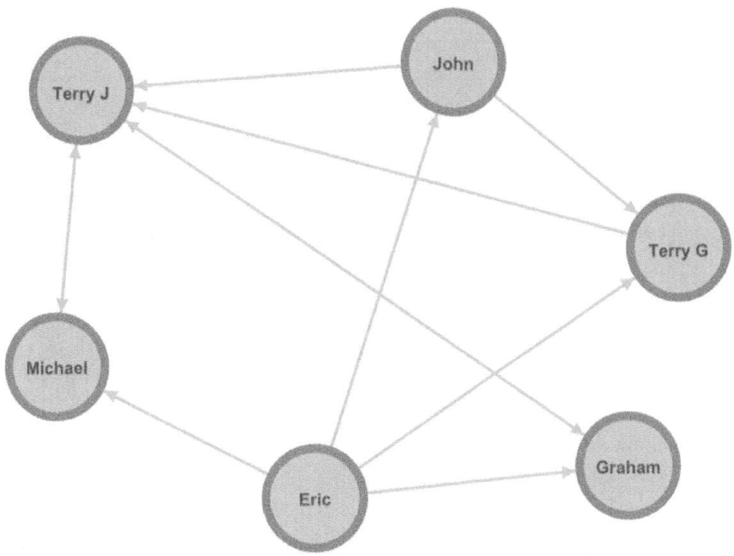

Figure 3.1: An example of a social network with directed edges.

In the network shown in Figure 3.1, we can see a directed network where the arrows indicate the direction of the relationship. We can see that Michael and Terry J have a mutual relationship, as well as Terry J and Graham. John has two outgoing relationships (with Terry J and Terry G) and one incoming relationship with Eric.

We know it is directed as the edges are represented with arrows.

Sometimes it is useful to concentrate our exploration of a network on a specific node. Within a social network context, we refer to those subsets as *ego networks*. The ego network for Terry G in our example can be seen in Figure 3.2. As you can see, this enables us to focus only on the edges that connect the node of interest with the rest of the network.

Ego networks concentrate on a specific node in the network.

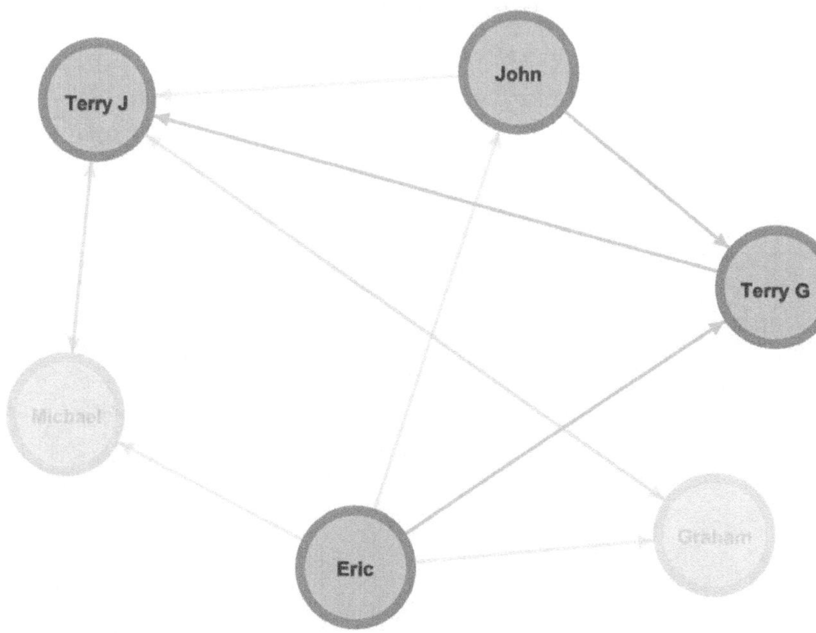

Figure 3.2: The ego network for Terry G. Only the related nodes are highlighted, and the rest are dimmed down for clarity.

The ties that connect the nodes in the network can tell us things regarding how strongly (or weakly) the actors interact. We can identify clusters in the network exhibiting characteristics such as **homophily**, that is the tendency of individuals to associate and bond with similar actors, or **transitivity**, i.e., when there is a tie from node i to node j, and also from node j to node k the relationship is transitive if there is also a tie from i to k (see Figure 3.3). We can also

Homophily → "Birds of a feather flock together".

Transitivity → "Friends of my friends are my friends".

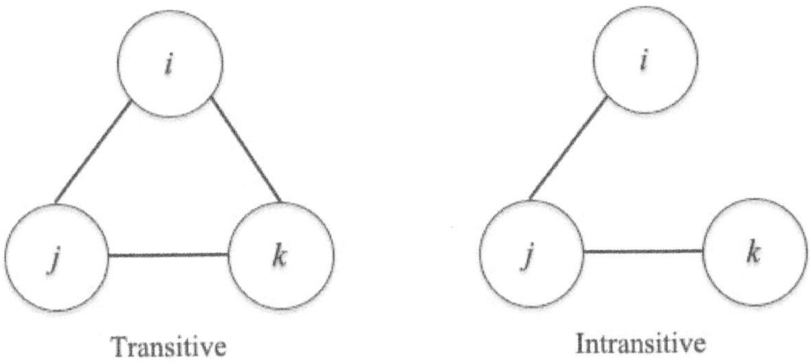

Figure 3.3: Transitivity in a network.

distinguish **cliques** which are densely, fully connected components in the network.

All these relationships can be uncovered, studied and understood using the tools developed by the branch of mathematics known as graph theory. It has a long and distinguished history starting in the 18th century with the Swiss mathematician Leonhard Euler solving a pass-time puzzle that entertained people in the old Prussian city of Königsberg, now Kaliningrad, Russia. The layout of the city connected four land masses, divided by the Pregel river, by seven bridges. The puzzle challenged the walker to find a way through the city crossing each bridge only once.

Graph theory is at the heart of social network analysis.

Leaving behind the geographical position of the land masses, and the bridges, Euler's solution consisted instead of concentrating on the connections[1]. The result can be represented with a graph. See our depiction in Figure 3.4. Euler's approach laid the foundations of network theory as we know it today.

[1] Euler, L. (1736). Solutio problematis ad geometriam situs pertinentis. *Comment. Acad. Sci. U. Petrop. 8*, 128–140.

The nodes in Figure 3.4 represent the land masses and the edges are the bridges. When looking at the problem in this

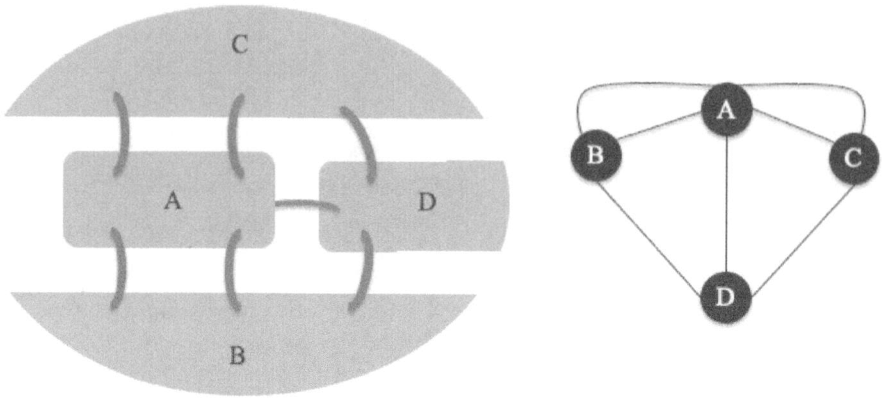

Figure 3.4: A schematic geographical representation of the seven bridges of Königsberg and a network highlighting the connectivity of the four land masses in question.

way and according to the puzzle rules, you can see that when you arrive to any particular node via an edge, you will need to leave it via a different line (unless it is the final destination!). This means that any node that is neither the starting, nor the ending position requires to have an even number of lines; in other words, for every bridge used to enter, there needs to be one bridge to leave. We can see that to be able to have a walking journey that crosses every edge once, at most two nodes can have an odd number of edges. As we can see from the graph in Figure 3.4, all nodes have an odd number of edges and as such the puzzle has no solution. Voilà!

You can follow this discussion with the network shown in Figure 3.4.

Either two nodes, or none at all!

Graph theory is therefore the study of relationships: Given a set of edges and nodes, which can be references to people, computer networks, companies, atoms, etc., it is possible to quantify and understand a variety of dynamic systems. If the nodes were cities, and the edges refer to routes connecting those cities, we end up with a classical problem known as the *travelling salesman problem* where given a finite number of cities, along with the cost of travel between each

The travelling salesman problem is a classic algorithm problem in computer science.

pair of cities, the task is to find the cheapest way of visiting all of the places and returning home, i.e., the starting point.

The problem can be posed in a variety of ways. A great example is the puzzle game invented in the late 1850s by the mathematician William R. Hamilton known as the Icosian game[2] where the aim is to find a Hamiltonian cycle; in other words, a graph that visits each node only once, along the edges of a dodecahedron. The travelling salesman problem is a computationally difficult problem, and a large number of heuristics and exact methods are known to tackle it; in some instances, a solution can be found for tens of thousands of cities.

[2] Ball, W.W.R. and Coxeter, H.S.M. (1987). *Mathematical Recreations and Essays*. Dover Recreational Math Series. Dover Publications.

Actually, it is an NP-Hard problem.

Ever since Euler's incursion in the field, mathematicians, physicists, biologists, chemists, engineers and social scientists have found uses for graphs. Given our interest in social analysis, perhaps it is illustrative to explore some of these applications. A great place to start is the game that the characters in Frigyes Karinthy's short story *Chains*[3] create: Find the chain that connects two individuals through at most five acquaintances. This is the beginning of the **small-world** experiments that gave us the notion of the *six degrees of separation*.

[3] Karinthy, F. (1929). Chains in Everything is Different. Online at http://bit.ly/karinthy_chains. Translated from Hungarian and annotated by Adam Makkai. Edited by E Jankó.

During the 1960s the experimental psychologist Stanley Milgram devised a series of experiments to prove the existence of short paths (the eponymous six degrees) among social connections[4]. The main aim was to test the notion that the world has shrunk in an ever-interconnected world. Today the experiment may seem a bit rudimentary given the

[4] Milgram, S. (1967). The small world problem. *Psych. Today 1*(1), 60–67.

social media tools we have at our disposal, but back in the 1960s the mere idea of interconnectedness was put to the test. In one of the experiments for example, Milgram arranged for 96 packages to be sent randomly to chosen people living in Omaha, Nebraska. Each package contained instructions for each recipient to get the package back to a friend of his who lived in Boston, Massachusetts. The name of the ultimate recipient was provided, along with his address and his occupation.

They were randomly chosen from a telephone directory!

He was (a stockbroker if you must know.

The task requested that each recipient of a package send it to a person they knew on a first-name basis and who they felt would be socially closer to the ultimate addressee. These new recipients were in turn asked to do the same until, of course, the package was hopefully received by the stockbroker in Boston. The lucky Bostonian received 18 of the 96 original packages, and the mean number of the connections from start to end turned out to be around 5.9, leading to the famous 6 degrees everyone, including ourselves, is talking about.

18 of the 96 packages reached their destination with a mean number of connections equal to 5.9.

Our collective imagination has been captured by this "small world" phenomenon, but the real surprise is the easiness with which, using local information, it is possible to navigate a large social network. So much so, that similar challenges have kept film trivia boffins entertained with calculating the so-called *Bacon number* where the aim is to find the shortest path that connects any given actor to Kevin Bacon in terms of having worked together. In that way someone with a Bacon number of 1 has appeared with the Mr. Bacon in a project directly. For example, Tom Hanks has

The Bacon number connects any given actor to Kevin Bacon.

a Bacon number of 1 having appeared alongside our central node in the 1995 film *Apollo 13*. Someone with a Bacon number of 2 would have appeared in a movie alongside someone with a Bacon number of 1, and so on. For example, Leonard Nimoy has a Bacon number of 2. I leave it as an exercise to find out the connecting path.

Fascinating!

The Bacon number is in fact an application of the *Erdös number* used and abused by mathematicians to describe the distance of academic collaboration with the prolific Hungarian mathematician Paul Erdös. The measurement is the authorship of papers that connect mathematicians: Erdös himself has number 0; those mathematicians who co-authored a paper with him have an Erdös number of 1, co-authors who have penned a paper with a scientist whose Erdös number is n have an Erdös number equal to $n + 1$. The calculation is given by the so-called shortest path algorithm which aims to find a path between two nodes such that the sum of the weights of the edges is minimal.

The Erdös number connects any given mathematician to Paul Erdös.

There is even a combined Erdös-Bacon number which is the sum of someone's Erdös number with their Bacon number. Some of my favourite nodes in the network that intersects thespians with scientists include Mayim Bialik of *The Big Bang Theory* fame and Natalie Portman (aka *Star Wars*'s Queen Amidala, among other characters) both have an Erdös number of 5 and a Bacon number of 2 (as of 2018), leaving them with an Erdös-Bacon number of 7. Carl Sagan and Stephen Hawking both have an Erdös-Bacon number equal to 6 (Bacon= 4, Erdös= 2).

The sitcom by the way, not the event that created the Universe.

The work of Duncan Watts and Steve Strogatz on small-world networks[5] has become so influential that these networks are often referred to as Watts-Strogatz networks. It is important to mention that the wide preference is to use the term specifically to describe graphs with a small mean geodesic path length and significant local clustering. We will come to explain these terms in the next section.

[5] Watts, D. and Strogatz, S. (1998). Collective dynamics of small-world networks. *Nature* 393(1), 440–442.

These days, the opportunities to analyse social media data are open to a lot of us, from using Twitter (now known as X) data to help better define the term digital humanities[6], all the way through to finding what combinations of flavours make some dishes taste great[7]. Some applications could be as complex as understanding the symptoms experienced by cancer patients undergoing chemotherapy[8]; or simply visualising the relationships between philosophers over centuries[9]. We need to be mindful, of course, of the data privacy issues that may arise when sourcing information from various social media platforms and other sources of information. This is not just important in the analysis of social networks, but indeed more general to any data science work we are involved with. Be a good Jackalope data scientist!

[6] Grandjean, M. (2016). A social network analysis of Twitter: Mapping the digital humanities community. *Cogent Arts and Humanities* 3, 1–14.
[7] Simas, T. et al. (2017). Food-Bridging: A new network construction to unveil the principles of cooking. *Frontiers in ICT* 4, 14.
[8] Papachristou, N. et al. (2019). Network Analysis of the Multidimensional Symptom Experience of Oncology. *Scientific Reports* 9(1), 2258.
[9] Noichl, M. (2017). Relationships between Philosophers, 600 b.c - 160 b.c. https://homepage.univie.ac.at/noichlm94/full/Greeks/index.html. Accessed: 2019-02-18.

3.2 *Let's Make a Connection: Graphs and Networks*

Now that we have a better idea of the applications and usefulness of networks, it is time to provide some of the notions that underpin the framework that enables us to understand the connections (edges) between the actors (nodes) in a given network. That framework is largely built around graph theory, a branch of mathematics interested in the properties of graphs. As we saw in the previous section, the basic idea of graphs was introduced by Euler, and in this section we will address some important aspects we need to understand to work with graphs, but we will not cover graph theory in its full glorious interconnectedness.

Graph theory is a branch of mathematics interested in the properties of graphs.

Up until now we have defined a graph in a loose way. Let us correct that and define a graph G as an object that consists of a collection of nodes or vertices V, and arcs or edges E, that connect pairs of vertices and can be expressed as $G = (V, E)$. We will refer to an arc as a directed connection between two nodes. If we consider two nodes v_1 and v_2 in G, an arc will be denoted as the ordered pair (v_1, v_2). If the connection is undirected, we will refer to it as an edge and will be denoted as $(v_1 : v_2)$. Notice that the order in this case is irrelevant.

$G = (V, E)$ denotes the graph G with nodes V and edges E.

Consider a graph G containing an node v_i. The neighbours of node v_i are denoted as $N(v_i)$, and they are all the nodes immediately connected to it. A walk in graph G is a sequence that traverses the graph from neighbour to neighbour. The length $|s|$ of the walk is the number of lines it contains. A walk is **closed** if the starting and ending points are one and the same node. There are other kinds of walks:

A walk is a sequence that traverses a graph from neighbour to neighbour.

- A **trail** is a walk where no lines (i.e., arcs or edges) are repeated. This was the aim in Euler's Königsberg puzzle: We cannot use the same bridge again.

* A **path** is a walk where no nodes are repeated. Using the Königsberg arrangement, this would be a case where we cannot visit the same land mass more than once.

* A **cycle** is a closed walk where all the nodes are different. In contrast, an **acyclic graph** does not contain any cycles.

* A **chain** or **semi-walk** is a walk where the direction of the lines is not considered.

There are other kinds of walks, such as trails, paths, cycles and chains.

The distance of shortest length between two nodes is denoted as $d(v_i, v_j)$. We can take a look at the largest (maximum) distance between any two vertices in the graph, i.e., $\max_{v_i,v_j \in V} d(v_i, v_j)$. This is the diameter of the graph and is denoted as $diam(G)$. On the other hand, the shortest paths are called **geodesic** paths.

The diameter of a graph is the path of maximum length.

Remember: No repeated nodes in a path.

Consider the graph in Figure 3.5, the distance from node 1 to 2 is $d(1,2) = 1$ and the distance from node 1 to 4 is $d(1,4) = 2$.

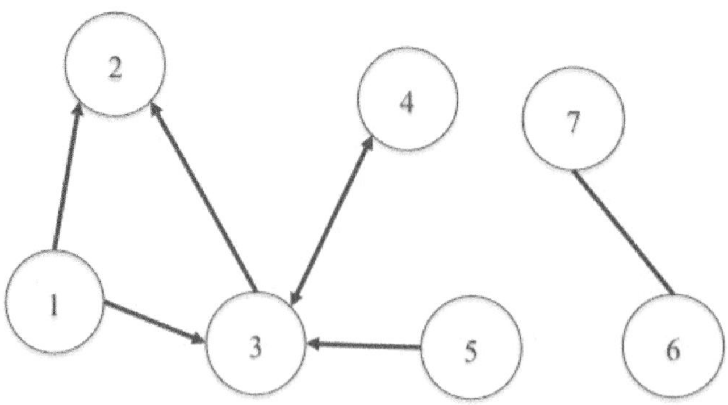

Figure 3.5: An example graph with seven nodes, and two sub-graphs.

If the nodes are not connected, then $d(v_i, v_j) = \infty$. This means that the graph is disconnected, and thus the vertices

v_i and v_j live in separate parts of the graph, such as nodes 1 and 7 in Figure 3.5, where we can clearly see the disconnection too. If the relationship in the graph was communication between actors, this situation would mean that there is no way for any messages to be passed between nodes $1, 2, 3, 4, 5$ and $6, 7$ in our example graph.

A disconnected graph has paths with distances equal to infinity (∞).

We say that node v_j is **reachable** from node v_i if and only if (iff) there is a walk starting at v_i and ending at v_j. We have a **weakly connected** node iff there is a semi-walk between nodes v_i and v_j. Iff both nodes are reachable, then we have a **strongly connected** pair of nodes. In our example graph, node 4 is reachable from node 1 (as are nodes 2 and 3); node 5 is weakly connected to 1. Nodes 3 and 4 are strongly connected. Notice that nodes 6 and 7 are also strongly connected, as we are assuming that the lack of arrows in the line indicates bidirectionality and therefore the relationship is undirected.

As we can see, it is possible to characterise the connectedness of our graphs.

We have seen a typical depiction of a network showing the connections among neighbours and, if appropriate, the direction of those connections. It is possible to represent a graph with the help of an **adjacency matrix**, i.e., a square matrix whose elements indicate whether a pair of vertices are connected or not. In an undirected graph, the matrix is symmetric, and typically we will show a 0 if the nodes are not connected and a 1 if they are. Values different from 1 are possible, and this would indicate the strength or weight of the connection. The adjacency matrix for the graph in

An adjacency matrix indicates whether two nodes are connected or not.

Figure 3.5 is given by:

$$\begin{array}{c} \\ \mathbf{1} \\ \mathbf{2} \\ \mathbf{3} \\ \mathbf{4} \\ \mathbf{5} \\ \mathbf{6} \\ \mathbf{7} \end{array} \begin{array}{c} \begin{array}{ccccccc} \mathbf{1} & \mathbf{2} & \mathbf{3} & \mathbf{4} & \mathbf{5} & \mathbf{6} & \mathbf{7} \end{array} \\ \begin{bmatrix} 0 & 1 & 1 & 0 & 0 & 0 & 0 \\ 0 & 0 & 0 & 0 & 0 & 0 & 0 \\ 0 & 1 & 0 & 1 & 0 & 0 & 0 \\ 0 & 0 & 1 & 0 & 0 & 0 & 0 \\ 0 & 0 & 1 & 0 & 0 & 0 & 0 \\ 0 & 0 & 0 & 0 & 0 & 0 & 1 \\ 0 & 0 & 0 & 0 & 0 & 1 & 0 \end{bmatrix} \end{array}. \qquad (3.1)$$

This is the adjacency matrix for the graph in Figure 3.5.

Notice that only the entries for nodes 3 and 4, and 6 and 7 are symmetric. For the rest, we need to read the matrix row-by-row to find the connections.

You may have noticed that there is a large number of zero entries in the adjacency matrix. Computationally speaking, it may be possible to store this information in a sparse matrix. An alternative way to store the information contained in the adjacency matrix is via an **edge list** where each entry is given by a pair of vertices that are connected. The edge list for our example graph is given by:

If the graph is weighted, the entry is a triplet: The first two elements are the nodes, and the third one is the weight.

$$G = [[1,2],[1,3],[3,2],[3,4],[4,3],[5,3],[6,7],[7,6]]. \qquad (3.2)$$

Finally, a way that combines the connectivity format of an adjacency matrix with the briefness of an edge list is the **adjacency list**. In this case, for each node in the graph we store a list that contains the nodes adjacent to it. If the graph is weighted, we can add the weight to the connected

An adjacency list combines the connectivity format of an adjacency matrix, with the briefness of an edge list.

node too. The adjacency list for our example graph is as follows:

$$\begin{aligned} G = & [[1 \to [2,3]], \\ & [3 \to [2,4]], \\ & [4 \to [3]], [5 \to [3]], \\ & [6 \to [7]], [7 \to [6]]]. \end{aligned} \tag{3.3}$$

It is possible to define a **partition** of nodes V as the set of subsets of nodes $\mathbf{C} = \{C_i\}$ such that the union of C_i is equal to V and for subsets $C_i \cap C_j = \emptyset$ (with $i \neq j$). In other words, the subsets do not overlap and when looking at them together as a whole they regenerate the original set V. We can also define an **equivalence** relation R on V iff it is reflexive ($\forall v \in V : vRv$), symmetric ($\forall u, v \in V : uRv \to vRu$) and transitive ($\forall u, v, z \in V : uRz \wedge zRu \to uRv$). Each equivalence relation determines a partion into equivalence classes $[v] = \{u : vRu\}$; and each partition determines an equivalence relation. Weak and strong connectivities as defined above are equivalence relations, defining weak and strong components.

Each equivalence relation determines a partition into equivalence classes, and vice versa.

3.2.1 *Taking the Measure: Degree, Centrality and More*

WE ARE NOW WELL CONNECTED with the idea of a graph and we have defined a number of attributes related to it. In this section we will define characteristics of the nodes themselves as well as characterise the relationship between the nodes in a graph.

Pun definitely intended!

Let us start by defining the **degree** of a node v, $deg(v)$, as the number of edges that are connected to node v. In Figure 3.5 the degrees of nodes 1 and 3 are $deg(1) = 2$ and $deg(3) = 4$, respectively. The **outdegree** is only applicable for directed graphs and $outdeg(v)$ is the number of arcs outgoing from node v. Similarly, the **indegree**, $indeg(v)$ is the number of arcs incoming to node v. In our example graph above, for node 1 we have that $outdeg(1) = 2$, and $indeg(1) = 0$; whereas for node 3, the measures are $outdeg(3) = 1$, and $indeg(3) = 3$.

The degree of a node is the number of edges that are connected to it. The in- and outdegrees are only applicable to directed graphs.

The centrality of the nodes is another important attribute that gives us information about the most prominent actors in a network. Centrality in this case refers to how well connected a node is to the rest of the network. We can think of highly connected nodes as power centres, or information hubs. As such, a higher centrality is judged to be an important asset for a node. We already know how to calculate the **degree centrality** of a node: It is simply the degree measures we defined earlier on.

In other words, how *central* the node is.

There are other types of centrality, such as the so-called **betweenness**, which is useful in measuring the influence that a particular node has over a network. We can think of this measure as a way to finding bridges between different components of a graph. Betweenness centrality is calculated by the shortest (weighted) path between every pair of nodes and is given by:

Betweenness tells us about the influence of nodes over the graph, thinking of them as bridges over the network.

$$g(v) = \sum_{a \neq v \neq b} \frac{\sigma_{ab}(v)}{\sigma_{ab}}, \quad (3.4)$$

where σ_{ab} is the number of geodesic paths from node a to node b, and $\sigma_{ab}(v)$ is the number of those paths that pass through node v.

There are cases where we may be interested in finding out which nodes are able to spread information more efficiently through the network. In those cases, the centrality measure we are interested in is called **closeness**. The closeness centrality of a node is proportional to the inverse of the average distance from the node to the rest of the network. In this way, a node with high closeness centrality has the shortest distances to all the other nodes. This can be expressed as follows:

Closeness centrality tells us about the nodes that are able to spread information more efficiently in the network.

$$C(v) = \frac{N}{\sum_x d(v,x)}, \tag{3.5}$$

where $d(v,x)$ is the distance between nodes v and x, and N is the number of nodes in the graph. Closeness centrality is sensitive to the size of the graph. As you intuitively know, it is harder to keep a close relationship with every single one of the members in a network, and as the network grows in size, this gets harder and harder. Multiplying by the number of nodes provides a form of correction for this situation.

Closeness centrality is sensitive to the size of the network.

In some cases, instead of asking how efficient the communication between nodes may be, we may be interested in finding out how well connected the actors in our network are. This can be seen as an extension to the degree centrality we discussed earlier on. The indegree centrality scores a point for every link a node receives; however, in a more general case, not all nodes are equivalent

This is the equivalent of "having friends in high places".

and there may be some that are more relevant / powerful / important than others. This is effectively a case of being endorsed by influential nodes. It can be measured by the **eigenvector centrality** which tells us that a node is important if it is linked to other important nodes.

Eigenvector centrality tells us that a node is important if it is connected to other important nodes.

A node receiving many connections does not necessarily have a high eigenvector centrality score (the actor can have a lot of friends, but none are in high places); furthermore, a node with a high eigenvector centrality score is not necessarily highly linked (the actor has a few but very important friends). To calculate the eigenvector centrality, we take advantage of the matrix representation of the graph and calculate its eigenvectors. First of all, we need to calculate a measure that is proportional to the sum of the scores of all nodes connected to a given node, i.e.:

Hence the name!

$$x_i = \frac{1}{\lambda} \sum_{j \in M(i)} x_j, \tag{3.6}$$

where the sum is over all $j \in M(i)$ such that the nodes j are connected to the node in question (i). Another way to calculate this is using the adjacency matrix A and we let $\mathbf{x}$ be the vector that has the centrality scores enabling us to write the following eigenvector equation:

$$A\mathbf{x} = \lambda \mathbf{x}, \tag{3.7}$$

Surely you can recognise this as an eigenvector equation.

where λ is called the eigenvalue. Our task is to find λ, and in general there may be multiple non-trivial solutions to the problem. We need to use an extra tool from our Jackalope data scientist belt: If we require that all the entries in the eigenvector are non-negative, thanks to the Perron-Frobenius theorem[10], there is only one eigenvalue that satisfies this requirement! This corresponds to the largest eigenvalue and that is good enough for ranking our nodes in terms of this centrality measure.

[10] Bapat, R., T. Raghavan, C. U. Press, T. S, G. Rota, B. Doran, P. Flajolet, M. Ismail, T. Lam, et al. (1997). *Nonnegative Matrices and Applications*. Encyclopedia of Mathematics and its Applications. Cambridge University Press.

The **PageRank** algorithm, famously used by Google Search to rank webpages, is a variant of eigenvector centrality. It is used to determine the importance of a webpage considering the number of links it gets, the link propensity of other pages and the centrality of those pages. We can calculate the PageRank centrality of a node as follows:

PageRank is a variant of eigenvector centrality.

$$x_i = \alpha \sum_k \frac{a_{k,i}}{outdeg(k)} x_k + \beta, \tag{3.8}$$

where α and β are constants, $outdeg(k)$ is the outdegree of node k, and $a_{k,i}$ is the (k, i) entry in the adjacency matrix for the graph. We can write this equation in matrix form as

Note that if the outdegree of k is null, we require that $outdeg(k) = 1$ in this calculation.

$$x = \alpha x D^{-1} A + \beta, \tag{3.9}$$

with D^{-1} being a diagonal matrix with k-th diagonal element equal to $1/outdeg(k)$. We can solve for x as $x = \beta(I - \alpha D^{-1} A)^{-1}$. We call α the damping factor, and its value should be chosen between 0 and $1/\rho(D^{-1}A)$, where $\rho(D^{-1}A)$ is the largest eigenvalue of $D^{-1}A$. It must be said that for large networks, it is more efficient to compute the PageRank via power iteration, as it does not have to deal with matrix decomposition, and it works very well with sparse matrices.

See more about power iteration in Appendix B.

3.2.2 *Connecting the Dots: Network Properties*

WE HAVE DESCRIBED A FEW attributes that characterise the individual nodes in a graph, and although they are important, the power comes from the collective properties that the nodes provide to the whole network, as they show the structure in the relationships between the actors. The emerging properties of the network as a whole provide us with a view of the aggregate effects individual nodes have on the whole.

We are interested in understanding the aggregate effects individual nodes have on the whole network.

For instance, looking at the different centrality measures discussed in the previous subsection, we can take a look at the **centralisation** of the overall graph. In other words, we can measure how even the scores of the nodes are. If they are evenly distributed we can talk about distributed networks, where every node is as central as any other. If the scores are not even, we refer to centralised networks, where one node is maximally central, and the rest are not.

Centralisation is an important characteristic of a network as a whole.

This brings us to the concept of the **density** of the network. It is a measure of how the network nodes are connected to each other. In the case where all the nodes are connected to one another, we have a complete graph and the density is equal to one. Formally speaking, the density $D(G)$ of graph G is defined by the number of existing edges, m, in the graph, compared to the total number of all possible edges:

The density measures how nodes are connected to one another.

$$D(G) = \frac{2m}{n(n-1)}. \tag{3.10}$$

The total number of possible edges is given by $n(n-1)/2$.

The value of $D(G)$ ranges between 0 and 1. In many real situations, the density of a graph is low. Think of a typical network in social media: A user will be connected to a few other users, while the actual network contains many, many more.

Now that we know about network density, it is straightforward to talk about **cliques** or **clusters** in the network. We are interested in knowing how much the nodes tend to form dense subgraphs, i.e., cliques or clusters. In a way, this is related to figuring out if two people are friends given that each person is friends with a common third party. We call this the **local clustering coefficient**, and it is given by the following expression:

Cliques are densely, fully connected components in the network.

$$C_i = \frac{2T(i)}{deg(i)\,(deg(i)-1)}. \tag{3.11}$$

The local clustering coefficient.

In other words, this is the ratio of the pairs of friends of v_i who are friends among themselves, $T(i)$, and the total number of pairs of v_i's friends. $T(i)$ is given by the number of closed triangles with node v_i as one of the vertices, whereas the total number of pairs of v_i's friends is given by:

$$\frac{deg(i)}{2}\,(deg(i)-1)\,. \tag{3.12}$$

In turn, the clustering in the network can be measured by the average **clustering coefficient**:

$$C = \frac{1}{n}\sum C_i, \tag{3.13}$$

The average clustering coefficient.

where n is the number of nodes in the graph.

A closely related measure to the clustering coefficient is the transitivity of the network. The average transitivity of a network is defined over the number of triangles in the graph:

We introduced the concept of transitivity on page 168.

$$Transitivity = \frac{3(\text{num. of triangles})}{(\text{num. of connected triples})}, \qquad (3.14)$$

where a connected triple is any trio of nodes i, j, k that forms an open triangle, for example with connections between i and j, and i and k. Notice that a closed triangle can be thought of as being composed of three open triangles. Transitivity measures the fraction of open triangles that are actually closed.

Hence the factor of 3 in the formula.

We are interested in the clustering coefficient and the transitivity of a graph, as they can be used to check for structural holes in the network. In other words, these measures show missing links between neighbours of a node. They give us information about the efficiency of information diffusion in the network, as well as how robust it may be to disruptions.

We may also be interested in identifying the **giant component** of a network. This is the largest strongly connected subgraph in a large network such that its size is a constant fraction of the entire graph as the latter grows in size. If N_1 is the size of a connected component K in a network with N nodes, then K is a giant component if:

The giant component is the largest strongly connected graph in a network.

$$\lim_{N\to\infty} \frac{N_1}{N} = c > 0, \qquad (3.15)$$

with c being a constant.

Once we are able to detect cliques and giant components, it is natural to ask if the network exhibits clusters that are not densely connected to others, but which are densely connected within themselves. We can think of these situations as having different "communities" within the network. **Community detection** is a hot research topic, as it is an NP-complete problem and in many cases the full exploration of the entire network is required. The task in community detection is to find a subgraph S of $G(V, E)$ where the nodes $V_S \in V$ share some similarity.

NP-complete means that we can verify the answer *quickly*, but sadly there is no known way to find a solution quickly.

One way we can start detecting groupings in a network is by finding sub-graphs which keep nodes connected as we traverse the graph. In other words, we need to find a k-component of the graph. We define a k-component as a maximal subgraph with, at least, connectivity k. Put in a different way, if we wanted to break that subgraph into more components, we would need to remove at least k nodes from it. The algorithm from Moody and White[11] can help us with this task. Note that there is a hierarchical nature to the structure of k-components in that the subgraphs are nested from a connectivity point of view: A given network can have a number of 2-components, which in turn can have one or more 3-components, and so on.

[11] Moody, J. and White, D. (2003). Social cohesion and embeddedness: A hierarchical conception of social groups. *Am. Soc. Rev. 68*(1), 103–128.

In terms of community detection, an algorithm usually employed for this purpose is the Girvan-Newman algorithm[12]. It aims to find the communities in a network by iteratively removing edges from the initial graph; as such, the remaining connected components are deemed to be the communities. The algorithm extends the definition of

[12] Girvan, M. and Newman, M.E.J (2002). Community structure in social and biological networks. *Proc. Natl. Acad. Sci. USA 99*, 7821–7826.

betweenness to the edges of the network, with **edge betweenness** being the number of geodesic paths between pairs of nodes that pass through a given edge. The idea is that separate communities are connected via edges with high edge betweenness. If we remove these edges, the community structure is unraveled.

There are a number of algorithms attempting to find community structures in networks[13] from graph partitioning and hierarchical clustering through to optimisation and generative model techniques. Unfortunately, we do not have the remit to cover these methods at length, but we can highlight the **Louvain** method[14] used to detect communities in large network settings based on a greedy optimisation approach. At the heart of both the Girvan-Newman and Louvain methods lies the concept of **modularity** as a way to quantify how cohesive the communities in a network are.

[13] Fortunato, S. (2010). Community detection in graphs. *Phys. Rep.* *486*(3-5), 75–174.

[14] Vincent D. Blondel, Guillaume, J.-L., Lambiotte, R., and Lefebvre, E. (2008, Oct.). Fast unfolding of communities in large networks. *J. Stat. Mech-Theory E* *2008*(10), P10008.

We can define modularity in terms of the adjacency matrix of the graph, A and the sum of the edge weights attached to a node i given by $k_i = \sum_j A_{ij}$:

$$Q = \frac{1}{2m}\sum_{i,j}\left[A_{ij} - \frac{k_i k_j}{2m}\right]\delta(c_i, c_j). \tag{3.16}$$

Each term in the sum contributes to the overall modularity measure by comparing nodes in the same community c_i. The Kronecker delta function $\delta(c_i, c_j)$ is equal to 1 if

$i = j$; if not, the nodes are not in the same community and $\delta(c_i, c_j) = 0$. The total edge weight in the entire network is given by $m = \frac{1}{2}\sum_{i,j} A_{ij}$.

In other words, if both nodes are in the same community, we multiply the contribution by 1, otherwise by 0.

Let us try to get a better understanding of each contribution to the expression above: We know that k_i is the total of the edge weight attached to i. We can consider a situation where node i assigns this edge weight randomly to other nodes in a way that is proportional to their own edge weight values. In that case, $\frac{k_j}{2m}$ is the average fraction of node i's edge weight that would be assigned to node j. Each contribution tells us how strongly nodes i and j are connected in the actual graph, in contrast to the case where the nodes are connected in a random network.

A dissection of the modularity terms in Equation (3.16).

The Louvain method proceeds in two steps. In the first step, we start up by assigning each node to its own community. We calculate the change in the modularity score defined above caused by removing each and every node from its current community, and placing them in the community of one of their neighbours. If the changes are negative, we keep the node in the current community, but if the changes are positive we assign the node to the community that generated the highest change.

In a network with N nodes, we start with N communities.

The second step makes use of the newly created communities from the first step. These communities are effectively the nodes of a new network. In this new network, the edge weight is given by the total of all the edge weights between the new nodes. There are also self-loops whose weights are given by the edge weights within each

Iterations over the two steps in the Louvain algorithm return the communities in the network.

community. We then simply do repeated iterations of these two steps until there is no improvement in the modularity measure, and the communities are therefore said to be stable.

The Louvain algorithm is fast compared to other methods and provides a hierarchical community structure that can shed light to the networks under scrutiny. However, due to the merging of communities that happens during the second step detailed above, detecting small groupings in a large network results in poor resolution. It is important therefore to be aware that for sufficiently large networks, the algorithm may not return the expected communities. The other fact that we need to take into account is determining a global maximum may not be possible, resulting in a degeneracy where several solutions with maximum modularity scores are possible.

Be aware that the Louvain algorithm may result in poor resolution of the communities in the network.

3.3 *Social Networks with Python: NetworkX*

We are going to use NetworkX to analyse networks, but before we do that, let us get acquainted with the module. NetworkX is a Python module that enables us to carry out computational network modelling tasks. It is effectively a memory graph database with some good rendering capabilities that let us draw the graphs we analyse. Although it is not ideal for truly large-scale applications, it is a good package that a Jackalope data scientist can use for analysing networks (social or otherwise). It strikes a useful

NetworkX is a Python module for analysing network/graph data.

balance between accessibility and functionality, allowing us to focus on exploring the structure and properties of graphs.

It is possible to represent various network types with NetworkX including directed and undirected graphs, as well as multigraphs. Furthermore, the nodes in our graphs can be any hashable object, and the edges can contain arbitrary data. The package comes with a variety of useful algorithms, and it is easy to use. Its integration with other Python libraries such as Matplotlib and pandas also makes it particularly convenient for embedding network analysis within broader data workflows.

Think metadata!

3.3.1 *NetworkX: A Quick Intro*

LET US START BY IMPORTING the NetworkX module, alongside some other useful ones:

```
import networkx as nx
import numpy as np
import matplotlib.pyplot as plt
```

A canonical abbreviation for NetworkX is `nx`.

We need to instantiate a graph object to which we can add nodes:

```
g = nx.Graph()
g.add_node('A')
```

We need to instantiate a graph object with `Graph()`.

The nodes can also be added from a given list. In this case we will need to use the `add_nodes_from` method:

```
g.add_nodes_from(['B', 'C'])
```

Adding nodes and edges to the object is straightforward.

From our discussion in Section 3.2 we know that apart from nodes, we also need edges. These can be added as follows:

```
g.add_edge('A', 'B')
```

In this case we are adding an edge between nodes A and B. We can also add edges from a list of tuples:

```
g.add_edges_from([('C', 'D'),
    ('E', 'F')])
```

Edges can be added by specifying the two nodes connected.

Note that in this case we are adding edges between nodes C and D on the one hand, and E and F on the other one. NetworkX is smart enough to figure out that although the nodes have not been defined, they get created as required.

Finally, we can also add weighted edges. In this case we require a tuple with three entries, the first two entries correspond to the nodes to be connected, and the third entry is the weight:

```
g.add_weighted_edges_from([(1, 'E', 2),
    ('C', 2, 3.5)])
```

Weighted edges are defined with a third value in the tuple.

Notice that the nodes can also be numbers, not just strings. In the example above, we are creating an edge between nodes 1 and E with a weight of 2, and an edge between nodes C and 2 with a weight of 3.5. Let us now take a look at the nodes of graph `g`:

```
> g.nodes()


NodeView(('A', 'B', 'C', 'D', 'E', 'F', 1, 2))
```

We can look at the nodes in a network with the nodes() method.

and its edges:

```
> g.edges(data=True)


EdgeDataView([('A', 'B', {}),
('C', 'D', {}),
('C', 2, {'weight': 3.5}),
('E', 'F', {}),
('E', 1, {'weight': 2})])
```

To see the metadata, we can add data=True to both the nodes or edges methods.

We are requesting information about the edges by passing the parameter data=True; otherwise (the default), we will simply get a list of existing edges.

We can render the network with the draw_network method as follows:

```
nx.draw_networkx(g,
    node_color='black',
    font_color='white',
    node_size=800)
```

We can plot the network with draw_network.

Here we are requesting that the nodes be coloured in black and that the font be white with a size of 800 pt. The result can be seen in Figure 3.6. Remember that the position of the nodes is not important, and indeed the rendering may look different in your screen.

The position of the nodes is not important (until it is! ... for ease of visualisation!)

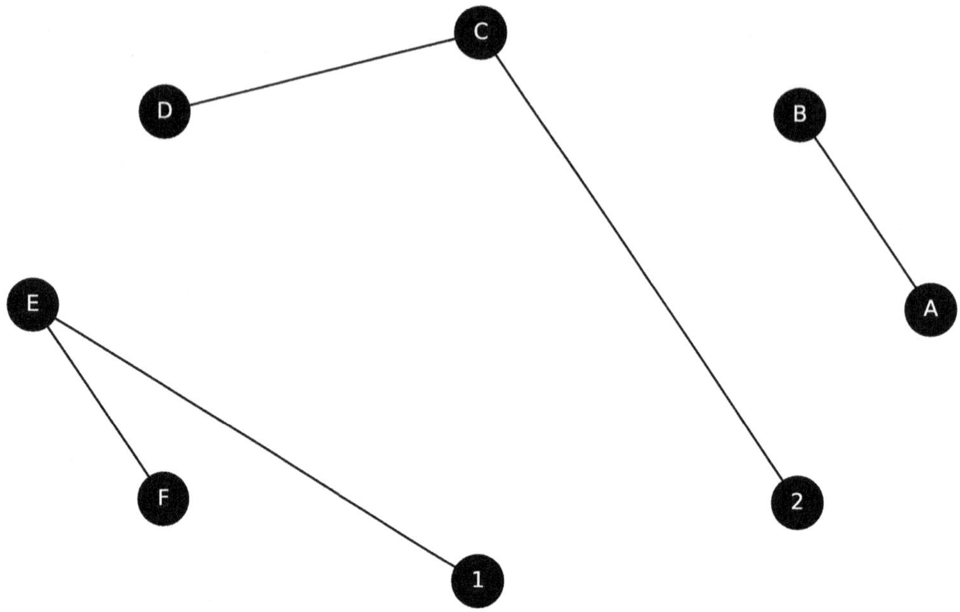

Figure 3.6: A simple graph depicting eight nodes and five edges.

We know that it is possible to represent a graph with the help of an adjacency matrix. For the undirected graph shown in Figure 3.6 the adjacency matrix is symmetric, and it can be expressed as:

$$
\begin{array}{c} \\ \mathbf{A} \\ \mathbf{B} \\ \mathbf{C} \\ \mathbf{D} \\ \mathbf{E} \\ \mathbf{F} \\ \mathbf{1} \\ \mathbf{2} \end{array}
\begin{array}{c}
\begin{array}{cccccccc} \mathbf{A} & \mathbf{B} & \mathbf{C} & \mathbf{D} & \mathbf{E} & \mathbf{F} & \mathbf{1} & \mathbf{2} \end{array} \\
\begin{bmatrix}
0 & 1 & 0 & 0 & 0 & 0 & 0 & 0 \\
1 & 0 & 0 & 0 & 0 & 0 & 0 & 0 \\
0 & 0 & 0 & 1 & 0 & 0 & 0 & 3.5 \\
0 & 0 & 1 & 0 & 0 & 0 & 0 & 0 \\
0 & 0 & 0 & 0 & 0 & 1 & 2 & 0 \\
0 & 0 & 0 & 0 & 1 & 0 & 0 & 0 \\
0 & 0 & 0 & 0 & 2 & 0 & 0 & 0 \\
0 & 0 & 3.5 & 0 & 0 & 0 & 0 & 0
\end{bmatrix}
\end{array}. \tag{3.17}
$$

Notice that the weighted edges we created above are shown in the corresponding elements of the matrix. We can see the adjacency matrix for our graph in NetworkX as follows:

```
adj_matrix = nx.adjacency_matrix(g)
> print(adj_matrix.todense())

[[0.  1.  0.  0.  0.  0.  0.  0. ]
 [1.  0.  0.  0.  0.  0.  0.  0. ]
 [0.  0.  0.  1.  0.  0.  0.  3.5]
 [0.  0.  1.  0.  0.  0.  0.  0. ]
 [0.  0.  0.  0.  0.  1.  2.  0. ]
 [0.  0.  0.  0.  1.  0.  0.  0. ]
 [0.  0.  0.  0.  2.  0.  0.  0. ]
 [0.  0.  3.5 0.  0.  0.  0.  0. ]]
```

We can see the adjacency matrix with the adj_matrix method.

We need to use the todense() method, as the matrix is stored as a sparse matrix. It is easy to see why this is the case, particularly when we consider the number of zero entries in matrix (3.17). An alternative representation for the matrix is as an edge list:

```
> edge_list = nx.to_edgelist(g)
> print(edge_list)

[('A', 'B', {}), ('C', 'D', {}),
('C', 2, {'weight': 3.5}), ('E', 'F', {}),
('E', 1, {'weight': 2})]
```

The edgelist methods shows us the edge list of our network.

Finally, it is possible to define the graph as an adjacency list. This is actually a dictionary object where the keys are nodes in the graph and the values are themselves dictionaries. The latter contain the nodes to which the key node is connected, and the values can store the weight of the edge (if required). The adjacency list for our graph is:

```
> for n in g.adjacency():
    print(n)


('A', {'B': {}})
('B', {'A': {}})
('C', {'D': {}, 2: {'weight': 3.5}})
('D', {'C': {}})
('E', {'F': {}, 1: {'weight': 2}})
('F', {'E': {}})
(1, {'E': {'weight': 2}})
(2, {'C': {'weight': 3.5}})
```

The adjacency list can be obtained with the `adjacency` method.

As it is the case in many applications, we usually require to read and write our data in a more expedient manner. NetworkX is no exception, and it is possible to read and write graph data in a variety of commonly used formats such as the ones described above, i.e., edge lists or adjacency lists, as well as others such as GML, GraphML, pickle, LEDA, JSON, etc.

NetworkX supports formats such as GML, GraphML, pickle, LEDA, JSON, etc.

3.4 *Social Network Analysis in Action*

IN THIS SECTION, WE WILL take a look at using the concepts and techniques described earlier in the chapter and start

We will analyse data for Zachary's karate club, and *Star Wars*!

to answer questions we may have about specific networks at hand. First, we will take a look at a classic example of social network analysis given by the Zachary karate club network. We will look at some social dynamics shaping the network. Second, we will analyse the interactions of Jedis, Siths, Droids and Princesses with a *Star Wars* network.

Punch it!

3.4.1 *Karate Kids: Conflict and Fission in a Network*

THE ART OF EMPTY-HAND FIGHTING, karate, is a relatively recent martial art originated on the island of Okinawa, but influenced by ancient Chinese martial arts known as kung-fu. Today, karate is a widespread sport, with karatekas all over the world and plenty of dōjōs from which to choose.

空手 is read as karate. 空 (kara) means "empty" and 手 (te) means "hand". *Karaoke*, meaning "empty orchestra" shares the same first word with karate!

Konishi Yasuhiro, an early karate sensei, is quoted to say that "Karate aims to build character, improve human behaviour, and cultivate modesty; it does not, however, guarantee it". And indeed this is something that can be corroborated with some karate clubs out there. A case in point is a now famous karate club studied over three years by Wayne W. Zachary[15] in the 1970s to analyse conflict and fission in small groups.

[15] Zachary, W. W. (1977). An information flow model for conflict and fission in small groups. *J. Anthropol. Res.* 33(4), 452–473.

The club was based at a university, and tensions between the club president, John A., and a part-time instructor, Mr. Hi, had been brewing for some time due to the setting of fees. Over time, the club became divided over these issues with the eventual separation of the club into two: One that supported Mr. Hi's teachings, and another one that followed John A. and the club officers.

The club was eventually split into two factions.

Zachary collected information about the original club, and the dataset obtained is now known as "Zachary's karate club" network. The groups that emerged from the fission of the karate club were factions not necessarily recognised by the club members. Instead, the friendship network among members gave rise to them during a moment of conflict.

The dataset called `karate.gml` can be obtained at `https://doi.org/10.6084/m9.figshare.7985174.v1`[16] and we will use it in the rest of this section. It contains 34 nodes representing individuals within the karate club. The edges in the network are given by interactions between two individuals outside the activities of the club such as actual lessons or meetings.

[16] Rogel-Salazar, J. (2019c, Apr). Zachary's karate club. https://doi.org/10.6084/m9.figshare.7985174.v1

Let us take a look at the data in the network. We can read the GML directly with NetworkX as follows:

GML - Graph Modelling Language.

Remember to refer to the correct path for the file!

```
import networkx as nx
fname = 'karate.gml'
K = nx.read_gml(fname)
```

We can plot the network with the `draw_networkx` method. In this case, we will colour the nodes black, with white labels and a size of 800. By default, the method uses a force-directed layout to position the nodes, and in this case we make this explicit:

In a force-directed layout the edges are roughly of equal length, and crossings are reduced by assigning forces to the edges similar to spring-like forces based on Hooke's law.

```
nx.draw_networkx(K, node_color='black',
    font_color='white', node_size=800,
```

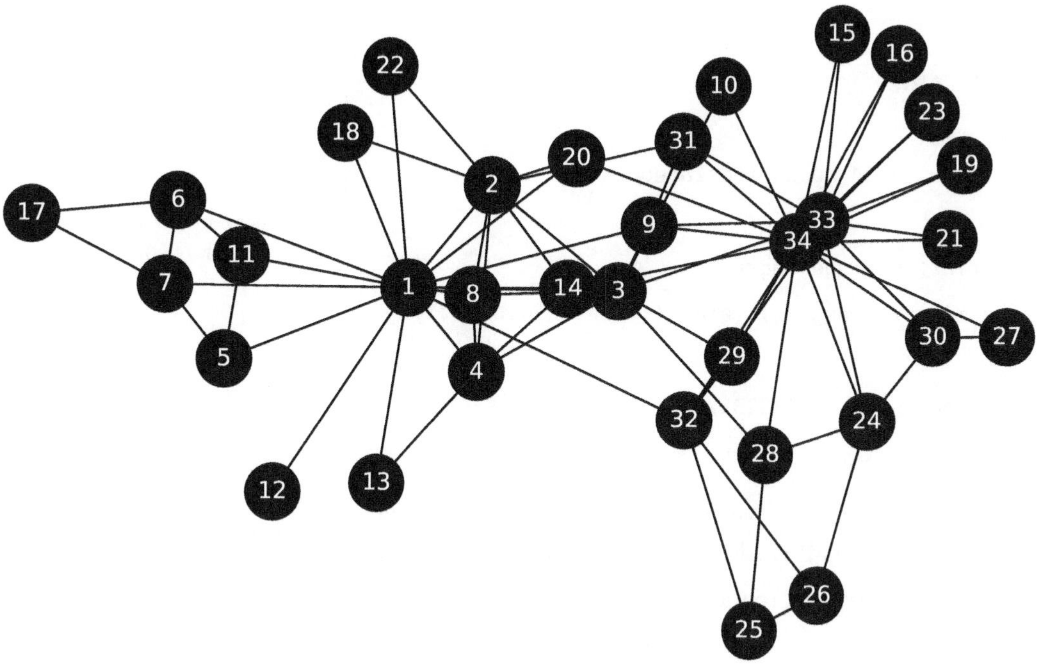

Figure 3.7: Zachary's karate club: 34 individuals at the verge of a club split. Edges correspond to friendship relationships among club members.

```
    pos=nx.spring_layout(K))
limits = plt.axis('off')
plt.show()
```

We can see the connections among members in the network depicted in Figure 3.7. Node number 1 is Mr. Hi (the instructor) and node 34 is John A. (the administrator). Let us see some basic information about the network:

```
> print(K)

Graph with 34 nodes and 78 edges

> print('Average degree', \
  sum(dict(K.degree).values()) / len(K.nodes))

Average degree 4.588235294117647
```

General information about the network is obtained by printing it.

We can see that the average degree of the network (4.5882) falls within the small world networks discussed earlier on in the chapter. We can request the degree of Mr. Hi and John A. with the help of the `degree` method for the network object:

```
> K.degree(['1', '34'])

DegreeView('1': 16, '34': 17)
```

Degree information for individual nodes from a list.

More information can be obtained for each node, for instance the degree:

```
> print('Degree: ', nx.degree(K,'1'))

Degree: 16
```

And a list of neighbours:

```
> print('Neighbours: ', list(nx.neighbors(K, '1')))

Neighbours: ['2', '3', '4', '5', '6', '7',
'8', '9', '11', '12', '13',
'14', '18', '20', '22', '32']
```

Decisions in the club structure were made by consensus during club meetings. This meant that having a majority in a meeting would result in decisions being swayed in favour of one faction over the other. If Mr. Hi called for a meeting, it would be advantageous for him if his supporters received the information, but not the opposers. This effectively means that the connections between individuals enable the flow of communication among parties. Those individuals that were undecided about giving support to one group over the other one become key players. They are able to pass on the information more readily than others.

Information transmission in Zachary's karate club network was important in the decision-making process, and eventual split.

According to the information provided by Zachary, once the unity of the club was unsustainable, two groups formed and the membership for each of them is listed in the paper. Nodes 1 – 9, 11 – 14, 17, 18, 20 and 22 became Mr. Hi's club, and the rest remained with John A. Let us add this information as metadata to our network. First we create a dictionary called `club` holding the membership for each node:

We know what actors in the network moved to each of the two groups after the split.

```
mr_hi = [*range(1, 10), *range(11, 15),
    17, 18, 20, 22]
```

In the expression above we have used `*range()` to unpack the values of the iterable so that we can pass them as separate arguments. We can use the list above to create membership for the nodes:

```
club = {}
for m in range(1, 35):
    if m in mr_hi:
        club[str(m)] = ''Mr. Hi''
    else:
        club[str(m)] = ''John A.''
```

We can encode this metadata in our network with the help of a dictionary.

We can now add this dictionary as an attribute to the nodes in the network:

```
nx.set_node_attributes(K, club, 'club')
```

And add the dictionary as an attribute to our network.

Let us check the information we just added:

```
> nodes = K.nodes(data=True)
> print(list(nodes)[:3])

[('1', 'club': 'Mr. Hi'), ('2', 'club': 'Mr. Hi'),
('3', 'club': 'Mr. Hi')]
```

Remember that `data=True` provides us with metadata of both nodes and edges.

We know that the degree centrality of a node tells us the number of connections to that node. We obtained above the degrees for Mr. Hi and John A. What about the rest of the nodes? We can answer this question very easily:

```
kdeg = K.degree()
```

The degree of the nodes is obtained with the `degree` method.

The result is a dictionary that we can query at will. For instance, we can check the degree of node 9:

```
> kdeg['9']
5
```

We can query the dictionary as usual.

Node 9 is an interesting one as mentioned by Zachary. Individual 9 backed (weakly) John A. but ended up joining Mr. Hi's club after the split. The explanation provided was that the person was only three weeks away from a black belt test and staying with Mr. Hi ensured that the test could be taken.

Node 9 in the karate network is an interesting one. Read on!

We can plot a network encoding the degree of the nodes in the size of the circles depicting them and use colour to show the final affiliation of the new clubs. Let us start by defining the colour map we will use:

```
import itertools
nodes = K.nodes(data=True)
clubs = set(nx.get_node_attributes(\
    K, 'club').values())
mapping = dict(zip(sorted(clubs),\
    itertools.count()))
colours = list(mapping[n[1]['club']] for n\
    in nodes)
```

In order to add colour or size attributes to the nodes, we need to create appropriate mappings.

The third line in the code above creates a set (unique values) of the clubs in the node attributes. We use this to create a mapping between the unique clubs and a count to serve as an index. Finally, we use the mapping to create a list that will be used to assign the colour index to each of the nodes.

Let us now create the plot:

```
nx.draw_networkx(K, node_color=colors,
  node_size=[200*val for (node, val) in kdeg])
limits = plt.axis('off')
plt.show()
```

Notice that we need to pass a value for each of the node sizes. In this case, the values are given by the degree centrality of the node in question.

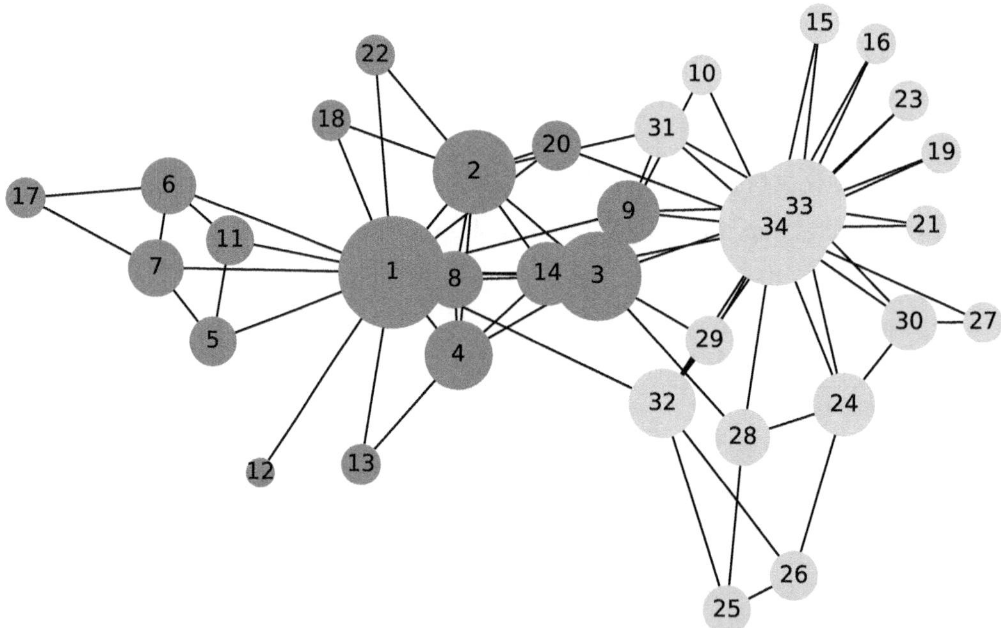

Figure 3.8: Degree measure of the Zachary karate club network. The size of the nodes denotes the degree, and the colour corresponds to the groups formed after the split of the club. The darker grey nodes are Mr. Hi's group, and the light grey ones are John A's supporters.

It is possible to customise the plot defining the colour map, font colour, position, etc. The result can be seen in Figure 3.8. The size of the nodes corresponds to their degree, and the colour indicates the affiliation to the groups formed after the split, with the darker grey nodes being Mr. Hi's group and the light grey ones John A.'s supporters.

The largest nodes seem to be nodes 1, 34 and 33. We can corroborate this with the information that we calculated before. In order to make it easier to grab this information, let us create a function that lists the top n nodes given a centrality measure (as a dictionary):

```
def get_top_nodes(cdict, num=5):
  top_nodes = {}
  for i in range(num):
    top_nodes = dict(
      sorted(cdict.items(), key=lambda x: x[1],
        reverse=True)[:num]
    )
  return top_nodes
```

We will use this function in the rest of this chapter. Remember it well!

As we can see from the result below, the nodes with the largest degree in descending order are 34 with degree 17, 1 with degree 16, node 33 with 12, followed by nodes 3 with 10, and 2 with 9:

```
> get_top_nodes(dict(kdeg))

 {'34': 17, '1': 16, '33': 12, '3': 10, '2': 9}
```

Not surprising to see 34 and 1 in the top nodes... right?

The total number of connections is a good start, but what about if we weight this measure by the maximum possible degree in a simple graph $n - 1$, where n is the number of nodes in the network. We can calculate this in NetworkX with the `degree_centrality` function:

```
degree_centrality = nx.degree_centrality(K)
nx.set_node_attributes(K, degree_centrality, 'dc')
```

Calculate the degree centrality with `degree_centrality`. Simple, right?

We can use this normalised measure to look at a histogram of the degree centrality for the karate club. We can obtain the frequencies by sorting the values of the measure and use the `Counter` from the `collections` module:

```
from collections import Counter


deg_values = sorted(set(degree_centrality.\
  values()))
value_counts = Counter(degree_centrality.values())
deg_hist = [value_counts[x] for x in deg_values]
```

Counting the number of nodes with a particular degree centrality is straightforward.

In Figure 3.9 we can see the result of the calculations above. There are only a few nodes with degree centralities higher than 0.4. The bulk of the nodes in our network has lower scores for this measure. Let us create a plot of the network using the size as the degree centrality:

```
nx.draw_networkx(K, node_color=colors,
  node_size=[3000 * v for v in
    nx.get_node_attributes(K, 'dc').values()])
```

We have left out the commands to avoid showing the axis and the plot itself.

We can see in Figure 3.10 how the degree centrality keeps the information about the network. We perhaps have learnt nothing new. However, the normalised version provides us

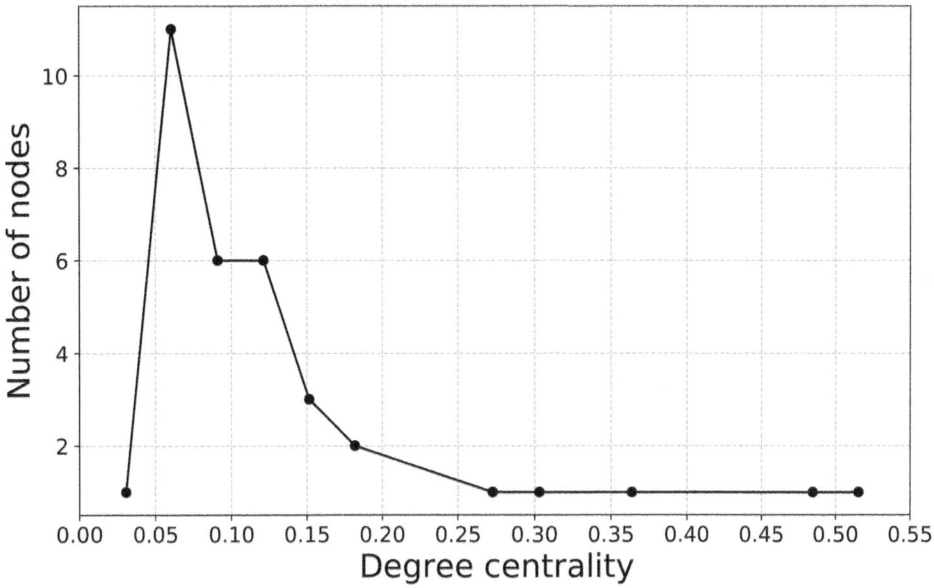

Figure 3.9: Frequencies of the degree centrality measure for the karate club network.

with an easier way to make comparisons between the nodes than the degree directly.

We know that the betweenness tells us about the influence of particular nodes over the network. Let us calculate the betweenness for our karate club. This can be done with the `betweenness_centrality` function as follows:

```
betweenness_centrality = \
  nx.betweenness_centrality(K)
nx.set_node_attributes(K,
  betweenness_centrality, 'bc')
```

Calculate the betweenness with `betweenness_centrality`.

We mentioned before that betweenness can be seen as a measure of nodes serving as a bridge between different

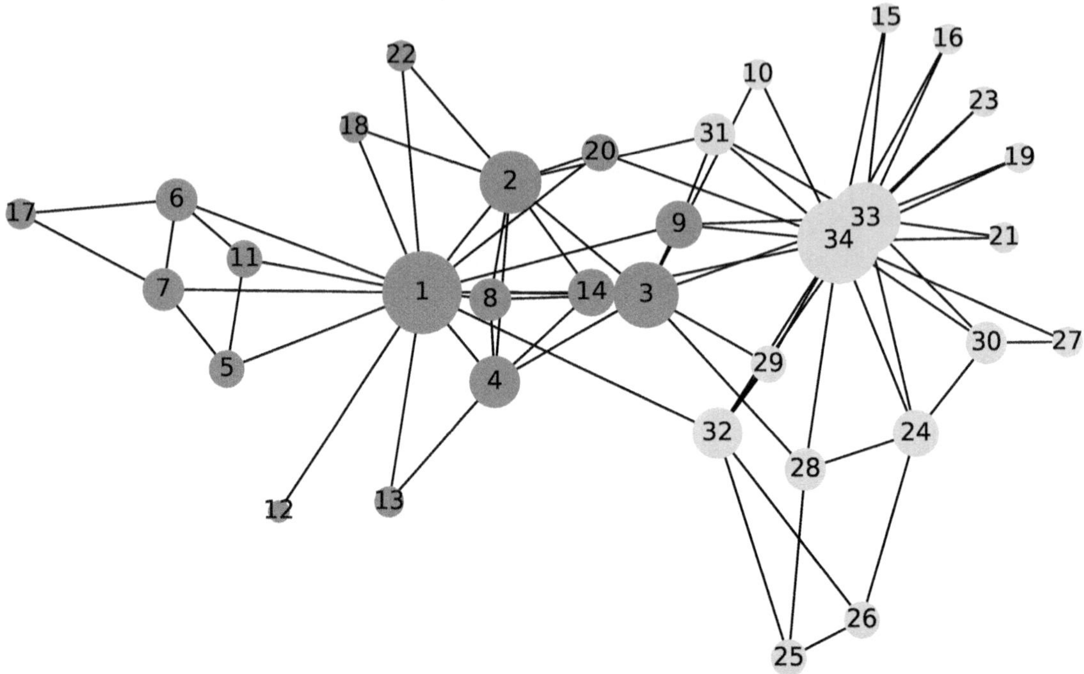

Figure 3.10: Degree centrality measure of Zachary's karate club. The size of the nodes denotes the degree centrality. We can see the importance of not only nodes 1, 34, 33, but also 2 and 3.

components of a graph. Let us have a look at these "bridges" by getting the top 5 nodes by betweenness.

```
> get_top_nodes(betweenness_centrality)


{'1': 0.43763528138528146,
 '34': 0.30407497594997596,
 '33': 0.145247113997114,
 '3': 0.14365680615680618,
 '32': 0.13827561327561325}
```

Remember the function `get_top_nodes` we defined above?

Mr. Hi (1) and John A. (34) are indeed prominent in the network. We can see the presence of nodes 33 and 3 as before, but a newcomer has appeared in the top 5: Node

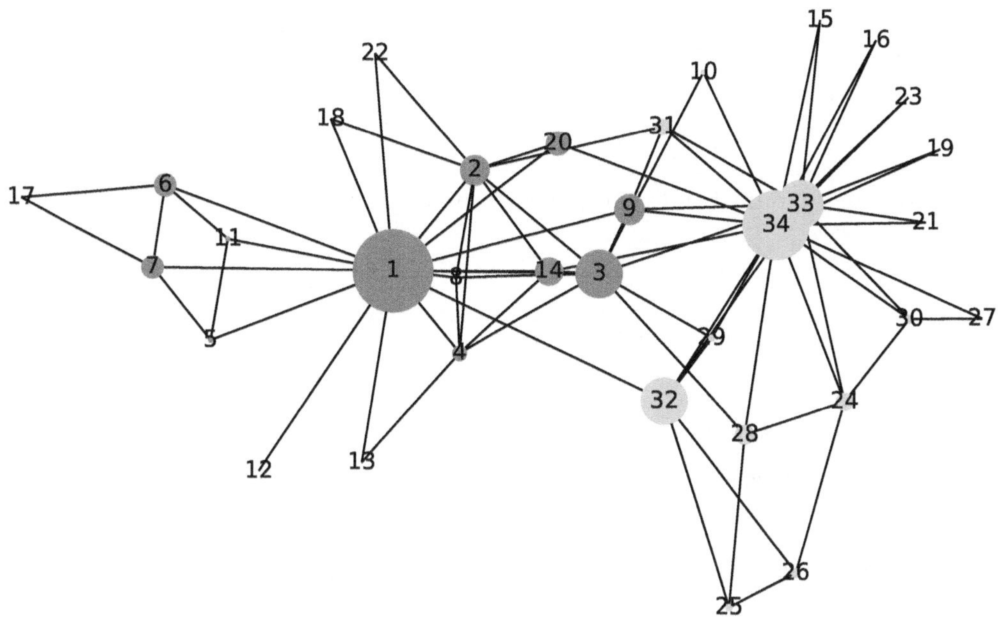

Figure 3.11: Betweenness of Zachary's karate club network. The size of the nodes denotes the betweenness. We can see the importance of nodes 1, 34, as well as 33 and 3. Node 32 is a bridge in the network.

32. We can see the relative importance of the betweenness measure in Figure 3.11. The code for this plot is as follows:

```
nx.draw_networkx(K, node_color=colors,
  node_size=[4000 * v for v in
    nx.get_node_attributes(K, 'bc').values()])
```

We know that the flow of information in the network was an important way to ensure that decisions taken during meetings favoured the faction with a majority. A way to assess which nodes are able to spread information more efficiently is given by the closeness. We can calculate the closeness as follows:

```
closeness_centrality = nx.closeness_centrality(K)
nx.set_node_attributes(K,
  closeness_centrality, 'cc')
```

The closeness_centrality lets us calculate the closeness of the nodes in the network.

The "closest" nodes in the karate club network are as follows:

```
> get_top_nodes(closeness_centrality)

{'1': 0.5689655172413793,
 '3': 0.559322033898305,
 '34': 0.55,
 '32': 0.5409836065573771,
 '9': 0.515625}
```

We finally see node 9 appear as an important, close, node in the network!

Things are getting interesting. We can still see Mr. Hi (1) and John A. (34) as important nodes. Nothing is surprising there, or indeed by having node 3 in the top "closest" nodes. We again have node 32 appearing, and now we finally see node 9 in there. It is through these nodes that information about meetings would have flowed.

The closeness measure of the nodes is very similar, and showing this measure as the size of the nodes results in a plot that does not showcase the importance of certain nodes. Instead, we will show this measure as the colour of the nodes. This requires us to draw the network's parts separately as follows:

Encoding information in the network representation is flexible, including size and colour for nodes and edges.

```
pos = nx.spring_layout(K)
ec = nx.draw_networkx_edges(K, pos=pos)
nc = nx.draw_networkx_nodes(K, pos=pos,
  node_color=[v for v in
    nx.get_node_attributes(K, 'cc').values()],
  node_size=[1200 * v for v in
    nx.get_node_attributes(K, 'cc').values()])
lb = nx.draw_networkx_labels(K, pos=pos)
```

We can use separate methods to render the network in the way we want. Using `draw_networkx_edges` for the edges, `draw_networkx_nodes` for the nodes and `draw_networkx_labels` for the labels. Notice that all have the same position attribute.

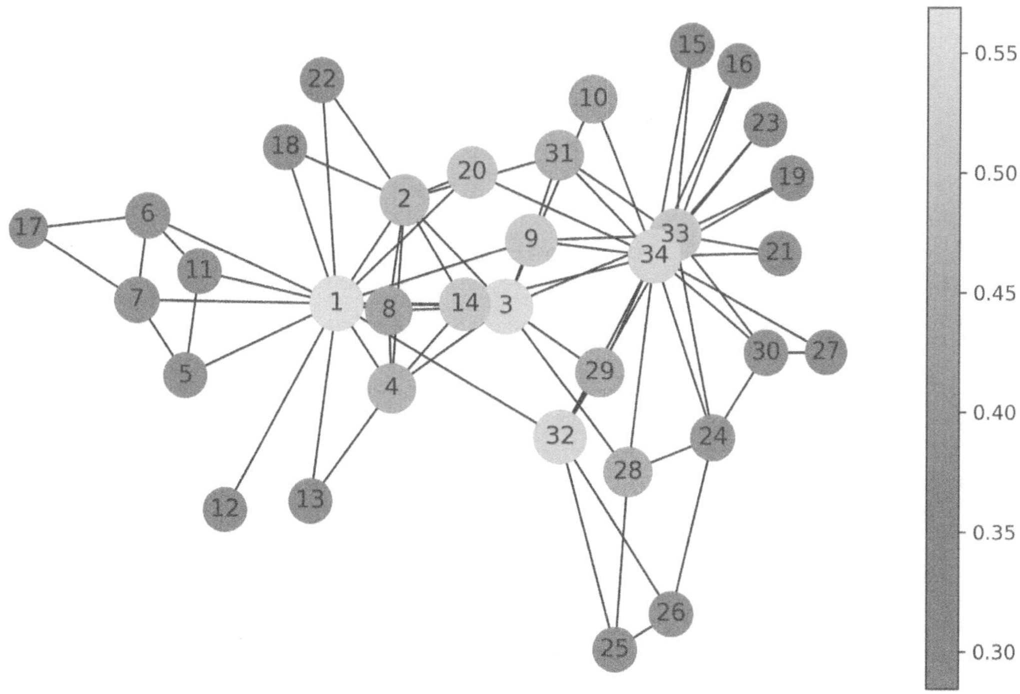

Figure 3.12: Closeness of Zachary's karate club network. The size of the nodes denotes the closeness. We can see the importance of the nodes we already know about: 1, 34, 33 and 3. Node 9 is a close node in the network too.

We are drawing separately the edges, nodes and labels, all with the same position layout. Note that we are encoding the closeness measure both in the size of the node and in its colour. Figure 3.12 shows the result of the commands above. You can see that the size alone would not tell us much about the closeness; however, the colour lets us obtain the information desired.

We can now turn our attention to what nodes are best connected within the network. We have seen that the eigenvector centrality provides a view of the nodes that are endorsed by influential actors. We can calculate the eigenvector centrality as follows:

Eigenvector centrality shows nodes that are important because they link to other important nodes.

```
eigenvector_centrality = \
  nx.eigenvector_centrality(K)
nx.set_node_attributes(K, eigenvector_centrality,
  'ec')
```

The best connected nodes in our network are:

```
get_top_nodes(eigenvector_centrality)


{'34': 0.373371213013235,
 '1': 0.3554834941851943,
 '3': 0.31718938996844476,
 '33': 0.3086510477336959,
 '2': 0.2659538704545025}
```

Get the eigenvector centrality with `eigenvector_centrality`. Getting the gist of it, right?

We see John A. be an influencer, with a higher eigenvector centrality than Mr. Hi. Once again, node 2 makes an appearance, together with nodes 3 and 33. The eigenvector centrality network can be seen in Figure 3.13.

```
nx.draw_networkx(K, node_color=colors,
  node_size=[2400 * v for v in
    nx.get_node_attributes(K, 'ec').values()])
```

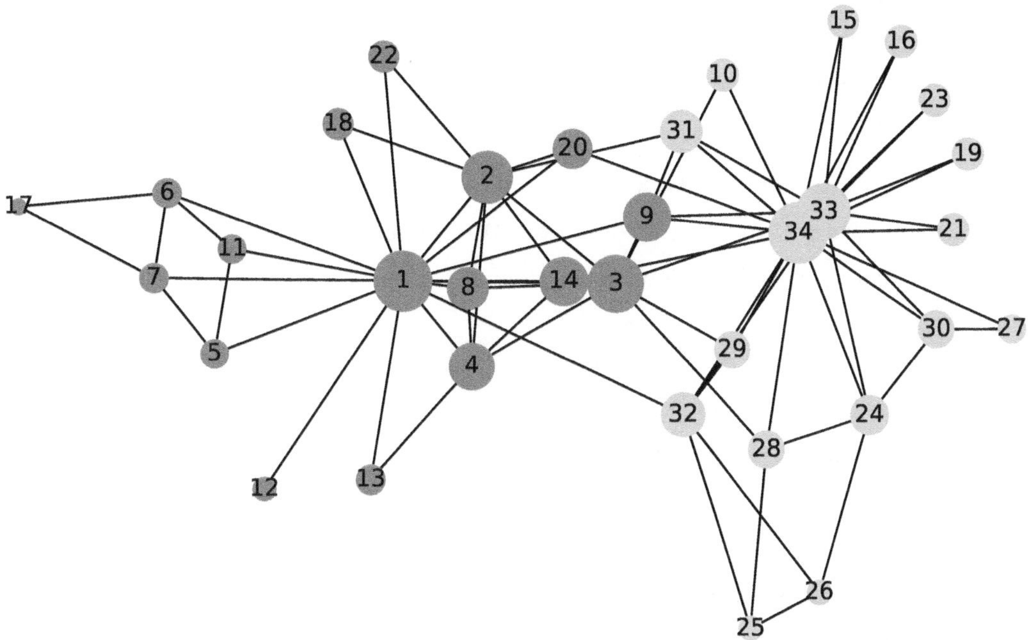

Figure 3.13: Eigenvector centrality of Zachary's karate club network. The size of the nodes denotes the eigenvector centrality of the network.

Once we have taken a look at the eigenvector centrality, the next logical step is to calculate the PageRank. As you can imagine, there is a handy function in NetworkX to let us do this: `pagerank`.

```
pagerank_centrality = nx.pagerank(K,\
nx.set_node_attributes(K,\
  pagerank_centrality, 'pr')
```

The PageRank can be calculated with `pagerank`.

The top five nodes per PageRank are as follows:

```
> get_top_nodes(pagerank_centrality)

{'34': 0.10345460652842152,
 '1': 0.09923208031303203,
 '33': 0.07330616298815512,
 '3': 0.05919704684187155,
 '2': 0.0543403155825792}
```

The ranking of the nodes with PageRank returns the usual karate kids.

We can see the usual karate kids: In this case though, nodes 33 and 3 have swapped places in the ranking. We can get a plot of the network as we have done in the previous cases:

```
nx.draw_networkx(K, node_color=colors,
  node_size=[5000 * v for v in
    nx.get_node_attributes(K, 'pr').values()],
    pos=pos)
```

We can see the result in Figure 3.14, where, as usual, we have encoded the PageRank centrality score in the size of the node. We can see the prestige of nodes 34, 1, 33, 3 and 2. We can start thinking of the factions that were created during the conflict and look at those nodes that are central to the network. We will keep Mr. Hi and John A. in the network for obvious reasons. However, we can consider what happens when we remove some of the nodes whose centrality measures indicate importance, i.e., nodes 2, 3, 9 and 32 for example.

We can consider what happens to the graph when we remove certain nodes.

```
k = K.copy()
k.remove_nodes_from(['2', '3', '32', '9'])
```

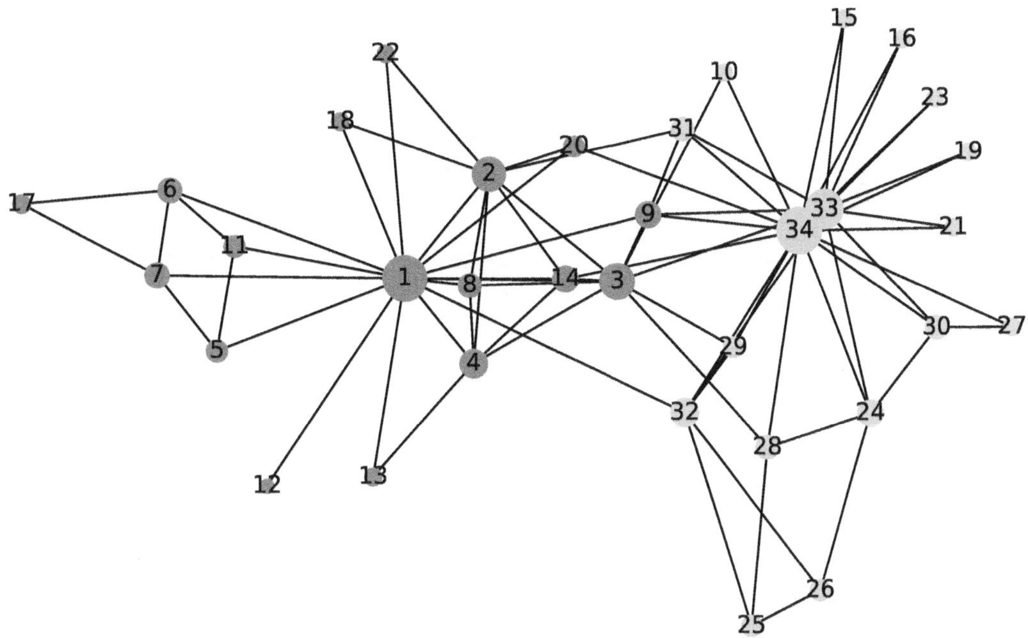

Figure 3.14: PageRank of Zachary's karate club network. The size of the nodes denotes the PageRank scores of the network.

The result of this removal can be seen in Figure 3.15. It is clear that a number of connections have disappeared in this reduced network, and these individuals can be thought of as being important for the cohesion of the network.

The clustering coefficient for the nodes in the karate network can be obtained with the `clustering` function. Notice that the result is a dictionary where the keys are the individual nodes, and the values are the clustering coefficients:

We can remove nodes with `remove_nodes_from` and provide a list with the nodes we want expunged.

```
> ccoeff = nx.clustering(K)
> print(ccoeff['1'])


0.15
```

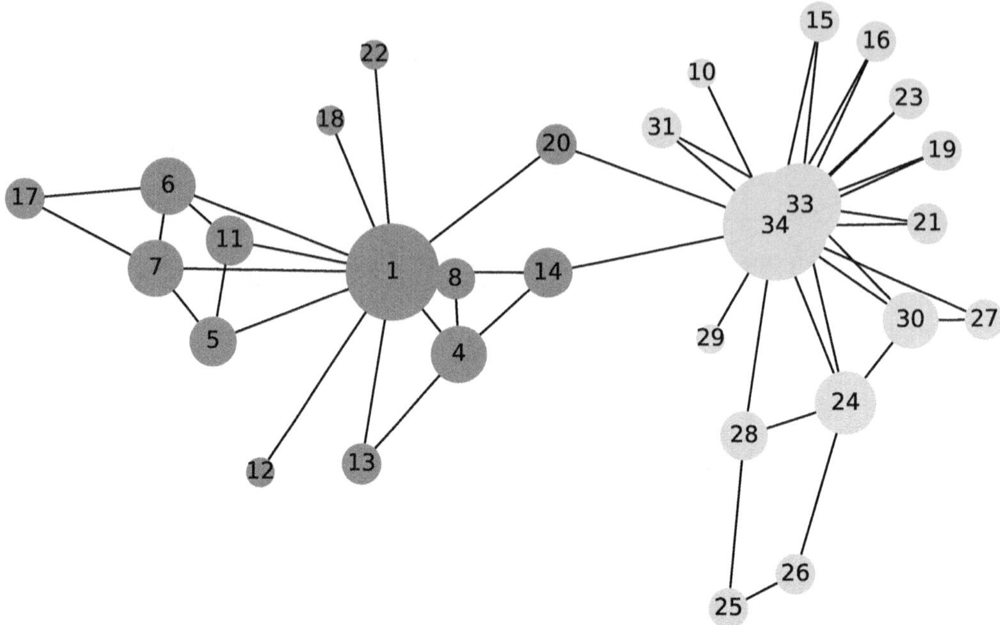

Figure 3.15: Reduced network for Zachary's karate club. We have removed nodes 2, 3, 9 and 32 that are important for the cohesion of the network. The size of the nodes denotes the degree centrality of the nodes.

The average clustering coefficient is given by the `average_clustering` function:

Calculate the clustering coefficient of the network with `average_clustering`.

```
> avg_ccoeff = nx.average_clustering(K)
> print(avg_ccoeff)


0.5706384782076823
```

Now that we started looking at removing nodes and at the clustering of the network, we can consider calculating the *k*-components of the karate club. The `k_components` function enables us to do this in NetworkX.

Remember that a *k*-component is a maximal subgraph with, at least, connectivity *k*.

```
components = nx.k_components(K)
```

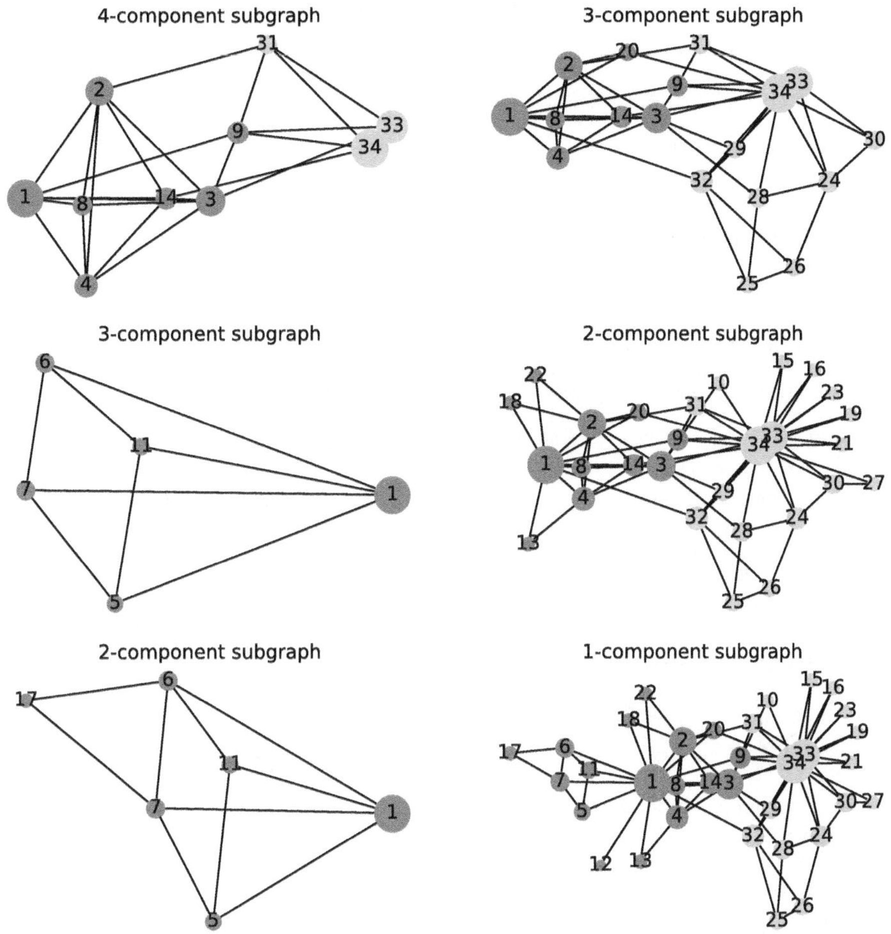

Figure 3.16: *k*-components of Zachary's karate club network.

The result is a dictionary with connectivity level *k* as key, and a list of sets of nodes that form a *k*-component of level *k*. For instance, the network has one single 4-level component and is given by:

```
> print(components[4])


[{'14', '34', '3', '8', '31',
'9', '4', '33', '1', '2'}]
```

We can see the different *k*-components of Zachary's karate club network in Figure 3.16.

It is also possible to answer the question regarding the fully connected components in the network, in other words the cliques. As you can imagine, NetworkX provides a way to find the cliques: `find_cliques`.

```
cl = nx.find_cliques(K)
```

The result is an iterator over maximal cliques, providing a list of nodes in the network. You can verify that there are 36 cliques, and we show 4 of these in Figure 3.17.

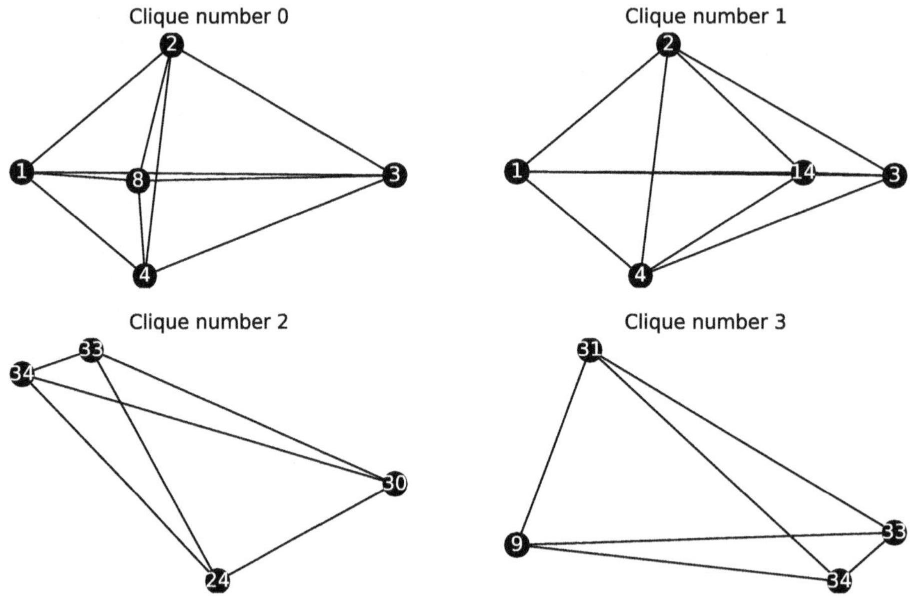

Figure 3.17: Some of the cliques in Zachary's karate club network.

There are several ways to detect communities in the network. One simple way is to look at hierarchical clustering which we discussed in Chapter 7 of *Data Science and Analytics with Python*[17] where we learnt how to construct dendrograms. Let us use the shortest path lengths between the nodes in our network:

[17] Rogel-Salazar, J. (2025). *Data Science and Analytics with Python*. Chapman & Hall/CRC Data Mining and Knowledge Discovery Series. CRC Press.

```
path_length = nx.all_pairs_shortest_path_length(K)
```

We will now use this information to get a distance measure between the nodes and build a dendrogram:

```
n = len(K.nodes())
distances = np.zeros((n, n))

from scipy.cluster import hierarchy
from scipy.spatial import distance

for u, p in path_length:
    for v, d in p.items():
        distances[int(u) - 1][int(v) - 1] = d
sd = distance.squareform(distances)
h = hierarchy.average(sd)
```

We are using scipy to calculate hierarchical clustering in our network.

The resulting dendrogram can be seen in Figure 3.18 where we can see a hierarchy of 2 and then 4 clusters, or communities.

We discussed in this chapter how the Girvan-Newman algorithm discovers communities in a network. NetworkX provides us with a function to do just this: `girvan_newman()` in `community`.

The `girvan_newman()` function in `community` from `networkx.algorithms` does what it says on the tin.

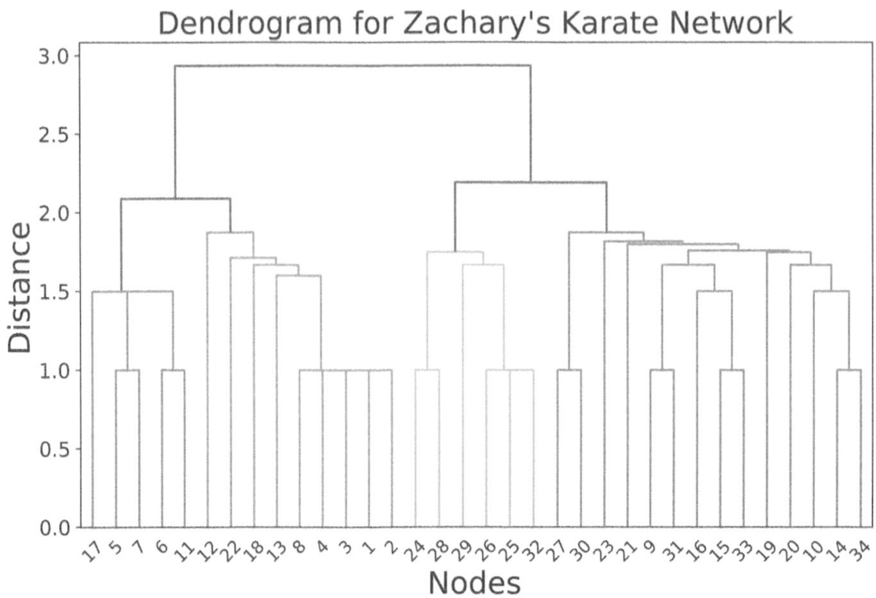

Figure 3.18: Hierarchical clustering over Zachary's karate club network.

```
from networkx.algorithms import community


comp = community.girvan_newman(K)
communities = tuple(sorted(c) for c in next(comp))
```

The algorithm has found 2 communities in the network:

The function returns an iterator over tuples, and each tuple is a sequence of communities.

```
> len(communities)


2
```

Let us add this information to the metadata of our network. First let us create two sub-graphs, one for each community:

```
c_1 = K.subgraph(communities[0])
c_2 = K.subgraph(communities[1])
```

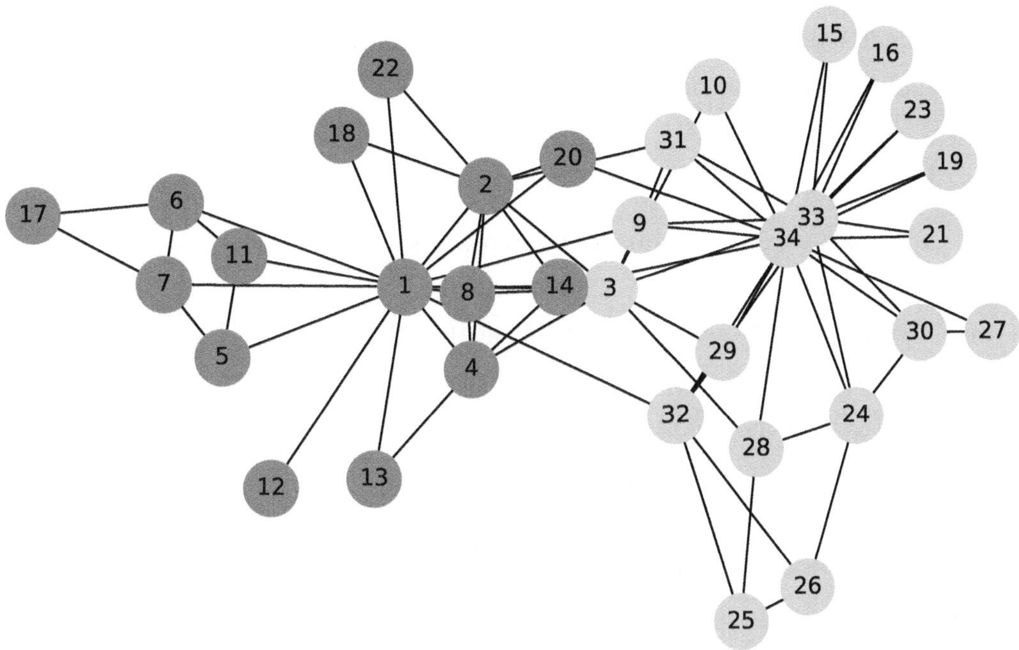

Figure 3.19: Communities discovered by the Girvan-Newman algorithm on Zachary's karate club network. Notice that nodes 3 and 9 have been assigned to John A.'s faction.

We can now use the nodes in each community to add a new attribute to our network:

```
comm = {}
for c in c_1:
  comm[str(c)] = 'community 1'

for c in c_2:
  comm[str(c)] = 'community 2'

nx.set_node_attributes(K, comm, 'comm')
```

This calculation could be reduced to a single for loop. See next section for this.

In Figure 3.19 we can see the plot of the network with the nodes coloured by the community to which they were assigned by the algorithm. We can see that the network looks roughly the same as that in Figure 3.8. However, if you closely inspect the nodes, you will see that nodes 3 and 9 have been assigned to John A.'s faction and not to Mr. Hi. We knew about node 9 and his black belt test, perhaps node 3 had similar reasons to join one group over the other.

Girvan-Newman has found that two nodes would naturally switch sides. This confirms explanations provided by Zachary.

Finally, let us see what the Louvain algorithm has to say about the communities in Zachary's karate network. NetworkX provides the `louvain_communities` method that help us find the best partition of a graph using the Louvain community detection algorithm to extract the community structure of a network.

We can detect communities with `louvain_communities`.

```
louvain = nx.community.louvain_communities(K)
```

The result is a list of node sets. Each set corresponds to a community detected with the algorithm. We can take a look at the communities discovered in Figure 3.20.

We can take a look at what nodes have been assigned to each of the four communities that the algorithm has discovered:

The result is returned as a list of sets.

```
for i, community in enumerate(louvain):
    print('Community {}'.format(i))
    print(community)
```

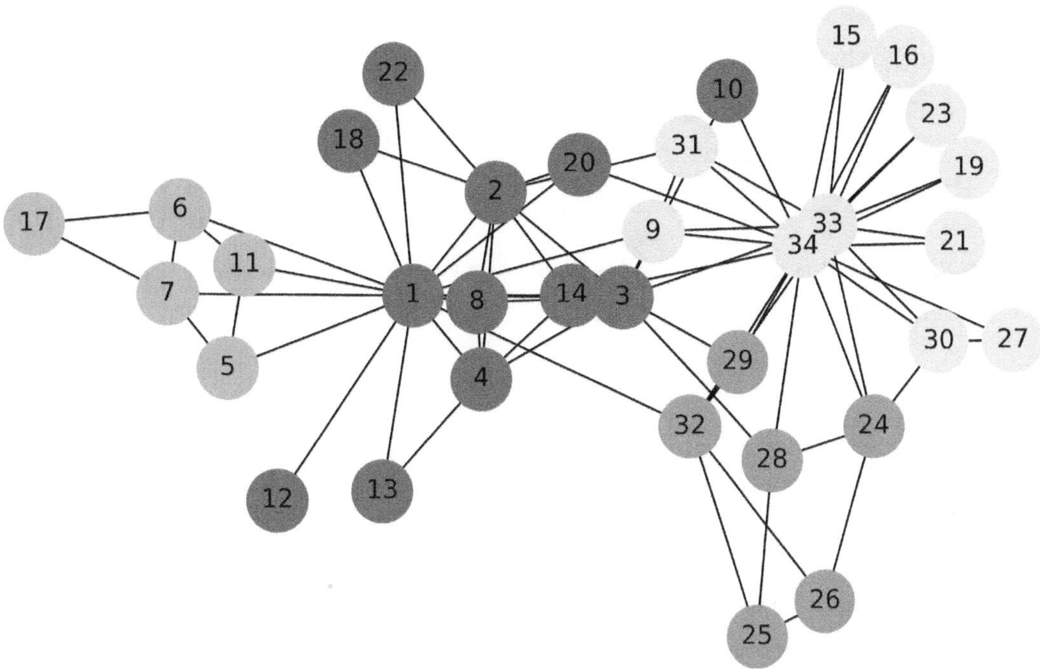

Figure 3.20: Communities discovered by the Louvain algorithm on Zachary's karate club network. We have four communities denoted by different shades of grey.

For completeness, let us show the result of the code above. We can see how each community contains non-overlapping nodes:

```
Community 0
{'22', '13', '2', '4', '12', '20', '18', '10',
'8', '1', '3', '14'}
Community 1
{'5', '11', '7', '17', '6'}
Community 2
{'25', '29', '32', '28', '26', '24'}
Community 3
{'30', '23', '33', '21', '16', '31', '27', '19',
'34', '9', '15'}
```

In this case, we have four communities. Notice that we start counting in a Pythonic style — from 0.

Let us finish this section by mentioning that the karate club network we have been playing with is also part of NetworkX, and you can load it as follows:

You will be glad to know that Zachary's karate club network is included in NetworkX.

```
G = nx.karate_club_graph()
```

Please note that in this graph the nodes have been labelled in a Pythonic style starting from 0: Hi is node 0 and John A. is node 33.

3.4.2 *In a Galaxy Far, Far Away: Central Characters in a Network*

From ancient Japan to galaxies far, far away..., it is widely known that George Lucas is a fan of Akira Kurosawa's work and the influence of films such as *The Hidden Fortress* from 1958 is patent in the story of *Star Wars*, from the spiritual elements of the Force to the use of swords in battle and the armour of Lord Vader himself. Much has been written about these influences, and in this case we are interested in finding out more about the interactions among our favourite characters in this space opera.

From ancient Japan to galaxies far, far away.

The first step in the process is to get hold of the data that we will use to analyse our characters. In this case, we will be using data from the work that Evelina Gabasova[18] has done in a series of blog posts. The nodes in the network represent our beloved characters. The connections between them represent interactions between the characters in the form of dialogue in the films scenes. The data can be obtained directly from Gabasova's reference above. For completeness,

[18] Gabasova, E. (2016). *Star Wars* social network. https://doi.org/10.5281/zenodo.1411479

a GML format file with the network can be obtained at `https://doi.org/10.6084/ m9.figshare.7993292.v1`[19] with the same information as the original JSON files provided by Gabasova.

[19] Rogel-Salazar, J. (2019a, Apr). *Star Wars* Network. https://doi.org/10.6084/m9.figshare.7993292.v1

The network contains information for Episodes I through to VII and it is an undirected graph. The edges in the network are weighted by the amount of dialogue between the characters. As you may imagine, there are some assumptions that Gabasova has made to keep the network manageable. For example, separate nodes are kept for Anakin Skywalker and Darth Vader. But those for the Emperor and Senator Palpatine, or Queen Amidala and Padmé have been merged. Similarly, non-speaking characters such as R2-D2 and Chewbacca were added via mentions in the screenplay. For further information on these aspects, please refer to the excellent post from Evelina Gabasova.

aka Darth Sidious too!

As usual, let us load some useful libraries, including NetworkX, matplotlib, pandas and NumPy:

```
import networkx as nx
import numpy as np
import matplotlib.pyplot as plt
```

These libraries will be with you. Always...

The network can be loaded as follows:

```
fname = 'starwars_network.gml'


S = nx.read_gml(fname)
```

As we did for the karate network, let us print some information about the *Star Wars* network:

```
> print(S)
> print('Average degree', sum(\
  dict(S.degree).values()) / len(S.nodes))

Graph with 112 nodes and 450 edges
Average degree 8.035714285714286
```

Our dataset contains 112 characters with 450 edges and the average degree for this Universe is 8.0357.

We have 112 characters with 450 edges and the average degree for this Universe is 8.0357, a bit higher than the six degrees of separation! Let us take a look at the network.

Before we do that, given the number of characters, it would be good to pick out some of the nodes that we may be interested in tracking. We will define a list of main characters as follows:

```
main_characters = ['Darth Vader',
  'Emperor (Palpatine)', 'Luke', 'Leia',
  'Yoda', 'Anakin', 'R2-D2', 'Han',
  'Chewbacca', 'Padme (Queen Amidala)',
  'Poe', 'BB-8', 'Jabba', 'Count Dooku',
  'Jar Jar', 'Rey', 'Darth Maul',
  'Admiral Ackbar', 'Snoke', 'Qui-Gon',
  'Kylo Ren', 'Obi-Wan', 'C-3PO',
  'Darth Maul', 'Niv Lek', 'Boba Fett']
```

Oh, my dear friends. How I've missed you!

We will use this list to create a dictionary so that we can label these characters in the plots we will create as we go along this analysis:

```
labels = {}
for character in main_characters:
  labels[character] = character
```

Plotting labels in our network is managed with a dictionary.

In the original network, each node is assigned a value that represents the number of scenes where the character speaks, similarly a colour is also assigned. Although the plots in this book are in black and white, you can see the results in full colour in your machine. Let us extract these attributes from the network so that we can use them in our plots:

```
node_sizes = [3 * float(v) for v in
  nx.get_node_attributes(S, 'value').values()]

colours = [c for c in
  nx.get_node_attributes(S, 'colour').values()]
```

We extract node attributes such as size and colour from the network to create our plot.

We mentioned above that the edges are weighted, and we can use the values to represent the thickness of the connections in the network:

```
edges = S.edges()
edge_width = [S[u][v]['value'] for u, v in edges]
```

We read the value for each existing connection in the network.

It is well known that both Jedis and Siths are able to use the Force, and very appropriately we can use a force-directed layout to plot our network.

```
pos_force=nx.spring_layout(S)
```

May the (spring) Force be with you!

We are now ready to use the Force too. We will plot the nodes, edges and the node positions separately, giving us more control over the representation of our network. Let us take a look:

But our training is not yet complete!

```
nx.draw_networkx_nodes(
  S, node_color=colours,
  node_size=node_sizes,
  alpha=0.9, pos=pos_force)

nx.draw_networkx_edges(S, alpha=0.15,
  edge_color='gray', width=edge_width,
  pos=pos_force)

nx.draw_networkx_labels(S, labels=labels,
  font_size=10, font_color='#000099',
  font_weight='bold', pos=pos_force)
```

We are plotting the nodes, edges and labels separately, but in the same figure and the same layout.

I could not help playing with the network and decided to show an initial rendering inspired by the famous Death Star space station. We can see the network in Figure 3.21.

Degree centrality is the first measure we will look at when analysing our network.

```
degree_centrality = nx.degree_centrality(S)
nx.set_node_attributes(S, degree_centrality, 'dc')
```

Remember that the degree centrality tells us how well connected a node is to the rest of the network.

The distribution of the degree centrality is shown in Figure 3.22 where we can see only a handful of characters with

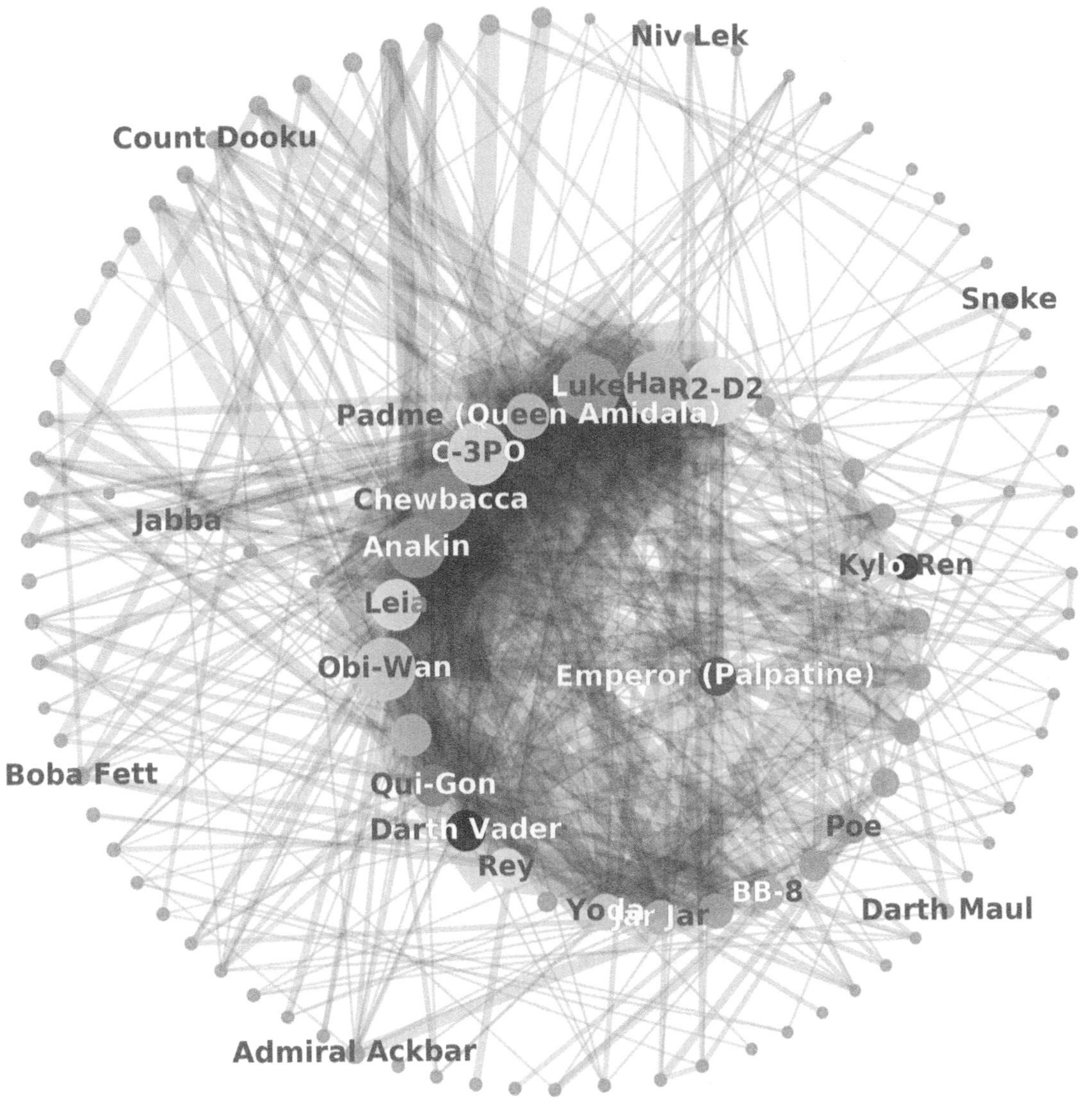

Figure 3.21: *Star Wars* network covering Episodes I-VII. Layout inspired by the famous Death Star.

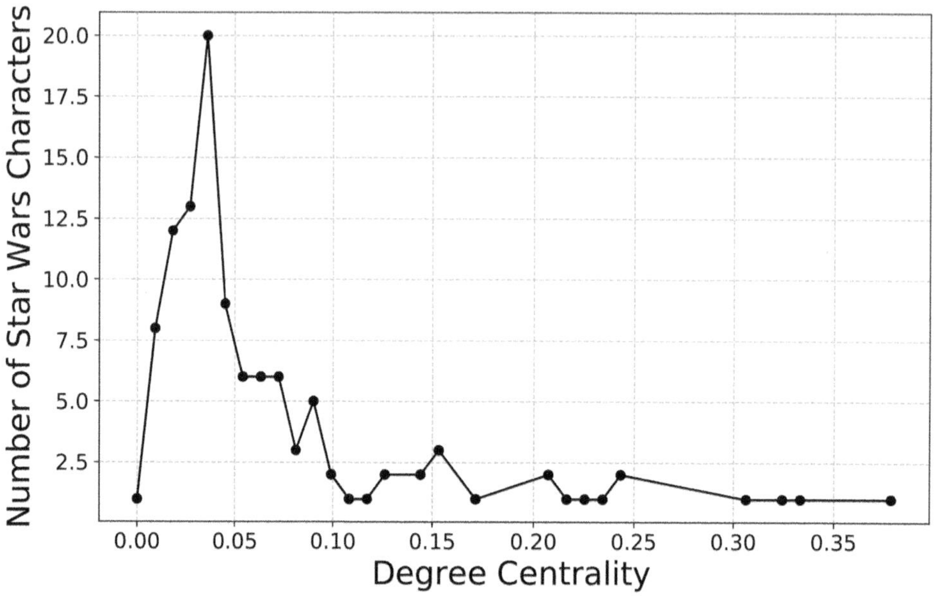

Figure 3.22: Distribution of the degree centrality for the *Star Wars* network.

degree centralities higher than 0.20 and a large number of nodes with very small scores in this centrality measure.

Before we continue, in order to make our life a bit easier, let us define a function to plot networks in a more straightforward fashion. We will pass a network object, an attribute that will be encoded as the node sizes, a threshold to filter the network, a factor to modify the size of the nodes, the position where the nodes will be plotted and the width of the edges in the network. We will also accept a named parameter to show the labels of the chosen nodes. The function is as follows:

```
def plot_graph(G, att, att_threshold, size_factor,
  position, edge_width, **kwargs):

    labels = kwargs.get('labels', None)

    nodes = [x for x, y in G.nodes(data=True)
      if y[att] >= att_threshold]
    sg = G.subgraph(nodes)

    gcolors = [c for c in
      nx.get_node_attributes(sg,'colour').values()]

    nx.draw_networkx_nodes(sg, node_color=gcolors,
      node_size=[size_factor * v for v in
        nx.get_node_attributes(sg, att).values()],
      pos=position, alpha=0.5)

    nx.draw_networkx_edges(sg, alpha=0.2,
      edge_color='gray', pos=position,
      width=edge_width)

    nx.draw_networkx_labels(sg, labels=labels,
      pos=position)
```

First we check if a set of labels is provided.

We then select the nodes that meet the threshold provided and obtain a subgraph.

We use the colour attribute to render our nodes.

We then draw the nodes with the appropriate size.

Then the edges.

And finally, the labels.

Using the same function that we defined in the previous section to obtain the top nodes for a centrality measure, we can see the top 5 characters by degree.

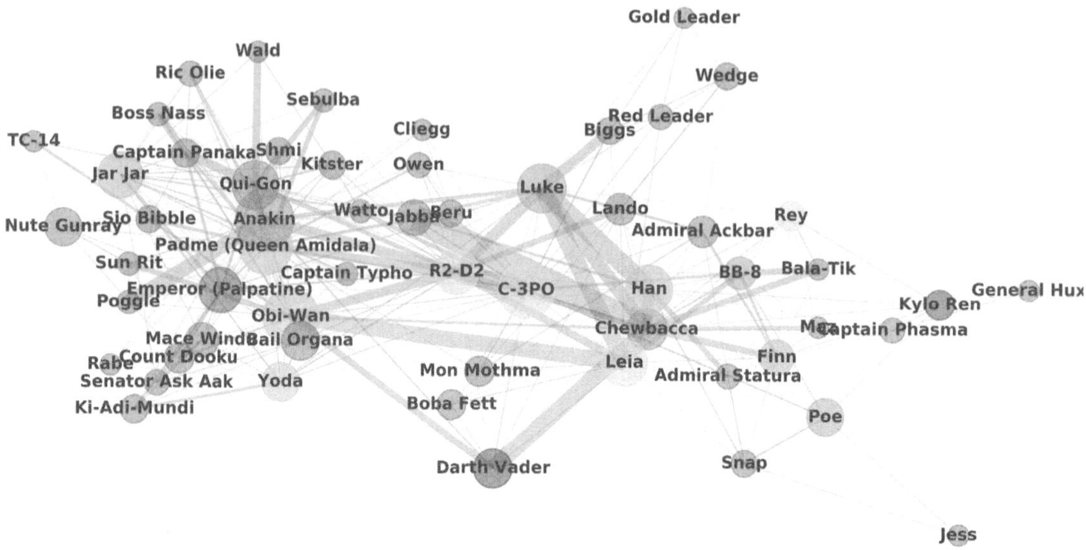

Figure 3.23: Degree measure of the *Star Wars* network. The size of the nodes denotes the degree centrality of the node.

```
> get_top_nodes(degree_centrality)


{'Anakin': 0.3783783783783784,
 'Obi-Wan': 0.3333333333333333,
 'C-3PO': 0.32432432432432434,
 'Padme (Queen Amidala)': 0.3063063063063063,
 'Qui-Gon': 0.24324324324324323}
```

Anakin and Obi-Wan are the characters with the highest number of connections.

It is not surprising to see there Anakin and Obi-Wan, but Qui-Gon⁇ Well, without him Anakin would not have become a prominent figure in the Empire! We can see the filtered network for degree centrality in Figure 3.23, and the code is as follows:

You see, it only took a line with our new function!

```
plot_graph(S, 'dc', 0.04, 5000, pos_force,
  edge_width)
```

The bridges in the network can be obtained with the help of the closeness centrality, let us take a look:

```
closeness_centrality = nx.closeness_centrality(S)
nx.set_node_attributes(S, closeness_centrality,
  'cc')
nodes_cc = get_top_nodes(closeness_centrality)
```

Closeness centrality shows us the bridge nodes in the network.

The bridge characters are:

```
> print(nodes_cc)


{'C-3PO': 0.5619021082938609,
 'Obi-Wan': 0.559020559020559,
 'Anakin': 0.5505505505505506,
 'Luke': 0.526613570091831,
 'R2-D2': 0.5166303744502797}
```

In this case, we have C-3PO and Obi-Wan as those bridges.

It is great to see both C-3PO and R2-D2 appear in the top 5 characters by closeness, together with Luke and Obi-Wan. The androids are indeed integral to the story line, without R2-D2 and his protocol sidekick the Death Star plans would not have been delivered from General Organa (aka Princess Leia) to Obi-Kan, enabling Luke to destroy the deadly weapon.

These were indeed the droids we were looking for!

Let us see the eigenvector centrality:

```
eigenvector_centrality=nx.eigenvector_centrality(S)
nx.set_node_attributes(S, eigenvector_centrality,
  'ec')
nodes_ec = get_top_nodes(eigenvector_centrality)
```

The top 5 characters by eigenvector centrality are:

```
> print(nodes_ec)

{'Anakin': 0.29656614921513724,
 'Obi-Wan': 0.2810463592564618,
 'C-3PO': 0.2753430975993982,
 'Padme (Queen Amidala)': 0.2580025161393472,
 'Qui-Gon': 0.22896839403488994}
```

We have Anakin, Obi-Wan and C-3PO in the first three places.

Let us turn our attention to the PageRank for our network:

```
pagerank_centrality = nx.pagerank(S, alpha=0.9)
nx.set_node_attributes(S, pagerank_centrality,'pr')
nodes_pr = get_top_nodes(pagerank_centrality)
```

If we look at the top 5 characters by PageRange, we have roughly the same order, but instead of having Qui-Gon in 5th place, we have Luke:

```
> print(nodes_pr)

{'Anakin': 0.042419290139533466,
 'Obi-Wan': 0.03851822264942938,
 'C-3PO': 0.035812500857126256,
 'Padme (Queen Amidala)': 0.03369795977341906,
 'Luke': 0.029121630268795225}
```

The order for PageRank is similar, but we finally get to see Luke!

The network resulting from encoding the eigenvector centrality in the size of the nodes and filtering for nodes with values higher than 0.06 can be seen in Figure 3.24.

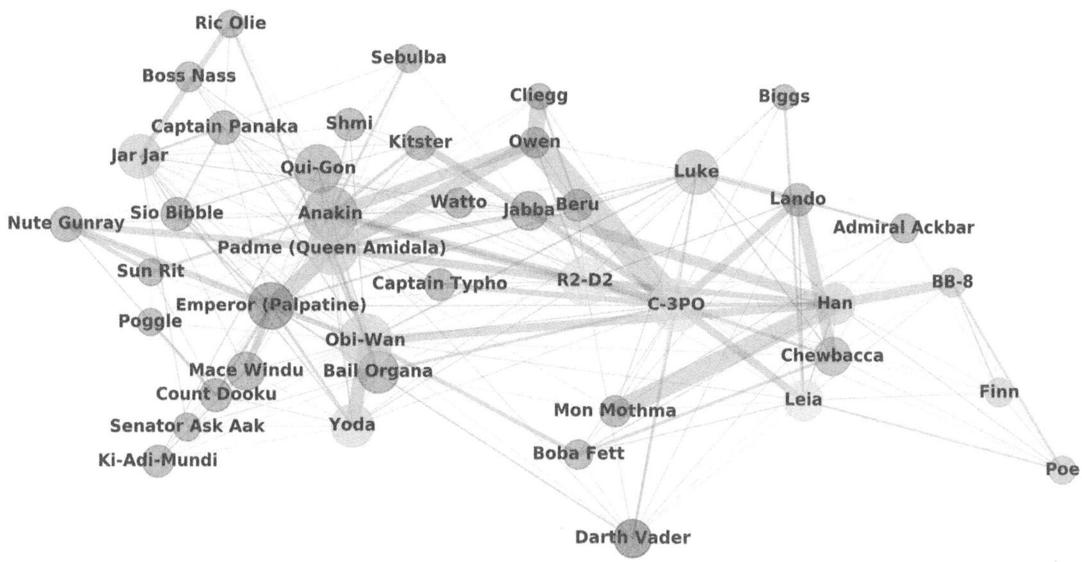

Figure 3.24: Eigenvector centrality for the *Star Wars* network. The size of the nodes denotes the eigenvector centrality of the node.

```
plot_graph(S, 'ec', 0.06, 5000,
  pos_force, edge_width)
```

The network encoding the PageRank scores for nodes with values higher than 0.006 is shown in Figure 3.25.

```
plot_graph(S, 'pr', 0.006, 25000,
  pos_force, edge_width)
```

It is an inescapable fact of the *Star Wars* story that Anakin Skywalker gets seduced by the Dark Side of the Force, and we can think of the two characters as being one and the same person. Let us consider the network where the nodes for these two central characters get merged. The merging can be done with NetworkX with the `contracted_nodes` function:

Remember, fear is the path to the Dark Side.

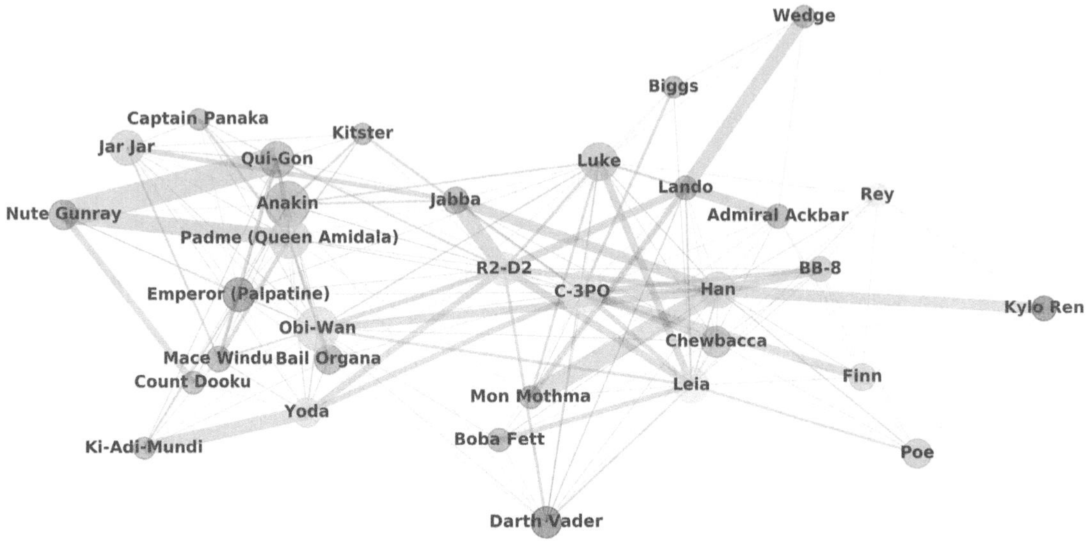

Figure 3.25: PageRange for the nodes in the *Star Wars* network. The size of the nodes denotes the PageRank score for the node.

```
V = nx.contracted_nodes(S, 'Darth Vader', 'Anakin')
```

Similar calculations to the ones carried out above can be done on this new network. The results for degree centrality, eigenvector centrality, PageRank and betweenness can be seen in Table 3.1. As we can see, the rankings are very stable, keeping the first three places for Darth Vader, Obi-Wan and C-3PO, we then have Padmé, Luke, Qui-Gon and Han, followed by Leia, Chewbacca, the Emperor, R2-D2, Poe, and even Jar Jar.... Plots of the resulting (filtered) networks can be seen in Figure 3.26.

C-3PO!! Not R2!! Really??

Jar Jar... Oh well!!!

We can definitely see who the central characters in this galaxy are and how they interact. The story of the Light versus the Dark Side of the Force is right there with Darth Vader and Obi-Wan in the first places. The presence of the

This is definitely not a trap!

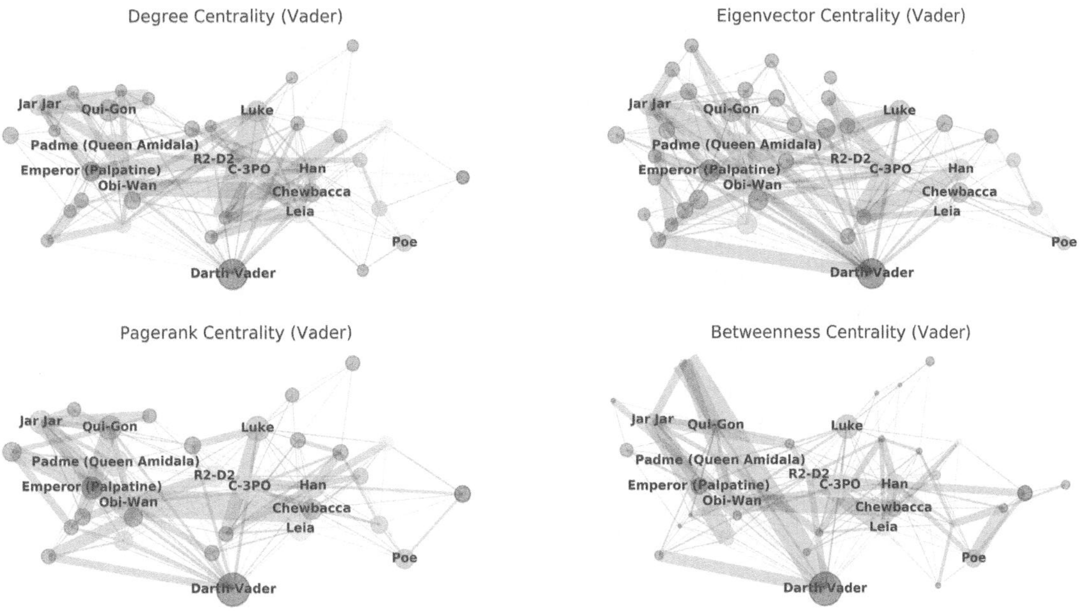

Figure 3.26: Vader networks for the following centrality measures: Degree centrality, eigenvector centrality, PageRank and betweenness.

droids in the first 10 places pays homage to the influence of the feudal peasants from Kurosawa's film *The Hidden Fortress*.

The data we have used contains information from Episodes I through VII, and having characters from the prequel (I-III) in the form of Qui-Gon, Padmé and even Jar Jar tells us that part of the story. It is interesting to see Poe as the only character from Episode VII that made the cut in the first 10 places and only for the betweenness centrality. This tells us about his importance in bringing together other characters in the story. This makes sense as he meets Finn first while escaping from the First Order, even giving him a name (FN-2187 is not deemed good enough) and introduces him to the rest of the resistance. Interesting to see that although

Rey is not in the first 10 places. But then again, we only have data up to episode VI.

Ranking	Degree Centrality	Eigenvector Centrality	PageRank	Betweenness
1	Vader (0.4909)	Vader (0.3559)	Vader (0.0561)	Vader (0.2843)
2	Obi-Wan (0.3273)	Obi-Wan (0.2689)	Obi-Wan (0.0381)	Obi-Wan (0.1627)
3	C-3PO (0.3182)	C-3PO (0.2637)	C-3PO (0.0352)	C-3PO (0.1391)
4	Padmé (0.3091)	Padmé (0.2529)	Padmé (0.0344)	Luke (0.1309)
5	Qui-Gon (0.2455)	Qui-Gon (0.2243)	Luke (0.0284)	Han (0.104)
6	Luke (0.2364)	R2-D2 (0.2166)	Qui-Gon (0.0273)	Poe (0.073)
7	Han (0.2364)	Emperor (0.1966)	Han (0.0268)	Chewbacca (0.0681)
8	Leia (0.2273)	Jar Jar (0.183)	Leia (0.026)	Emperor (0.0641)
9	Jar Jar (0.2182)	Luke (0.1809)	Jar Jar (0.0251)	Padmé (0.0621)
10	R2-D2 (0.2)	Han (0.1765)	Emperor (0.0226)	Leia (0.0586)

Table 3.1: Character rankings for the most central characters in the *Star Wars* saga given by various centrality measures.

the Emperor is an important character in the story, his presence is not outwardly revealed. This makes sense when we consider the plottings and cover-ups he had to concoct to get his plans to fruition.

We finish this section by looking at the communities that arise from the connections in the network. Will we be able to distinguish the Dark Side from the Light one? Can we tell which are the shady characters? Let us take a look. We

Light versus Dark Side? Not quite, as we shall see.

start by reducing the number of nodes in the network by concentrating on those that have degree centralities higher than 0.05:

```
nodes = [x for x, y in V.nodes(data=True)
  if y['dc'] >= 0.05]
VDC = V.subgraph(nodes)
```

We filter the graph for nodes with degree centrality higher than 0.05.

We can apply the Girvan-Newman algorithm as follows:

```
gn_side = community.girvan_newman(VDC)
sw_sides = tuple(sorted(c) for c
  in next(gn_side))
```

In this case, we have found two communities. We will now add this metadata to the network itself:

```
comm = {}
for i, side in enumerate(sw_sides):
  for character in side:
    comm[str(character)] = 'side {0}'.format(i)
nx.set_node_attributes(VDC, comm, 'side')
```

If we colour the nodes in the network by the side that was found by the algorithm, we end up with the network shown in Figure 3.27. As we can see, it is perhaps telling us more about the episodes in the story, with the characters from Episodes I-III on one side, and the ones from IV-VI and VII on the other one. This makes sense when we consider the meaning of the edges in the network: They are dialogue interactions among characters; we know that Rey interacts with Han and Luke, but Poe never talked to Yoda or Padmé.

The communities tell us about the different chapters in the story, not about the two sides of the Force.

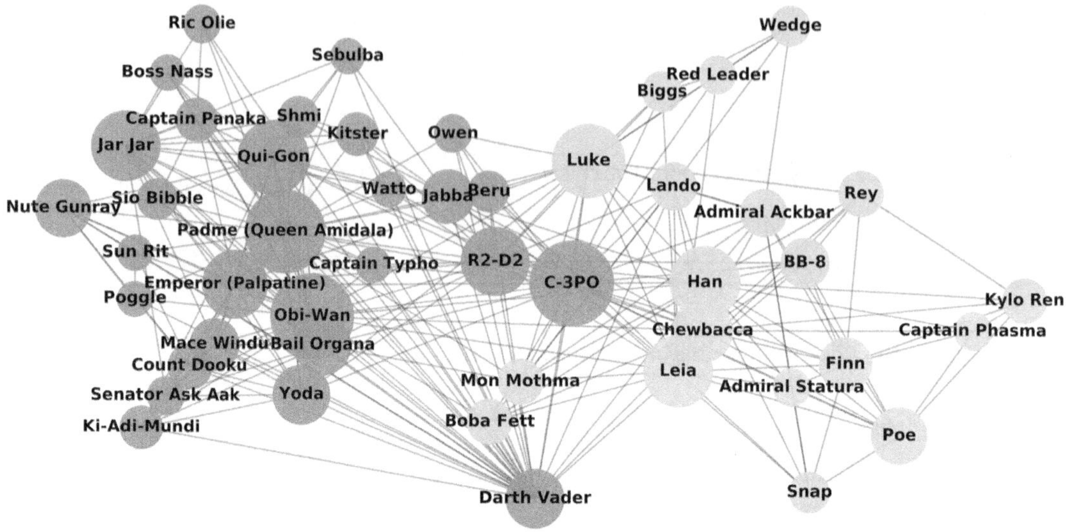

Figure 3.27: *Star Wars* sides (communities) obtained with the application of the Girvan-Newman algorithms.

3.5 *Graph Representation Learning and Embeddings*

TRADITIONAL GRAPH ALGORITHMS SUCH AS those we discussed in this chapter so far rely on explicitly defined features such as degree, centrality, or connectivity. While effective in many settings, these approaches may fall short when graphs become large, noisy, or lack clear structure. In such cases, we require a means of representing graph elements—particularly nodes—in a form that is more amenable to modern machine learning models. This has given rise to the field of *graph representation learning*, where the objective is to learn low-dimensional vector embeddings that capture structural properties of the graph.

Graph representation learning lets us capture structural properties of a graph.

Graph Representation Learning is a set of techniques used to convert parts of a graph—such as nodes, edges, subgraphs, or even entire graphs—into vector representations (embeddings) that capture their structural and relational properties. These vector embeddings can then be used as input to standard machine learning models for tasks like classification, clustering, or prediction.

The aim is to convert a graph into vectors that capture the relations in the graph.

In supervised learning tasks, features are typically represented as vectors in $\mathbb{R}^n$. However, nodes in a graph are inherently discrete and interdependent, with properties defined more by their position in the graph than by any individual attribute. The aim of graph embeddings is to map each node $v \in V$ to a vector $\mathbf{z}_v \in \mathbb{R}^d$, where $d \ll |V|$. These embeddings should preserve graph proximity, structure, and—where applicable—semantics.

The embeddings should preserve graph semantics.

Graphs are complex, non-Euclidean structures and unlike actual images, or for that matter, tabular data, they do not have a fixed size or shape, they have arbitrary connectivity between elements and typically encode rich relational and structural information. In contrast, traditional machine learning algorithms expect fixed-size, continuous-valued feature vectors as input. As such, we need a way to represent graph components in a format they can consume.

The resulting vectors enable us to use a variety of machine learning models on our networks.

3.5.1 *Random Walk Based Methods*

One popular class of embedding methods draws inspiration from natural language processing. Algorithms like Node2Vec generate node embeddings by performing

See Section 2.7 for more about embeddings in natural language processing and Section 5.2 for context within neural networks.

truncated biased random walks to produce sequences of nodes, treating these walks like "sentences" and applying a skip-gram model to learn embeddings. The skip-gram model is a simple neural netwok algorithm. Instead of predicting the next word given previous words, the skip-gram tries to predict surrounding context words given a center word. It does so by selecting a context word with which to start. It then randomly picks target words within a defined window and uses the information to train a model to predict the probability of seeing those target words given the context word. This is a useful way to explore our network.

We will talk about neural networks in Chapter 4.

The Node2Vec algorithm generates node embeddings by simulating biased random walks on the graph. The walker's behaviour is governed by two parameters, p and q, to bias the walk towards breadth-first (BFS) or depth-first (DFS) exploration:

The walker may prefer to explore close to the starting node or venture outwards.

- p – Return parameter: Controls the likelihood of revisiting the previous node.
- q – In-out (exploration) parameter: Controls the likelihood of exploring outward (BFS vs. DFS).

Think of this as a walk around your city, and you have just arrived at a junction (node). From here, you can make a number of choices:

The city is your graph, and the junction is a node. And the world is your oyster!!

- Go back where you came from (controlled by p)
- Stay near your last location (BFS-like)
- Go further into unfamiliar areas (DFS-like)

The parameters have different effects:

- Low p (< 1): Encourages returning — more "local loops"
- High p (> 1): Discourages returning — forces exploration
- Low q (< 1): Encourages outward movement — DFS-style
- High q (> 1): Encourages staying close — BFS style

Effects of the parameters p and q.

In other words p controls how much the walk resists or encourages going back, whereas q controls whether the walk prefers local clusters (BFS) or structure-hopping (DFS). Tuning these gives Node2Vec its power to learn different structural roles (e.g., neighbourhood vs. structural similarity).

Let us take a look at drawing some random walks. We will use the implementation in Stellar Graph[20], a Python library for machine learning on graphs and networks. Please ensure that you install the library to run the code shown below. We will work with Zachary's Karate network from Section 3.4.1:

[20] Data61, C. (2018). Stellargraph machine learning library. `https://github.com/stellargraph/stellargraph`

```
import networkx as nx
import matplotlib.pyplot as plt
from stellargraph import StellarGraph
from stellargraph.data import BiasedRandomWalk


K = nx.read_gml(fname)
KS = StellarGraph.from_networkx(K)
```

Notice that we need to convert our graph into a Stellar Graph object.

Note that we need to load our NetworkX data into a Stellar Graph object. This is done with the `from_network` method as shown in the last line in the code above. Remember that in the version of the network that we have been using the nodes are being labelled from 1, and the labels are strings.

Node labels being strings will be useful later on. You will see.

We will create a function to explore different values of p and q in the algorithm:

```
def plot_random_walks(p, q, title):
  rw = BiasedRandomWalk(KS)
  walks = rw.run(nodes=['1'],
    length=10,n=1, p=p, q=q, seed=42)
  walk = walks[0]
  walk_int = [n for n in walk]
  pos = nx.spring_layout(K)
  nx.draw(K, pos, node_color='lightgrey',
    with_labels=True, node_size=800,
    edge_color='lightblue')
  nx.draw_networkx_nodes(K, pos,
    nodelist=walk_int,
    node_color='gray')
  nx.draw_networkx_edges(K, pos,
    edgelist=[(walk_int[i], walk_int[i+1])
      for i in range(len(walk_int)-1)],
    edge_color='black', width=2)
  plt.title(f'Random Walk with p={p}, q={q} -
    {title}')
  plt.axis('off')
  plt.show()
```

A useful function to explore the effects of the parameters p and q.

The function above takes parameters `p`, `q` and `title` to generate random walks in a graph with `BiasedRandomWalk`. We are going to run a walk from node `'1'` with a length of 10 and parameters `p` and `q`. We obtain the nodes that the walk will visit in the list `walk_int` and draw the components of the network highlighting the random walk by colouring the nodes and edges visited. We can see the result of different values of p and q in Figure 3.28. In panel a) we can see how the walk stays close to the starting node with $p = 0.25$ and $q = 2$. Panel b) shows an unbiased walk, i.e., $p = q = 1$. Finally, panel c) shows a random walk that explores the network outwards with $p = 2$ and $q = 0.25$.

We walk through our network with the help of `BiasedRandomWalks`.

Stellar Graph provides a scalable and customisable way for learning node embeddings using biased random walks and embedding layers. First we will use random walks as shown above to generate tailored node sequences from the graph, where parameters p and q govern the exploration of the graph. This will help us capture both local community structure (homophily) and broader structural roles. These sequences effectively convert graph topology into "sentences" of node tokens.

The result of our random walks provides us with "sentences", i.e., sequences of visited nodes.

We then leverage Gensim's Word2Vec[21] to learn embedding vectors that predict the surrounding context of each node within these walks, mirroring how word embeddings are trained in natural language processing. The resulting embeddings are versatile, serving as powerful features for downstream tasks such as node classification, link prediction, and clustering—bringing the best of NLP techniques into graph representation learning.

[21] Řehůřek, R. and P. Sojka (2010, May). Software Framework for Topic Modelling with Large Corpora. In *Proceedings of the LREC 2010 Workshop on New Challenges for NLP Frameworks*, Valletta, Malta, pp. 45–50. ELRA. `http://is.muni.cz/publication/884893/en`

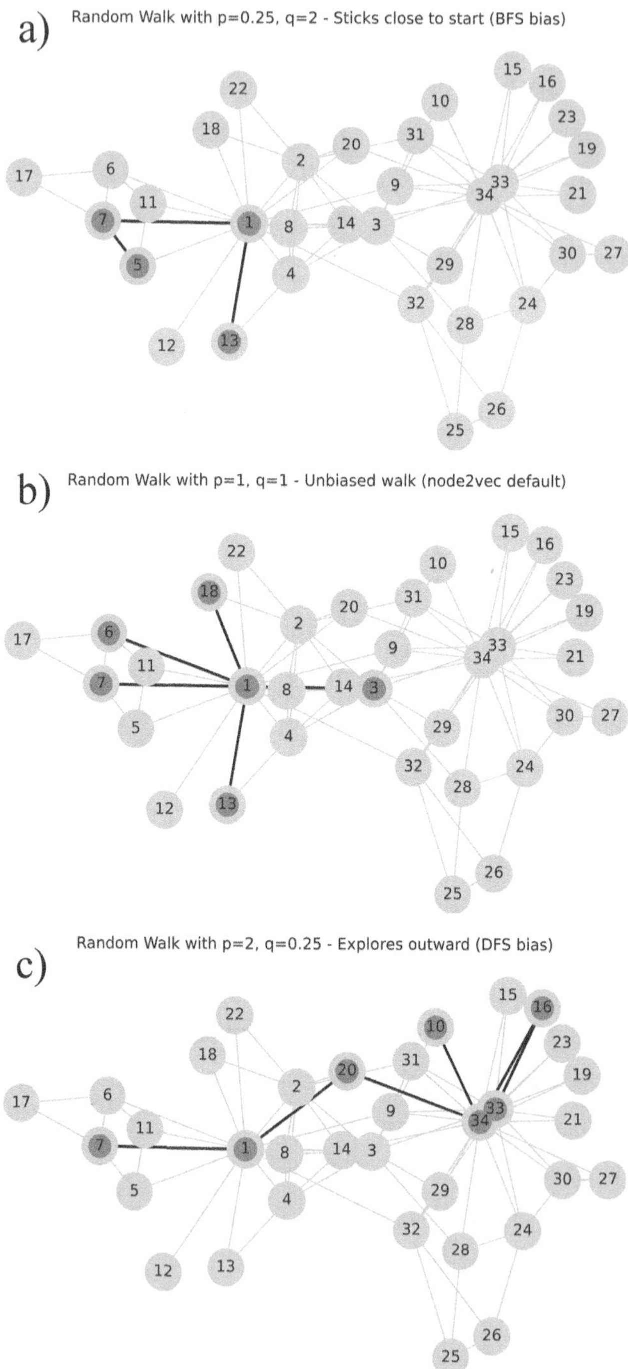

Figure 3.28: Random walks with Node2Vec across Zachary's Karate netwok using different values for parameters p and q.

Let us see how this works for the now-familiar karate club network. We are working with KS as per the example above, we will generate 10 random walks along the nodes of the network with a length of 20, and in this case we will use parameters $p = 1.0$ and $q = 0.5$ to explore the network:

```
rw = BiasedRandomWalk(KS)
walks = rw.run(nodes=list(KS.nodes()),length=20,
  n=10, p=1.0, q=0.5)
str_walks = [[str(n) for n in walk]
  for walk in walks]
```

We perform a series of random walks on the karate club network.

In the last line of the code above, we are capturing the "sentences" created by the random walks each of which is a list of the nodes visited along the walk.

We are now ready to pass these "sentences" to Gensim's Word2Vec. Since our labels are strings, we are actually embedding the sequence of nodes as if they were sentences whose meaning is given by the way in which the nodes are linked:

For more information about Word2Vec see Section 2.7.

```
from gensim.models import Word2Vec


model = Word2Vec(sentences=str_walks,
  vector_size=64, window=5,
  min_count=1, sg=1,
  workers=2, epochs=5)
```

Word2Vec will provide us with vector embeddings we are looking for.

In the Word2Vec model we pass our sentences i.e., str_walks. In the code above we are requiring the dimensionality of word vectors to be 64. The maximum distance between the current and predicted word within a sentence is given by `window`. We can ignore all words with a total frequency lower than `min_count`. We will use the skip-gram algorithm (`sg=1`) with 2 workers and 5 epochs, i.e., iterations over the corpus.

Let us now extract the embeddings:

```
node_ids = list(KS.nodes())
embeddings = [model.wv[node_id]
  for node_id in node_ids]
```

The actual embeddings are obtained with the wv method.

In the code above we are obtaining the trained word vectors for each node with the `wv` method. We can now visualise the representations of link embeddings. In this case we are going to use Principal Component Analysis (PCA)[22]. In this case learned link embeddings have 64 dimensions, but for visualisation we project them down to 2 dimensions using the PCA algorithm.

[22] Rogel-Salazar, J. (2025). *Data Science and Analytics with Python*. Chapman & Hall/CRC Data Mining and Knowledge Discovery Series. CRC Press.

```
pca = PCA(n_components=2)
X_pca = pca.fit_transform(embeddings)
plt.scatter(X_pca[:, 0], X_pca[:, 1])
```

A stylised version of the scatterplot above showing the 2-dimensional projection of Node2Vec embeddings for the Zachary's karate network can be seen in Figure 3.29 where the data points have been labelled with the corresponding node label.

PCA reduces the dimensionality of data while preserving as much variance as possible.

The result is a set of continuous-valued node embeddings that reflect structural similarities and can be used as input

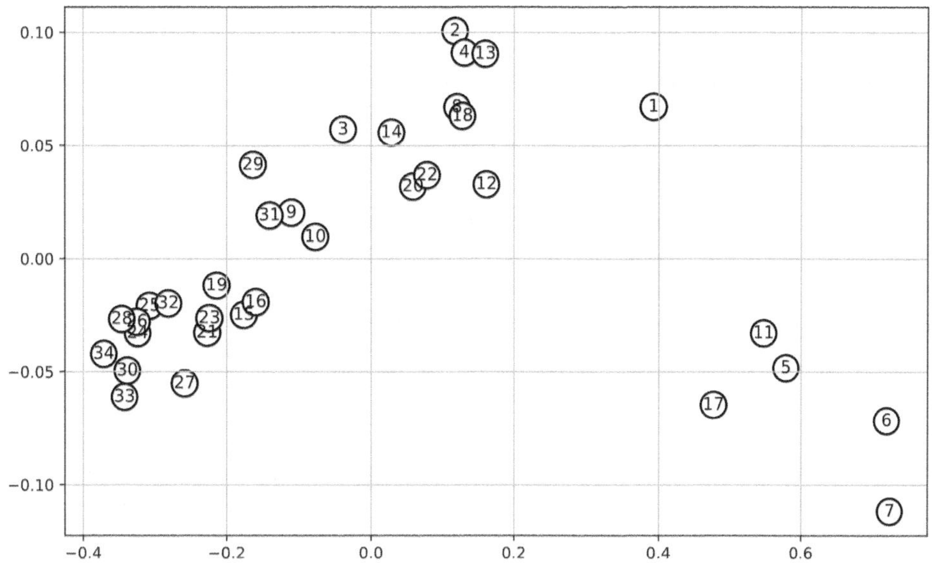

Figure 3.29: 2-dimensional projection of Node2Vec embeddings for the Zachary's karate network.

to a variety of downstream tasks, such as node classification, clustering, or link prediction where relational information is key, for example in:

- **Node classification:** Assigning labels to nodes based on local structure or attributes.
- **Link prediction:** Estimating the likelihood of a future or missing edge.
- **Community detection:** Using clustering techniques on embeddings to reveal groups or modules.
- **Recommendation systems:** Suggesting connections based on similarity in embedding space.

Some useful things we can do with embeddings for our networks.

As an example, let us use a basic classifier to predict node labels using the learned embeddings from the Karate Club graph. Let us use logistic regression in this example[23]:

[23] Rogel-Salazar, J. (2025). *Data Science and Analytics with Python*. Chapman & Hall/CRC Data Mining and Knowledge Discovery Series. CRC Press.

```
from sklearn.linear_model import LogisticRegression
from sklearn.model_selection\
  import train_test_split
from sklearn.metrics import classification_report
```

We can extract the features and labels. We will use the graph that comes with NetworkX to extract the final club affiliation:

```
X = [model.wv[node_id] for node_id in node_ids]
G = nx.karate_club_graph()
y = [G.nodes[int(node_id)-1]['club'] == 'Mr. Hi'
  for node_id in node_ids]
```

We obtain the final club affiliation from the network provided by NetworkX.

The features for our classification are the vector embeddings and the club affiliations are our labels for supervised learning. We are now ready to split our data and train our logistic regression model:

```
X_train, X_test, y_train, y_test =
  train_test_split(X, y, test_size=0.3,
  random_state=42)

clf = LogisticRegression()
clf.fit(X_train, y_train)
y_pred = clf.predict(X_test)
```

We train a logistic regression model with our vector embeddings.

Let us see our results:

```
> print(classification_report(y_test, y_pred))

              precision    recall  f1-score   support
       False       0.86      1.00      0.92         6
        True       1.00      0.80      0.89         5
    accuracy                           0.91        11
   macro avg       0.93      0.90      0.91        11
weighted avg       0.92      0.91      0.91        11
```

The classification report for our logistic regression.

The classifier performs very well overall with a 91% accuracy and strong precision and recall for both classes. The model is slightly better at identifying John A.'s club members (False class).

3.6 *Summary*

IN THIS CHAPTER WE HAVE covered many of the fundamental concepts used in the analysis of networks, whether social or otherwise. We have seen the wide variety of applications that networks have and the discussion was framed in terms of social network analysis, although I trust you can see the relevance in other areas of interest.

The work of the brilliant Leonhard Euler opened up a new way of understanding relationships between actors in a network. These actors are referred to as nodes or vertices, and the ties are known as edges. We understand the difference between directed and undirected graphs as well as some of the characteristics that make these networks interesting. Graph theory provides the basis to understand the relationships encoded in networks of interest.

We discussed the ideas behind a small-world network, leading to the popular idea of the six degrees of separation proposed by Milgram in the 1960s. Similarly, we talked about related measures such as the Bacon and Erdös numbers as ways to gauge the distance between actors, literally in the case of the Bacon number, in a network.

Encoding the information of a network in the form of a graph enables us to represent it using matrices, and we described how an adjacency matrix can be used for this purpose. We covered other formats to encode this information in terms of edge and adjacency lists. In this way we introduced concepts around graphs such as trails, paths, cycles and semi-walks. We also described the use of NetworkX as a tool to analyse graph/network data with Python.

Furthermore, we described different measures that provide information about the importance of agents in the network. Measures such as degree centrality, closeness, betweenness, eigenvector centrality and PageRank let us describe the relationships in the graph and establish patterns that otherwise would not be easy to spot. We talked about cliques and clustering coefficients leading to the discussion of community detection with Girvan-Newman and Louvain algorithms.

We then looked at the application of these ideas to a couple of networks. The first one is the data provided by Wayne W. Zachary about a karate club with an infighting issue leading to the split of the club. The second one covers the interactions of the characters in the *Star Wars* films.

Finally, we talked about graph representation learning. It offers a powerful bridge between discrete network structure and continuous machine learning models. By converting nodes into vector embeddings, we unlock the full potential of standard machine learning techniques while preserving the rich information encoded in graph topology. So, do as Yoda says and pass on what you have learnt.

4 Thinking Deeply: Neural Networks and Deep Learning

AN ARTIFICIAL NEURAL NETWORK (ANN) is effectively a computing system that takes into account inputs that are combined, typically in a nonlinear manner, to calculate for example outputs that can be compared to expected outcomes. The motivation behind ANNs is loosely inspired by the biological neural networks of animal brains.

For simplicity, we will also refer to them as *neural nets*.

The fact that expected outcomes are available to us should immediately make our Jackalope data scientist brains consider using neural nets for supervised learning. In that sense, neural nets are said to be able to *learn* how to carry out tasks based on the label data provided (data samples), without the need of being specifically programmed with rules.

Learning without having to be programmed!

Before we get into the deep end, understanding how neural networks work, we will first cover some historical aspects

Pun definitely intended!

of their development. Then we will explain the general architecture of a neural network in terms of layers and nodes, cover forward and backward propagation and finish the chapter with a discussion on convolutional neural networks and reinforcement learning.

4.1 *A Trip Down Memory Lane*

GIVEN ALL THE REPORTED ACHIEVEMENTS accomplished with the use of neural networks, we may think that the field is quite new. However, a lot of the ideas behind modern neural network implementations can be traced back to the 1940s. A good starting point is the work of McCulloch and Pitts[1] taking an electrical engineering approach to describing the use of *logical units* to model an artificial neuron. This can be seen as the basis of what we now call artificial neural networks. The inspiration was indeed the mimicking of the functions of a brain through electrical circuits, culminating with the coinage of the term *artificial intelligence* by John McCarthy.

Some ideas may be even older, but we need to draw the line somewhere.

[1] McCulloch, W. S. and Pitts, W. (1943). A logical calculus of the ideas immanent in nervous activity. *Bull. of Math. Biophysics* 5(4), 115–133.

The neuron doctrine as proposed around 1888 by Spanish Nobel Prize winner Santiago Ramón y Cajal is the basis of modern neuroscience. It states that neurons are individual separate cells and they behave as biochemically distinct cells rather than a single entity in an interlinked network. A crude approximation to model some of the functions of the human brain is the electrical connectivity that takes place between the more than 10 billion neurons that compose it. The neuronal cell body, or soma, receives electrochemical

The inspiration is indeed the electrochemical activity of biological neurons.

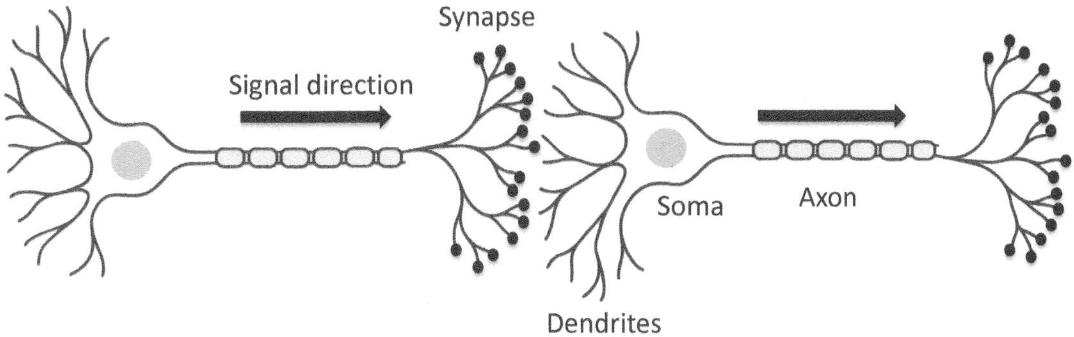

Figure 4.1: Schematic view of the structure of neurons.

signals (input) via the neuron's dendrites. If the combined signal received meets a given threshold, the neuron transmits a new signal (output) along its axon to other neurons' dendrites. This is the process the artificial neurons from McCulloch and Pitts emulated. See Figure 4.1 for a schematic view of this process.

Continuing with the inspiration of a brain as a model, Frank Rosenblatt developed the concept of the *perceptron*[2] in which a neuron receives information from other neurons in the form of electrical impulses of varied strengths (positive or negative). The receiving neuron combines these impulses, and if the result is larger than a certain given threshold, then the neuron "fires", transmitting the resulting impulse to other neurons. As we shall see in the rest of this chapter, today we refer to this as a one-layer neural network. Interestingly, the perceptron was conceived to be a custom-made machine, rather than an algorithm. If you find yourself in Washington D.C., you can pay a visit to the Mark I Perceptron in the Smithsonian Institution.

[2] Rosenblatt, F. (1962). *Principles of neurodynamics: perceptrons and the theory of brain mechanisms*. Report (Cornell Aeronautical Laboratory). Spartan Books.

You can visit a perceptron in Washington D.C.

The perceptron combines the receiving inputs as a weighted sum, and the firing happens if the sum exceeds the threshold C. With inputs x_1 and x_2 and weights w_1 and w_2 the output of the perceptron can be written as follows:

$$P_{output} = \begin{cases} 1, \text{ if } w_1 x_1 + w_2 x_2 > C, \\ 0, \text{ if } w_1 x_1 + w_2 x_2 \leq C. \end{cases} \quad (4.1)$$

The perceptron is able to separate regions linearly.

We are effectively separating two regions in a plane with a line and thus the perceptron is able to separate regions linearly.

During the 1960s other advances helped bring these early neurons to be applied in the real world. For example, Bernard Widrow and Marcian Hoff devised the first learning rules for feedforward networks with multiple adaptive elements, naming their models "ADALINE" and "MADALINE". The rules required examining the values before updating the weights. Each weight adjustment was proportional to the product of the previous value and the error, normalised by the number of inputs. This approach ensured that, even if a single perceptron produced a large error, the adjustment process could redistribute that error across neighbouring perceptrons.

We will expand on feedforward nets in Section 4.2.3.

ADAptive LINear Elements and Multiple ADAptive LINear Elements, respectively.

With a perceptron, we can implement circuits that recreate logic operators such as AND and OR. However, it is not possible to implement a nonlinearly separable operation like XOR. Marvin Minsky and Seymour Papert showed[3] that not only it was not possible to compute an XOR operation with a single perceptron, but also it provided arguments about it being achievable with multiple layers of perceptrons. The

[3] Minsky, M., S. Papert, and L. Bottou (2017). *Perceptrons: An Introduction to Computational Geometry*. The MIT Press. MIT Press.

idea is to combine multiple neurons to perform more complicated tasks, if only we can add another and another layer of neurons to our model. As it turns out, the learning algorithm proposed by Rosenblatt did not work for multilayer neural nets.

XOR requires a multilayer architecture.

The supervised nature of the task means that the correct output expected is only specified for the final layer. We can use this information to adjust the weights for the layer in question, but... how do we get to the hidden layers sandwiched between the output and input ones? The answer, i.e., backpropagation, will have to wait for the lift of the first AI winter to be widely spread. Nonetheless, the ideas behind it were floating around much before then.

We will cover backpropagation in Section 4.3.3.

AI winter refers to a period when enthusiasm, funding, and progress in AI sharply decline after earlier hype fails to deliver expected results.

In the early 1970s the work of Paul Werbos to extend beyond MADALINE enabled the development of a backpropagation algorithm[4]. This was largely unknown until 1986 when Rumelhart, Hinton, and Williams rediscovered it[5] and formalised it. They were able to set a clear framework for the technique, finally making it the well-known methodology we have today. Later in Section 4.3.3 we will address in more detail the workings of backpropagation. In the meantime, it suffices to say that the key aspect in its development is the realisation that if the neurons are not perceptrons per se, but instead they are able to compute their output with a nonlinear, differentiable function, then it is possible to use the derivative to minimise the errors incurred during training. In this way, with the aid of the well-known chain rule we can calculate the derivative for all the neurons in the prior layers.

[4] Werbos, P. (1994). *The Roots of Backpropagation: From Ordered Derivatives to Neural Networks and Political Forecasting*. Adaptive and Cognitive Dynamic Systems: Signal Processing, Learning, Communications and Control. Wiley.

[5] Rumelhart, D. E., G. E. Hinton, and R. J. Williams (1986). Learning representations by back-propagating errors. *Nature* 323(6088), 533–536.

With the advent of the backpropagation algorithm, it was possible to train multilayer architectures, opening the door to the development of convolutional neural networks (CNNs), first used by Yann LeCun et al.[6] to recognise handwritten digits with application in optical character recognition. By the end of the 1980s the interest in neural networks slowed down again as the approach to-date was not able to scale. Instead, algorithms such as the support vector machine gained prominence, and it was not for another decade or so that neural nets regained interest.

[6] LeCun, Y., Boser, B., Denker, J. S., et al. (1989). Backpropagation applied to handwritten zip code recognition. *Neural Computation 1*(4), 541–551.

We discussed SVMs in chapter 9 of *Data Science and Analytics with Python*.

In 1997 a recurrent neural network (RNN) framework known as long short-term memory (LSTM) was proposed by Hochreiter and Schimdhuber[7], improving the efficiency and practical use of RNNs as we shall discuss in Section 5.2. By the mid-2000s, the term *deep learning* became ever more popular thanks to the use of the word "deep" by Geoffrey Hinton[8,9] and others to describe their approach to the development of large-scale neural networks. There are many more advances that merit more in-depth analysis than we can do justice here, and largely speaking, areas of research in Transfer Learning (TL), Generative Adversarial Networks (GANs), Reinforcement Learning (RL), hardware and software developments will give us more food for thought in the years to come.

[7] Hochreiter, S. and Schmidhuber, J. (1997). Long short-term memory. *Neural. Comput.* 9(8), 1735–1780.

[8] Hinton, G. E., Osindero, S., and Teh, Y.-W. (2006). A Fast Learning Algorithm for Deep Belief Nets. *Neural Computation 18*, 1527–1554.

[9] Hinton, G. E. and R. Salakhutdinov (2006). Reducing the dimensionality of data with neural networks. *Science 313 5786*, 504–7.

The attention mechanism[10] is an important area of development that is worth exploring. It introduced the Transformer, a novel architecture built entirely on an attention mechanism and dispensing with recurrent and convolutional layers. Thanks to its parallelisable design, the

[10] Vaswani, A., N. Shazeer, N. Parmar, et al. (2017). Attention Is All You Need. In *Advances in Neural Information Processing Systems*, pp. 5998–6008. Curran Associates, Inc.

transformer handles long-range dependencies with remarkable efficiency. Its encoder-decoder stacks of multi-head attention and feedforward layers dramatically improve translation fluency and training speed.

The Transformer is built entirely on attention. After all, that is all you need!

The scalable nature of transformers paved the way for a new generation of text-based models that have revolutionised the are of Natural Language Processing (NPL). Early implementations like Generative Pre-trained Transformers such as GPT-1 and GPT-2 explored unsupervised pre-training on large text corpora, followed by task-specific fine-tuning. The real inflection point came in 2020 with GPT-3,[11] an autoregressive transformer with a staggering 175 billion parameters, trained on vast amounts of text. It demonstrated few-shot and even zero-shot learning capabilities, performing tasks from translation to arithmetic through in-context prompts—without weight updates. Zero-shot learning means the model tackles a new task with no examples. Few-shot learning, by contrast, is when the model sees a few examples (usually between 1 and 5) within the same prompt.

See Chapter 2 for more on NLP.

[11] Brown, T., F. Mann, N. Ryder, M. Subbiah, et al. (2020). Language models are few-shot learners. In H. Larochelle, M. Ranzato, R. Hadsell, M. Balcan, and H. Lin (Eds.), *Advances in Neural Information Processing Systems*, Volume 33, pp. 1877–1901. Curran Associates, Inc.

GPT-3's capabilities heralded the Large Language Model (LLM) era, spotlighting both the promise and cost of gigantic, pre-trained systems. At the same time, practical considerations—compute footprint, latency, and accessibility—galvanised the development of small language models: Distilled or efficiently fine-tuned transformer variants optimised for on-device deployment or low-resource environments.

Small-language models: Compact models derived via distillation or efficient fine-tuning for deployment under constrained resources.

Meanwhile, ChatGPT[12] and its peers exemplify the harmonious convergence of scale, interactivity, and alignment. Though fundamentally decoder-only transformer models, they are fine-tuned using Reinforcement Learning from Human Feedback (RLHF) to produce conversational, contextual, and more aligned outputs. The AI ecosystem now spans a spectrum—from lean, specialised models to sprawling LLMs—reflecting a dual imperative: The pursuit of broader capabilities and the need for practical, sustainable deployment.

[12] OpenAI (2023a). ChatGPT (Mar 14 version) Large Language Model. `https://chat.openai.com/chat`

All in all, for the different types of neural network architectures we have mentioned above, the analogy of neurons connecting with each other via their axons and dendrites is a first image that comes to mind. We can therefore start our journey by describing a general neural network architecture as a collection of nodes connected with each other so as to enable the transfer and manipulation of information. The nodes are aggregated into layers, and thus the information flows from one layer to the next in a directed manner. A typical neural network architecture can be seen in Figure 4.2 where the nodes are represented by open circles, and the connections between them are shown as directed edges.

A neural network is a collection of nodes arranged in layers, enabling information to flow from one layer to the next.

As we can imagine, the graphical representation we have is similar to the graphs we discussed in Chapter 3. In this case we have a directed graph where the nodes belong to tiered layers, and the information in the network flows in a single direction from one layer to the next.

For more on graphs, see Chapter 3.

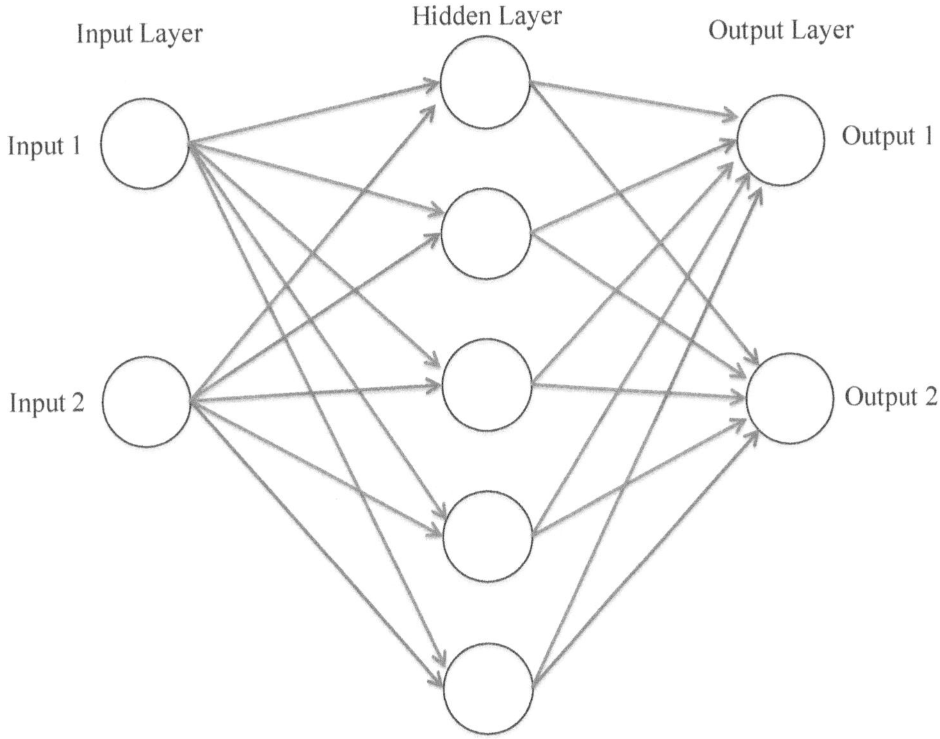

Figure 4.2: Neural network architecture with a single hidden layer.

Each of the edges in the network carries a weight, and each node is able to take the inputs provided and combine them before passing them to the next tier of nodes. The learning process enables us to adjust or "learn" the optimal weights for the edges as the training proceeds, so that we make predictions with the network. Let us now go deeper inside this architecture.

Each edge in the graph has its own weight, and adjusting those weights is the learning process for a neural net.

4.2 *No-Brainer: What Are Neural Networks?*

As WE HAVE SEEN IN the previous section, artificial neural networks can be understood in terms of their diagrammatic representations as graphs. Let us start delving into the workings of these graphs and see how they are able to *learn* patterns, *see* images, *recognise* speech and capture our collective imagination.

Neural nets are amazing!

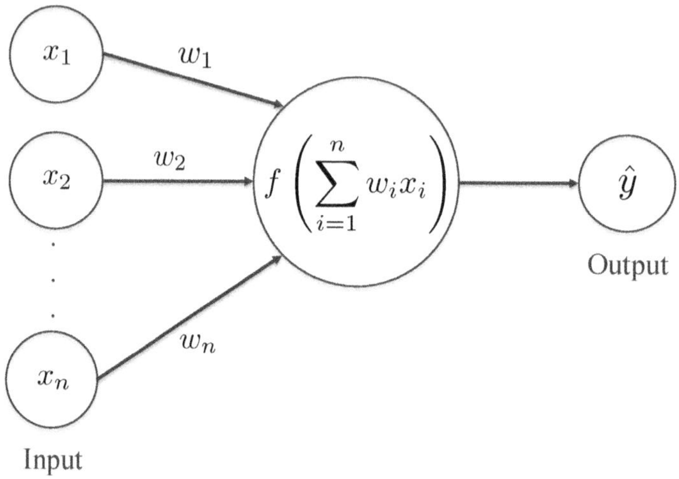

Figure 4.3: An artificial neural network takes up an input and combines the contributions of the nodes to calculate an output $\hat{y}$ with the aid of a nonlinear function with the sum of its inputs.

The first thing to point out is that, unlike the graphs that we analysed in Chapter 3, the information present in this graph is not embedded in the architecture of the network. Instead an external input is required. This information is then used to compute an output with a function of the sum of its inputs. We can represent this as shown in Figure 4.3 where we can see n nodes providing a contribution to the calculation of the output $\hat{y}$ via a function $f(\cdot)$. Notice that each edge i has its own weight w_i.

Typically a nonlinear function.

The network architecture that we have in place is a weighted directed graph and our aim is to adjust the edge weights w_i as the learning takes place. We can think of this process as having a set of dials to adjust the strength of a signal at

A neural net is a weighted directed graph.

a given connection in the network. As it is the case in its biological counterpart, the synapses between neurons may actually fire, or be activated, if the aggregate signal is above a certain threshold.

To continue using the brain analogy, this would be the strength of the synapses between neurons.

4.2.1 *Neural Network Architecture: Layers and Nodes*

AN IMPORTANT FEATURE OF THE architecture of our neural networks is the fact that the nodes are arranged in layers. In other words, the information in the network flows from one layer to the next in the direction prescribed by the directed edges. We count the number of layers starting effectively from zero. That first layer is usually called the input layer, and it is made out of passive nodes that take the input. The last layer is usually called the output layer and is made of active nodes. That is to say that they take the outcomes of the previous layer and modify the signals received. In between the input and output layers, we can have any number of so-called hidden layers. These hidden layers are also made out of active nodes. In Figure 4.2 we showed a typical example of a single layer neural network.

How Pythonic... but actually just a happy coincidence!

Each of the layers in the neural network architecture can have any number of nodes, and as such both the number of hidden layers as well as the number of nodes in each layer are a couple of the parameters you need to decide upon first. As the number of hidden layers in our architecture increases, the deeper and deeper the input information needs to flow. I do use the word "deeper" with a bit of intent, as this is what gives rise to the term *deep learning* to describe the

We shall talk about the number of nodes later in this section.

work done with large artificial neural networks. Today, deep learning architectures have a wide range of applications including speech recognition, computer vision, automatic machine translation, text generation, image captioning, etc. We will talk more about deep learning in Section 4.4.

Deep learning refers to the use of neural networks with a large number of hidden layers.

Different layers in the architecture will perform different kinds of manipulations and transformations on their respective inputs. The nodes in the input layer perform no computation; they simply, but importantly, pass on the information to the nodes in the first hidden layer. The hidden nodes carry out computation on the inputs received and transfer the result to the next layers, all the way through to the output layer. This process is usually known as *feedforward* where the information moves in one direction only; there are no cycles or loops.

In other words, the nodes in a hidden layer.

Not yet!

The single layer perceptron that we mentioned in the previous section is the simplest feedforward neural network: It does not have hidden layers and it is only capable of learning linear separable patterns. As the number of hidden layers grows, we are able to accomplish more complex tasks as shown in Table 4.1. The more layers we add, the more effectively we can perform automatic feature engineering.

The more layers we add, the more effectively we can perform automatic feature engineering.

We mentioned above that each layer can contain, in principle, any number of nodes. Deciding how many nodes we put in each layer is as important as making up our minds about the number of layers. Although the hidden layers do not directly interact with the outside world, they do have a profound impact on the final output returned by

Deciding on the number of layers and the number of nodes in each is an important step.

Number of Hidden Layers	Capability
0	Capable of representing only linear separable patterns.
1	Able to approximate any function with a continuous mapping from one finite space to another.
2	Able to represent any arbitrary decision boundary to arbitrary accuracy; can approximate any smooth mapping to any accuracy.
3 or more	Complex representations can be learnt by performing automatic feature engineering of sorts.

Table 4.1: Capabilities of neural networks with a different number of hidden layers.

the neural network. On the one hand, having too few nodes in the hidden layers gives rise to underfitting, as there are not enough nodes to detect the potential complex patterns in our data. On the other hand, the presence of too many nodes can also result in other issues. Overfitting is one of them, as the extra capacity in the network enables the system to memorise the attributes in the data, particularly when the set is not large enough. Even in cases where there is enough data, we need to take into consideration that the more nodes we have in the hidden layers results in longer training times. Some rule-of-thumb recommendations include having hidden layers with a number of nodes bounded by the size of the input and output layers. A good start is having around 60-70% of the number of nodes in the

Choosing the size of the hidden layers is more data art than data science.

input layer plus the number of nodes in the output layer. Finally, do not include more than twice the size of the input layer and remember that the ultimate architecture setup is a matter of striking a balance, as it is the case in many other areas of machine learning.

Do bear these recommendations in mind.

4.2.2 *Firing Away: Neurons, Activate!*

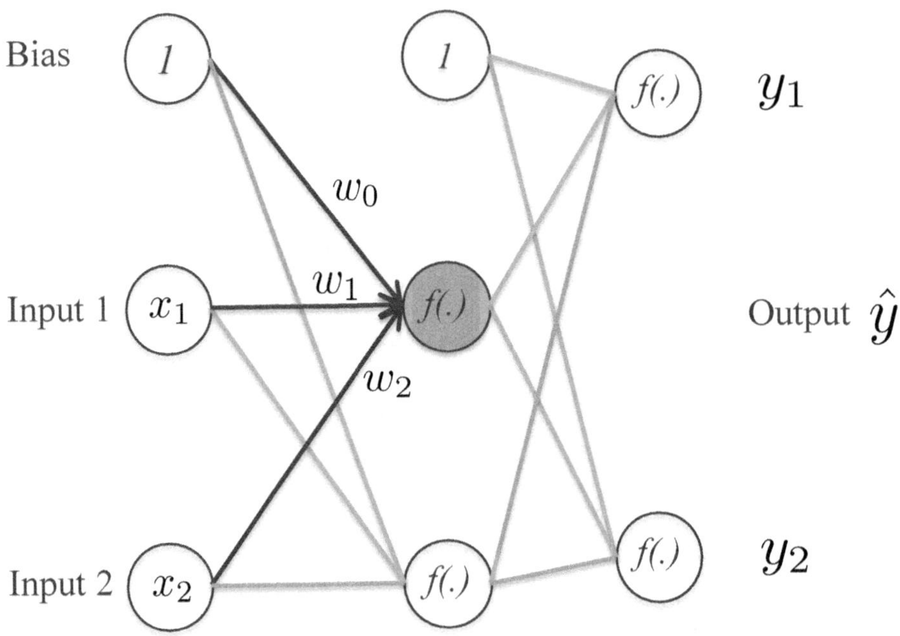

Figure 4.4: Neural network architecture with a single hidden layer, including bias. The inputs to a node (marked in grey) are used in conjunction with the weights w_i to calculate the output with the help of the activation function $f(\cdot)$.

Now that we have a better understanding of the architecture of our neural networks, we can delve deeper into their inner workings. Let us consider a one-hidden layer neural network as shown in Figure 4.4. Not only is this architecture able to represent linear functions, but also nonlinear ones. The input layer has three nodes, one of which we have marked as bias with a value of 1, the other two nodes take the values x_1 and x_2. These inputs are passed to the next layer along with their associated weights.

Let us take a node in the (first) hidden layer of this neural network (highlighted in grey). Actually, we can zoom in to see what is happening there: See Figure 4.5. This hidden node receives the inputs $(1, x_1, x_2)$ along with the associated weights $(w_0, w_1 w_2)$ and uses the values to compute the function $f(\cdot)$ whose argument is a sum of the inputs as $\sum w_i x_i$. This function is referred to as the *activation function*, and we shall talk more about it in the next pages.

We can extend this analysis to a larger number of nodes.

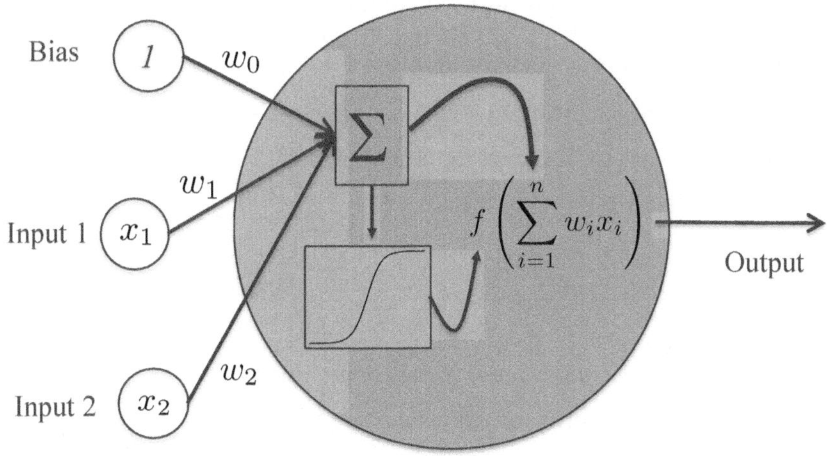

Figure 4.5: Zooming into one of the hidden nodes in our neural network architecture.

The process described above is carried out for each of the nodes in the first layer, and the resulting value from the activation function is used as the input for the next layer, and so on. In the architecture shown in Figure 4.4, we have two output nodes. After executing the same process with the activation function $f(\cdot)$, their results (y_1, y_2) are the output of the neural network.

The activation function is a nonlinear function. This is because we are interested in representing complex, real-world data with our neural networks. The activation function therefore introduces a non-linearity to the outputs of the node, enabling the architecture to learn these complex representations.

The activation function is a nonlinear function.

We have been talking about the activation function as an important part of our neural network, but so far we have not said much about its structure. This is because there may be many options available to us. Each of these options offers different ways in which the inputs are combined, and the most common activation functions include the following:

- **Sigmoid**: This function takes a real-valued input and maps it to a range of values between 0 and 1. The sigmoid function is given by the expression below and we can see a plot in the top panel of Figure 4.6

  We have encountered this function in the context of logistic regression!

$$S(x) = \frac{\exp(x)}{1 + \exp(x)}. \tag{4.2}$$

- **Hyperbolic tangent**: This function also takes real-valued inputs and maps them to a range of values in the interval $[-1, 1]$. It is effectively a rescaling of the sigmoid function:

  This is a rescaled sigmoid function.

$$\tanh(x) = 2S(2x) - 1 = \frac{\exp(2x) - 1}{\exp(2x) + 1}. \tag{4.3}$$

  We can see the shape of the tanh function in the middle panel of Figure 4.6.

- **Rectified Linear Unit** (ReLU): This function places a minimal threshold of zero to negative inputs and maps

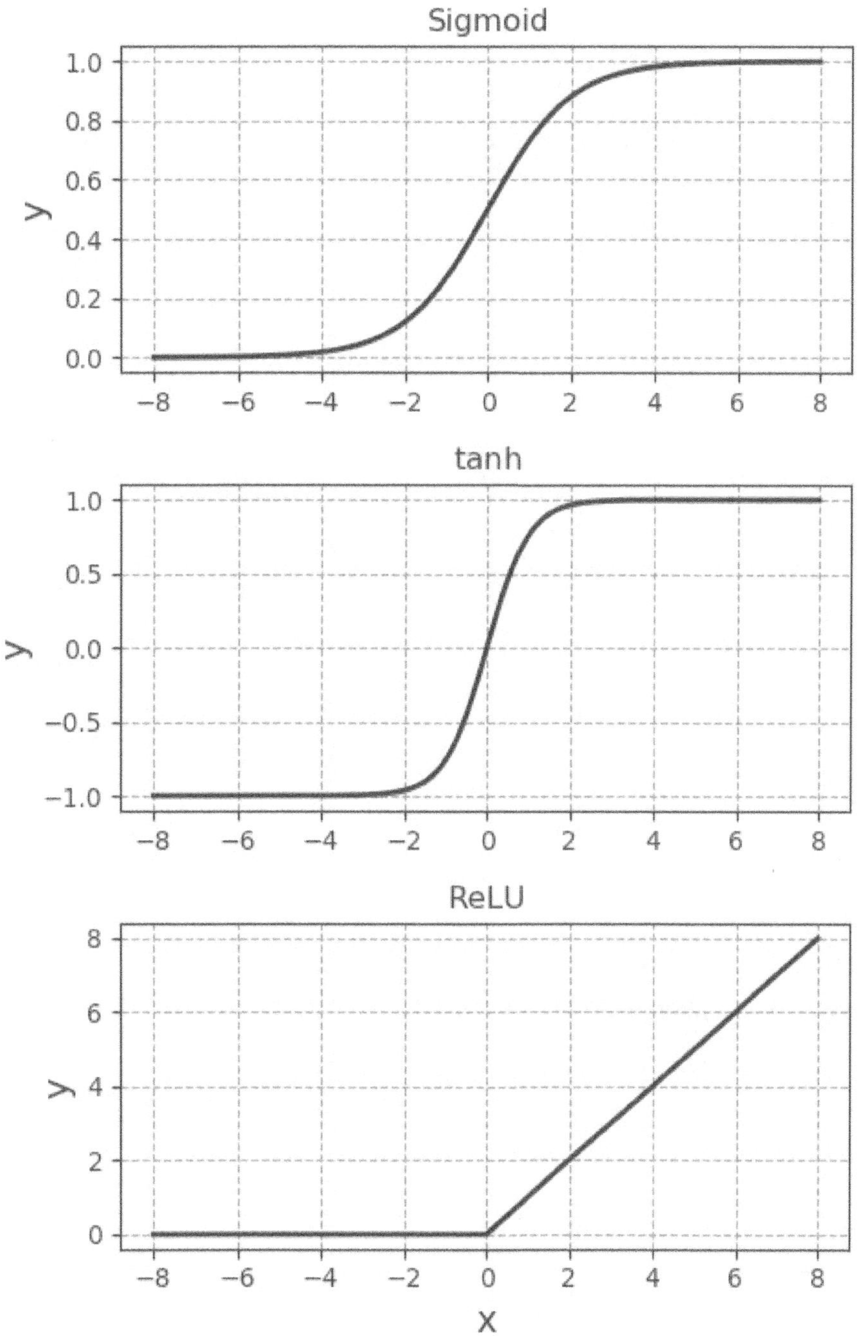

Figure 4.6: Some common activation functions, including sigmoid, tanh and ReLU.

positive values to themselves:

$$f(x) = \max(0, x). \tag{4.4}$$

The bottom panel of Figure 4.6 depicts a ReLU function.

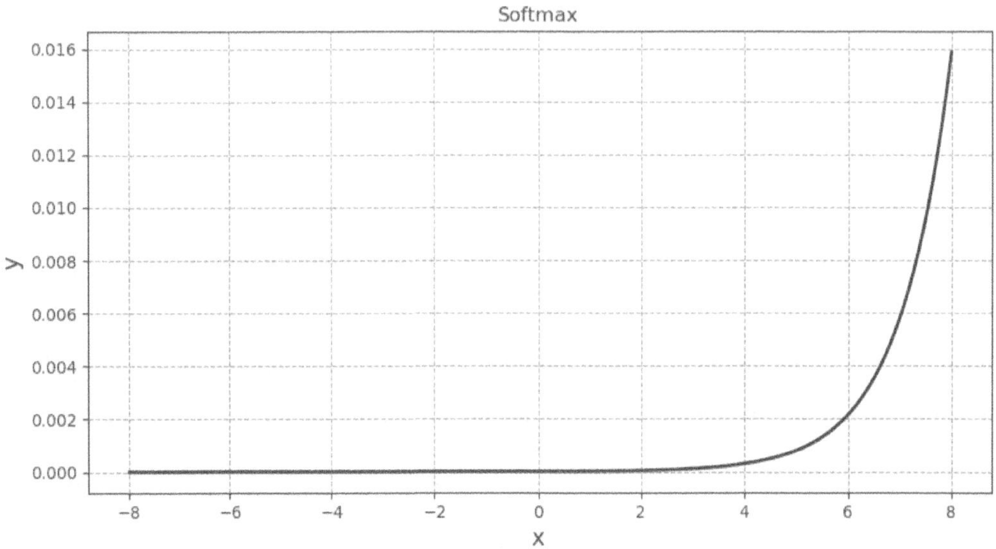

Figure 4.7: A plot of the softmax function.

It may be the case that for our application we are interested in generating probabilities as the outcomes of the activation layer. In this case, we can make use of the **softmax** activation function. This function is effectively a generalisation of the sigmoid function. It takes real values as input and maps them to a probability distribution where entry is in the range $(0, 1]$. Furthermore, all the entries add up to 1. The softmax activation function is given by Equation (4.5), and a plot can be seen in Figure 4.7.

As the entries of a softmax function add up to 1, it can be used to draw probabilities.

$$\text{softmax}(x_i) = \sigma(z_i) = \frac{\exp(x_i)}{\sum_{j=1}^{N} \exp(x_j)}, \text{ for } i = 1, \ldots, k. \tag{4.5}$$

Once we have applied the activation function to the inputs of the node in question, we are ready to pass the outcome to the next layer in our neural network. We do this until we reach the last layer, where the outputs are actually the predictions made by the entire neural network architecture. Et voilà!

4.2.3 *Going Forwards and Backwards*

THE OUTPUT OF THE NEURAL networks we have discussed so far has been obtained by taking forward the inputs from one layer to the next. This kind of neural network is called a feedforward network and the flow of information goes in one single direction, not allowing for loops or cycles. Feedback is therefore not possible. What happens if the response we obtain from training our neural network is not satisfactory? Well, in the case of a feedforward network, as described above, there is not much we can do.

So far, we have only fed the information forward from the input to the output layers.

Nonetheless, it is possible to consider the following scenario: Once we have obtained the final output of our neural network, we can compare it to the labelled data used for training. If the error is negligible, we are done; however, if the error is not acceptable, we would like to provide this as feedback to the neural network. In other words, we would like the neural network to "learn from its mistakes".

We would like to be able to learn from our mistakes.

The process to enable this form of *learning* in a neural network is known as backward propagation of errors, or **backpropagation** for short. Following up the analogy about learning from our mistakes, we are, in a sense, asking the

Or actually the neural network's mistakes!

machine to guess the value of the labelled data. The error in the guess is calculated and backpropagated so that a better estimate can be made.

OK! OK! Estimate...

In this way, we are going forwards and backwards, and forwards again, and again, until the error is within an accepted level of tolerance. The way in which backpropagation estimates the error is by minimising a cost function, and therefore we need to make use of calculus. A well-known optimisation method used in this kind of tasks is **gradient descent**.

Or until we give up...

In the following sections we will cover in more detail the implementation of backpropagation, but for the time being let us spend some more time getting familiar with what is happening at a high level. Let us start with our forward propagation network as depicted in Figure 4.8, in panel a) we have the situation described in the previous section. For our purposes, we have a neural network with one hidden layer and three nodes in the input layer.

We start with the forward propagation step. Nothing unusual here.

We need to bring the inputs (and bias) together with the initial weights w_0, w_1 and w_2 and make the appropriate calculations with them. In order to track what is happening to the weights, we are adding the superscript $[0]$ to denote the initial forward pass. In this way, the weights ${w_i}^{[0]}$ and the inputs are combined in the hidden nodes by a given activation function. The results are then passed forward to the output layer, where we get a target prediction, in this case the output is either a 1 or a 0. Please note that in Figure 4.8 we are only labelling the weights that go from the input

We are not explicitly showing the weights used from the hidden layer to the output later, but the same process applies.

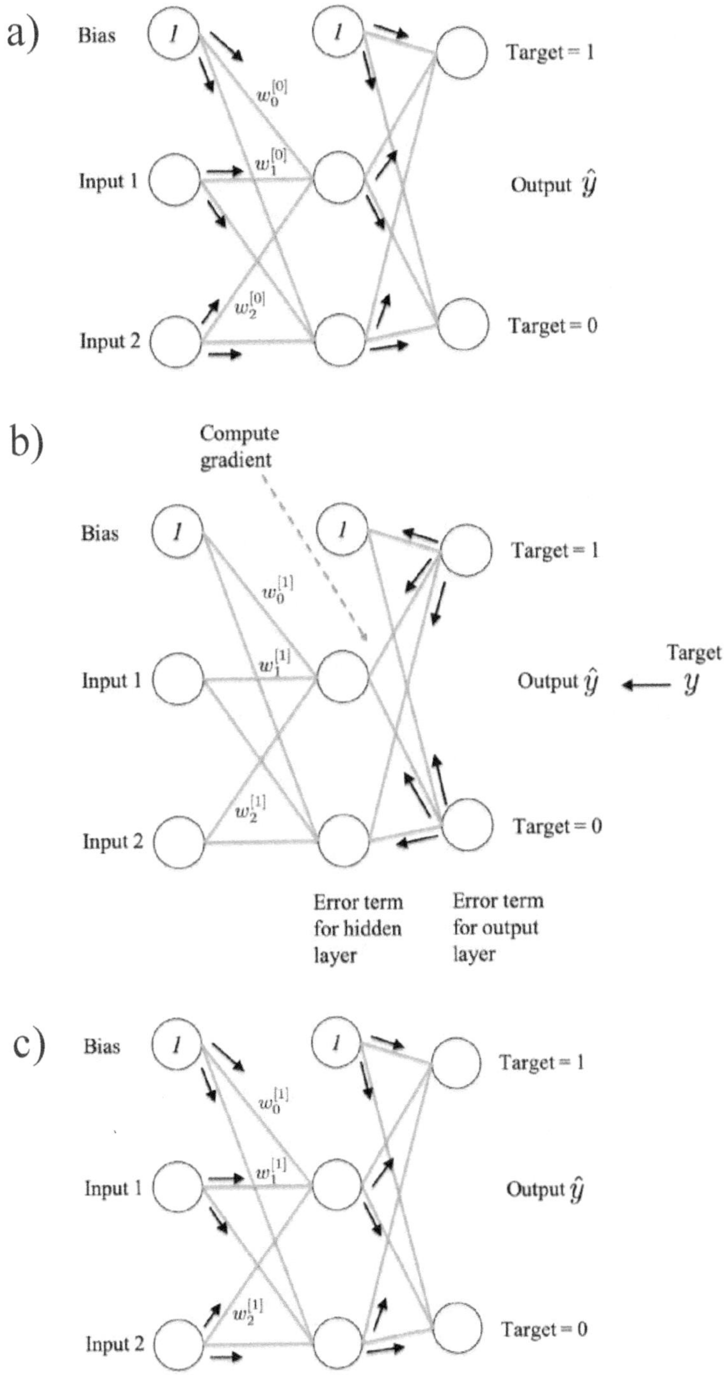

Figure 4.8: Backward propagation of errors, or backpropagation, enables the neural network to learn from its mistakes.

to the first hidden layer. The other edges in the architecture carry their own weights too.

We are now interested in checking if the prediction labels obtained from the 0th forward pass are any good. We can denote the output result as $\hat{y}$ and compare it to the actual target y. The result of the comparison between y and $\hat{y}$ contains useful information for the neural network, as it enables it to learn from its mistakes. In order to do this, we make use of a loss (or cost) function, which enables us to evaluate how well our chosen algorithm models the training data provided. If our predictions are off the mark, the loss function will return a higher value. However, if they are good, the result of the loss function will be smaller.

The comparison between actual and predicted values enables the network to learn from its mistakes.

It is possible to propagate this information from the output layer back to the hidden nodes, until it reaches the edges of the input layer. In this way it is possible to enable the neural network to identify the weights that need to be adjusted to improve the predictions made. On the one hand, in the cases where the prediction is different from the target label, the neural network can adjust the weight that made this prediction and improve the result. On the other hand, for labels that have been correctly predicted, no adjustment is needed. In order to propagate back the information, we are in effect solving an optimisation problem for the loss function chosen.

Please note that since the weights are combined by the activation, changes in one may require further changes in others.

As mentioned above, a well-known algorithm such as *gradient descent* can be used for the optimisation step, and it requires us to be able to compute gradients. We will provide further details about it in the next section. The backpropagation step is depicted in Figure 4.8, panel b). Note the direction of the arrows depicting the flow of information.

The direction of the flow is now reversed.

We are now in the situation shown in panel c) of Figure 4.8 where we reach the start of our learning loop. Now that we have passed information back about the weights, the neural network can make adjustments, and the new weights let us start a new forward pass. This step starts and follows exactly the same logic as before, except that this time we have new values $w_0^{[1]}$, $w_1^{[1]}$ and $w_2^{[1]}$. Notice that we are using the superscript 1 to denote the fact that we have a new iteration.

We start a new forward pass with the new adjusted weights.

From here on, the process continues as before: We use the weights and inputs to make calculations using the activation function, and pass the results to the next layer. When we reach the output layer, the new prediction results are compared with the targets. The fact that we are using a minimisation process indicates that we are expecting lower and lower values from our loss function. We continue iterating over our neural network sending information back and forth until we reach a chosen tolerance on the values of our loss function. At that point, we can stop the iterations, and we have a neural network that has learnt from its mistakes in making predictions when comparing to the target labels provided. We are ready to unleash the model to the world and confront real data. Let us now take a look at implementing this workflow in more detail.

We iteratively adjust the weights until we reach an optimal solution, sending information forth and back through the layers of the network. You are right, the phrase goes "back and forth", but that seems wrong for an ANN!

4.3 *Neural Networks: From the Ground up*

We have covered quite a few of the concepts behind a neural network architecture and understand the main ideas behind their "learning". In this section we are going to implement an artificial neural network with three layers: The input and output layers and one hidden layer. The goal is to see how the concepts described above translate into code with Python. The code is not meant to be the most efficient implementation ever, and there may be other ways to achieve the same results in a better way. Take this implementation for what it is, and we will cover other alternatives later on in this chapter.

Take this implementation with a "brain" of salt!

Let us imagine that we are interested in discriminating between two classes of animals, say, cats and dogs. In chapter 5 of *Data Science and Analytics with Python*[13], we encountered a friendly alien life-form that was tasked with clustering animals on Earth based on similarities and differences between them: Cats have pointy triangular ears, whereas rabbits have long oval ones; horses have manes, and deer have antlers. This provided our alien friend with rules that can be used in classification based on the labels we have obtained for the animals shown to it. In this case we are assuming that the labels have already been identified and that we have a dataset containing animals with their corresponding label: Cat or dog. The next task for the alien is therefore to obtain a model that enables it to correctly predict whether she has a cat or a dog in front of him, given the different features provided to them.

[13] Rogel-Salazar, J. (2025). *Data Science and Analytics with Python*. Chapman & Hall/CRC Data Mining and Knowledge Discovery Series. CRC Press.

It? him? her? them!

We should have asked for a name and preferred pronoun! Ma-Sha from Gazorpazorp?

From our previous discussion, we know that training an artificial neural network involves choosing a number of nodes in our hidden layer(s). It stands to reason that the more nodes we include, the more complex our neural network becomes, and the hope is that we will be able to fit more complex functions with it. However, we need to take into account the balancing between high dimensionality and hence complexity, versus the computational cost incurred.

Higher complexity may mean higher computational cost.

We did mention in Section 4.2.1 that choosing the right number of hidden nodes is more data art than data science. For our current purposes, we are going to consider playing with the number of hidden nodes in the architecture and see how this affects our output.

We will see the effect of different numbers of hidden nodes in our architecture.

4.3.1 *Going Forwards*

WE START BY MAKING OUR way forwards from the input layer and into the depth of our neural network architecture. In practice, the way to achieve this is via the application of matrix multiplication, and of course of the activation function chosen for the task. Let us consider our input to be given by a 2-dimensional matrix X which will render our prediction denoted by $\hat{y}$. We will denote the vector of weights from the input layer to the first hidden layer as W_1, and thus we can calculate the combination of the inputs with the weights as:

We will use matrices to represent our neural network model.

$$z_1 = XW_1 + b_1, \tag{4.6}$$

This is the combined result of our inputs.

please note that both W_1 and b_1 are parameters of our network that need to be learnt from training data.

We can pass the result z_1 to the activation function, and here we will use the hyperbolic tangent for the hidden layer. This means that the output will be given by:

$$a_1 = \tanh(z_1). \tag{4.7}$$

This is the output of the hidden layer.

We are now able to take the output a_1 of the hidden layer and pass it as the input to the next layer in our network. Remember that in this particular architecture, this is actually the output layer. In this case we have that the combination of the input a_1 and the weight vector W_2 is given by:

$$z_2 = a_1 W_2 + b_2. \tag{4.8}$$

Once more, we calculate the combination of inputs.

For the activation function in the output layer, we will use the softmax function which will let us convert our scores to probabilities:

$$a_2 = \hat{y} = \sigma(z_2). \tag{4.9}$$

And this is the output of the entire network.

Although we have written the expressions above specifically for our three-layer neural network, it is easy to generalise the equations noting that z_i corresponds to the weighted sum of inputs of layer i, and thus a_i is the output of the i-th layer after applying the activation function chosen for that layer. In effect we have a pipeline of matrices that transform our data from one layer to the next, along the way enabloing some featuring engineering in an automatic way.

With one hidden layer in our architecture.

We can do automatic feature engineering! Yay!

Let us stop for a moment to consider the dimensionality of our matrices. For a 2-dimensional input X, with a single hidden layer comprising n hidden nodes we have that our parameters are $W_1 \in \mathbb{R}^{2\times n}$, $b_1 \in \mathbb{R}^n$, $W_2 \in \mathbb{R}^{n\times 2}$, $b_2 \in \mathbb{R}^2$. We can see how the complexity becomes larger not only as we increase the number of nodes in the layer, but also as we increase the number of layers, and indeed the number of nodes in them. Keeping track of all the transformations that larger, deeper neural networks perform could become a truly gargantuan task.

Checking the dimensions of our matrices is a good practice.

The calculations above can be generalised to a neural network with L layers. We denote the activation of the nodes in layer l as a column-vector $\mathbf{a}^l$, the edges from the nodes in layer $l-1$ to layer l are stored in the weight matrix $\mathbf{W}^l$ and the biases in the column vector $\mathbf{b}^l$. For the forward pass, given the activation function f_l, we have that:

Let us generalise the ideas above to L layers.

$$\mathbf{a}^l = f_l\left(\mathbf{W}^l\mathbf{a}^{l-1} + \mathbf{b}^l\right). \tag{4.10}$$

Note that we are taking into account the possibility that the activation function on each layer may be different, perhaps ReLU, softmax or even a hyperbolic tangent. The general architecture of the network can be seen in Figure 4.9.

The activation function can be different for each layer.

To calculate the input sums and move forward in the network, let us consider three adjacent layers in the architecture as shown in the middle part of Figure 4.9. Let us index the nodes in the layers $l-1$, l and $l+1$ as m, p and q, respectively. The input sum of a node p in layer l is:

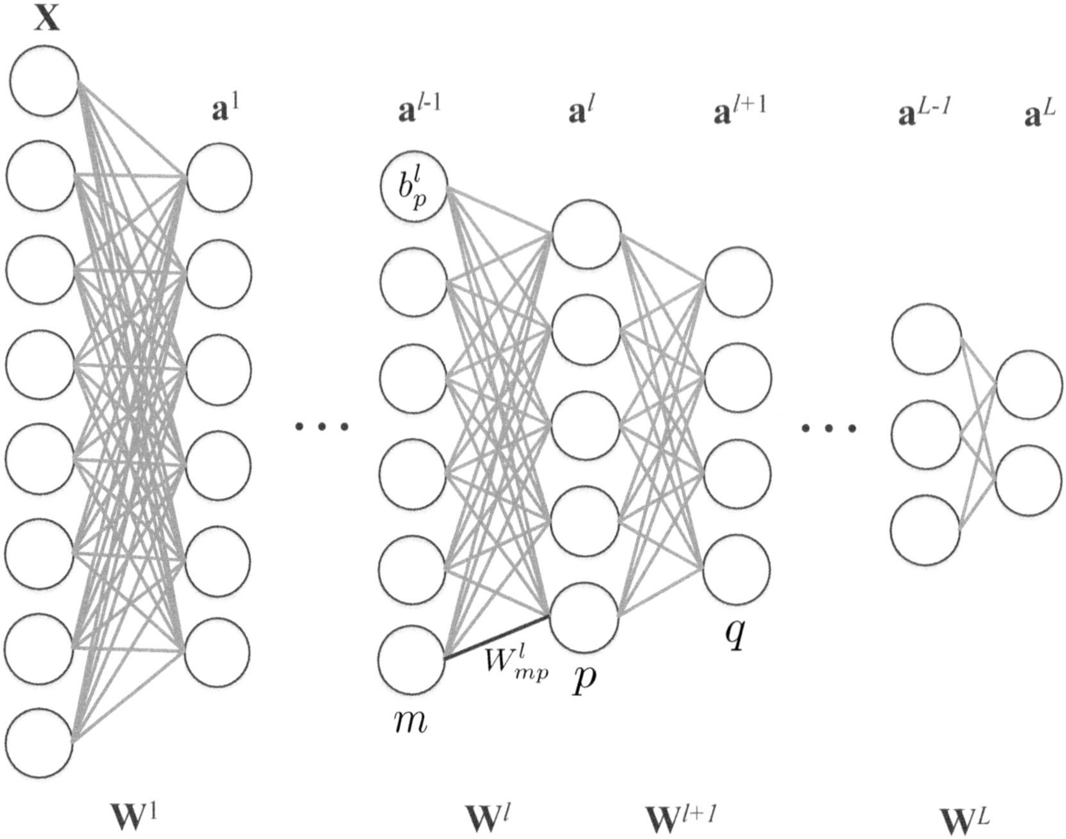

Figure 4.9: General architecture of a neural network; we are showing the labels of the different L layers in the network.

$$z_p^l = \sum_m W_{mp}^l a_m^{l-1} + b_p^l, \tag{4.11}$$

where we are adding the contributions of all nodes m in layer $l-1$. We can calculate the activations in layer l as $a_p^l = f_l(z_p^l)$ and thus the input sum of a node q in layer $l+1$ is:

Equation (4.11) corresponds to the generalised combination of inputs.

$$z_q^{l+1} = \sum_p W_{qp}^{l+1} a_p^l + b_q^{l+1}. \tag{4.12}$$

In this way we have moved forwards in the network from one layer to the next. We continue doing this until reaching the output layer. So far so good, and now how do we learn the parameters? Let us take a look.

We have moved forwards...

4.3.2 *Learning the Parameters*

THE TASK DEFINED ABOVE REQUIRES us to determine the paramaters (W_1, b_1, W_2, b_2) such that we get a minimum error on our training data. Crucially, we need to define what we mean by error in terms of a suitable loss function. In the high-level description in Section 4.2.3, we mentioned that a comparison between our prediction $\hat{y}$ and the true class labels of y would be ideal.

We need to minimise a cost/loss function.

A suitable choice, with the softmax activation function we have for our output layer, is the cross-entropy loss. Given a model for which c classes are predicted, the hypothetical occurrence probabilities are $\hat{y}_1, \hat{y}_2, \ldots, \hat{y}_c$. If we observed k_1 instances for the first class, k_2 for the second, and so on we have that the likelihood is $P(data|model) = \Pi_c \hat{y}_c^{k_c}$. For $N = k_1 + k_2 + \ldots + k_c$ observations we can write the following expression:

The cross-entropy loss function is a suitable choice for many situations.

$$
\begin{aligned}
L(y, \hat{y}) &= -\frac{1}{N} \log \Pi_c \hat{y}_c^{k_n} \\
&= -\frac{1}{N} \sum_i k_i \log \hat{y}_i \\
&= -\sum_i y_i \log \hat{y}_i \qquad (4.13)
\end{aligned}
$$

The log-likelihood function helps us define our loss.

where $y_i = k_i/N$ correspond to the empirical probabilities. For the case of two classes, we have that the true observed probabilities are such that $y_2 = 1 - y_1 = 1 - y$, and the same applies to the predicted values. Therefore we can write Equation (4.13) as:

Binary classification is a good typical case.

$$L(y, \hat{y}) = -y \log \hat{y} - (1 - y) \log(1 - \hat{y}). \qquad (4.14)$$

In practice the loss function implemented in applications including logistic regression is an average of all cross-entropies. In the case where we have N data samples, the loss function is calculated as:

$$L(y, \hat{y}) = -\frac{1}{N} \sum_{n=1}^{N} \sum_{i=1}^{C} y_i^{(n)} \log \hat{y}_i^{(n)}. \qquad (4.15)$$

Remember that it is possible to add a regularisation term to the loss function.

This expression lets us sum over each of our training data points, and whenever we predict the incorrect class, we add to the loss. In other words, in cases where the two probability distributions y and $\hat{y}$ are far away, we have a greater loss. Our goal is to find parameters that minimise the loss, and thus maximise our predictions to match our training dataset. Let us see how the minimisation can be done.

The bigger the difference against our target, $\hat{y}$, the bigger the loss.

4.3.3 *Backpropagation and Gradient Descent*

Now that we have a loss function, we need to use an optimisation method to find its minimum. Gradient descent algorithms find the optimal for a loss or cost function by changing the parameters of a model such that the gradient

Gradient descent is a popular optimisation method.

of the errors points down to a minimum error value. I like thinking of gradient descent in terms of a seasoned skier going down a slope: the skier always heads in the direction of steepest descent, aiming to reach the lowest point of the valley. If the slope is too steep and they take overly long strides, they might overshoot and crash into another ridge; if the strides are too small, the journey becomes painfully slow. Just like a skier adjusting their pace and trajectory to reach the bottom smoothly, gradient descent relies on carefully tuned step sizes (learning rates) to converge towards the optimal solution.

Watch out—too much speed and you will overshoot the optimum; too little, and you will be skiing in circles until spring thaw.

We can use any optimisation technique we prefer and there are many out there from which to choose, ranging from brute-force search, all the way through to generic algorithms. The important thing is to be able to change the parameters of the neural network. However, as the complexity of our network increases, we must take into account that the number of parameters to track becomes larger and larger, and we would like it to be as computationally efficient as possible. Calculus is a good ally to every savvy Jackalope data scientist.

In principle, any good optimisation method can be applied.

A useful and fundamental concept from calculus is that of the derivative of a function. It basically provides a gauge to the rate of change the function experiences at a given point. In our case we can use this tool to check how much the error in our predictions changes when we change one of the parameters we would like to learn. Consider for instance the 2-dimensional function f depicted in Figure 4.10, where a clear minimum is shown.

Not to be derivative, but the derivative of a function is a useful tool in many applications.

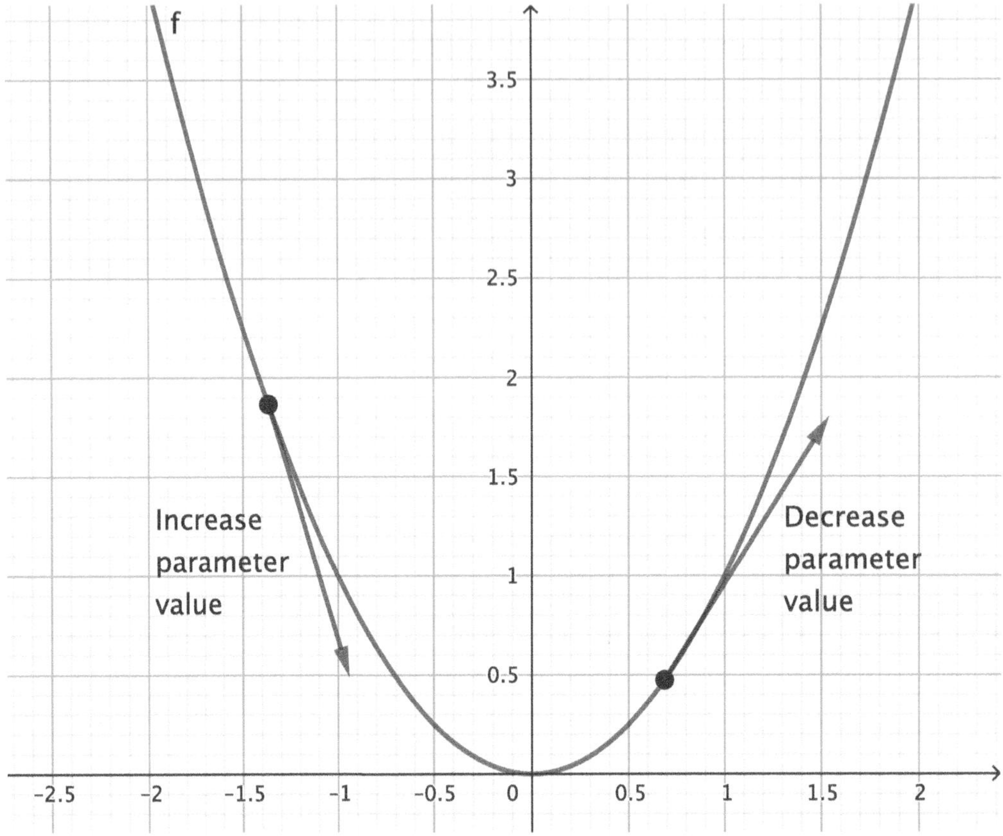

Figure 4.10: The derivative of a function f indicates the rate of change at a given point. This information lets us change our parameters accordingly.

If the function represents the cost, a positive value for its derivative indicates that the error increases if we increase the value of our parameter. If that is the case, we need to reduce it and hence we move towards the function's minimum. If, however, the derivative is negative, the error is decreasing, and therefore increasing the value of our parameter gets us closer to the minimum. If the derivative has a value of 0, we have reached a stable point, i.e., the minimum, and we are done.

Local minimum...

Let us go back to our analogy of a skier trying to reach the valley and stop for a well-deserved refreshment. She would like to get to the lodge as swiftly as possible, and that means finding the slope with steepest descent to reach her destination. If she chooses a path where the slope is increasing, she should change direction. The case shown in Figure 4.10 can be described in terms of an ordinary derivative; however, when we have multiple parameters, we will require the use of partial derivatives.

Think of the algorithm in terms of a skier that wants to reach the lodge as swiftly as possible.

For the backpropagation of the errors in our neural net, we can apply the derivative trick and trace back our steps in the network architecture. Our starting point now is the output layer. We calculate the partial derivatives of the loss function with respect to our parameters and propagate the errors back to the input layer. The gradient descent algorithm requires as input the gradients of the loss function:

We are going backwards now...

In other words, the vector of derivatives.

$$\frac{\partial L}{\partial W_1}, \frac{\partial L}{\partial b_1}, \frac{\partial L}{\partial W_2}, \frac{\partial L}{\partial b_2}.$$

Remember that our neural network carries out the following computations:

$$z_1 = XW_1 + b_1, \tag{4.16}$$

$$a_1 = \tanh(z_1), \tag{4.17}$$

We obtained these expressions in Section 4.3.1.

$$z_2 = a_1 W_2 + b_2, \tag{4.18}$$

$$a_2 = \sigma(z_2) = \hat{y}. \tag{4.19}$$

We use this information to update our parameters, and we do this with a particular **learning rate**, α, such that for a parameter W_i the update is given by:

$$W_i := W_i - \alpha \frac{\partial L}{\partial W_i}, \tag{4.20}$$

The learning rate, α, is a hyperparameter of our model.

and for b_i we have:

$$b_i := b_i - \alpha \frac{\partial L}{\partial b_i}. \tag{4.21}$$

We need to calculate each of the gradients, and the application of the chain rule makes this task easier. Let us start with the derivative of the loss function with respect to the parameter b_2:

$$\frac{\partial L}{\partial b_2} = \frac{\partial L}{\partial z_2}\frac{\partial z_2}{\partial b_2}. \tag{4.22}$$

We have that:

$$\frac{\partial z_2}{\partial b_2} = \frac{\partial(a_1 W_2 + b_2)}{\partial b_2} = 1. \tag{4.23}$$

The chain rule to the rescue!

For the partial derivative of the loss function with respect to the variable z_2 we have that:

$$\begin{aligned}
\frac{\partial L}{\partial z_2} &= -y\frac{\partial \log \sigma(z_2)}{\partial z_2} - (1-y)\frac{\partial \log(1-\sigma(z_2)))}{\partial z_2}, \\
&= \frac{-y}{\sigma(z_2)}\frac{\partial \sigma(z_2)}{\partial z_2} - \frac{1-y}{1-\sigma(z_2)}\frac{\partial(1-\sigma(z_2))}{\partial z_2}, \qquad (4.24) \\
&= -y(1-\sigma(z_2)) + (1-y)\sigma(z_2), \\
&= \sigma(z_2) - y = \hat{y} - y. \qquad (4.25)
\end{aligned}$$

We need to calculate the derivative of the softmax function.

Expression (4.24) requires us to compute the derivative of the softmax function, and more information can be found in Appendix C. Furthermore, a general derivative of the loss function with respect to parameter z_j can be found in Appendix D.

See Appendices C and D for more information.

We have now all the information we need to calculate the derivative of the loss function with respect to the parameter b_2. Let us take a look:

$$\frac{\partial L}{\partial b_2} = \frac{\partial L}{\partial z_2}\frac{\partial z_2}{\partial b_2} = \hat{y} - y. \qquad (4.26)$$

Once more, we use the chain rule.

The derivative of the loss function with respect to the parameter W_2 is given by:

$$\frac{\partial L}{\partial W_2} = \frac{\partial L}{\partial z_2}\frac{\partial z_2}{\partial W_2} = a_1(\hat{y} - y). \qquad (4.27)$$

And again...

In a similar way, we can make use of the chain rule to calculate the derivative of the loss function with respect to b_1 as follows:

$$\begin{aligned} \frac{\partial L}{\partial b_1} &= \frac{\partial L}{\partial z_2}\frac{\partial z_2}{\partial a_1}\frac{\partial a_1}{\partial z_1}\frac{\partial z_1}{\partial b_1}, \\ &= (\hat{y} - y)W_2(1 - \tanh^2(z_1)). \qquad (4.28) \end{aligned}$$

We know the drill by now...

Following the same train of thought, finally the derivative of the loss function with respect to W_1 is:

$$\frac{\partial L}{\partial W_1} = \frac{\partial L}{\partial z_2}\frac{\partial z_2}{\partial a_1}\frac{\partial a_1}{\partial z_1}\frac{\partial z_1}{\partial W_1},$$

$$= (\hat{y} - y)W_2(1 - \tanh^2(z_1))X. \quad (4.29)$$

We definitely do know the drill, don't we??

Let us now go back to the generalisation introduced in Section 4.3.1 and use the indexing shown in Figure 4.9. Given a loss function L, we can calculate its derivative with respect to a single weight in layer l:

$$\frac{\partial L}{\partial W^l_{mp}} = \frac{\partial L}{\partial z^l_p}\frac{\partial z^l_p}{\partial W^l_{mp}},$$

$$= \frac{\partial L}{\partial a^l_p}\frac{\partial a^l_p}{\partial z^l_p}\frac{\partial z^l_p}{\partial W^l_{mp}},$$

$$= \left(\sum_q \frac{\partial L}{\partial z^{l+1}_q}\frac{\partial z^{l+1}_q}{\partial a^{l+1}_p}\right)\frac{\partial a^l_p}{\partial z^l_p}\frac{\partial z^l_p}{\partial W^l_{mp}},$$

$$= \left(\sum_q \frac{\partial L}{\partial z^{l+1}_q}W^{l+1}_{qp}\right)f'_l(z^l_p)a^{l-1}_m. \quad (4.30)$$

We can now generalise our calculations.

We are including a sum to account for all the contributions from the nodes in layer $l+1$. This is because their values have an effect on the overall error, as they depend on the weights with respect to which we are taking the derivative. In other words, we are taking the contribution of all the input nodes.

Remember that we need to take into account the contributions from all input nodes.

Furthermore, in the expression above we are fixing p and m and as a result we can see what happens to the error when changing one single weight. We can also look at how the total error changes when the input sum into a node is modified:

$$\delta_p^l \equiv \frac{\partial L}{\partial z_p^l} = \left(\sum_q \frac{\partial L}{\partial z_q^{l+1}} W_{qp}^{l+1} \right) f_l'(z_p^l), \tag{4.31}$$

This is the total error change given by the change in the input sum to a node.

where we have used the result in expression (4.30). This hints to a recursive formula such that:

$$\delta_p^l = \left(\sum_q \delta_q^{l+1} W_{qp}^{l+1} \right) f_l'(z_p^l). \tag{4.32}$$

We have obtained a recursive function that can be applied to our model.

As for the derivatives of the loss function with respect to the biases we have:

$$\frac{\partial L}{\partial b_p^l} = \frac{\partial L}{\partial z_p^l} \frac{\partial z_p^l}{\partial b_p^l} = \frac{\partial L}{\partial z_p^l}(1) = \delta_p^l. \tag{4.33}$$

Which turns out to be very handy!

We can now use our recursive formula to obtain the error of the nodes in the final layer L:

$$\delta_m^L = \frac{\partial L}{\partial z_m^L} = \frac{\partial L}{\partial a_m^L} \frac{\partial a_m^L}{\partial z_m^L} = \frac{\partial L}{\partial a_m^L} f_l'(z_m^L). \tag{4.34}$$

Using these recursion formulas, we can verify the expressions we obtained before:

$$\delta^{(2)} = \frac{\partial L}{\partial b_2} = \frac{\partial L}{\partial a_2}\frac{\partial \sigma(z_2)}{\partial z_2} = \hat{y} - y \quad (4.35)$$

$$\delta^{(1)} = \frac{\partial L}{\partial b_1} = \delta^{(2)} W_2 \frac{\partial \tanh(z_1)}{\partial z_1}$$

$$= \delta^{(2)} W_2 \left(1 - \tanh^2(z_1)\right) \quad (4.36)$$

We obtained these expressions at the beginning of this section.

$$\frac{\partial L}{\partial W_2} = \delta^{(2)} \frac{\partial z_2}{\partial W_2} = \delta^{(2)} a_1 \quad (4.37)$$

$$\frac{\partial L}{\partial W_1} = \delta^{(1)} \frac{\partial z_1}{\partial W_1} = \delta^{(1)} X \quad (4.38)$$

Now that we have the equations that enable us to backpropagate errors, we can consider some aspects of the computational implementation of the optimisation algorithm. There are different variations and one of the most common is the so-called **stochastic gradient descent** where the model is changed for each training example in the dataset. In this case, the data effectively becomes available to the algorithm in sequential order. This kind of methodology is sometimes called *online machine learning*. Although we may get a more immediate view of the performance of the model, it is a computationally intensive affair as well as being prone to be affected by noise.

In stochastic gradient descent, we update the model for every training data sample.

A variation on this theme is the use of the so-called **batch gradient descent** where the changes in the model are calculated for each training sample, but crucially, the model

In batch gradient descent, the model is updated after all the training samples are considered.

is updated once all the training samples have been considered. A full loop through the complete training dataset is called an **epoch**, and we update the model at the end of each epoch. The batch methodology makes our computation more efficient compared to the stochastic approach. It also provides us with a more stable error estimation. However, we need to be mindful of potential premature convergence given that stability. Similarly, large training datasets may give us very slow execution times.

An epoch is a full loop through the complete training dataset.

A variation on the batch methodology that splits the training dataset into small batches can be used too. This is called **mini-batch gradient descent** and serves as a balance between the stochastic and batch methodologies described above. Mini-batch lets us update the model with a higher frequency than batch while being more efficient than the stochastic approach. The batching of the training dataset also makes it more manageable for large sets. The batch size needs to be adjusted depending on our application.

In mini-batch gradient descent, we split the training set in smaller batches.

The batch size describes the size of the mini-batch!

Note that although our goal is to find the parameters of the model, we need to be aware of any hyperparameters for our model. In the case of mini-batch, not only do we need to find a suitable number of epochs but also the batch size. When the batch size is equal to the size of the training dataset we recover the batch methodology, whereas when the batch size is equal to a single data point we have the stochastic one. Masters and Luschi[14] advocate the use of small batch sizes, between 2 and 32 for example. Some popular batch sizes include values such as 32, 64 or 128.

[14] Masters, D. and C. Luschi (2018). Revisiting Small Batch Training for Deep Neural Networks. *Computing Research Repository http://arxiv.org/abs/1804.07612.*

As for the epochs, let us recall that they refer to the number of iterations our algorithm runs through the entire training dataset. Each epoch has therefore one or more batches. When the number of batches per epoch is equal to 1, we have a batch gradient descent implementation! In cases where we have 2 or more batches per epoch, we effectively have a couple of nested loops. One loop is over the number of epochs, where the entire training dataset is utilised; inside this loop we have another one that runs through the number of batches specified. In general the number of epochs can be typically on the order of hundreds so that the algorithm has enough time to learn the parameters that minimise the
error.

Remember that an epoch has one or more batches.

Even thousands!

What does this all mean in more concrete terms? Let us assume that we have a dataset with 1000 data points, and we have chosen a batch size of 32 with 2000 epochs. We are requiring our dataset to be divided into 31 batches of 32 samples, and therefore we will update our model 31 times per epoch. With 2000 epochs we have 62,000 batches to go through while training our neural network.

Note that we are leaving 8 samples out... We can choose a better batch size to use all our data!

4.3.4 *Neural Network: A First Implementation*

We have been thinking about ANNs and the way they work, and you may be asking yourselves where the code is. Without further ado, let us provide a first implementation. Remember the caveat we clarified at the beginning of Section 4.3: This may not be the best implementation, and

We did mention to take this implementation with a "brain" of salt!

the aim is to demonstrate the concepts discussed above.

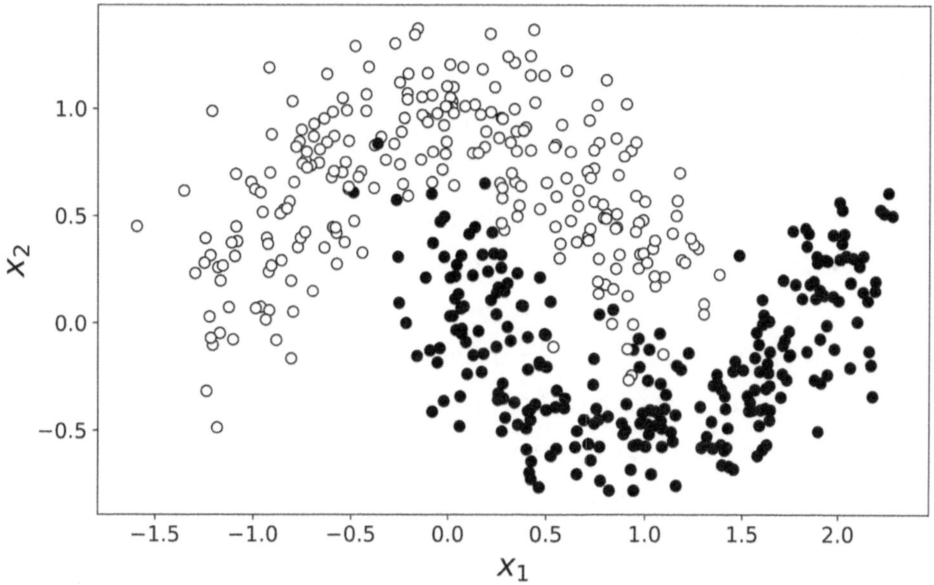

Figure 4.11: Observations corresponding to two classes, 0 and 1, described by features x_1 and x_2. We will use this data to train a neural network.

Let us consider the dataset shown in Figure 4.11. It contains observations corresponding to two classes labelled 0 and 1 described by two features x_1 and x_2. The dataset called `neuralnet_dataset.csv`[15] can be obtained at `https://doi.org/10.6084/m9.figshare.9249074.v1`. We can see that a linear classifier may be able to do a satisfactory job in separating the two classes, but it would be a hard task to improve the discrimination given the semi-circular trends shown in the plot. Similar datasets can be generated with scikit-learn with the help of the `make_moons` command. Let us start by reading the data:

[15] Rogel-Salazar, J. (2019b, Aug). Neural Network - Observation dataset. https://doi.org/10.6084/m9.figshare.9249074.v1

```
df = pd.read_csv('neuralnet_dataset.csv')
X = df[['x1', 'x2']].values
y = df['label'].values
```

We are reading our data into a pandas dataframe.

Let us define a few parameters that will be used in determining the architecture of the neural network as described in the previous sections. We need to keep information about the number of samples in the training set as well as the number of nodes in the input and output layers. We are building a one-layer neural network, with its corresponding input and output layers. For the input layer we will have two nodes, one for each of the two features, x_1 and x_2 in our dataset. For the output layer we will also have two nodes, one for each class to be predicted. We can then see how this can be extended for multi-class problems. The architecture is the one shown in Figure 4.2.

We could actually use one node in the case of binary classification.

```
n_training = df.shape[0]
input_layer = 2
output_layer = 2
```

We have 2 nodes in the input and output layers.

We also provide a value for the learning rate α, and should we require a regularisation term in the cost function we also need the value for the hyperparameter λ:

```
alpha = 0.01
lambda_reg = 0.01
```

We define α and λ, our hyperparameters.

In order to keep track of the neural network parameters W_i and b_i, we will store and modify the values in a Python dictionary. We will provide the number of nodes in each of the layers to initialise the model. The number of nodes in the hidden layer is one parameter we will need to decide upon, and in this case we are going to show the effect of the number of hidden nodes in the layer. Let us start with a hidden layer comprising 3 nodes.

We also need to decide the number of nodes in the hidden layer.

```
def init_model(input_layer=2, output_layer=2,\
               hidden_layer=3):
    np.random.seed(42)
    W1 = np.random.randn(input_layer,\
      hidden_layer) / np.sqrt(input_layer)
    b1 = np.zeros((1, hidden_layer))
    W2 = np.random.randn(hidden_layer,\
      output_layer) / np.sqrt(hidden_layer)
    b2 = np.zeros((1, output_layer))

    nn_params = {}
    nn_params = {'W1': W1, 'b1': b1, 'W2': W2,\
      'b2': b2}
    return nn_params
```

This function initialises our model.

Our model can be initialised as follows:

```
nn_model = init_model(input_layer,\
    output_layer, 3)
```

In this case we have a model with 3 nodes in the hidden layer.

With the help of Equations (4.6)-(4.9), we can write a function that implements the forward propagation step in our neural network. For the hidden layer we are using a hyperbolic tangent activation function. Since the output will be given in terms of probabilities for each of the two classes, we use the softmax activation function:

```
def forwardprop(nn_model, X):
    W1, b1, W2, b2=nn_model['W1'], nn_model['b1'],\
        nn_model['W2'], nn_model['b2']
    z1 = X.dot(W1) + b1
    a1 = np.tanh(z1)
    z2 = a1.dot(W2) + b2
    e_scores = np.exp(z2)
    prob = e_scores / np.sum(e_scores, axis=1,\
        keepdims=True)
    return prob
```

This function implements the feedforward step in our neural network. We are using a hyperbolic tangent as the activation function.

Once we have the forward propagation step, we need to evaluate the loss incurred, and therefore a function to this end is required. We will implement the cross-entropy loss function including a regularisation term as follows:

```
def loss_eval(nn_model, X, y, lambda_reg):
    W1, b1, W2, b2=nn_model['W1'], nn_model['b1'],\
        nn_model['W2'], nn_model['b2']
    prob = forwardprop(nn_model, X)
    logprobs = -np.log(prob[range(n_training), y])
    data_loss = np.sum(logprobs)
    data_loss+=lambda_reg/2 *\
        (np.sum(np.square(W1))+\
        np.sum(np.square(W2)))
    return data_loss * (1./n_training)
```

We evaluate the cross-entropy loss function with this implementation.

Now that we have an evaluation of the loss, we can start the backpropagation step with learning rate α. In this case we are making use of our formulation from Equations (4.35)-(4.38).

And now the backpropagation step.

Remember that we are seeking to update the parameters of the model, and thus we return a dictionary with the required information after the backpropagation step is completed. This in turn can be used as the input for the next forward propagation step:

Et voilà, the backpropagation implementation.

```
def backprop(nn_model, X, y, prob, alpha=0.01):
    W1, b1, W2, b2=nn_model['W1'], nn_model['b1'],\
        nn_model['W2'], nn_model['b2']
    z1 = X.dot(W1) + b1
    a1 = np.tanh(z1)
    delta2 = prob
    delta2[range(n_training), y] -= 1
    dW2 = (a1.T).dot(delta2)
    db2 = np.sum(delta2, axis=0, keepdims=True)
    delta1 = delta2.dot(W2.T)*(1-np.power(a1, 2))
    dW1 = np.dot(X.T, delta1)
    db1 = np.sum(delta1, axis=0)

    W1 += -alpha * dW1
    b1 += -alpha * db1
    W2 += -alpha * dW2
    b2 += -alpha * db2
    nn_model = {'W1': W1, 'b1': b1,\
        'W2': W2, 'b2': b2}
    return nn_model
```

In order to get a final prediction from the model, we implement a function for this purpose:

```
def predict(nn_model, x):
    prob = forwardprop(nn_model, x)

    return np.argmax(prob, axis=1)
```

We can obtain predictions with this piece of code.

With all the parts, we can build our neural network and implement a batch gradient descent for a chosen number of epochs:

```
def neural_net(X, y, input_layer, output_layer,\
  hidden_layer, alpha=0.01, lambda_reg=0.01,
  epochs=30000, print_loss=False):
    nn_model = init_model(input_layer,\
        output_layer, hidden_layer)

    for i in range(0, epochs):
        prob = forwardprop(nn_model, X)
        nn_model=backprop(nn_model, X, y,\
            prob, alpha)

        if print_loss and i % 1000==0:
            print('Epoch {0} loss: {1:.{2}f}'.\
                format(i, loss_eval(nn_model,\
                X, y, lambda_reg), 4))

  return nn_model
```

We can now put it all together in a batch gradient descent implementation.

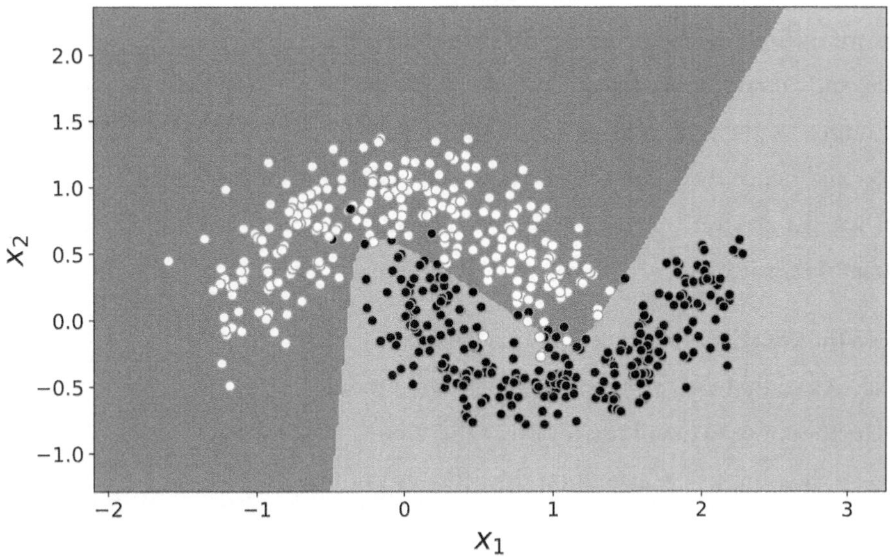

Figure 4.12: Classification boundary obtained with a 3-node hidden layer neural network. The discrimination is modelled well with a cubic-like function.

Let us train our neural network with a 3-node hidden layer:

```
nnet = neural_net(X, y, input_layer, output_layer,\
    3, alpha, lambda_reg, print_loss=True)


Epoch 0 loss: 0.4451
Epoch 1000 loss: 0.0942
...
Epoch 28000 loss: 0.0921
Epoch 29000 loss: 0.0922
```

A typical run of a neural net training provides information about the loss at the end of each epoch.

We can see the decision boundary obtained with this architecture in Figure 4.12 where we can see how the discrimination of the two classes is modelled with a cubic-like function.

It is now easy to implement a loop so that we investigate the effect that hidden layers of different sizes have in the predictions we make. Let us consider hidden layers with 1, 2, 3, 10, 30 and 50 nodes. We know that the larger the number of nodes in the hidden layer, the more complex the network, and hence the more complex the classification boundaries we can generate. This of course comes at the cost of potential overfitting.

Different hidden layer sizes provide different boundaries.

We will store the weights of each model in a dictionary called nn_models so that we can retrieve the chosen model with ease. Furthermore, we will make use of the time library to get a measure of the execution time for each of the architectures:

```
hidden_layers = [1, 2, 3, 10, 30, 50]


import time
nn_models = {}


for hidden_node in hidden_layers:
  print('{0}-node hidden layer'.\
    format(hidden_node))
  start = time.time()
  nn_models[str(hidden_node)] = neural_net(X, y,\
    input_layer, output_layer, hidden_node,
    alpha, lambda_reg)
  stop = time.time()
  d = stop-start
  print('Execution time: {0:.{1}f} sec'.\
    format(d, 2))
```

We can see the effect of various layer sizes. In this case, a layer with 1, 2, 3, 10, 30 and 50 nodes.

A typical run of the loop defined above would look similar to the following output:

```
1-node hidden layer
Execution time: 2.53 sec

2-node hidden layer
Execution time: 3.02 sec
...

50-node hidden layer
Execution time: 16.54 sec
```

Note that the times may vary from run to run and computer to computer.

Let us now write a function to create predictions with our neural network model:

```
def predict(nn_model, x):
    prob = forwardprop(nn_model, x)
    return np.argmax(prob, axis=1)
```

We need to be able to create predictions with our neural network model.

We can then use it as follows:

```
ypred = predict(nn_model, X)
```

In Figure 4.13 we can see some classification boundaries resulting from the code above. Notice that the neural network with 1 hidden node is effectively a linear classifier, not dissimilar to an implementation of logistic regression for example. The classification boundary is a straight line, and empirically we can see a number of misclassified data points.

A hidden layer with 1 node is as good as a linear classifier.

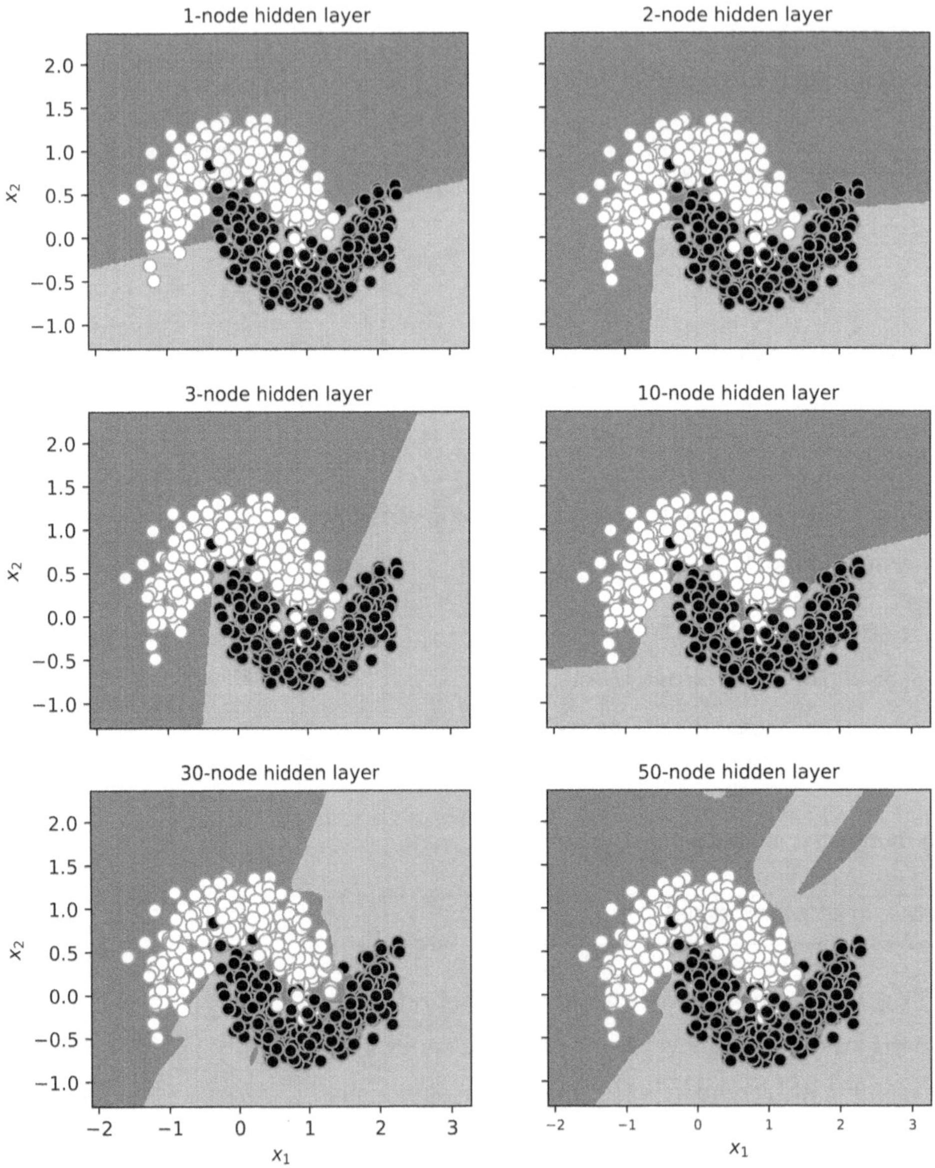

Figure 4.13: Classification boundaries for a neural network with one hidden layer comprising 1, 2, 3, 10, 30 and 50 hidden nodes.

As we move to 2 nodes we, start seeing the nonlinearity in the boundary. We had already seen the 3-node case in Figure 4.12, and it is great to see the result in context. By the time we reach 10 nodes, the boundary starts becoming more intricate. In the cases with 30 and 50 nodes the boundaries are increasingly curvier, trying to separate the two classes more and more. We can see the balancing act we need to perform between getting a good enough prediction and avoiding memorising our training dataset.

As we add more nodes, we get more intricate boundaries and separate our classes better. Beware overfitting though!

4.4 *Neural Networks and Deep Learning*

WE HAVE SUCCESSFULLY BUILT OUR first neural network from scratch, deserving a celebration worth remembering. Not only have we covered a lot of the foundational concepts in neural networks, but also we have paved the road to addressing useful extensions to those ideas. A case in point is the explosion in the use of deep learning and large language models for a variety of applications, from automatic machine translation, document summarisation, image and video creation to computer vision and even medical diagnosis.

Who's for fruit cake? Maybe two dozens fruit cakes, a dozen macaroons and some nice vanilla sponge would do for celebrations.

In Section 4.2.1 we first introduced the term *deep learning* in the context of explaining the layers and nodes inside a neural network. As we add more and more hidden layers to our network, with a larger and larger number of nodes we require for our inputs to flow deeper and deeper into the architecture we built. In that sense, we are moving from having 1, 2 or 3 hidden layers to having hundreds of them.

Deep learning refers to the use of large multi-layer networks.

A complex architecture like that is suitable to be used when having large sets of labelled data, with rich features and patterns to be learnt by the deep neural network.

Given their usefulness, deep neural networks have gathered a lot of attention, and constructing them in the way we did for our humble 1-layer network in the previous section is no longer feasible. Instead, there are a number of frameworks and libraries that make this task much easier and more understandable, as well as enabling us to make use of better implementations and the best in class in terms of hardware, such as graphics processing units (GPUs).

We need a better framework to build large networks.

A notable framework is Google's TensorFlow[16] with low-level implementations for deep learning and a low-level API. Modern research and industry are also turning to JAX[17] for high-performance scientific computing and model training, and to the Hugging Face Transformers library[18]as a cornerstone for pre-trained models across NLP, vision, and multimodal AI. For scaling very large models efficiently, DeepSpeed[19] offers memory optimisation and parallelism tools, while OpenVINO[20] provides deployment optimisation for edge and Intel hardware. Earlier frameworks such as Theano, CNTK, Caffe, and MXNet have been deprecated or largely superseded. I would not be surprised if some of the names mentioned above will also change in coming years. It is important to mention that in many cases some of these frameworks are not Python libraries *per se*; however, they do offer bindings into Python and suitable APIs, making things more approachable for us while keeping our programming language of choice.

[16] Abadi, M. et al. (2015). TensorFlow: Large-scale machine learning on heterogeneous systems. http://tensorflow.org/. Software available from tensorflow.org.

[17] JAX Authors (2024). JAX: High Performance Array Computing. `https://docs.jax.dev/en/latest/`. Accessed: 2025-09-22

[18] Wolf, T., L. Début, V. Sanh, J. Chaumond, C. Delangue, et al. (2020, October). Transformers: State-of-the-art natural language processing. In *Proceedings of the 2020 Conference on Empirical Methods in Natural Language Processing: System Demonstrations*, Online, pp. 38–45. Association for Computational Linguistics.

[19] Microsoft DeepSpeed Team (2025). Deepspeed documentation. `https://deepspeed.readthedocs.io/en/latest/`. Accessed: 2025-09-22

[20] Intel OpenVINO Team (2025). OpenVINO Documentation. `https://docs.openvino.ai/`. Accessed: 2025-09-22

As you can see, the ecosystem is a vast one, and there are many more tools out there than we would be able to cover in this book. All in all, we are interested in a framework that enables us to use some of the most up-to-date techniques in the deep learning arena, while keeping a high-level language interface. This will enable Jackalope data scientists like us to abstract some of the low-level implementations and use modular libraries to carry out deep learning tasks. For these reasons, we are going to cover the use of Keras in this book.

In this book we are going to concentrate on the use of Keras.

Keras[21] offers a high-level API written in Python supporting backends such as TensorFlow, PyTorch, JAX and OpenVINO. Keras enables experimentation and rapid prototyping, while keeping with the Pythonic philosophy of readability and user friendliness. It started life as part of the ONEIROS research effort. The name is the Greek word for "horn" (κὲρας) in reference to the Hellenic literary image of the gates of horn and ivory that distinguish between true (horn) and false (ivory) visions or dreams. Homer makes reference to these gates in the Odyssey[22], when Penelope herself is trying to decide whether her dream about her husband's return to Ithaca is but a false vision.

[21] Chollet, F. et al. (2015). Keras. `https://github.com/fchollet/keras`

ONEIROS stands for Open-ended Neuro-Electronic Intelligent Robot Operating System.

[22] Fagles, R. (1997). *The Odyssey*. A Penguin Book. Penguin Books.

In any event, Keras is a modular library that enables us to put together deep neural networks using a high-level syntax making it ideal for our purposes. It enables millions of users to build and train models for NLP, computer vision, audio processing, recommendation systems, etc. In this book we will make use of the TensorFlow backend, but other options are possible as we mentioned above. Keras

Here, we will use a TensorFlow backend.

enables us to build sequential networks, i.e., where the flow of information moves forward in a linear way as we have described in the previous sections. Similarly, it also lets us construct graph-based networks with the help of a functional API. With it, we can let inputs "jump" to specific layers and obtain more complex network architectures as a result.

Keras is flexible enough to let us build complex networks easily.

For us to be able to use Keras with TensorFlow, we will need to make appropriate installations in our machines. We are assuming that we are working with Anaconda and creating a conda environment is probably the best option. You can try something like this:

Please make sure you check the documentation for your own system requirements.

```
> conda create -n tfenv pandas scikit-learn
    jupyter matplotlib
```

Remember to activate your environment (in this case called `tfenv`) every time you need to use Keras:

```
> conda activate tfenv


(tfenv)
> pip install tensorflow
> pip install keras
```

We are assuming the use of conda. Other virtual environments can also be used.

You can also consider installing other libraries to make your workflow better for you. Let us recreate with Keras the neural network architecture we built in Section 4.3.4. We will use the sequential API to create a layer-by-layer model, and as usual we will import some useful libraries first:

```
import pandas as pd
import tensorflow as tf
import keras
from keras.utils import to_categorical
from keras.models import Sequential
```

We will be using the sequential API.

We know why we require the first three import statements above; as for the fourth one, we will use this to wrangle our data so that we can transform our output into categorical data. The last import statement enables us to use the sequential API in Keras.

We will treat this example as a categorical classification problem.

We instantiate a sequential model as follows:

```
model = keras.Sequential()
```

We need to instantiate our model.

Now that we have an instance of our model, we can proceed to the creation of each of the layers in our network. Keras offers different types of layers, and one of the most common is the dense layer. It is a layer where all the nodes have edges to the previous layer. We need to provide the number of units (i.e., nodes) that this layer must have. Since this is our first hidden layer, we pass an argument to tell it how many nodes are in the input layer. We can do this with a shape tuple called `input_shape`, or for layers such as dense ones we can use a parameter called `input_dim`. We also need to specify the activation function that will be used at this point of the neural network architecture. This is how we do this:

A dense layer is a fully connected layer.

```
hnodes = 3
hidden_layer = keras.layers.Dense(units=hnodes,
  input_shape=(2, ), activation='tanh')
```

Our hidden layer.

In this case we are creating a hidden layer with 3 hidden nodes, the input layer has 2 entries and the activation function is the hyperbolic tangent. We can see how easy it would be to change the number of hidden nodes in this case. Notice that we did not have to declare explicitly the existence of an input layer. We simply provide information about its shape or dimensions. It is important to mention that `input_shape` tells the first layer of our model what shape to expect for each input sample (not counting the batch size). In the case above, each sample is a 1D vector of length 2. Internally, Keras uses this information to build the weight matrices for the first layer. Note that this is needed for the first layer of a sequential model because Keras needs to know what to connect. Otherwise, it cannot initialise the layer weights. For subsequent layers, Keras can infer their input shapes from the output shape of the previous layer.

This is only possible for Sequential models.

In other words, how many input weights to create per neuron.

The next layer in our architecture is the output layer, so let us declare it in Keras:

```
output_layer = keras.layers.Dense(units=2,
  activation='softmax')
```

And our output layer.

In this case we have an output layer with two nodes, and the activation function applied is a softmax function. Notice that we do not have to declare explicitly the shape of the input received by this layer. It is implied by the sequencing of layers once we "stitch" them together. Let us do that:

```
model.add(hidden_layer)
model.add(output_layer)
```

Remember that the order in which you add the layers is important.

We simply use the `add` method of the sequential model to add the layers in the order they go in the architecture.

Usually when training a neural network model, it is useful to lower the learning rate as the training process takes place. In Keras we can do this with the help of a learning rate schedule. Let us create an exponential decay schedule as follows:

```
from tensorflow.keras.optimizers.schedules\
  import ExponentialDecay

schedule = ExponentialDecay(
    initial_learning_rate=0.01, decay_steps=100000,
    decay_rate=0.96, staircase=True)
```

This is a learning rate schedule that uses an exponential decay function.

The arguments of `ExponentialDecay` control how the learning rate decreases as training progresses. The `initial_learning_rate`, *irl* sets the starting value before any decay is applied. The `decay_steps` parameter determines how often the rate should drop. The learning rate decays once every `decay_steps` training steps. The `decay_rate` specifies the factor by which the learning rate is multiplied at each decay point, so values less than 1 gradually reduce it. If `staircase=False`, the decay is applied smoothly as a continuous exponential function of `step/decay_steps`; if `staircase=True`, the decay happens in

Keras lets us control how the learning rate decreases as training progresses.

discrete jumps at multiples of decay_steps. The decayed learning rate, *dlr*, is essentially given by:

$$dlr = (irl)\,(\texttt{decay\_rate})^{\left(\frac{\texttt{step}}{\texttt{decay\_steps}}\right)}, \qquad (4.39)$$

The decayed learning rate (dlr) is a function of the initial learning rate (ilr) and the decay rate and the decay steps.

which steadily reduces the learning rate over time.

We now need to decide on the optimisation algorithm that we are going to use in our neural network. Keras offers a variety of them including stochastic gradient descent (SGD), Adagrad, RMSprop or Adaptive Moment Estimation (Adam)[23] . In this case we will use SGD in conjunction with our learning rate schedule above:

[23] Kingma, D. P. and J. Ba (2014). Adam: A method for stochastic optimization. arxXiv:1412.6980. Comment: Published as a conference paper at the 3rd International Conference for Learning Representations, San Diego, 2015.

```
sgd = keras.optimizers.SGD(
  learning_rate=schedule, momentum=0.9,
  nesterov=True)
```

where momentum is a parameter that encourages the algorithm to move in the direction of descent and is related to the velocity of descent:

$$\texttt{v} := \texttt{momentum} * \texttt{m} - \texttt{learning\_rate} * \texttt{g}, \qquad (4.40)$$

The momentum is related to the velocity of descent.

where m is the previous weight update, and g is the current gradient with respect to parameter p. We can use this velocity to calculate the new value of p:

$$\texttt{p}_{new} = \begin{cases} \texttt{p} + \texttt{v}, \text{ if } \texttt{nesterov} == \texttt{False}, \\ \texttt{p} + \texttt{momentum} * \texttt{v} - \texttt{learning\_rate} * \texttt{g}, \\ \quad \text{otherwise.} \end{cases} \qquad (4.41)$$

If you are interested in reading more about Nesterov momentum, take a look at the paper by Sutskever et al.[24] where a good description of initialisation and momentum is presented.

[24] Sutskever, I., J. Martens, G. Dahl, and G. Hinton (2013, 17–19 Jun). On the importance of initialization and momentum in deep learning. In S. Dasgupta and D. McAllester (Eds.), *Proceedings of the 30th International Conference on Machine Learning*, Volume 28 of *Proceedings of Machine Learning Research*, Atlanta, Georgia, USA, pp. 1139–1147. PMLR.

We now need to compile our model, this step configures the learning process for our neural network architecture. We need to provide three arguments to the `compile` method: The optimisation algorithm to be used, the loss function to be optimised, and a list of metrics:

```
model.compile(optimizer=sgd,
    loss='categorical_crossentropy',
    metrics=['accuracy'])
```

In this case we are using the stochastic gradient descent algorithm we instantiated above; the loss function is for categorical cross-entropy as we are trying to distinguish between two classes.

We compile our model to use stochastic gradient descent.

We are finally in a position to start the learning process with the aid of the `fit` method, but before we do that let us make a couple of manipulations to the input data. Remember that we read our data from a pandas dataframe as follows:

```
df = pd.read_csv('neuralnet_dataset.csv')
X = df[['x1', 'x2']].values
y = df['label'].values
```

We use pandas to read our data. Other methods can also be used.

We will convert the labels in the y vector into a binary class matrix to be used with the categorical cross-entropy cost function:

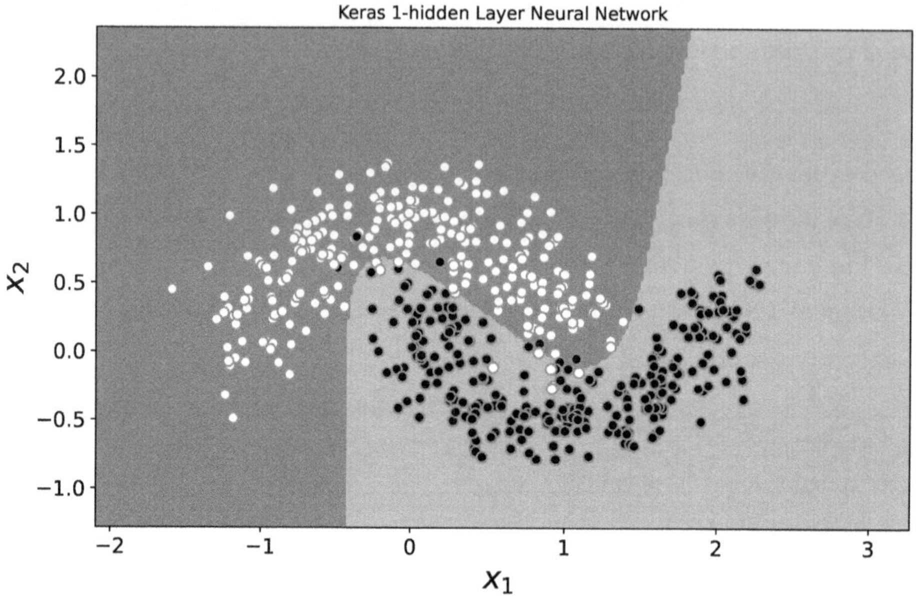

Figure 4.14: Classification boundary obtained with a sequential model for a neural network implemented in Keras.

```
y = np_utils.to_categorical(y)
```

and now we fit our model:

```
model.fit(X, y, batch_size=100, epochs=5000,
  verbose=0)
```

We converted the target labels into categorical variables, finally, we train our model.

Notice that we can change the batch size and the number of epochs directly in the `fit` method. You can see how the learning progresses with `verbose=1`. The result of our learning process can be seen in Figure 4.14.

We can customise the batch size and epochs when fitting the model.

We can look at a summary of the architecture we just created as follows:

```
> model.summary()


Model: "sequential"
Layer (type)          Output Shape          Param #
=====================================================
dense (Dense)         (None, 3)             9
dense_1 (Dense)       (None, 2)             8
=====================================================
Total params: 35 (144.00 B)
Trainable params: 17 (68.00 B)
Non-trainable params: 0 (0.00 B)
Optimizer params: 18 (76.00 B)
```

We can see the layers created and the number of parameters to learn.

As we can see, there are 2 dense layers, one with 3 nodes and one with 2. There are thus 17 parameters that need to be fitted in this model. We can also see the number of parameters for the optimiser, in this case 18, making the total of parameters equal to 35. We are able to see the 17 weights obtained with the `get_weights` method:

```
> model.get_weights()


[array([[-3.828975  , -1.7090695 ,  2.818843  ],
        [ 0.6450384 , -2.0851789 ,  0.02288325]],
        dtype=float32),
array([5.379173 , 1.6936812, 1.4065304],
        dtype=float32),
array([[ 4.086628 , -5.372559 ],
        [-3.7643743,  4.1487727],
        [-3.8150563,  3.2673843]], dtype=float32),
```

The weights are readily available to us. Beware their numbers for deep networks.

```
array([-0.08712076,  0.0871227 ],
dtype=float32)]
```

Please note that the weights you obtain in your machine may vary from the ones shown above; after all we are relying on different starting points. Finally, remember that you should apply best practices in your work by splitting your data into training and testing. You can also apply cross-validation while finding the best hyperparameters for your
model.

Remember to apply best practices, and split your data into training and testing datasets.

We can see how the use of a high-level framework like Keras enables us to implement neural network architectures in an easy and friendly way. This opens up the opportunities to build more complex networks such as convolutional and recurrent neural networks. Let us take a
look.

4.4.1 *Convolutional Neural Networks*

A CONVOLUTIONAL NEURAL NETWORK IS a type of artificial neutral network that relies on convolution to learn patterns in the training data provided. The architecture—including input, hidden and output layers—is the same as we have discussed above. The main difference is the fact that the hidden layers use more than a simple activation function; they also convolve their input with a filter or kernel. Convolution is a mathematical operation that combines two functions by flipping, shifting, and multiplying them to

CNN for short. Not to be confused with a certain news organisation!

Think of convolution as sliding one function over another to see how much they overlap at each point.

produce a third function that shows how one modifies or "blends" into the other. CNNs have been gaining traction in applications such as image processing and computer vision for example.

Many image editing tools make use of convolution to apply different filters to a picture. Different kernels result in blurring, sharpening or detecting edges in the image. For example an identity kernel can help scale a picture down, while sharper images can result from the application of a sharpening kernel such as:

An identity kernel is given by
$$I = \begin{bmatrix} 0 & 0 & 0 \\ 0 & 1 & 0 \\ 0 & 0 & 0 \end{bmatrix}.$$

$$F_s = \begin{bmatrix} 0 & -1 & 0 \\ -1 & 5 & -1 \\ 0 & -1 & 0 \end{bmatrix}. \tag{4.42}$$

Consider the image of a (pixelated) letter J as shown on the left-hand side of Figure 4.15. The application of an identity kernel to this image results in a smaller one. The convolution of the original picture with the kernel chosen requires the element-wise multiplication of a portion of the image of equal size as the kernel. We then add up all the product outputs as the result, which we show on the right-hand side of Figure 4.15.

Convolution requires element-wise multiplication of image portions of the same size as the kernel applied.

The application of the filter is done as if we were scanning the original image, moving the filter by a stride S. Think of the filter as a torch that is used to illuminate portions of the image as we move across it, letting us concentrate on the details highlighted by the torch's light. In our example above, for a stride $S = 1$ we go from an image of 11×8 to a scaled image of 9×6. If you want to avoid the scaling down, you can apply **padding** to the image with zeros. You

Think of the convolution operation as a torch that scans the image to highlight details.

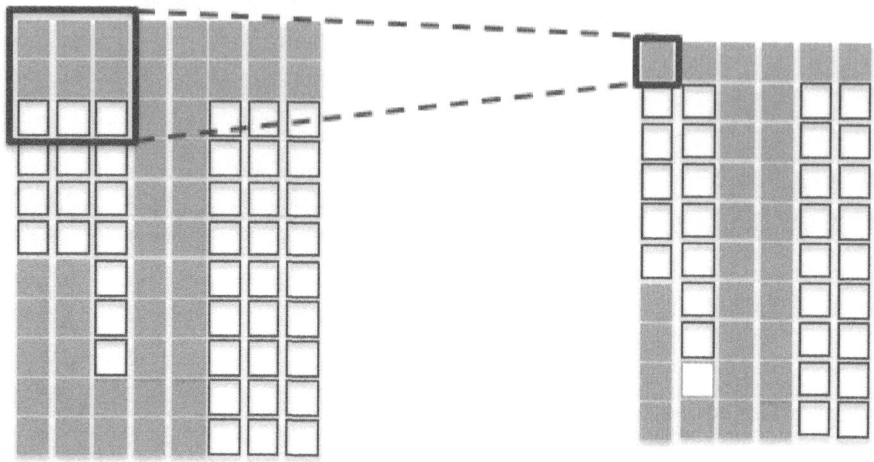

Figure 4.15: An image of a letter J (on the left). After applying an identity kernel, the result is a scaled-down version of the image (on the right).

can determine the size of the final figure with the following formula:

$$\text{output\_side} = 1 + \frac{1}{S}(\text{input\_side} + \text{kernel\_side} + 2(\text{padding})) \,. \quad (4.43)$$

Let us take a look at a more realistic image manipulation. In Figure 4.16 we can see the result of applying the sharpening filter of Equation (4.42) to the image of a Jackalope icon. Let

us take a look at what is happening with a portion of the image. Here are is a 5×5 patch of the image:

$$P = \begin{bmatrix} 0 & 1 & 1 & 1 & 1 \\ 0 & 0 & 1 & 1 & 1 \\ 0 & 0 & 1 & 1 & 1 \\ 0 & 0 & 1 & 1 & 1 \\ 0 & 0 & 1 & 1 & 1 \end{bmatrix} . \quad (4.44)$$

We have chosen a portion containing an edge, 0 being blank and 1 black pixels.

Figure 4.16: An image of a Jackalope icon (on the left). After applying a sharpening filter, we obtain the image on the right.

The convolution of patch P with the filter F_s is given by:

$$P \circledast F_S = \begin{bmatrix} -2 & 2 & 1 \\ -1 & 2 & 1 \\ -1 & 2 & 1 \end{bmatrix}, \qquad (4.45)$$

This is the result of convolving a 3×3 filter with a 5×5 image portion.

where $\circledast$ denotes the convolution operation, and the first element of the result is given by $(0)(0) + (1)(-1) + (1)(0) + (0)(-1) + (0)(5) + (1)(-1) + (0)(0) + (0)(-1) + (1)(0) = -2$. Think of this as a "piece-wise" matrix multiplication, where we select the right-sized piece to multiply with the filter, then we move to the next piece.

The same sort of calculation is done for each of the entries in the given patch. For a colour image, we have red, blue, green and transparency channels and the convolution

The same operation will have to be applied to each layer of the image.

has to be done for each layer. The output channel of the convolution is called a **feature map**, and it encodes the degree of presence of the feature detected.

Once the convolution is completed, it is possible to apply an operation to further reduce the size of the image and make the whole process more manageable. One such operation is **pooling**: Given an $n \times n$ pooling window, we keep only the maximum value in the window. This is called *max-pooling*. Another option could be to obtain the average, and this is called *average-pooling*. In the example above, max-pooling on a 2×2 window will result in:

Pooling is a down-sampling process that reduces the size of our matrices.

$$\text{max\_pooling}(P \circledast F_S) = \begin{bmatrix} 2 & 2 \\ 2 & 2 \end{bmatrix}. \qquad (4.46)$$

The operations outlined above will need us to sweep the entire image with our filter. The result is a filtered image with the resolution given by the formula shown in Equation (4.43).

Remember the analogy of using a torch.

So far so good, but... what is the relationship with neural networks? Well, if we use various filters that detect different features such as vertical and horizontal edges, curved features, etc. we can use the results to determine, for example, the presence of objects. In practice, a CNN learns these feature maps as the training process is executed. A typical architecture for a CNN is shown in Figure 4.17.

This is useful in computer vision problems.

The setup involves the use of one or more convolutional layers with pooling and a ReLU activation, followed by

Or other activation functions.

a **flattening** layer. Flattening enables us to convert our 2D matrices into a column vector ready to be used in a dense layer. Sometimes, it is useful to drop a random set of activations forcing the network to generalise better. These layers are referred to as **dropout** layers.

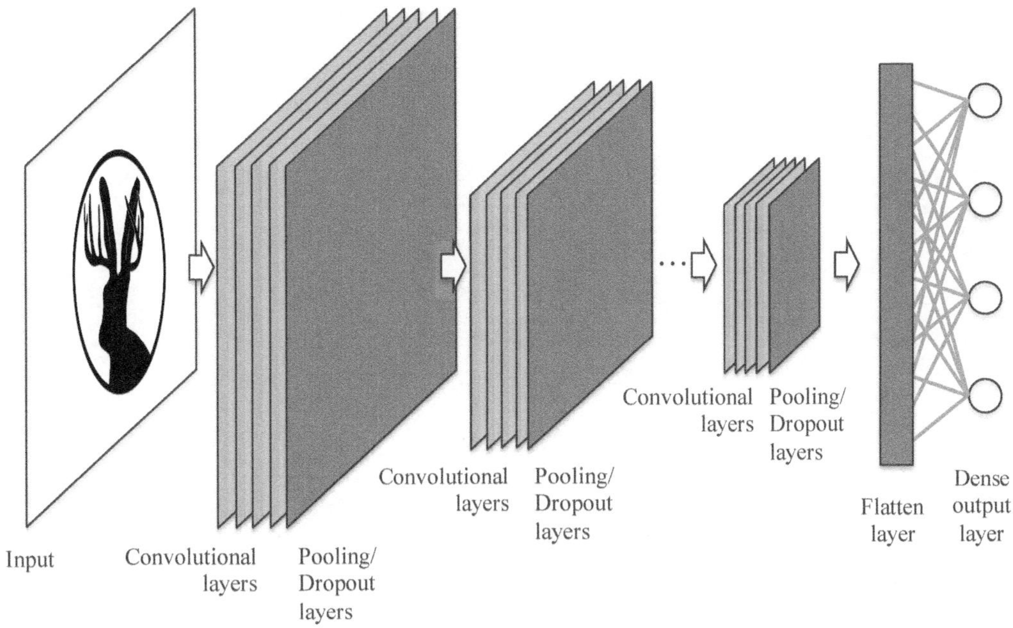

Figure 4.17: Architecture of a convolutional neural network.

4.4.2 *Convolutional Neural Networks in Action*

LET US CREATE A NEURAL network classifier for images based on the CIFAR-10 dataset[25]. The dataset contains 60,000 images with 32×32 resolution. They are divided into 10 balanced classes. The dataset is split into 50,000 training images and 10,000 testing ones. The ten classes in the dataset are: Airplane, automobile, bird, cat, deer, dog, frog, horse, ship and truck. An example for each of the

[25] Krizhevsky, A. (2009). Learning multiple layers of features from tiny images. Technical Report TR-2009, University of Toronto, Toronto.

classes is shown in Figure 4.18. Let us define a list with the classes:

```
class_names = ['airplane','automobile','bird',
  'cat','deer','dog', 'frog','horse','ship',
  'truck']
```

We will use this list to make human-readable predictions later on.

Figure 4.18: Example images for each of the 10 classes in the CIFAR-10 dataset. The pixelation is the result of the images being 32×32.

The dataset is included with Keras and can be imported as follows:

```
from keras.datasets import cifar10
(X_tr, y_tr), (X_tst, y_tst) = cifar10.load_data()
```

The images are stored as integer numpy arrays. In order to ensure their correct manipulation, we will normalise our data. First we will cast the arrays as float.

Please note that the data will need to be downloaded the first time you use the dataset. This may take some time.

```
X_train = X_tr.astype('float32')
X_test = X_tst.astype('float32')
```

We will then calculate a mean and standard deviation and apply it to the data:

```
mean = np.mean(X_train,axis=(0,1,2,3))
std = np.std(X_train,axis=(0,1,2,3))
X_train = (X_train-mean)/(std+1e-7)
X_test = (X_test-mean)/(std+1e-7)
```

We obtain the mean and standard deviation to normalise our data.

In order to use categorical cross-entropy as our loss function, we will use one-hot encoding to get suitable classes for our task. We will have to specify the number of classes in our dataset so that we have the appropriate number of nodes in the output layer:

```
from tensorflow.keras.utils import to_categorical
y_train = to_categorical(y_tr)
y_test = to_categorical(y_tst)
num_classes = y_train.shape[1]
```

In this way we ensure the labels are categorical variables.

We are going to build our convolutional neural network using the Keras functional API. Let us import some useful libraries first:

```
import numpy as np
import keras
from tensorflow.keras.models import Model
from tensorflow.keras.layers import Dense, \
  Activation, Flatten, Dropout, Input, \
  BatchNormalization
from tensorflow.keras.layers import Conv2D, \
  MaxPooling2D
from tensorflow.keras import regularizers
from tensorflow.keras.optimizers import RMSprop
from tensorflow.keras.callbacks import \
  LearningRateScheduler
from tensorflow.keras.preprocessing.image import \
  ImageDataGenerator
```

We import a number of useful libraries from Keras.

We can see some familiar words such as `Dense` and `Flatten`. As for others, they tend to do what they describe: Convolutional layers can be defined with `Conv2D`, and max-pooling can be achieved with `MaxPooling2D`. For others, we will provide explanations as we use them.

`Conv2D` implements a convolutional layer.

When using the functional API, we must define an input layer explicitly with a shape argument determining the dimensionality of the training data. In this case we have images of size $32 \times 32 \times 3$.

Remember that we have 3 channels in the images.

```
in_layer = Input(shape=(32, 32, 3))
```

The layers are connected pairwise, and the connection specifies the source of the input as given by the arrangement in our architecture. We explicitly name the inputting layer

We explicitly name the inputting layer in parentheses.

in parentheses after the desired connecting layer. It is easier when we see it; let us create a first convolutional layer taking input from in_layer defined above:

```
weight_decay=1e-4
conv1 = Conv2D(32, kernel_size=(3, 3),\
    activation='relu', padding='same',\
    kernel_regularizer=\
    regularizers.l2(weight_decay))(in_layer)
```

We define a convolutional layer with Conv2D.

Our convolutional layer takes first the number of filters to be learnt. This represents the dimensionality of the output space for the layer. In this case we request 32 filters. kernel_size specifies the window size for the convolution. The activation function applied to the layer is specified with activation, and in this case we are using a ReLU function. It is possible to apply padding; here we request for the output to be the same size as the input. We also apply a penalty to the parameters of this layer, in this case an $L2$ penalty with a weight decay of 1×10^{-4}. Finally, we can see that in_layer is the input for this convolutional layer. The next step in our architecture is the application of a normalisation[26] transformation maintaining the mean activation close to 0 and its standard deviation near 1.

The kernel_size is a tuple defining height and width of the window.

Other padding options include valid and casual.

[26] Ioffe, S. and C. Szegedy (2015). Batch normalization: Accelerating deep network training by reducing internal covariate shift. *CoRR abs/1502.03167*.

```
batchn1 = BatchNormalization()(conv1)
```

We apply another combination of a convolution layer and batch normalisation:

```
conv2 = Conv2D(32, (3, 3), activation='relu',\
    padding='same', kernel_regularizer\
    = regularizers.l2(weight_decay))(batchn1)
batchn2 = BatchNormalization()(conv2)
```

We can easily add more layers to our architecture.

Our next layer is a pooling layer. `MaxPooling2D` takes an argument defining the pooling window size:

```
pool1 = MaxPooling2D(pool_size=(2,2))(batchn2)
```

We define a pooling layer with `MaxPooling2D`.

As we can see, the input for this layer is given by the `batchn2` layer. In order to help with generalisation, we will now set a random fraction of the input units to 0:

In this case we drop out 20%.

```
drop1 = Dropout(0.2)(pool1)
```

We are getting the hang of this. We will add a few more convolution layers together with batch normalisation, pooling and dropout. Here, we will be requesting 64 filters in each of the next two convolution layers, followed by two more with 128 filters, with dropouts of 30% and 40%, respectively:

```
conv3 = Conv2D(64, (3, 3), activation='relu',\
    padding='same', kernel_regularizer\
    =regularizers.l2(weight_decay))(drop1)
batchn3 = BatchNormalization()(conv3)
conv4 = Conv2D(64, (3, 3), activation='relu',\
    padding='same', kernel_regularizer=\
    regularizers.l2(weight_decay))(batchn3)
```

We are adding layer upon layer to our convolutional neural network.

```
batchn4 = BatchNormalization()(conv4)
pool2 = MaxPooling2D(pool_size=(2,2))(batchn4)
drop2 = Dropout(0.3)(pool2)
conv5 = Conv2D(128, (3, 3), activation='relu',\
    padding='same', kernel_regularizer=\
    regularizers.l2(weight_decay))(drop2)
batchn5 = BatchNormalization()(conv5)
conv6 = Conv2D(128, (3, 3), activation='relu',\
    padding='same', kernel_regularizer=\
    regularizers.l2(weight_decay))(batchn5)
batchn6 = BatchNormalization()(conv6)
pool3 = MaxPooling2D(pool_size=(2,2))(batchn6)
drop3 = Dropout(0.4)(pool3)
```

We have convolutional, batch normalisation and pooling layers, one after the next.

We can add as many convolutional layers as we desire, and remember that as you add more, the number of parameters to be fitted grows too. Let us flatten the input up until now, and add a dense layer.

```
flat = Flatten()(drop3)
dense1 = Dense(num_classes,\
  activation='softmax')(flat)
```

Finally, we connect to a dense output layer.

We can now stitch our model together:

```
model = Model(inputs=in_layer, outputs=dense1)
```

Note that the output layer has `num_classes=10` nodes, one for each class in our training data, and the activation function is a softmax function. We can see the final version of our architecture with the summary:

We can see the different layers in our CNN, and the number of parameters to learn.

```
> model.summary()

________________________________________________________________
Layer (type)              Output Shape            Param #
================================================================
input_layer (InputLayer) (None, 32, 32, 3)    0
conv2d (Conv2D)          (None, 32, 32, 32)  896
batch_normalization      (None, 32, 32, 32)  128
conv2d_1 (Conv2D)        (None, 32, 32, 32)  9248
batch_normalization_1    (None, 32, 32, 32)  128
max_pooling2d (Max       (None, 16, 16, 32)  0
dropout (Dropout)        (None, 16, 16, 32)  0
conv2d_2 (Conv2D)        (None, 16, 16, 64)  18496
batch_normalization_2    (None, 16, 16, 64)  256
conv2d_3 (Conv2D)        (None, 16, 16, 64)  36928
batch_normalization_3    (None, 16, 16, 64)  256
max_pooling2d_1 (MaxP    (None, 8, 8, 64)    0
dropout_1 (Dropout)      (None, 8, 8, 64)    0
conv2d_4 (Conv2D)        (None, 8, 8, 128)   73856
batch_normalization_4    (None, 8, 8, 128)   512
conv2d_5 (Conv2D)        (None, 8, 8, 128)   147584
batch_normalization_5    (None, 8, 8, 128)   512
max_pooling2d_2 (MaxP    (None, 4, 4, 128)   0
dropout_2 (Dropout)      (None, 4, 4, 128)   0
flatten (Flatten)        (None, 2048)        0
dense (Dense)            (None, 10)          20490
================================================================
Total params: 309,290 (1.18 MB)
Trainable params: 308,394 (1.18 MB)
Non-trainable params: 896 (3.5 MB)
```

In this case we have 308,394 parameters to train.

This model has a total of 309, 290 parameters, of which we need to train 308, 394. Let us now compile our model. We define a batch size of 64 and use an RMS optimiser:

```
batch_size = 64
opt_rms = RMSprop(learning_rate=0.001)
model.compile(loss='categorical_crossentropy',
  optimizer=opt_rms, metrics=['accuracy'])
```

Do not forget to compile the model before training.

We can define a schedule for the learning rate: As the number of epochs increases, our learning rate gets smaller.

```
def lr_schedule(epoch):
    if epoch>100:
        lrate = 0.0003
    elif 75 < epoch <= 100:
        lrate = 0.0005
    else:
        lrate = 0.001
    return lrate
```

As training goes on, we make our learning rate smaller.

This is a custom schedule, and we can use other learning schedules as shown in the previous section.

We will also use Keras to augment our data by making transformations to the inputs; we will use the `ImageDataGenerator` function to create modifications enabling for rotation of the image, height and width shifts and even horizontal flips:

Keras can help us augment our data.

```
datagen = ImageDataGenerator(
  rotation_range=15, width_shift_range=0.1,
  height_shift_range=0.1, horizontal_flip=True)

datagen.fit(X_train)
```

ImageDataGenerator generates new images by applying transformations to our data.

We are ready to fit our model: Keras enables us to fit the model on batches with real-time data augmentation through the `fit` method for the model, and the `flow` method for the data augmentation.

```
history = model.fit(
  datagen.flow(X_train, y_train,
    batch_size=batch_size),
  steps_per_epoch=X_train.shape[0] // batch_size,
  epochs=125,
  verbose=1,
  validation_data=(X_test, y_test),
  callbacks=[LearningRateScheduler(lr_schedule)]
)
```

Please note that this step may take several hours, depending on the computer architecture you use.

We can evaluate the model on the test data as follows:

```
> scores = model.evaluate(X_test, y_test,\
  batch_size=128, verbose=1)
> print('Evaluation result: {0:.2f}, Loss:\
  {1:.2f}'.format(scores[1]*100, scores[0]))

Evaluation result: 87.94, Loss: 0.48
```

Evaluating our model is very easy.

Let us pick 10 images at random to create predictions for them:

```
import numpy as np


ixs = np.random.choice(X_test.shape[0],
  size=10, replace=False)
sub_X_test = X_test[ixs]
```

Using the good old `random.choice` method.

First let us look at the indices of the pictures:

```
> print(ixs)


[8203 6614 4601  414 9480
9850 3121  103  865 8574
```

In case you want to check the labels predicted...

For the pictures chosen randomly, the prediction can be calculated as:

Our model can now be used to predict the class of a given image.

```
preds = model.predict(sub_X_test)
mypred = np.argmax(preds, axis=1)
```

In the first line above we are obtaining the predictions for the batch, and in the second one we convert to class indices. The predicted classes are:

```
> print([class_names[x] for x in mypred])


['cat', 'dog', 'bird', 'automobile', 'bird',
'deer', 'truck', 'frog', 'automobile', 'deer']
```

We are able to compare the labels predicted with the actual ones.

The actual labels can be retrieved as follows:

```
> print([class_names[y_tst[i][0]] for i in ixs])

['cat', 'dog', 'bird', 'automobile', 'bird',
'horse', 'truck', 'cat', 'automobile', 'deer']
```

You may want to use something like a confusion matrix instead.

Finally, let us make a prediction with a totally new image. Let us try the picture shown in Figure 4.19 saved into a file called picbo001.jpg. First we will need to read the image and ensure that it has the right dimensions:

You can also make predictions for images not in the dataset!

```
import matplotlib.image as mpimg
from skimage.transform import resize

img=mpimg.imread('picbo001.jpg')
img_resized = resize(img, (32, 32),\
    anti_aliasing=True)
```

This code requires the installation of scikit-image.

In this case, the resized image has values between 0 and 1. We will therefore multiply the image by 255 to apply the normalisation used for the training images:

We need to ensure the image has the right dimensions and range of values.

```
img_resized = (img_resized*255-mean)/(std+1e-7)
proc_img = img_resized.reshape((1,) +\
  img_resized.shape)
```

The last step is needed so that the image has dimensions $(1, 32, 32, 3)$ as expected by the model. Finally we can make our prediction:

Figure 4.19: A picture of a nice feline friend to test our convolutional neural network.

```
> pr = model.predict(proc_img)
> pr_label = np.argmax(pr, axis=1)[0]
> print('The image has a {0}'.format(\
  class_names[pr_label]))

The image has a cat
```

Indeed, the convolutional neural network can see our feline friend and tell us about it!

Et voilà, we have an image classifier from a convolutional neural network ready to be used.

4.5 *Reinforcement Learning: Learning by Reward and Regret*

IF SUPERVISED AND UNSUPERVISED LEARNING are two sides of the same coin, then *Reinforcement Learning* (RL) is the moment the coin decides to roll off the table and learn how to bounce. At its heart, RL is about an *agent* interacting with an *environment*, taking actions and receiving feedback in the form of *rewards*. Over time, the agent learns a policy that maximises its expected cumulative reward. Think of it as a game of chess where the agent improves by playing countless rounds against itself, gradually learning what works. In this context, an agent is the decision-maker. In other words, it is the thing that *learns* and chooses an action at each timestep. The environment is everything the agent interacts with. It is the "world" around the agent giving it a state, a response to its actions and hence produces the next state. The reward is the feedback signal that tells the agent how well, or not, it is doing. Consider a self-driving vacuum cleaner as an example:

Yes, this one learns through trial and error. Literally.

Not only what works, but also what really, really does not.

Think of agent, environment, and reward as the holy trinity in RL.

- Environment: House with rooms, carpets, dust, etc.
- Agent: The vacuum's navigation and decision module.
- Reward: Different actions are assigned values to reward (or punish) the vacuum cleaner, for example:
  - $+1$ for collecting dust
  - -5 for hitting a wall
  - $+20$ for cleaning a room completely

A self-driving vacuum cleaner as an example. The agent's job is to learn to maximise cleaning while minimising chaos!

Reinforcement Learning problems are often modelled as a *Markov Decision Process* (MDP)[27], represented by the tuple (S, A, R, P, γ) where:

[27] Puterman, M. L. (1994). *Markov Decision Processes: Discrete Stochastic Dynamic Programming*. John Wiley & Sons.

- S is the set of states of the environment,
- A is the set of possible actions,
- R is the reward function,
- P is the transition probability between states, and
- γ is the discount factor determining how much future rewards matter.

Teenagers, for example, tend to operate with a discount factor very close to zero.

Given a state s of the environment at a given time and an action a taken by the agent at state s, we have the goal of finding a policy $\pi(a|s)$ that maximises the expected return:

$$G_t = \mathbb{E}_\pi \left[\sum_{k=0}^{\infty} \gamma^k R_{t+k+1} \right]. \tag{4.47}$$

Reinforcement Learning is therefore a computational framework in which an autonomous decision-maker learns to act by interacting with its surroundings. Unlike supervised learning, where each input comes lovingly labelled with the correct answer, RL must operate in a world that does not provide such luxuries. Instead, it relies on experience, exploration, and feedback, much like an energetic toddler learning not to touch hot stoves.

Reinforcement Learning relies on experience, exploration, and feedback.

In essence, RL consists of an agent learning to maximise a notion of cumulative reward by taking actions in an environment. Each timestep follows the same loop: The environment presents a state s_t; the agent chooses an action a_t; the environment transitions to a new state s_{t+1} and returns a reward r_t. The agent's challenge is to discover a policy that leads to the greatest expected long-term return.

Every Reinforcement Learning system implements some variant of that learning loop:

```
initialise agent
repeat:
    observe state s_t
    select action a_t
    send action to environment
    receive (s_{t+1}, r_t)
    store or process experience
    update policy/value network
until convergence or budget exceeded
```

We can see a schematic representation of the loop in Figure 4.20. In more advanced setups, this loop may be distributed across multiple parallel actors (collecting data), one or more learners (updating networks), or replay servers (storing transitions).

The RL loop can be made more advanced if required, but the same essence remains.

To guide learning, we define value functions, i.e., quantities estimating how good it is to be in a state, or to take an action under a given policy. These can be:

- Action value (Q-function):

$$Q^{\pi}(s,a) = \mathbb{E}_{\pi}\left[G_t \mid s_t = s, a_t = a\right]. \qquad (4.48)$$

Value functions for actions or states support the learning for RL systems.

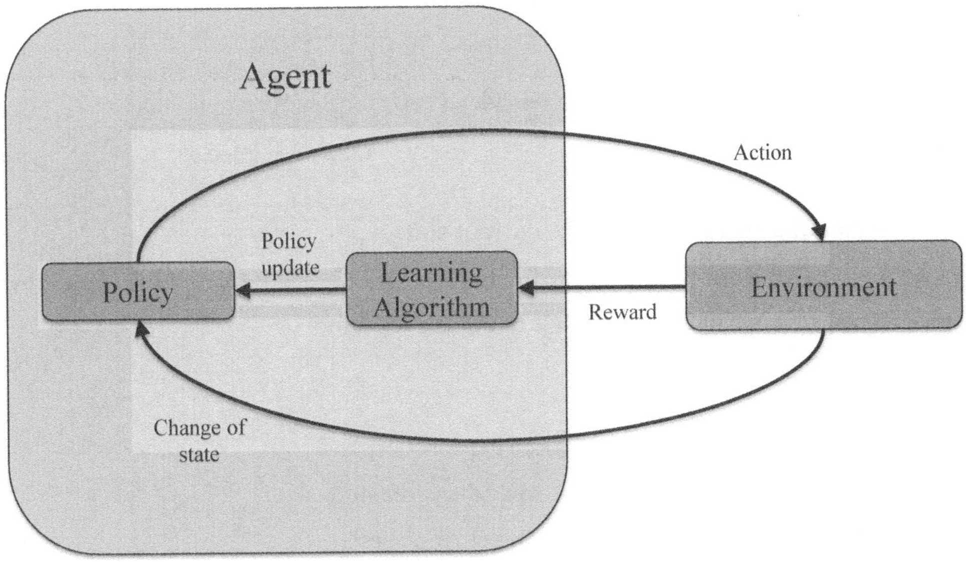

Figure 4.20: Reinforcement Learning loop.

- State value:

$$V^{\pi}(s) = \mathbb{E}_{\pi}\left[G_t \mid s_t = s\right]. \tag{4.49}$$

These values allow the agent to compare actions not just in terms of immediate reward but in terms of long-term consequences, an ability some humans spend a lifetime acquiring. As you can imagine, there are several families of RL algorithms, each using value estimates differently. Typically this can be done with value-based or policy-based methods.

These values allow the agent to compare actions and learn from their mistakes and their successes.

4.5.1 *Q-Learning: Value-based methods*

VALUE-BASED METHODS ASSUME THAT THE agent learns the optimal Q-function, $Q^*(s,a)$, and thus acts greedily with respect to it. The classic example is Q-learning and is

In Q-Learning, the agent acts greedily with respect to a function $Q^*(s,a)$.

defined by the following update rule:

$$Q(s_t, a_t) \leftarrow Q(s_t, a_t) + \alpha \left(r_t + \gamma \max_a Q(s_{t+1}, a) - Q(s_t, a_t) \right). \quad (4.50)$$

At each timestep the agent observes the current state s_t, selects an action a_t and receives a reward r_t finally transitioning to the next state s_{t+1}, with α being the learning rate.

Using an exploration strategy such as ε-greedy.

A simple, and widely used, way to balance exploration and exploitation is the ε-greedy strategy: At each decision step, with probability $1 - \varepsilon$, the agent chooses the current best action (i.e., the action with the highest estimated value), and with probability ε it chooses an action at random, uniformly among all possible actions:

ε-greedy keeps you curious just often enough.

$$a_t = \begin{cases} \text{random action}, & \text{with probability } \varepsilon, \\ \arg\max_a Q(s_t, a), & \text{with probability } 1 - \varepsilon. \end{cases} \quad (4.51)$$

If the agent knows this Q^*, the optimal policy is trivial: In each state, choose the action with the highest Q-value. So the whole game is to incrementally improve the estimates of Q-values over time. The update rule aims to update the current estimate of the value of taking action a_t in state s_t by nudging it toward a target built from the reward and the best future value $\max_a Q(s_{t+1}, a)$.

Most of the time you exploit what you know; occasionally you take a deliberate wander to discover something better.

Tabular Q-learning is the simplest and most classical form of Q-learning, and it sits at the very heart of RL. It estimates the optimal action–value function $Q^*(s, a)$ using a table where each entry corresponds to a particular state s and

Literally a multidimensional array.

particular action a. We need to store an estimate of how good that action is in that state. The goal of Q-learning is to approximate:

$$Q^*(s,a) = \max_{\pi} \mathbb{E}\left[\sum_{t=0}^{\infty} \gamma^t r_t \mid s_0 = s,\ a_0 = a\right], \tag{4.52}$$

Q-learning acts perfectly greedy tomorrow, even if it is a bit chaotic today; that is the power of being off-policy.

and it builds up this estimate incrementally through experience. Tabular Q-learning is an off-policy algorithm in the sense that the agent may behave with exploration during training, but updates assume it will act greedily in the future. As the update uses $\max_a Q(s_{t+1}, a)$, it always updates toward the best predicted future behaviour, regardless of how the agent behaved in this step. This off-policy nature makes tabular Q-learning powerful and widely
applicable.

It is called tabular because the Q-function is literally stored in a table rather than represented by a neural network. It works well when the state space is discrete, or a continuous state space is discretised (e.g., using bin), and the total number of discrete states is small enough to store in a table.

Tabular Q-learning works well when the state space is discrete.

4.5.2 *Policy-based methods*

INSTEAD OF LEARNING VALUES, WE can get the agent to learn directly a parameterised policy $\pi_\theta(a|s)$, i.e., a mapping from states to actions. It is possible to cast the problems in the form of the optimisation of an objective function J parametrised by θ, which are typically the weights of a neural network. This approach is, in a way, more elegant

Here the agent skips the value estimates and goes straight for learning "how to act".

because it directly optimises behaviour, rather than relying on intermediate signals like Q-values.

The policy gradient theorem[28] tells us that to improve our policy, we need to nudge the parameters in the direction that increases the probability of good actions, and decreases the probability of bad ones, weighted by how good/bad they were. For a policy $J(\theta)$ that we want to maximise, we have that $\nabla_\theta J(\theta)$ is the gradient of that objective with respect to the policy parameters. This can be written mathematically as:

[28] Sutton, R. S., D. McAllester, S. Singh, and Y. Mansour (2000). Policy gradient methods for reinforcement learning with function approximation. In *Advances in Neural Information Processing Systems*, pp. 1057–1063.

$$J(\theta) = \mathbb{E}_\pi \left[\nabla_\theta \log \pi_\theta(a|s) \, Q^\pi(s,a) \right]. \qquad (4.53)$$

In other words, "How should we change the policy's neural network weights to make performance go up?"

In the expression above, $\nabla_\theta \log \pi_\theta(a|s)$ tells us how to change the policy to make action a more (or less) likely. This is the direction in parameter space that increases the probability of taking action a. $Q^\pi(s,a)$ tell us how good that action was in hindsight; if it is high, the algorithm strengthens the tendency to choose that action, if it is low, the policy is discouraged from repeating it.

Think of this as the *reputational system* in Reinforcement Learning!

Policy-based methods work naturally with continuous action spaces, as there is no need for value tables or discretisation since we use neural networks directly over continuous inputs; furthermore, stochastic policies are essential for proper exploration in many tasks. They often lead to more stable learning than bootstrapped value methods. In general we run an episode using the current policy, we collect log probabilities of actions chosen and rewards obtained and compute returns. Finally we update policy parameters using $\theta \leftarrow \theta + \alpha \, G_t \nabla_\theta \log \pi_\theta(a|s)$. It must

Policy-based methods are ideal in continuous action spaces.

be said that policy gradients suffer from high variance, and that is why sometimes Actor–Critic methods are used, as they improve stability by introducing a critic:

- The actor is the policy network $\pi_\theta(a|s)$.
- The critic estimates a value function $V^\pi(s)$.

The actor chooses actions, the critic judges the actors' performance.

The critic provides a low-variance learning signal, while the actor still learns the policy. This combination stabilises and accelerates learning.

4.5.3 *Reinforcement Learning in Action*

IN PRACTICE THE DISCUSSION ABOVE may sound scarier than it is. Once a Reinforcement Learning agent has been equipped with a value function and a policy, however rudimentary, it is natural to ask a simple but crucial question: *Is it learning anything at all?* In the context of tabular Q-learning, the answer lies in observing the agent's behaviour along two complementary dimensions:

So, how do we know the agent is learning?

1. Performance **during training**, when exploration is required, and
2. Performance **after training**, when the learned value function can be used deterministically.

To answer that question, we can look at its performance during and after training.

These two views allow us to distinguish between what the agent *tries* to do while learning and what it has *actually internalised* as a useful control policy.

During training, the agent typically follows an ε-greedy policy, balancing exploration and exploitation. When $\varepsilon > 0$, the agent occasionally takes random actions regardless of what the Q-table suggests. This randomness is not a bug; it is an essential component of the learning process, as we saw from Equation (4.51). To assess learning in this exploratory regime, we track the total reward per episode:

Exploration prevents the agent from getting stuck thinking that falling over is the optimal strategy.

$$R_{\text{episode}} = \sum_{t=0}^{T} r_t. \tag{4.54}$$

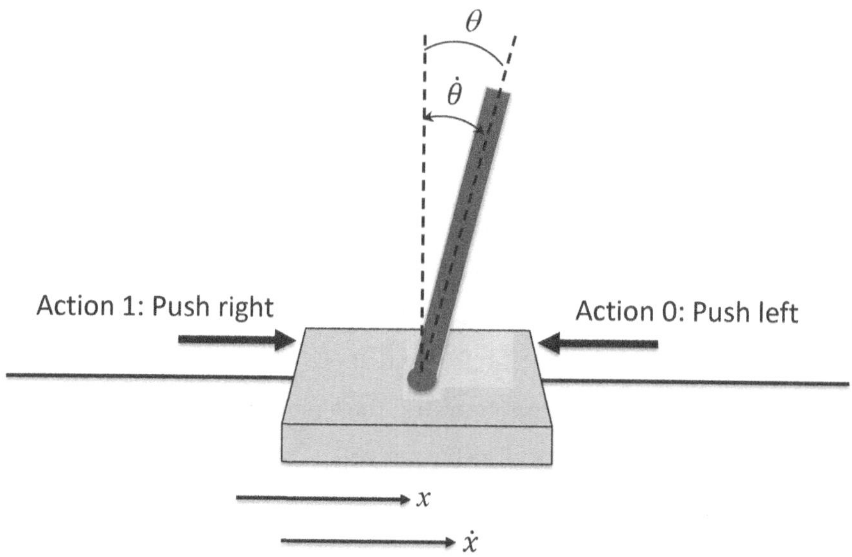

Figure 4.21: Cart Pole setup.

Let us see a simple example using `gymnasium`, a common RL toolkit designed for developing and testing Reinforcement Learning algorithms, providing various environments for training agents. In this case we are going to use Cart Pole[29] which is a classic RL environment where the goal is to balance a pole on a moving cart by applying forces in either direction as shown in Figure 4.21. The cart moves along a frictionless track, and a pole is attached to it by

[29] Barto, A. G., R. S. Sutton, and C. W. Anderson (1983). Neuronlike adaptive elements that can solve difficult learning control problems. *IEEE Transactions on Systems, Man, and Cybernetics SMC-13*(5), 834–846.

an un-actuated joint, the goal is to balance the pole by applying forces in the left and right direction on the cart. The observation space comprises values corresponding to the positions and velocities as shown in Table 4.2. The goal is to keep the pole upright for as long as possible and a rewards of +1 is given at every step taken, with a reward threshold of 500 for version 1 and 200 for version 0 due to the time limit on the environment.

Described by arrays with shape (4,).

Num	Observation	Min	Max
0	Cart Position (x)	-4.8	4.8
1	Cart Velocity ($\dot{x}$)	$-\infty$	∞
2	Pole Angle (θ)	≈ -0.418 rad (-24°)	≈ 0.418 rad (24°)
3	Pole Angular Velocity ($\dot{\theta}$)	$-\infty$	∞

Table 4.2: Observation space ranges for the `CartPole-v1` environment.

Let us import the necessary libraries and create an instance of the Cart Pole environment using Gymnasium.

```
import gymnasium as gym
import numpy as np
import matplotlib.pyplot as plt


env = gym.make('CartPole-v1')
n_actions = env.action_space.n
```

We are using version 1 in this example.

The last line in the code above retrieves the number of possible actions the agent can take, i.e., `env.action_space` describes what actions are allowed and `n` is used for discrete action spaces.

Classical tabular Reinforcement Learning methods such as Q-learning require the state space to be *discrete*. Each possible state corresponds to a row in the Q-table, and each action to a column. In many control problems, however, the agent does not observe tidy symbolic states but rather *continuous* quantities. The Cart Pole environment is a good example: At each timestep the agent receives a four-dimensional real-valued state vector consisting of the cart position and velocity, and the pole angle and angular velocity. These values vary smoothly and cannot be used directly as indices into a table.

Numerical values such as 0.032 or −0.157 do not make good array indices.

In such cases we must convert the continuous state into a discrete representation. The most common approach is **state discretisation**. The underlying idea is simple: Subdivide each dimension of the continuous state space into a fixed number of intervals, or *bins*, and map any continuous value to the index of the interval into which it falls. In effect, we approximate the continuous space by a coarse grid. More formally, suppose the state s has components

State discretisation requires us to subdivide each dimension into a fixed number of intervals.

$$s = \left(s^{(1)}, s^{(2)}, \ldots, s^{(d)}\right), \tag{4.55}$$

and each dimension is divided into B bins. Let $\{b_1^{(i)}, b_2^{(i)}, \ldots, b_B^{(i)}\}$ denote the bin edges for the i–th component. The discretised state $\hat{s}$ is defined component-wise as

$$\hat{s}^{(i)} = \texttt{digitize}\left(s^{(i)}, \{b_j^{(i)}\}\right), \tag{4.56}$$

The `digitize()` function returns the indices of the bins to which each value in an input array belongs.

where `digitize` returns the index of the bin that contains the value $s^{(i)}$.

In the case of Cart Pole, for example, we might choose ten bins per dimension, namely:

$$\begin{aligned} \text{cart position} &\in [-4.8, 4.8], \\ \text{cart velocity} &\in [-4.0, 4.0], \\ \text{pole angle} &\in [-0.418, 0.418], \\ \text{angular velocity} &\in [-4.0, 4.0]. \end{aligned} \tag{4.57}$$

These are the dimensions at play in Cart Pole.

Applying discretisation then yields a tuple of integers, $\hat{s} = (i_1, i_2, i_3, i_4)$, each $i_k \in \{0, 1, \ldots, B-1\}$, which can be used directly to index the Q-table. With $B = 10$ bins in four dimensions, the resulting table has 10^4 rows, a size that is computationally manageable while still providing a useful approximation of the underlying continuous dynamics.

```
NUM_BINS = 10
EPISODES = 500


bins = [
    np.linspace(-4.8, 4.8, NUM_BINS),
    np.linspace(-4.0, 4.0, NUM_BINS),
    np.linspace(-0.418, 0.418, NUM_BINS),
    np.linspace(-4.0, 4.0, NUM_BINS)
]
```

Here we simply define the bins with the help of `linspace`.

Discretisation introduces an approximation error, but for low–dimensional systems such as Cart Pole it strikes an effective balance between tractability and representational power. It allows us to retain the conceptual simplicity of tabular RL methods while extending them to environments with continuous observations. Let us discretise the state:

```
def discretise_state(state):
  return tuple(
    np.clip(np.digitize(state[i], bins[i]) - 1,
      0, NUM_BINS - 1)
    for i in range(len(state))
  )
```

We convert a continuous environment state into a discrete one.

The function above converts a continuous environment state into a discrete one. For each element of the state vector, it places the value into one of several predefined bins; `np.clip` ensures the index stays within valid bounds. The function returns a tuple of bin indices, one per state dimension, which can be used as a lookup key in a tabular Q-table.

I.e., between 0 and `NUM_BINS - 1`.

In the Cart Pole environment, the reward at each timestep is $+1$ as long as the pole remains upright. Thus, higher episode returns correspond to longer balancing times. Let us now create our Q-table and define some important parameters:

```
q_table = np.random.randn(*(NUM_BINS,) * 4, \
  n_actions)

learning_rate = 0.1
gamma = 0.9
epsilon = 0.1

training_rewards = []
```

Here, we setup some parameters such as our learning rate, the discount factor and ε.

We will use the `training_rewards` to track the performance. We are ready to define our learning loop. We start by reseting the environment and discretising the space as well as initialising the total reward:

```
for episode in range(EPISODES):
  state, _ = env.reset()
  state = discretise_state(state)
  done = False
  total_reward = 0

  while not done:
  if np.random.random() < epsilon:
    action = env.action_space.sample()
  else:
    action = np.argmax(q_table[state])
  next_state, reward, terminated, truncated, _ = \
    env.step(action)
  done = terminated or truncated
  next_state = discretise_state(next_state)
  total_reward += reward

  best_next = np.max(q_table[next_state])
  q_table[state][action] += learning_rate * ( \
    reward + gamma * best_next - \
    q_table[state][action])
  state = next_state
  training_rewards.append(total_reward)
  print(f'Learning Episode {episode+1}:\
    reward = {total_reward}")
```

Here we do our ε-greedy exploration.

Q-learning update happens here.

The loop runs over one entire episode, stopping when the environment signals that the episode is over either because the pole fell, the cart moved out of bounds or the time limit was reached. During the episode, we employ an ε-greedy strategy to explore the space and send the action to the environment returning the `next_state`, the reward and termination flags. Because Cart Pole's state is continuous, tabular Q-learning cannot use raw floats as indices, so we convert continuous values to discrete bins and accumulate the reward. Finally, we update the Q-value with the best next state based on what happened in the episode and move to the next state to start another round in the loop. Here is a typical output:

One episode = one full attempt. The agent keeps going until physics or patience says "stop".

Cart Pole speaks in continuous numbers, but Q-tables only understand tidy bins.

```
...
Learning Episode 496: reward = 60.0
Learning Episode 497: reward = 83.0
Learning Episode 498: reward = 49.0
Learning Episode 499: reward = 63.0
```

Exploration is essential during learning, but it obscures our view of the agent's true competence. To assess what the agent has *actually* learned, we freeze exploration by setting $\varepsilon = 0$ and evaluate the agent over several episodes. In this regime, the agent always selects the greedy action:

To evaluate the agent, we setup $\varepsilon = 0$.

$$a_t = \arg\max_a Q(s_t, a),$$

thus following the policy implied directly by the learned Q-table. No random actions are permitted. This produces a more accurate reflection of the agent's mature behaviour, untainted by exploratory noise.

```
def evaluate_agent(env, q_table, episodes=5):
  results = []
  for ep in range(episodes):
    state, _ = env.reset()
    state = discretise_state(state)
    done = False
    total_reward = 0

    while not done:
      # Greedy action
      action = np.argmax(q_table[state])
      next_state, reward, terminated, truncated, _\
        = env.step(action)
      done = terminated or truncated
      total_reward += reward
      state = discretise_state(next_state)

    results.append(total_reward)
    print(f'Evaluation Episode {ep}: \
      reward = {total_reward}')
  return results

evaluation_rewards = evaluate_agent(env, q_table,\
  10)
env.close()
```

Greedy action takes place here.

The total reward obtained in these evaluation episodes provides a post-training performance measure. If the learning procedure has been successful, these evaluation returns should be more stable and, one hopes, significantly

higher than the early training returns. Plotting R_{episode} against the episode index yields a learning curve, see Figure 4.22. A well-behaved curve typically begins with low, noisy values (the agent is still exploring wildly) and gradually increases as the agent learns to select stabilising actions more consistently. Although fluctuations will persist—exploration is still in effect—the upward trend serves as evidence that the Q-values are converging towards more useful
estimates.

Early chaos, later progress: A rising curve is the agent slowly getting its act together.

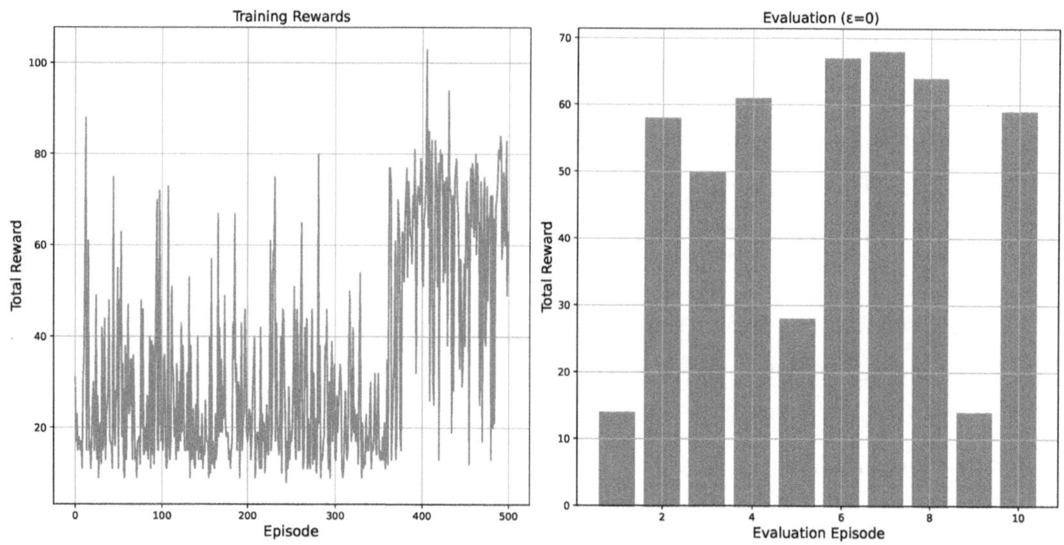

Figure 4.22: A learning curve for a round of Cart Pole using Q-learning. We compare this with a bar chart for a set of 10 evaluations.

As with many things in machine learning, what happens during learning is not always representative of what the agent is capable of doing when allowed to act calmly and without the occasional urge to "try something random". Here we have simply used a *random policy*. A proper RL

The equivalent of a toddler flailing the controls of a flight simulator.

agent learns a policy π through algorithms like Q-learning or policy gradients. These estimate the value of actions and adjust weights to favour those leading to higher long-term rewards.

Let us now implement a policy-based learning approach. We will be using Keras to build a neural network to manage our policy. Let us load our libraries:

```
import gymnasium as gym
import numpy as np
import tensorflow as tf
from tensorflow import keras
```

For our policy-based learning, we will employ Keras to build a neural network to manage the policy.

We are going to create `PolicyNetwork` with one dense hidden layer with a ReLu activation function that outputs action preferences (logits). This will be used for sampling actions in Reinforcement Learning.

```
class PolicyNetwork(keras.Model):
  def __init__(self, n_inputs, n_actions, \
      hidden_size=128):
    super().__init__()
    self.d1 = keras.layers.Dense(hidden_size, \
      activation='relu')
    self.logits = keras.layers.Dense(n_actions)

  def call(self, x):
    x = self.d1(x)
    return self.logits(x)
```

Two layers, one purpose: Turn states into action preferences the policy can learn to trust.

The class above defines a simple neural network for a policy gradient agent. It sets up two layers: A hidden dense layer with ReLU activation (`d1`), and an output layer (`logits`) that produces one raw score per possible action. In the `call` method, the input `x` is passed through the hidden layer and then through the output layer. The result is a vector of logits representing the unnormalised preferences for each action. Notice that `n_inputs` is the number of state variables, which in the case of Cart Pole is 4, `n_actions` is the number of possible actions the agent can take.

Our neural network sets up the policy for learning.

We now need a function to turn the network's logits into an actual decision.

```
def sample_action(logits):
  return int(tf.random.categorical( \
    logits, 1)[0, 0])
```

We turn the outputs into actual decisions with this function.

TensorFlow treats the logits as a categorical distribution and `tf.random.categorical` draws a single sample from it; no softmax ceremony required. The slightly ungainly `[0, 0]` simply extracts the scalar action index from TensorFlow's batch-shaped output, and `int()` hands back a clean Python integer.

In short: The policy suggests, probability nudges, and this function rolls the dice on the agent's behalf.

We can now write our main Reinforcement Learning loop. We will do so inside a function that takes the environment, the policy and an optimiser as inputs, we can also pass the number of episodes and the discount factor γ. We will explore the code that makes up that function by referring to portions marked with comments in the code listing below. Let us start with the code below the `## --- setup ---` comment where we keep track of the rewards in an array called `returns_history` and initialise arrays for states, actions and rewards as well as a stopping flag (`done`).

```
def reinforce(env, policy, optimiser, \
  episodes=500, gamma=0.99):

  ## ---- setup ----
  returns_history = []
  for episode in range(episodes):
    state, _ = env.reset()
    states = []
    actions = []
    rewards = []
    done = False

    ## ---- experience gathering ----
    while not done:
      states.append(state)
      s = tf.convert_to_tensor(state[None, :], \
        dtype=tf.float32)
      logits = policy(s)
      action = sample_action(logits)
      actions.append(action)

      next_state, reward, terminated, truncated, _\
        = env.step(action)
      rewards.append(reward)
```

We take an environment, policy and optimiser as inputs.

Setting up arrays for our Reinforcement Learning loop.

The agent is exploring different actions and getting the rewards (or punishment) for them.

Here we observe, decide, act, get paid, repeat.

```
    done = terminated or truncated
    state = next_state
```

```
    ## ---- discounted returns ----
  G = 0
  returns = []
  for r in reversed(rewards):
    G = r + gamma * G
    returns.insert(0, G)

  returns = np.array(returns, dtype=np.float32)
  returns = (returns - returns.mean()) / \
    (returns.std() + 1e-8)

  ## ---- update policy ----
  with tf.GradientTape() as tape:
    log_probs = []
    for s, a in zip(states, actions):
      s = tf.convert_to_tensor(s[None, :], \
        dtype=tf.float32)
      logits = policy(s)
      probs = tf.nn.softmax(logits)
      log_prob = tf.math.log(probs[0, a] + 1e-8)
      log_probs.append(log_prob)

      log_probs = tf.stack(log_probs)
      returns_tf = tf.convert_to_tensor(returns)
      loss=-tf.reduce_sum(log_probs*returns_tf)
```

Here we take a look back at the rewards received after an episode and smooth them into a learning signal.

We compute the log-probability of each action, weigh those by their discounted returns, and use the resulting loss to update the policy.

```
    ## ---- the learning ----
    grads = tape.gradient(loss, \
      policy.trainable_variables)
    optimiser.apply_gradients(zip(grads, \
      policy.trainable_variables))
    total_return = sum(rewards)
    returns_history.append(total_return)

    if episode % 50 == 0:
      print(f'Episode {episode:4d} | \
        Return = {total_return}')

  return returns_history
```

Then we compute gradients and update the policy, then log how much the agent earned this episode.

Let us now look at the code under the comment labelled `## --- experience gathering ---`, here at each step, the current state is recorded, converted into a TensorFlow-friendly batch shape, and fed through the policy network to produce logits. From these logits, the agent samples an action, storing that choice so we can later compute log-probabilities for the policy-gradient update later in the code. The action is then executed in the environment via `env.step(action)`, which returns the next state, the reward earned, and termination flags. Each reward is saved, and the loop continues until the environment declares the episode over (either `terminated` or `truncated`). In essence, we observe, decide, act, get paid, repeat; a Reinforcement Learning microcosm captured in a neatly structured loop.

Policy network → logits → sampled action: The agent's decision pipeline in miniature.

Observe, act, reward, repeat—the classic RL heartbeat played out one step at a time.

The code under `## --- discounted returns ---` is where the agent does some after-the-fact accounting. Once an episode is finished, we walk backwards through the collected rewards and compute the discounted return for each timestep. We initialise `G = 0`—the future contains no further riches—and then fold the rewards in reverse: Each new return is simply the immediate reward plus γ times whatever future value we have already accumulated. By inserting each `G` at the front of the list, we end up with a clean sequence of returns aligned with the original timeline. Finally, the whole vector is normalised to have zero mean and unit variance, a polite statistical smoothing that keeps gradient updates stable rather than melodramatic.

Walking backwards through the rewards turns chaos into a tidy map of future value.

This block converts raw "money earned per step" into a calm, well-behaved learning signal.

We are now at the moment where the agent turns reflection into improvement. Let us look at the code under `## --- update policy ---` where we are using a `GradientTape`, TensorFlow's equivalent of switching on the "track everything I do" button, to replay the episode, but only in the abstract: For every recorded state–action pair, we run the state back through the policy to get fresh logits, convert them to probabilities, and extract the log-probability of the action the agent actually took at the time. These log-probs form the backbone of the policy-gradient update. Once collected and stacked into a tidy tensor, they are paired with the previously computed discounted returns. Multiplying them together weights each decision by how good it ultimately turned out to be. The final loss is simply the negative of this sum, a gentle nudge telling the policy to increase the likelihood of decisions that led to high returns

`GradientTape` records operations performed on tensors, which can then be used to calculate gradients, making it essential for training machine learning models.

Or embarrassing!

and dial down the rest. In short: This block teaches the agent to repeat its triumphs and quietly forget its poor life choices.

In `## --- the learning ---` portion of our function is where the learning actually happens. Once the loss is computed, we ask the `GradientTape` to rewind its notes and produce gradients for every trainable parameter in the policy. These gradients are paired with the corresponding variables and handed to the optimiser, which performs the numerical elbow-grease of updating the weights. With the policy suitably nudged, we record the episode's total return for posterity, and every 50 episodes we print a small progress report to reassure ourselves that the agent is, indeed, getting less terrible over time. Finally, the full history of returns is sent back, giving a convenient record of how learning has unfolded across training. We are now ready to start our learning loop:

Effectively these are the directions for improvement.

This is the moment the policy actually learns, everything before was just collecting evidence.

```
env = gym.make('CartPole-v1')
n_inputs = env.observation_space.shape[0]
n_actions = env.action_space.n

policy = PolicyNetwork(n_inputs, n_actions)
optimiser = keras.optimizers.legacy.Adam(0.01)

rewards = reinforce(env, policy, optimiser, \
  episodes=200)

env.close()
```

Initialise the world, build a brain, choose an optimiser... then let `reinforce` take it for a spin.

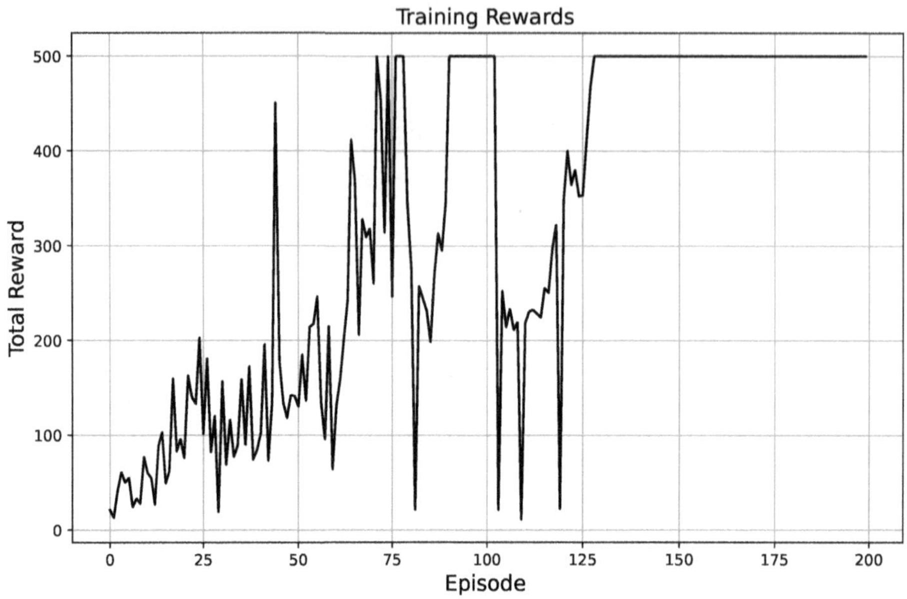

Figure 4.23: A learning curve for a round of Cart Pole using a policy-based method.

We start by instantiating the environment for Cart Pole and set up the spaces for inputs and actions. We then create our policy network and instantiate our optimiser. We then call our Reinforcement Learning function running over 200 episodes. The output may look as below, with a learning curve similar to that shown in Figure 4.23.

```
Episode    0 | Return = 21.0
Episode   50 | Return = 130.0
Episode  100 | Return = 500.0
Episode  150 | Return = 500.0
```

Remember that the results in your computer will likely be different.

As we can see, for this specific training session we have a system that has learnt how to receive the maximum number of points (500) in a consistent manner. This seems to be a better model than that obtained with Q-learning before. So, if traditional neural networks learn to predict, reinforcement learners learn to *survive*.

The neural Darwinism of machine learning.

4.6 *Generative Adversarial Networks: Learning through Rivalry*

IF REINFORCEMENT LEARNING IS ABOUT learning from experience, then Generative Adversarial Networks (GANs) are about learning through rivalry. As the name suggests, the learning mechanism requires an adversary to establish a friendly competition that results in improvement. Ask any sportsperson, and they will surely corroborate that competition is a great incentive. Generative Adversarial Networks were Introduced by Ian Goodfellow and colleagues in 2014,[30] and they consist of two neural networks locked in a cunning game: **Generator** G and **discriminator** D.

Two neural networks walk into a bar... only one comes out looking real.

[30] Goodfellow, I., J. Pouget-Abadie, M. Mirza, B. Xu, D. Warde-Farley, S. Ozair, A. Courville, and Y. Bengio (2014). Generative Adversarial Nets. In *Advances in Neural Information Processing Systems (NIPS)*, pp. 2672–2680.

In this adversarial friendly competition the generator G takes random noise z, sampled from a simple distribution like Gaussian or uniform, and it transforms it into synthetic data samples, aiming to forge outputs that resemble the real data. At the same time, the discriminator D receives either real samples (from the true dataset) or fake samples (from G) and attempts to distinguish real v. fake, outputting a high value for real and low for fake. We illustrate this flow in Figure 4.24.

I use the term "real" in the colloquial sense, not the mathematical one!

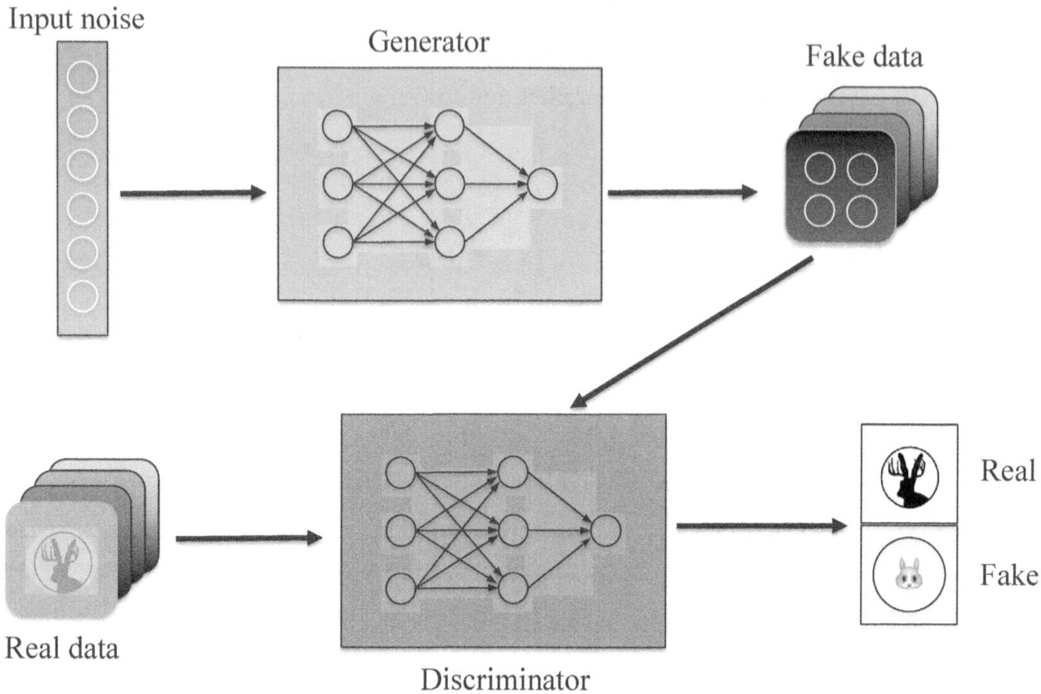

Figure 4.24: A schematic representation of the dynamics inside a Generative Adversarial Network.

In this cat-and-mouse setup, the two networks engage in a minimax game. Let us set the scene: The generator is our aspiring counterfeiter, and the discriminator is the overworked art critic trying to spot forgeries. Given an actual data distribution p_{data}, unknown, but sampled via our dataset, we can draw a sample $x \sim p_{data}$ representing "the real deal". The generator can draw a random noise vector $z \sim p_z$ from the chosen noise distribution p_z. If the noise distribution is Gaussian, then z is just a vector of values from a normal distribution. The generator uses this noise as raw material to sculpt a synthetic sample, i.e., a fake artwork. The plot of our play can be encapsulated by

In our analogy, a real artwork.

the following objective function:

$$\min_G \max_D V(D, G) = \mathbb{E}_x [\log D(x)] + \mathbb{E}_z [\log (1 - D(G(z)))] . \quad (4.58)$$

If you have ever looked at a formula and thought "that's either brilliant or trying too hard", don't worry, this one is mostly brilliant. The first term, $\mathbb{E}_{x \sim p_{data}}[\log D(x)]$, is the discriminator's reward. It feeds real examples x to the discriminator D, and it rewards D when it outputs something close to 1 indicating that it spots the real stuff correctly! The second term, $\mathbb{E}_{z \sim p_z}[\log(1 - D(G(z)))]$, is the "catch the forgery" term. It takes noise z and generates a fake sample $G(z)$. It rewards D when it outputs something close to 0 . So the discriminator is essentially doing its best Sherlock Holmes impression.

Let us unpack it before it starts unpacking us.

I.e., "no, this is fake!"

The outer $\max_D$ and $\min_G$ bring the adversarial nature to life. The discriminator wants to maximise the whole expression, giving high scores to real samples and low to fake ones. The generator on the other hand wants to minimise the same expression: Generate samples that force $D(G(z)) \rightarrow 1$, in other words make the fakes indistinguishable from the real.

Two networks, opposite goals: One exposes fakes, the other tries to fool it; adversaries locked in creative combat.

This is the classic forger–critic dynamic: As one improves, the other is forced to improve too. The whole objective is a dance of deception and detection, where G tries to minimise how well D can tell real from fake, and D tries to maximise it. By the end, if the stars align and optimisers behave, G learns to generate samples so realistic that even D shrugs

A creative arms race ensues.

and says, "Honestly, mate, I can't tell anymore!", ideally approaching a balance akin to a Nash equilibrium, where neither can improve without the other. At this equilibrium, G's output distribution matches the true data distribution, and D is maximally confused (outputting 0.5 for all inputs). In practice, reaching this theoretical equilibrium is tricky; training GANs is famously challenging due to issues like mode collapse and unstable convergence. Yet when it works, the results can be astonishing, all learned without any explicit labels, purely by this adversarial "game".

Which, in GAN-land, is a sign of success!

Perfect balance: A generator that imitates flawlessly and a discriminator too baffled to judge.

4.6.1 GANs in Action

In this example we will train G to generate samples that mimic the distribution of the "real" data. In practice, we would use for example convolutional GANs[31] (Deep Convolutional GANs or DCGANs) for image generation. It is possible to use other architectures from simple fully connected neural nets, to sequence models[32] (based on RNN/Transformers—we will cover these in the next chapter) for text and other discrete data. Indeed, generating text adversarially is much harder than images, because text is discrete and non-differentiable. Instead I advocate using Transformers—again refer to the next chapter.

[31] Radford, A., L. Metz, and S. Chintala (2016). Unsupervised Representation Learning with Deep Convolutional Generative Adversarial Networks. *arXiv preprint arXiv:1511.06434*

[32] Yu, L., W. Zhang, J. Wang, and Y. Yu (2017). SeqGAN: Sequence Generative Adversarial Nets with Policy Gradient. In *AAAI Conference on Artificial Intelligence*, pp. 2852–2858.

GAN-based text generators often rely on additional machinery to make training feasible, because discrete tokens break the clean flow of gradients that GANs depend on. As a result, Jackalope Data Scientists frequently turn to techniques such as Reinforcement Learning or differentiable relaxations to let the generator receive meaningful feedback. Nonetheless, the adversarial approach has been applied in many domains—images, audio, video, even molecule design[33]—often producing outputs of remarkable quality.

[33] Sanchez-Lengeling, B., C. Outeiral, G. Guimaraes, and A. Aspuru-Guzik (2017). Optimizing Distributions over Molecular Space with Deep Generative Models. ChemRxiv preprint, doi:10.26434/chemrxiv.5309668.v3.

To build intuition, here is a minimalist example of a GAN training loop using Keras. The generator and discriminator are as simple as possible. Think of this as a "hello world" GAN that tries to learn a distribution in $\mathbb{R}^{784}$, e.g., 28×28 images flattened. Both networks are trained in alternating steps: First update D, to better tell real vs. fake, then update G, to better fool D. In this case, we are going to use the MNIST dataset[34] which provides handwritten digit images. These will be our source of real images, and a GAN with Keras. Let us start by loading our libraries:

[34] LeCun, Y., L. Bottou, Y. Bengio, and P. Haffner (1998). Gradient-based learning applied to document recognition. *Proceedings of the IEEE 86*(11), 2278–2324

```
import tensorflow as tf
from tensorflow.keras import layers
import numpy as np
```

We are going to load the images from the set contained within Keras. The images are grayscale with 28×28 pixels stored as unsigned 8-bit integers. In this dataset, each pixel intensity can only take values in the range $[0, 255]$. To manage our GAN flow, we will scale the images to $[-1, 1]$ by dividing by half the range, and shifting the centre:

0 being black and 255 white.

```
(train_images, _), (_, _) = tf.keras.datasets.\
  mnist.load_data()
train_images = train_images.astype('float32')
train_images = (train_images - 127.5) / 127.5
```

This scaling will become clearer later, when we describe our generator.

We are going to create our generator and discriminator networks using convolutional neural networks which expect 4D tensors for batch, height, width and channel. Since the MNIST images are grayscale, each pixel has one intensity value, but Keras's convolution layers still expect a channel dimension. That is what we will add to our images:

We discuss CNNs in Section 4.4.1.

```
train_images = np.expand_dims(train_images,\
  axis=-1)
```

Let us now define our generator:

```
generator = tf.keras.Sequential([
  layers.Dense(7*7*128, use_bias=False, \
    input_shape=(100,)),
  layers.BatchNormalization(),
  layers.LeakyReLU(),
  layers.Reshape((7, 7, 128)),

  layers.Conv2DTranspose(64, kernel_size=5, \
    strides=2, padding='same', use_bias=False),
  layers.BatchNormalization(),
  layers.LeakyReLU(),

  layers.Conv2DTranspose(1, kernel_size=5, \
    strides=2, padding='same', \
    use_bias=False, activation='tanh')
])
```

Starting from pure noise, this stack progressively upsamples and shapes it into a 28×28 image; reverse-engineering reality one layer at a time.

Think of a generator a bit like the replicator on the Starship Enterprise: You feed it a meaningless pattern of quantum noise, and it somehow produces a recognisable object, in this case, an image of a handwritten digit instead of a hot Earl Grey tea. The architecture below is a carefully choreographed sequence of transformations that take a 100-dimensional noise vector and inflate it into a 28×28 grayscale image.

Unless it is a letter *T* and not the beverage of choice of J.L. Picard!

Our input is a 100-dimensional noise vector, pure randomness, no spatial structure, no meaning. The first dense layer explodes this tiny point into a large chunk of numbers: $7 \times 7 \times 128 = 6272$ activations, note that we are not requiring bias, this will be done later by batch normalisation. Batch normalisation stabilises training by keeping activations nicely distributed. In GANs, this is essential: Without BatchNorm, the generator tends to behave like someone who had too much coffee and not enough sleep, i.e., oscillatory, unstable, and prone to catastrophic mood swings. Instead of a hard cutoff at zero, `LeakyReLU` allows a tiny slope for negative values. This keeps gradients flowing, prevents dead neurons, and gives the generator a healthier mathematical metabolism. We then convert the flat vector output of the dense layer into a 7×7 feature map with 128 channels. This is the embryonic version of the final image.

BatchNorm keeps this explosive growth calm and learnable.

ReLU's dramatic "NOPE!!"

Think of it as the difference between a door slammed shut and a door politely left ajar.

Next, we use transpose convolutions to grow the $7 \times 7 \times 128$ seed into larger spatial structures. Strides of 2 double the spatial dimensions ($7 \rightarrow 14$), we reduce channels from 128 to 64, refining features. BatchNorm again keeps the activations from exploding and LeakyReLU keeps things flowing. Now our feature map is $14 \times 14 \times 64$. Finally, one last transposed convolution, spatially, $14 \rightarrow 28$ and we reach

This is the generator's equivalent of teenage growth: Everything doubles in size and becomes more expressive, if not entirely coordinated yet.

the MNIST image size. Channels drop from 64 to 1, because MNIST is grayscale and tanh squashes everything to the critical GAN range: $[-1,1]$. Now we see why we scaled our images. If the real data is not scaled to the same range, the discriminator instantly spots that the real images are in the range $[0,255]$ whereas the fake ones in $[-1,1]$. And like that we have our fully formed, fresh-out-of-the-replicator image. It may initially resemble an eldritch creature from the deep void—blurry, smudged, possibly digit-like—but as training progresses, it begins to resemble real MNIST digits.

That is the GAN equivalent of trying to counterfeit a £20 note using crayons.

Let us look at the discriminator:

```
discriminator = tf.keras.Sequential([
  layers.Conv2D(64, kernel_size=5, strides=2, \
    padding='same',input_shape=(28, 28, 1)),
  layers.LeakyReLU(alpha=0.2),
  layers.Dropout(0.3),

  layers.Conv2D(128, kernel_size=5, strides=2, \
    padding='same'),
  layers.LeakyReLU(alpha=0.2),
  layers.Dropout(0.3),

  layers.Flatten(),
  layers.Dense(1, activation='sigmoid')
])
```

A downward funnel of convolutions and dropout, distilling an image into a single verdict: Real or fake.

If the generator is the forger, then the discriminator is the art critic—the kind who can glance at a painting and immediately tell whether it's a masterpiece or something produced by a caffeinated octopus. In a GAN, this critic's job is simple but ruthless: Look at an image and say: "Fake or fortune". The code below builds such a critic using convolutional layers, because when judging images, fully connected layers are basically reading them with their eyes closed.

Fiona Bruce will surely be part of the reveal!

In the discriminator code above, with the help of `Conv2D`, the discriminator inspects the incoming image using 64 filters with a kernel size of 5×5. We have a large enough canvas to catch strokes and edges. Strides of length 2 half the image resolution ($28 \rightarrow 14$) and the same padding keeps spatial alignment tidy. `LeakyReLU(0.2)` avoids the "dead neuron" issues of plain ReLU, ensuring gradients keep flowing. TA downward funnel of convolutions and dropout—distilling an image into a single verdict: real or fake.he `Dropout(0.3)` randomly disables 30% of neurons, stopping the discriminator from becoming too confident too quickly, a common problem where D becomes so sharp it obliterates the generator before it can learn anything.

This is essentially the discriminator squinting at the image.

We then have another round of suspicious scrutiny:

- 128 filters: More feature extraction power
- Downsampling: $14 \rightarrow 7$
- The discriminator learns deeper features: Curves, digits, more abstract structures
- Same `LeakyReLU` and `Dropout` combo for stable, sceptical learning

Some of the steps performed by the discriminator.

At this stage, the discriminator has effectively turned the image into a $7 \times 7 \times 128$ tensor of high-level visual clues. The `Flatten` layer collapses the $7 \times 7 \times 128$ tensor into a single long vector of evidence. If the earlier layers were detectives gathering clues, this is the part where they hand everything to the judge in a neatly organised case file. Finally the last `Dense` layer is where the discriminator picks a side:

Much like the camera feed of a sci-fi security system analysing shapes for "fake" signatures.

- Output 1: "Fortune, looks real enough"
- Output 0: "Fake, nice try, generator!"

The sigmoid activation ensures the output is a probability which slots perfectly into the GAN loss function. This single neuron is the entire justice system of the adversarial game: Judge, jury, and executioner.

The following three lines look innocent enough, but they actually define the entire training dynamic of the GAN. They determine how the generator and discriminator learn, and how quickly and likely they are to spiral into chaos:

Like a quiet trio at the back of a lecture hall.

```
loss_fn = tf.keras.losses.BinaryCrossentropy()
opt_G = tf.keras.optimizers.Adam( \
  learning_rate=0.0002, beta_1=0.5)
opt_D = tf.keras.optimizers.Adam( \
  learning_rate=0.0002, beta_1=0.5)
```

GANs are temperamental creatures; choosing the wrong optimiser is like feeding gremlins after midnight.

The first one defines the loss function, which we will use as our lie detector. This is the same loss used in logistic regression and binary classifiers[35]. We then define the optimisers for the generator and the discriminator. We use identical optimisers to keep the networks balanced, like two

[35] Rogel-Salazar, J. (2025). *Data Science and Analytics with Python*. Chapman & Hall/CRC Data Mining and Knowledge Discovery Series. CRC Press.

fencers with matching weapons. Remember, training GANs is a delicate dance: If *D* learns too fast, it obliterates *G*; if *G* learns too fast, it confuses *D* and collapses.

We need to set the pace and structure for the GAN's training process. First, we choose a batch size of 64, meaning that during each update step the discriminator and generator will see 64 images at a time. We train for 30 epochs, so the model will loop over the entire MNIST dataset 30 times.

Small enough to keep training fast, but large enough to produce stable gradient estimates.

```
batch_size = 64
epochs = 30
steps_per_epoch = len(train_images) // batch_size

real_labels = tf.ones((batch_size, 1))
fake_labels = tf.zeros((batch_size, 1))
```

The `steps_per_epoch` simply calculates how many batches fit into one epoch, giving us the number of training iterations per cycle. Finally, we prepare two label tensors: `real_labels`, a batch of ones representing "genuine" MNIST images, and `fake_labels`, a batch of zeros representing generator-produced impostors. These labels form the basic currency of the adversarial game.

The discriminator tries to separate them, while the generator tries to turn fake-label predictions into real-label ones.

We are now ready to get our game going. For each epoch we start loading real images based on their indices. We need to ensure that they are converted into suitable tensors. Similarly, we generate some fake images sampling from a normal distribution and passing the sample to our generator:

See the code section marked as `1.` and `2.` in the listing below.

```
for epoch in range(epochs):
  for step in range(steps_per_epoch):

  # ---- 1. Load real images ----
  idx=np.random.randint(0, train_images.shape[0],\
    batch_size)
  x_real = tf.convert_to_tensor(train_images[idx])

  # ---- 2. Generate fake images ----
  z = tf.random.normal([batch_size, 100])
  x_fake = generator(z, training=False)

  # ---- 3. Train Discriminator ----
  with tf.GradientTape() as tape_D:
    D_real = discriminator(x_real, training=True)
    D_fake = discriminator(x_fake, training=True)
    loss_D = loss_fn(real_labels, D_real) + \
      loss_fn(fake_labels, D_fake)

  grads_D = tape_D.gradient(loss_D, \
    discriminator.trainable_weights)
  opt_D.apply_gradients(zip(grads_D, \
    discriminator.trainable_weights))

  # ---- 4. Train Generator ----
  with tf.GradientTape() as tape_G:
    x_fake = generator(z, training=True)
    D_fake = discriminator(x_fake, training=True)
```

We load real images based on their indices.

We then generate fake images with our generator.

The discriminator gets trained.

And in turn, the generator gets trained.

```
        # want fake to be labelled "real"
        loss_G = loss_fn(real_labels, D_fake)

    grads_G = tape_G.gradient(loss_G, \
        generator.trainable_weights)
    opt_G.apply_gradients(zip(grads_G, \
        generator.trainable_weights))

    # ---- Show progress ----
    print(f'Epoch {epoch}: \
        D_loss={loss_D.numpy():.3f}, \
        G_loss={loss_G.numpy():.3f}')
```

And we print some output to check our progress.

The code labelled `# --- 3. Train Discriminator ---` performs one full update step for the discriminator, teaching it to better distinguish real images from fake ones. Inside the `GradientTape`, we run two forward passes through the discriminator: One on a batch of real MNIST images and one on a batch of generator-produced images. Each pass produces a prediction. `D_real` should ideally be close to 1, while `D_fake` should be close to 0. We compute the discriminator's total loss by adding the binary-cross-entropy loss on real samples (labelled as 1) and fake samples (labelled as 0). This gives the discriminator a clear incentive: Reward correct classification of real images and penalise being fooled by the generator. Once the loss is computed, we ask the tape for the gradients of that loss with respect to the discriminator's trainable weights, and finally apply those gradients using its optimiser.

See the previous section for information on `GradientTape`.

This portion of the code strengthens the discriminator's ability to tell authentic images from the generator's fabrications.

The block of code labelled `# --- 4. Train Generator ---` indeed trains the generator by encouraging it to produce images that can successfully fool the discriminator. Inside the `GradientTape`, we begin by generating a fresh batch of fake images from noise z; these are then passed through the discriminator to obtain `D_fake`, the discriminator's judgement of how "real" the fakes look. Crucially, when calculating the generator's loss, we label these fake samples as real (`real_labels`), because the generator's objective is to maximise the discriminator's belief that its outputs are genuine. This inverted labelling is the essence of the adversarial trick: The generator improves by learning how to produce images the discriminator mistakes for real ones. Once we compute this loss, we extract the gradients with respect to the generator's weights and update those weights using the generator's optimiser. In effect, this code teaches the generator to become a better forger by analysing where its previous attempt failed in the eyes of the discriminator.

This network does the judging: Downsample, extract features, then deliver a single verdict: Real or fake.

The generator learns by pretending its fakes are real, and pushing the discriminator to believe the lie.

Finally, we print the losses incurred in the loop to check progress:

```
Epoch 26: D_loss=1.135, G_loss=1.348
Epoch 27: D_loss=1.153, G_loss=1.143
Epoch 28: D_loss=1.075, G_loss=1.215
Epoch 29: D_loss=1.059, G_loss=1.206
```

As we can see from the images in Figure 4.25, the images generated by the interplay between the discriminator and the generator in our simple Generative Adversarial Network are gradually getting better, with those at epoch 0 being

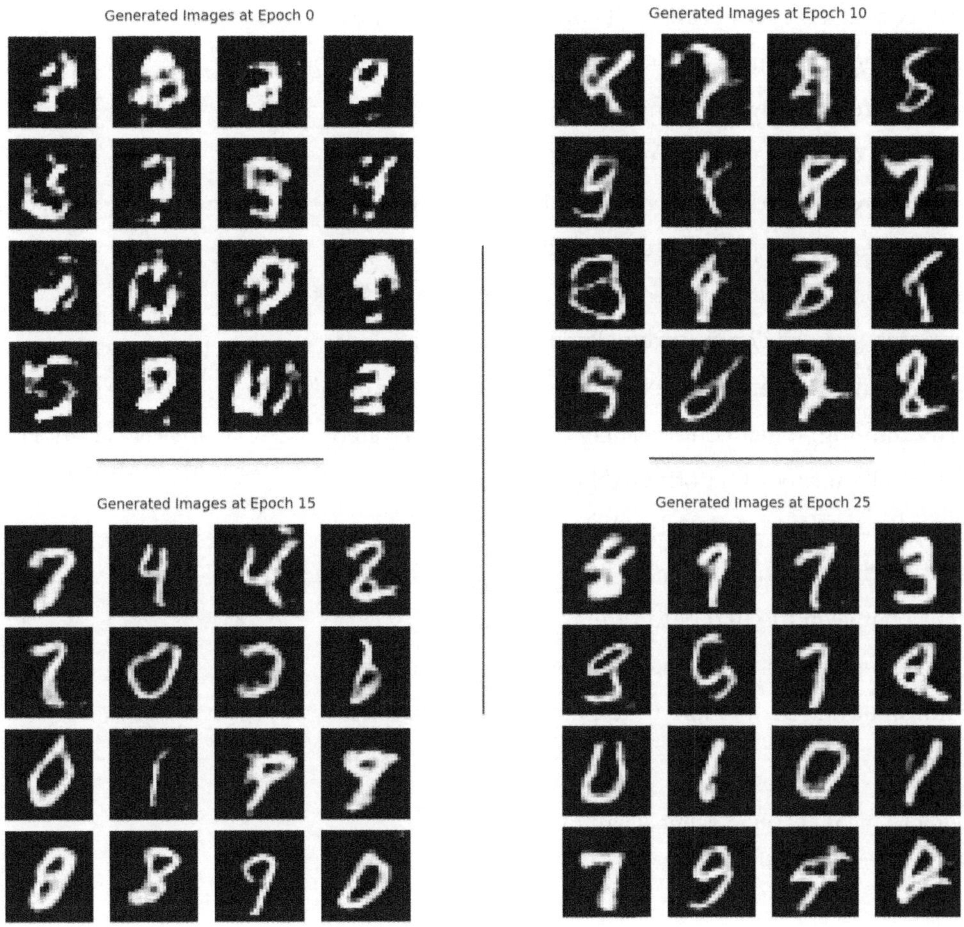

Figure 4.25: Images generated by a Generative Adversarial Network based on MNIST digits after 0, 10, 15 and 20 epochs.

rather poor imitations and those by epoch 20 being closer to numbers we would recognise.

The magic of GANs lies not only in their adversarial setup, but also in a certain philosophical elegance: Two opposing forces locked in a creative dance. One produces, the other critiques, and in doing so, both improve. This dynamic has an evolutionary flavour (mirroring the arms race of predator and prey in nature), and it is immediately rewarding: G gets

Two opposing forces locked in a creative dance: Light and Dark, Yin and Yang, a cat and a laser pointer...

instant feedback on how realistic its outputs are. In contrast, Reinforcement Learning agents often deal with delayed or sparse rewards and the challenge of exploration. An RL agent might only know it succeeded after a sequence of moves, whereas a GAN's generator knows right away (via D's gradients) which parts of its output look fake. The discriminator's output provides rich, differentiable feedback to G at each step, so G can update itself through standard backpropagation. There is no explicit notion of "exploration" in GAN training; it just continuously adjusts its generated samples to better fool D. Both GANs and RL involve learning through interaction, but the nature of that interaction differs fundamentally. Table 4.3 highlights some contrasts between the two paradigms. In short: Reinforcement Learning learns by exploration; GANs learn by confrontation. Or, as I like to tell my fellow Jackalope Data Scientists:

E.g., winning a game at the end

G does not need to try a long sequence of actions to get a reward.

> Reinforcement Learning agents learn to play the game;
> GANs learn to fake the board.

4.7 *Summary*

IT HAS BEEN A LONG journey, and I hope you have enjoyed the ride. In this chapter we have covered some of the most important aspects behind the magic and "unreasonable effectiveness" of neural networks. Given the influence that neural networks and deep learning have and with the number of use cases growing, this is truly an area in data science that any Jackalope data scientist needs to cover.

Aspect	Reinforcement Learning (RL)	Generative Adversarial Networks (GANs)
Learning paradigm	Trial-and-error: an agent learns by interacting with an environment and receiving rewards or punishments.	Adversarial: two models (generator and discriminator) learn by competing in a zero-sum game, each trying to outwit the other.
Objective	Maximise cumulative reward by finding an optimal policy (strategy of actions).	Achieve a Nash-like equilibrium where G's generated data distribution matches the real data and D can no longer tell the difference.
Feedback signal	Reward (often sparse or delayed): Feedback may come only after a sequence of actions (e.g., end of episode). Credit assignment is a challenge.	Differentiable feedback: The generator gets immediate gradients from the discriminator for each output, allowing direct tuning of G via backpropagation. No delayed reward, feedback is instant for each example.
Exploration vs. convergence	Needs to explore action space; trade-off between exploring new actions and exploiting known good ones. Convergence to optimal policy is target.	No explicit exploration of an environment. G explores the data space by continuous gradient-driven adjustments. Training seeks a balance (convergence) between G and D (often unstable if one overpowers the other).
Adversary/ Opponent	Optionally present in some environments (e.g., two-player games), but not required; the "opponent" is often the environment or nature, which does not actively adapt to undermine the agent.	Always present by design: The generator's opponent is the discriminator (and vice-versa), both learning and adapting simultaneously to each other's strategies. The environment here is the adversary.
Applications	Game playing, robotics, control systems, sequential decision-making tasks (e.g., AlphaGo in games, autonomous driving policies).	Generative modelling of data: image synthesis (e.g., deepfakes, Super-Resolution), data augmentation, creating music or text, etc.

Table 4.3: Comparison of Reinforcement Learning and GANs as learning paradigms.

We started our journey with a trip down memory lane, where we looked at an abridged historical account of some of the developments that have made neural networks shine. We saw how some of the ideas behind modern architectures started life much earlier than a lot of us imagine. Indeed the inspiration provided by biological neurons is a useful analogy, but realising the main differences is also important. The development of the perceptron is a clear step in the development of what we call deep learning and a good undestanding of its capabilities and limitations is a must.

Looking at the directed graphs used to represent neural nets, made out of nodes and layers, we get a clear picture of the flow of information, from layer to layer and node to node. We saw how the receiving nodes take both the input information and the weight of the connecting edges to compute a combined output. All this happens with the aid of an activation function. In turn this output is sent to the next set of nodes in the following layer. Deciding on the number of layers and nodes is an important task, and we saw how we can go from representing linear patterns through to more complex representations simply by changing the number of nodes in a hidden layer.

After getting a good understanding of the feedforward step in a neural network, we described the way the model can learn from its mistakes by looking at the errors incurred by the predictions after a single feedforward pass. The key to adjusting the weights in the network relies on the application of the chain rule to backpropagate the errors. Several round trips of feedforward and backpropagation enable the model to improve its predictions. With this information we were able to create our first neural network from scratch and looked at the effect that the number of nodes in a layer has in the overall classification boundaries generated by the model.

At this point we were able to take a look at expanding the number of layers, nodes and connections within a neural network and entered the world of deep learning. We used Keras to implement these architectures, as it offers a friendly and powerful manner to build our networks. We then talked about Reinforcement Learning, where learning is driven not by labelled examples but by trial, error, and the occasional triumph. We saw how agents interact with an environment, receiving rewards that guide their behaviour. We also ventured into the world of Generative Adversarial Networks (GANs), a domain where two neural networks engage in a rather elegant rivalry: One striving to create realistic data and the other attempting to expose its forgeries. By examining the dynamic between generator and discriminator, and the minimax objective that governs their interaction, we demonstrated how GANs have reshaped fields such as image synthesis, data augmentation, and creative and generative AI.

No brainer!

5

Attention, Memory and Meaning: A Journey Through Generative AI

SEQUENCE MODELS HAVE PLAYED A central role in the development of modern machine learning, quietly shaping the systems that translate languages, caption images, predict protein structures and, more recently, generate text that feels uncannily human.

Early architectures such as Recurrent Neural Networks (RNNs) and their more capable descendants, Long Short-Term Memory networks (LSTMs), marked the first serious attempt to give neural networks a sense of time. They could already carry information forward, step by step, making them powerful tools; with the addition of memory they could also retrieve past information making it possible to use them in applications using speech recognition, language modelling and a host of prediction tasks where order matters. Their limitations, however, became increasingly clear as datasets grew and ambitions expanded;

RNNs and LSTMs were the first to give neural nets a memory.

memory faded, gradients vanished, and computation struggled to scale.

The arrival of the Transformer architecture reshaped the field. By abandoning recurrence entirely and relying instead on attention mechanisms, Transformers demonstrated that models could capture both local and global structure more effectively than their sequential predecessors. This shift unlocked a new generation of pre-trained language models, from BERT, which excels at understanding and representation, to GPT-style models, which introduced the world to high-quality generative text. Today these approaches underpin the wider movement known as Generative AI.

And more efficiently!

In this chapter, we trace this journey from early recurrent models to the expansive capabilities of modern large language models, exploring the core ideas, motivations and practical considerations that have driven each step of this remarkable evolution.

5.1 *Architectures That Changed Language: RNNs to LLMs*

NATURAL LANGUAGE PROCESSING HAS ALWAYS wrestled with the fundamental challenge of representing meaning in a way that machines can work with. In Chapter 2 we explored the building blocks of this endeavour: How text is accessed, tokenised, tagged and transformed; how regular expressions help us tame messy inputs; and how embeddings allow us to move beyond sparse counts towards continuous, semantic

For a refresher on these topics, please refer back to Chapter 2.

representations. Those techniques provided the scaffolding on which early statistical and neural models were built. But as soon as we asked machines to model language, new architectural questions emerged. How should a model remember what came before? How should it decide which parts of a sentence, paragraph or document matter most?

In other words, to predict, translate, or generate language

Recurrent Neural Networks were the first major answer. They offered a simple but bold idea: Process text one token at a time, carrying a hidden state forward as a kind of rolling memory. Paired with the embedding methods we discussed earlier, RNNs could finally exploit the semantic closeness of words and phrases rather than rely on brittle surface forms. Yet, as Jackalope Data Scientists quickly discovered, their memory was rather more "goldfish" than "elephant". Gradients vanished, long-range dependencies slipped away and training became an uphill climb the moment the data had ideas above its station.

A noble early attempt at memory in motion—ingenious, but prone to forgetting anything beyond arm's reach.

LSTMs stepped in as more sophisticated successors, introducing gating mechanisms that controlled how information flowed and when it should be forgotten. This made them far more robust for tasks such as language modelling, sentiment analysis and machine translation. For a time, they were the state of the art, happily digesting tokenised text and building on the vector representations introduced in Chapter 2. However, as datasets expanded and expectations rose, the limits of strictly sequential processing became increasingly hard to ignore. Training was slow, parallelism was limited, and modelling subtle, global

Clever gatekeepers with far better memory, yet still shackled to the slow, one-step-at-a-time march.

relationships still felt like trying to read a novel through a letterbox.

The breakthrough came with the Transformer architecture. By replacing recurrence with attention, Transformers allowed models to examine all tokens simultaneously and decide which parts of the sequence were most relevant. This redefined the landscape. Not only could Transformers use embeddings more effectively, they could also scale to sizes previously unthinkable for sequential models.

We will explain what attention means in this context in Section 5.4.

Mathematically and mercifully free of bias.

From this foundation emerged a number of architectures that have quite literally revolutionised the landscape. One such architecture was the Bidirectional Encoder Representations from Transformers model, which specialised in deep linguistic understanding through masked language modelling, and Generative Pre-trained Transformer-style decoders, built to generate fluent, contextually rich text. Together they ushered in the era of Large Language Models.

BERT and GPT, more on these in Section 5.5.

These systems build on everything introduced earlier—the preprocessing, the tokenisation schemes, the embeddings—but amplify it with architectures capable of absorbing vast corpora and capturing patterns across documents, domains and even modalities. In the following sections, we will examine how these architectures work, what makes them so effective, and how the conceptual journey from RNNs to LLMs has reshaped our expectations of what machines can understand, and create, language.

Scale changes everything, including what we dare expect from machines that read and write.

5.2 *Recurrent Neural Networks*

MEMORY IS AN IMPORTANT FUNCTION that our brains enable us to perform. We are not pretending to explain here what memory is or is not, or even what it is for. I recommend reading A. Glenberg's paper on the subject instead[1]. If we think of memory as the function to encode, store and subsequently retrieve information, we would expect that, given the inspiration, an artificial neural network may be able to support a similar ability. So far, that has not been the case. The neural networks we have discussed pass information forwards and backwards, but at no point we have mentioned anything about retaining any memories. Carrying memories forwards is a helpful thing, as the Queen of Hearts[2] would remark , "It's a poor sort of memory that only works backward".

[1] Glenberg, A.M. (1997). What memory is for. *Behav. Brain Sci. 20*, 1–55.

[2] Carroll, L. and J. Tenniel (1897). *Through the Looking Glass: And what Alice Found There.* Altemus' illustrated young people's library. Henry Altemus Company.

The premise of a recurrent neural network architecture is such that we require it to remember previous inputs to be used in subsequent steps of the training. Up until now we have made the assumption that all inputs are independent of each other. However, there are certain tasks where this is not necessarily true. Think for example of applications where the past history is important in the prediction, such as in the time series we discussed in Chapter 1, or for example in speech recognition, language translation or image captioning. Remembering the previous inputs provide important information to the network. Later on, in Section 5.4, we will discuss extending the memory idea with the concept of *attention*.

And outputs for that matter...

See Section 5.4 for more on attention.

Performing the same task for every element of a sequence of inputs makes the task *recurrent* and hence the name of this type of neural networks. The output, as explained above, is dependent on the previous calculations carried out by the network, and therefore having the equivalent of a *memory* function that captures that information is important. Consider a section A of a neural network that receives an input X_t. The output of this section is a value y_t as shown in Figure 5.1. In a recurrent neural network we enable a loop that lets us pass the information from one portion of the network to the next. We can think of this loop in an unfolded way as shown in the right-hand side of Figure 5.1.

The same task occurs repeatedly for every element in the network, hence the name.

RNN for short.

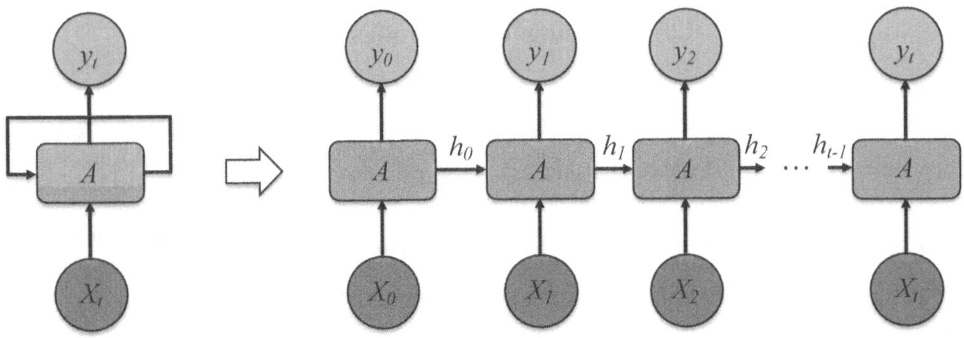

Figure 5.1: Diagrammatic representation of the architecture of a recurrent neural network.

The unfolded version of the recurrent neural network lets us see clearly the importance of the sequence of inputs and outputs during training. We have already mentioned some of the applications where RNNs have become the norm. A particular architecture that is widely used is the so-called *long short-term memory* or LSTM proposed in 1997 by Hochreiter and Schmidhuber[3], with several adjustments added in subsequent years. Before we get to see how LSTM networks work, let us highlight some of the differences

[3] Hochreiter, S. and Schmidhuber, J. (1997). Long short-term memory. *Neural. Comput.* 9(8), 1735–1780.

between RNNs and the neural network architectures we have seen so far.

Let us consider the task of predicting what the next word in a sentence is. We can choose a large corpus as our training data, think for example of a book such as *Erewhon; Or, Over the Range* [4] by Samuel Butler. First published in 1872, the book tells us about the adventures our narrator experiences in the eponymous country he discovers. Upon arrival on the land, the protagonist learns that, 500 years prior, Erewhonians were made aware of the danger of technological revolt, banning the use of anything but the most primitive machines. The decision is explained in a manifesto called *The Book of the Machines*. This is the literary mechanism that Butler uses to raise the possibility of conscious machines by Darwinian selection.

Indeed a sentence is a sequence of words.

[4] Butler, S. (1999). Erewhon; Or, Over the Range. Project Gutenberg https://www.gutenberg.org/ebooks/1906. Accessed: 2025-10-10.

But we digress... After training our neural network with the text from *Erewhon*, if we input the sequence:

> "There is no security"– to quote his own words– "against the ultimate development of mechanical...

The title of the novel is the word "Nowhere" spelt backwards, with the letters "w" and "h" transposed.

we would expect a reasonable word to follow, based on the training text provided. During training, we will take each word at a time and produce a result as in the feedforward neural networks we know and love. However, in this case we also need to be aware of the previous inputs that have been provided before we look at the result. This is what we are doing in the unfolded version of the RNN shown in Figure 5.1 where each $X_0, X_1, X_2, \ldots, X_t$ corresponds to the input words from the corpus. In turn, we produce the

Refer to the unfolded version of our RNN shown in Figure 5.1.

predicted follow-up word $y_0, y_1, y_2, \ldots, y_t$, and we hold in memory the information $h_0, h_1, h_2, \ldots, h_{t-1}$ about the previous words.

Remember, memory is the key.

In order to make the most out of our recurrent neural network architecture, we will need to consider using something like word embeddings to help us map words to vectors, for instance with the help of Word2Vec[5] which we discussed in the context of natural language processing in Sections 2.7.1 and 3.5.1. In this case, to make the explanation simpler, we consider a simplistic approach such as one-hot encoding to obtain vectors with dimension $(V, 1)$ where V is the number of words in the vocabulary. The values of the vectors are all zeros, except for a 1 at the position that corresponds to the entry in our dictionary of words. So if the vocabulary has three words: `[aardvark, iberian_lynx, zebra]`, the vector for `iberian_lynx` will be $[0, 1, 0]$.

[5] Mikolov, T., I. Sutskever, et al. (2013). Distributed Representations of Words and Phrases and Their Compositionality. In *Proceedings of the 26th International Conference on Neural Information Processing Systems - Volume 2*, NIPS'13, USA, pp. 3111–3119. Curran Associates Inc.

See Section 2.7 for more information on vector embeddings.

Back to *Erewhon*, let us imagine that we would like to use the RNN in Figure 5.1 to predict the next word in the proposed sequence. The network applies a recurrence formula in A to the input vector as well as to its previous state. For the first word (*There*) there is nothing before it, so nothing to remember. When we move to the next word (*is*) the network applies the recurrence formula to it and takes the previous state into consideration, i.e., the word *There*. The two words are used to calculate a new state, which will be fed back to the network in the next timestep. We say that at time t the input is *is*, at time $t - 1$ the input was *There*. We continue like this for the rest of the inputs, one at a time.

RNNs apply a recurrence formula to the input vector as well as to its previous state. This latter is the memory we want the network to retain.

We can think of the current state of the network to be given by a combination (via an activation function) of the previous state and the input vector as the current timestep:

We can see clearly the influence of the previous state.

$$h_t \simeq f(h_{t-1}, X_t), \tag{5.1}$$

where f is the activation function. From our discussions about the training of feedforward neural nets, we have seen that the weights associated with each of the nodes are the parameters we need to fit. We therefore need to take them into account here too. Let us denote the weight at the input node as W_{xh}, and the weight at the current node as W_{hh}, the state at time t will then be given by:

Not only the input and previous states, but we also need the weights.

$$h_t = \sigma(W_{hh}h_{t-1} + W_{xh}X_t), \tag{5.2}$$

where we are applying a softmax activation function. In this case the memory of the network is only of the immediate previous step. We can say that it has a short memory. Remembering more steps will require appropriate storage.

Remembering more steps requires more storage.

With this state we can calculate the output at time t as $y_t = W_{hy}h_t$. At this point, if this is the final output of the network, we can use backpropagation to enable us to update the weights as we have done before. In the case of our sample sentence, after obtaining the optimal weights, we input each of the words in the sequence, the RNN will produce $(h_1, h_2, h_3, \ldots, h_{15})$ and we calculate y_{16} using h_{15} and X_{16} (the one-hot encoded vector of the word *mechanical*). A successful training will give us a vector y_{16} corresponding to the word *consciousness*, which would have been the correct prediction.

The application of backpropagation still stands for recurrent neural networks.

The main difference between RNNs and the other neural nets we have discussed is the application of the feedback loop connecting the present state to the past decisions made. This is what we refer to as **memory** in the context of neural networks, and its main goal is to exploit the information contained in the sequence of inputs.

The feedback loop is the distinguishing feature of RNNs.

We mentioned above the application of backpropagation in a recurrent neural network. In this case we need to backpropagate through time (BPTT). We treat the full sequence (in this case, the sentence) as a single training sample; the error is given by the sum of errors at each timestep (each word). So for the total error E we have that:

In this case, backpropagation is actually backpropagation through time.

$$\frac{\partial E}{\partial \mathbf{W}} = \sum_t \frac{\partial E_t}{\partial \mathbf{W}}, \tag{5.3}$$

As before we can apply the chain rule, and as we can see from the unrolled version of the RNN, the gradient needs to be calculated for each timestep with respect to the weight parameter. For example for E_5 we have that:

$$\frac{\partial E_5}{\partial \mathbf{W}} = \frac{\partial E_5}{\partial \hat{y}_5}\frac{\partial \hat{y}_5}{\partial f_5}\frac{\partial f_5}{\partial \mathbf{W}}, \tag{5.4}$$

The chain rule still rules for BPTT.

where f_5 is the activation function at this time step. In turn, this activation function depends on $\mathbf{W}$ and f_4, which depends on f_3, and so on. With the weight being the same for all the timesteps in one single pass, we can combine all the gradients so long as we express the computations with a well-defined, ordered sequence of calculations. It is

sometimes preferred to use a truncated BPTT approach as the cost and time of going back over many timesteps can be quite
high.

It is clear now that recurrent neural nets get their predictive power from the dependency on previous timesteps. However, they may have some trouble remembering over long time dependencies. If the memory is only over one timestep, a recurrent neural network may have trouble with a sentence such as:

Not dissimilar to a lot of us humans anyway!

> The knight fleeing from the Jackalope is a coward

This must be the Jackalope of Caerbannog of course!

where the description of being a coward is for the knight and not for the Jackalope. The issue is not just one of interval length. As we propagate forward in the network, if we were to encounter a gradient that is smaller than 1 and we multiply it by a suitably small learning rate, the values become ever smaller. We then use this information to propagate the errors back through time making the problem bigger. This leads to an issue with recurrent neural networks called the **vanishing gradient** problem where the network has problems remembering information from far away in the sequence, making predictions based only on the most recent timesteps.

Vanishing gradients indicate issues with remembering long sequences.

Conversely, we can experience **exploding gradient** issues where the gradient values become increasingly large, assigning undue importance to certain weights for no good reason. Exploding gradients can be successfully managed by imposing a threshold on the gradients, for example.

Whereas exploding gradients assign undue importance to certain weights.

Another option is the truncated BPTT we mentioned above. In comparison, vanishing gradients are more concerning, and they can be dealt with by using architectures such as LSTM.

5.3 *Long Short-Term Memory Networks*

A LONG SHORT-TERM MEMORY NEURAL net is a type of RNN able to remember over longer-term dependencies. The chain of repeating modules we have described above still holds true in an LSTM. However, the inner workings of the module A shown in Figure 5.1 is no longer the simple application of an activation function such as a ReLU or a hyperbolic tangent.

Long short-term memory, or LSTM for short.

Instead, each module of the LSTM has 3 gates, namely the Forget Gate, the Input and the Output Gates. These are shown in Figure 5.2, and we will consider each of them in turn. The main cell state of the LSTM is the horizontal line that runs straight through the top of the diagram. The architecture of the network relies on the addition or removal of information to this cell state through the gates mentioned above.

LSTM gates act as valves that regulate what information is forgotten, added, or revealed from the cell state.

For example, in the Forget Gate we have a sigmoid neural network layer (the box marked with S) followed by a point-wise multiplication operation (the circle marked with X). This lets us decide what information is allowed to pass to the cell state. It takes information form the previous state h_{t-1} and the input X_t generating a value between 0 and 1 for each cell state C_{t-1}. The output g_t of this gate can be

Refer to the Forget, Input and Output Gates in Figure 5.2.

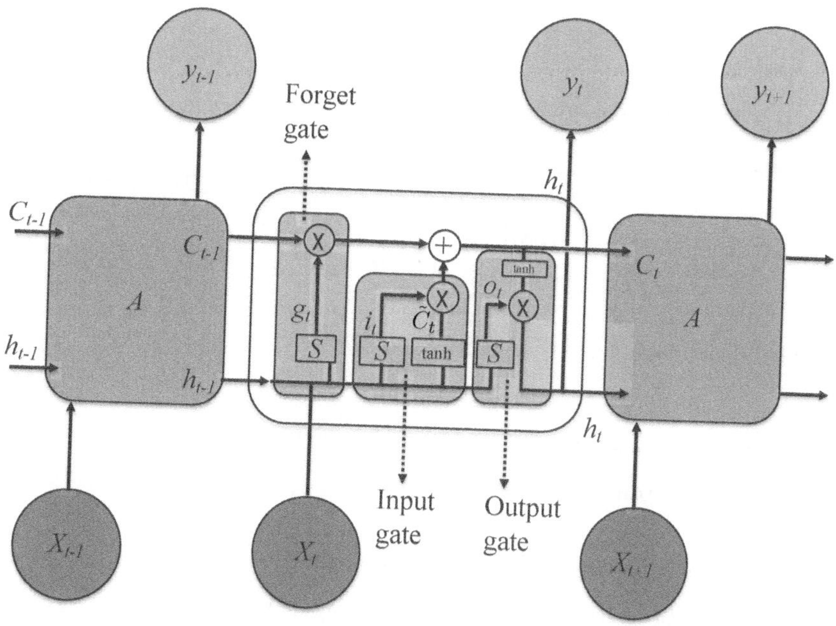

Figure 5.2: The inner workings of a long short-term memory neural network.

expressed as:

$$g_t = S\left(W_g \cdot [h_{t-1}, X_t] + b_g\right). \quad (5.5)$$

If the value generated is a 0, it indicates that the information will be forgotten, whereas a 1 will enable the information to be remembered. In short, the Forget Gate lets us decide how much past information we should remember.

The next stage in the process is the Input Gate where we are able to decide the amount of information that this module will add to the current cell state. In other words, if the Forget Gate enables us to forget information of the past state, this gate lets us decide what to remember in this cell state. The Input Gate has two stages, first a sigmoid layer that picks what values will be updated:

Also called Update Gate as we shall see.

$$i_t = S\left(W_i \cdot [h_{t-1}, X_t] + b_i\right). \tag{5.6}$$

Remember the 0s and 1s thrown by a sigmoid function.

Then we have a hyperbolic tangent layer that proposes new potential cell state values $\tilde{C}_t$:

$$\tilde{C}_t = \tanh\left(W_C \cdot [h_{t-1}, X_t] + b_C\right). \tag{5.7}$$

The importance of values is modulated by the $[-1, 1]$ output of the hyperbolic tangent.

The outputs of the two layers are then combined (circle marked with X in Figure 5.2 inside the Input Gate boundary), which will be used to update the state given by the top horizontal line in our diagram.

We need to update the old cell state C_{t-1}. In reality all the decisions have already been made in the previous stages, we just need to apply the calculations. First, we multiply the output of the Forget Gate g_t with the previous state C_{t-1}, forgetting parts of the old state. We then add the result to the filtered candidate values $\tilde{C}_t$ from the Input Gate (in the top horizontal line in the diagram):

At the circle marked with + in Figure 5.2.

$$C_t = g_t C_{t-1} + i_t \tilde{C}_t. \tag{5.8}$$

That is why we also call it the Update Gate.

We are now at the Output Gate of our module, where we decide the portion of the current cell that will make it to the output. We apply a sigmoid layer for this purpose:

$$o_t = S\left(W_o \cdot [h_{t-1}, X_t] + b_o\right). \tag{5.9}$$

And finally, to the Output Gate.

At the same time we put the cell state obtained from the previous stages C_t through a hyperbolic tangent layer to map the values between -1 and 1 and combine the outputs filtering out the portions of the cell state we want to output, i.e., h_t:

$$h_t = o_t \tanh(C_t). \quad (5.10)$$

The description presented above covers the main components in an LSTM. There are other variations such as the Gated Recurrent Unit (GRU)[6] which combines the Forget and Input Gates into a single unit. It also merges the cell state and hidden state resulting in simpler inner architecture.

[6] Cho, K., B. van Merrienboer, et al. (2014). Learning phrase representations using RNN encoder-decoder for statistical machine translation. *CoRR abs/1406.1078*.

If you are interested in a comparison of different LSTM architectures, take a look at *LSTM: A Search Space Odyssey*[7] where the authors present such comparison. They find that different LSTM architectures perform more or less the same as standard LSTM. They show that the Forget Gate and the output activation function are the most critical components in the general architecture of these networks. Well, it is time to take a look at the implementation of a long short-term memory neural network!

[7] Greff, K., Srivastava, R. K., Koutník, J., et al. (2017). LSTM: A Search Space Odyssey. *IEEE Trans. Neural Netw. and Learning Sys.* 28(10), 2222–2232.

5.3.1 *Long Short-Term Memory Networks in Action*

LET US CREATE A NEURAL network that is able to generate a plausible sequence given a set of training data. We will use a character-level language model. This means that we will give our LSTM recurrent neural network a number of character sequences and request for the probability distribution of the next character in the sequence. We can use the model to generate new sequences—hopefully

This kind of models is called generative... for obvious reasons.

coherent sentences—one character at a time. An interesting blog entry called *The Unreasonable Effectiveness of Recurrent Neural Networks*[8] covers this same challenge including different types of corpora.

[8] Karpathy, A. (2015). The Unreasonable Effectiveness of Recurrent Neural Networks. https://karpathy.github.io/2015/05/21/rnn-effectiveness/. Accessed: 2025-10-05.

Our starting point requires us to get hold of a large piece of text. We will use the text mentioned in Section 5.2, i.e., the 1872 fiction novel *Erewhon; Or, Over the Range*[9] by Samuel Butler. The text can be found in the Project Gutenberg site.

[9] Butler, S. (1999). Erewhon; Or, Over the Range. Project Gutenberg https://www.gutenberg.org/ebooks/1906. Accessed: 2025-10-10.

After downloading the text in UTF-8 format and it is saved in a plain file called `erewhon.txt`, we can start our journey over the range. As usual we start by loading some libraries:

We already know how to do this with our eyes closed.

```
import numpy as np
import random
from tensorflow.keras.models import Sequential, \
   Dense, Dropout, LSTM
from tensorflow.keras.callbacks import \
   ModelCheckpoint
from tensorflow.keras.utils to_categorical
```

We are familiar with the calls made above, except perhaps for `LSTM` and `ModelChekpoint`. The former should be pretty straightforward after reading the preceding section. The latter helps us request information from our architecture at desired points, e.g., at the end of every epoch. Let us load the text:

We open and read the file as usual.

```
book = 'erewhon.txt'
with open(book, 'r') as file:
```

```
    text = file.read().lower()
n_text = len(text)
```

We can see what the length of our corpus is:

```
> print('Book Text Length: {}'.format(n_text))

Book Text Length: 483134
```

The number of characters is the length of our text.

We have over 480k characters in the text. We will be generating text character-by-character, and therefore we require a set of the characters used in the text. It is this set that becomes our "vocabulary" for this task.

```
chars = sorted(list(set(text)))
n_vocab = len(chars)
```

We calculate a set from the characters in the corpus.

We can now ask about the cardinality of the character set used in the corpus:

```
> print('Number of characters used: {} '.\
    format(n_vocab))

Number of characters used: 62
```

There are 62 entries in the set, more than the usual 26 letters in English.

There are 62 different characters used, more than the typical 26 characters in the English alphabet. This is because there are some symbols, punctuation and other characters too:

```
> print(chars[:5], chars[-5:])


['\n', ' ', '!', '"', '#']
['y', 'z', '{', '}', '\ufeff']
```

Perhaps an opportunity to pre-process our data.

We will need to keep track of the characters used; but not only that, we will need to pass a numerical representation to the neural network. To that end, we will create an index for the characters:

```
char_ixs = dict((c, i)
    for i, c in enumerate(chars))
```

We are using a dictionary to create our vocabulary index. Great!

It may be needed to reverse back the index, so that any prediction can be traced back to the character in question:

```
ixs_char = dict((i, c)
    for i, c in enumerate(chars))
```

We also need the reverse index.

Another important decision that needs to be made is the length of the training sequences we will feed into the LSTM. In this case we are going to use a fixed length of 40 characters. Other approaches may include partitioning the text into sentences and pad them to take into account long and short sentences.

You can try other length sequences.

In order to keep things in check, we will generate sequences jumping a few characters. We do this with a step of 3. Finally, the training sequences, along with the next character in the sequence, will be stored in lists:

```
seq_len = 40
step = 3
rawX = []
rawy = []
```

We store the training sequences in rawX and the next characters in rawy.

Let us generate the sequences, i.e., sentences, that will be fed to the neural network:

```
for i in range(0, len(text) - seq_len, step):
    rawX.append(text[i: i+seq_len])
    rawy.append(text[i+seq_len])

n_sentences = len(rawX)
```

We append the sequences to the lists above.

We can check how many sequences have been generated:

```
> print(n_sentences)

161032
```

This is the number of sequences that will be used to train our recurrent neural network.

We have over 160k sentences to train our network. Let us take a look at one of them:

```
> print(rawX[900])

machines as an attempt to reduce mr. dar
```

This is sequence 900 in our dataset.

and the next character in this sequence is:

```
>  print(rawy[900])

w
```

And this is the next character for sequence 900.

We can get a glimpse to the Darwinian references used by Butler in the description of the Erewhonian machines. We need to encode these sentences and next characters to be able to pass them to the neural network. We will create some Boolean arrays to hold the information. For the sequences we need an array to hold the number of sentences (161,032) by the length of the sentence (40) by the number of characters in our vocabulary (62). For the next characters, we only need the number of sentences by the number of characters:

I am no RNN, but surely that would be a reference to Darwin himself!

```
X = np.zeros((len(rawX), seq_len, len(chars)),
    dtype=np.bool)

y = np.zeros((len(rawy), len(chars)),
    dtype=np.bool)
```

Our sequences and next characters are now transformed into Boolean arrays.

Each character in each sentence can now be encoded with the help of the index we created earlier on:

```
for i, sentence in enumerate(rawX):
    for t, char in enumerate(sentence):
        X[i, t, char_ixs[char]] = 1
    y[i, char_ixs[rawy[i]]]=1
```

We use our dictionary to encode the characters.

We have completed our data processing, and we are ready to define the architecture of our LSTM neural network. We will use the sequential API and try to keep the architecture simple at this stage:

```
model = Sequential()
model.add(LSTM(128, input_shape=(seq_len,
    len(chars))))
model.add(Dropout(0.2))
model.add(Dense(len(chars), activation='softmax'))
```

We use the sequential API in Keras for this implementation.

We start with a long short-term memory layer with 128 units expecting an input with dimensions of the length of the sequence by the number of characters. We then apply a dropout layer setting 20% of the inputs units to 0. Finally, we connect this to a dense output layer with a softmax activation function. Let us look at a summary of the model:

```
> print(model_summary())


_________________________________________________
Layer (type)              Output Shape         Param #
=================================================
lstm (LSTM)               (None, 128)          97792
dropout (Dropout)         (None, 128)          0
dense (Dense)             (None, 62)           7998
=================================================
Total params: 105,790
Trainable params: 105,790
Non-trainable params: 0
```

This is a very simple architecture for our first long short-term memory neural network.

This model requires us to train 105,790 parameters. For that purpose, we need to compile our model while providing an optimiser and an appropriate loss function:

```
from keras.optimizers import RMSprop


opt = RMSprop(learning_rate=0.01)
model.compile(loss='categorical_crossentropy',\
    optimizer=opt)
```

We need to train 105,790 parameters in this model.

We may be interested in a very accurate model that predicts each character in the text perfectly. That may take a more intricate architecture and a longer training time. In this case, we will request the model to provide us with a view of the improvements achieved in the training by recording a model to a file whenever this happens at the end of an epoch. This is why we are interested in the `ModelCheckpoint` method introduced earlier on in this section.

This model may not be the most accurate, but then again it is a very simple one.

We start by defining a file name including information about the given epoch and loss, we will pass this information to the model checkpoint and provide this as a list of callbacks to the model:

```
fname=''weights-improv-{epoch:02d}-{loss:.4f}.keras
checkpoint = ModelCheckpoint(fname,\
    monitor='loss', verbose=1,\
    save_best_only=True, mode='min')
```

`ModelCheckpoint` lets us keep track of the improvements in the model during training.

We can now start training our model:

```
model.fit(X, y, epochs=60, batch_size=128,
    callbacks=[checkpoint])
```

We are training the model for 60 epochs with batches of 128 sequences. In the instance when this model was run, the model did not manage to get any further improvements in the optimisation of the loss function after the 59th epoch. The latest file produced by the check point was `weights-improv-59-1.3969.keras`.

The model obtained can be used to generate some text. But before we do that, let us make sure that we are able to obtain appropriate samples out of the probability array. We will use the fact that we are using a softmax function and apply a "temperature" to control the randomness of the predictions made. If the network produces class probabilities with logit vector $\mathbf{z} = (z_1, z_2, \ldots, z_n)$ by applying a softmax function, then we are able to calculate the probability vector $\mathbf{q} = (q_1, q_2, \ldots, q_n)$ with q_i given by the following expression:

We need to ensure that we can obtain appropriate samples out of a probability array.

The temperature parameter adjusts how confidently the model chooses between possible outputs.

$$q_i = \frac{\exp(z_i/T)}{\sum_{j=1} \exp(z_j/T)}, \tag{5.11}$$

where T being the temperature parameter. When $T = 1$, we are computing the softmax function directly on the logits without scaling. When $T = 0.5$ for instance, we are effectively doubling the logits, and therefore we have larger values of the softmax function. This makes our predictions more confident but also more conservative. Let us create a function to calculate the sample:

Lower temperatures make predictions more deterministic, while higher ones increase creativity and randomness.

```
def sample(p, temperature=1.0):
    p = np.asarray(p).astype('float64')
    p = p**(1/temperature)
    p_sum = p.sum()
```

This function lets us obtain those samples.

```
    sample_temp = p/p_sum

    return np.argmax(np.random.multinomial(\
        1, sample_temp, 1))
```

Let us pick a random number to get a sequence. We will generate characters one at a time, and they will be added to the initial sentence:

```
start_ix=random.randint(0, len(text) - seq_len - 1)
generated= ''
sentence = text[start_ix: start_ix + seq_len]
generated += sentence
```

We pick a sequence at random.

An initial sentence will be given for example by:

```
> print(sentence)

gh he never\nwent beyond the bounds of mo
```

Your sentence will surely be different.

Let us generate 400 characters with the model. Remember that we will get predictions in terms of indices, and they will need to be translated back into characters using the dictionaries we defined earlier in this section:

```
for i in range(400):
    x_pred = np.zeros((1, seq_len, len(chars)))
    for t, char in enumerate(sentence):
        x_pred[0, t, char_ixs[char]] = 1.
```

We generate 400 characters with our LSTM. Remember that we need to translate back using our reverse index.

```
    preds = model.predict(x_pred, verbose=0)[0]

    next_index = sample(preds, diversity)
    next_char = ixs_char[next_index]
    generated += next_char
    sentence = sentence[1:] + next_char
```

The generated text for the sequence above would look similar to the following:

```
> print(generated)

'gh he never\nwent beyond the bounds of more so
long as they had been all the twing which i could
be the states of the man and some of them be made
his remembered of expecting and not the cently not
believe as a stranger for the statues of a
conscience and the man were right at the statues
of the old thing and man of the intention is the
work which they had my his and hand of conduct
with the machines which i had been weather with
which h'
```

This is an example of the text generated with our SLTM character by character. Yours will most likely be different.

It may not seem like much, but bearing in mind that the text was generated one character at a time and without prior knowledge to the English language, the model was able to generate word-like groups of characters, most of which are actual English words such as "remembered", "stranger", "machines", "intention" or "weather". The results are by no means perfect, but remember that the neural network architecture we build only had a single LSTM layer.

Not bad! It can also talk about the weather like a lot of us!

5.4 *Attention in Disguise: Transformers and Generative AI*

IF THE MENTION OF "TRANSFORMERS" brings to mind the adventures of autonomous robots in disguise, you are probably—like me—a child of the 1980s. As much as I would like to talk about that kind of transformer, the subject of this section is instead the architecture proposed by Vaswani *et al.* in their 2017 paper *Attention is All You Need* [10]. This model changed the landscape of deep learning by introducing a neural network that relies solely on the concept of *attention*, dispensing entirely with recurrence or convolution.

[10] Vaswani, A., N. Shazeer, N. Parmar, et al. (2017). Attention Is All You Need. In *Advances in Neural Information Processing Systems*, pp. 5998–6008. Curran Associates, Inc.

Before the advent of Transformers, sequence models relied heavily on recurrent neural networks (RNNs) and their more sophisticated cousins, such as Long Short-Term Memory networks (LSTMs). These models process sequences one element at a time, maintaining a hidden state that carries information forward. In theory, an RNN could learn long-range dependencies in data such as sentences or time series, but in practice this was limited by vanishing gradients and the inherently sequential nature of training.

We cover these in the previous section.

Researchers introduced the concept of *attention* as a way of mitigating these problems. In the context of a sequence-to-sequence model, the attention mechanism allows the decoder to look back at the entire input sequence, rather than relying solely on the final encoder state. In this way,

Attention lets the model peek at everything, not just the last breadcrumb, finally a way to focus on what truly matters.

the model can learn which parts of the input are most relevant for generating each output element.

Mathematically, attention computes a set of weights that determine how much each input contributes to a given output. This attention vector is then used to produce a new context representation for the decoder. In other words, attention lets the model decide *what to focus on*. The 2017 paper by Vaswani *et al.* took this concept a step further by introducing *self-attention*. Whereas attention in earlier models allowed the decoder to focus on parts of the encoder's output, self-attention enables every element in the input sequence to look at every other element. This provides the model with a powerful way of capturing relationships between distant parts of a sequence.

A neat bit of maths that boils down to this: Weighted focus, served fresh each step.

A sharper, faster way to transform one sequence into another.

Transformers are in essence a type of artificial neural network architecture that are used to solve the problem of *transduction* or transformation of input sequences into output sequences in deep learning applications. You may be wondering what we mean by input and output sequences: Think for example of speech recognition, protein structure prediction or machine translation. Let us concentrate on the latter.

A fresh take on turning one sequence into another: Fast, flexible, and built for more than just language.

Given a sentence in English (sequence input), we want to find the translation into Japanese (sequence output) that has the same meaning (or as close as possible) as the original sentence. So the input sentence:

"Optimus Prime is a cool robot"

requires us to produce the output

"コンボイはかっこいいロボットです。"

Yes, Optimus Prime is called Convoy/コンボイ in Japanese.

Simply translating word by word in the order of appearance may result in an output that a human Japanese speaker would consider ungrammatical. For instance, in Japanese the verbs are placed at the end of the utterance, whereas this never happens in English. One of the main questions in sequence transduction is the learning of representations for both the input and output sequences in a robust manner, so that no distortions are introduced.

Unless Master Yoda you are!

You do not want to mistranslate an important message! Ask Princess Leia!

An approach to tackle this question is the use of recurrent neural networks (RNNs) as we did in the previous section. The long short-term memory of the architectures we explored is a good start, but there are limitations in their use, for example finding out the length of the output sequence may be challenging given the fixed-sized input/output vector architecture of RNNs. A better approach is the use of a transformer.

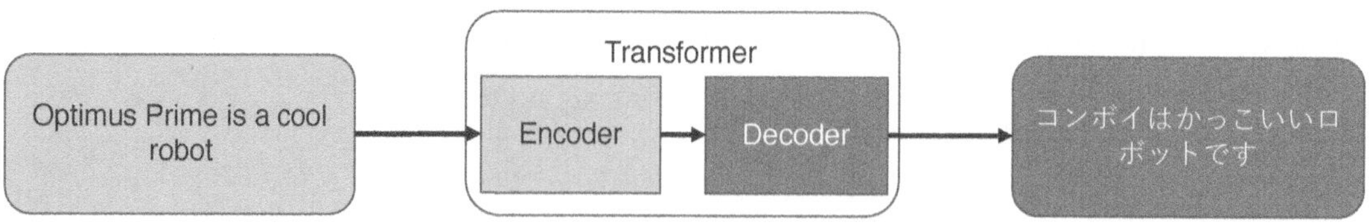

Figure 5.3: Schematic high-level of a Transformer including the encoder and decoder components to translate a sentence.

The magic of machine translation works thanks to two components in the architecture: the *encoder* and *decoder*, shown in Figure 5.3. The former is the element that receives each component of the input sequence, encoding it into a

Hence the names.

vector carrying the context information about the whole sequence. This is sent to the decoder whose job is to understand the context and resolve the output meaningfully. Since the important information of the original sequence is carried in the context vector, we can see this as the most important part of the architecture. Similarly, it may be the cause of a traffic jam in the system. This is where the concept of *attention* comes into place as it enables focussing on the significant parts of the input sequence as needed.

5.4.1 *Transformer Architecture*

THE TRANSFORMER ARCHITECTURE IS BUILT from stacks of identical layers that combine self-attention and feedforward neural networks. To understand the difference, it is useful to compare with a recurrent neural network (RNN), where data are processed sequentially, i.e., one element at a time. The hidden state is the mathematical representation of what the network has learned so far from the previous elements in that sequence. Think of the hidden state as a summary or compressed memory of all the previous inputs the network has seen up to that point. In a sequence-to-sequence mode the encoder passes only the last hidden state as the context to the decoder.

For instance, one word in a sentence or one frame in a time series.

Transformers do not have a recurrent hidden state. Instead, they replace it entirely with attention, where each token directly looks at all others in the sequence. The idea of "memory" is distributed across the entire attention mechanism, rather than stored in a single evolving vector. In

No recurrence, just tokens sharing context through attention. Memory becomes a team sport.

other words, the hidden state in an RNN is replaced in a Transformer by the contextual embeddings produced by attention layers.

When attention is used, the encoder passes not only the last hidden state, but actually all of them. This means that the decoder may have a bit more work to do than before. This extra processing is needed as now every hidden state received is associated to a given part of the input sequence. In our sample sentence *"Optimus Prime is a cool robot"*, the first hidden state is related to the word *Optimus*, the second to the word *Prime*, the third one to *is*, and so on. In this way, the decoder has more work, but also much more information.

The decoder now receives every hidden state, each one an Autobot with its own mission.

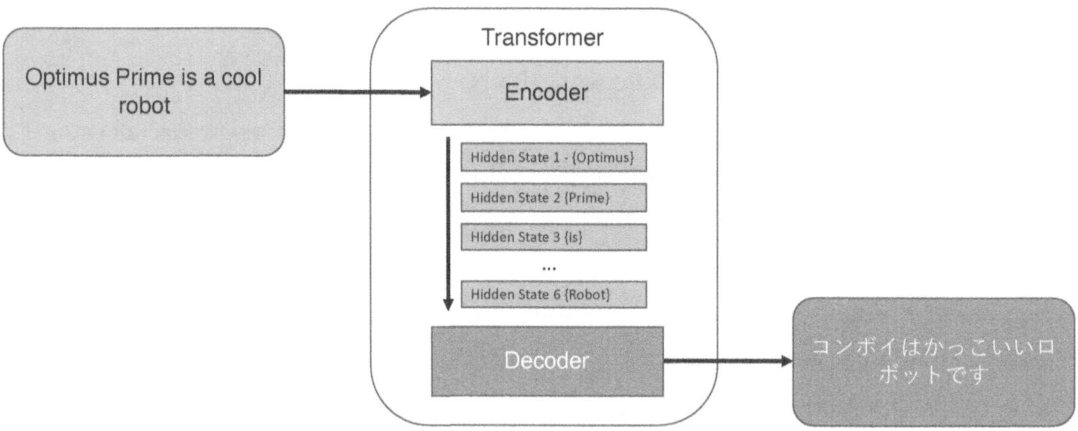

Figure 5.4: The transformer architecture relies on the decoder calculating the weight for each hidden state received from the encoder.

The job of the decoder is now to calculate the weight for each hidden state received from the encoder. This is done with the decoder's own hidden state, in other words, the output of the previous timestep in the model (see Figure

5.4). The aim is to provide greater importance to hidden states with higher weight values, and this is our new context vector. We can then use this context as input to the decoder's feedforward neural net to obtain the output sequence we are after. In turn, the output sequence is used as the hidden state of the decoder that is sued in the calculation of weights in the next timestep.

The model picks the heavy-hitters, blends them into a context vector, and uses that to steer the next move. Checkmate!

This cyclical process is what allows the decoder to "remember" what has already been generated, adjusting its focus at every step to ensure coherence and relevance. Each new token benefits from a weighted blend of past information and the encoder's representation of the input. The result is a model that does not merely translate word by word, but instead composes meaningfully—attending to what matters most as it goes.

Not word-by-word translation, but genuine composition, guided by what actually matters.

5.4.2 *Role of Self-Attention*

WHILE ATTENTION IS AN IMPORTANT trick under the sleeve of the decoder, we may ask whether the encoder has any tricks of its own. The answer is "yes", and it is called *self-attention*. Like attention, self-attention tracks associations from the input sequence, but this time it is the encoder who keeps track of other items to achieve a better encoding. Take for instance the following input sentence:

Self-attention gives the encoder its own Bumblebee mode: Tuning into every word so the whole message stays in harmony.

> "Bumblebee plays some catchy music and dances along to it".

If we only track the relationship of words that are close together, we can easily identify that the word *catchy* refers to *music*. If the tracking is only done between two consecutive words, we may end up in a situation where the word *it* at the end of the sentence loses its reference. To a human reader the *it* in the sentence is clearly referring to *music*. In a situation with low self-attention, however, a translating machine may not know this.

Without strong self-attention, long-range links get lost—"it" forgets who it belongs to.

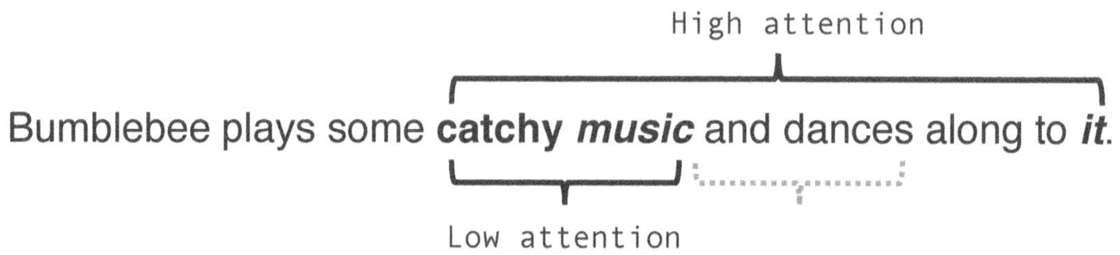

Figure 5.5: Self-attention in action with Bumblebee's sentence. High attention keeps "it" linked to "music," while low attention loses the rhythm — leaving our Transformer dancing out of sync.

The illustration in Figure 5.5 brings the idea to life. In the high-attention example, the model behaves a bit like the actual Bumblebee: Tuned in, alert, and happily syncing every beat. It keeps track of what is playing, linking *it* back to *music* just as our musical Autobot would never miss a cue. The connections stretch gracefully across the whole sentence, letting the encoder capture the rhythm and meaning in full. In the low-attention version, though, things fall apart—the model starts dancing to the wrong tune. With weak links between words, *it* loses track of *music*, and the sentence becomes a little tone-deaf. This shows why self-attention matters: When it is high, the model grooves along perfectly in time; when it is low, even Bumblebee's playlist goes out of sync.

Fittingly so, since our sentence stars Bumblebee himself.

In self-attention, the encoder looks for clues in the other elements of the sentence as it processes them. In this way self-attention can be used to extract understanding of each of the processed elements in the sequence from the rest of the elements. After embedding each element for processing, we need the following other components:

Self-attention lets each token borrow insight from the rest—context shared, meaning sharpened.

- **Key: Value pair** $(k : v)$: A key is label for an element in our sequence, used to distinguish it from the others. Each key has an associated value.
- **Query** (q): When we request specific information, we query the keys and select the best match for our request.

The understanding extraction is done with the following steps:

1. Calculate three arrays called query q, key k and value v from matrices created at training time.
2. Obtain a score for each element in the input sequence given by the dot product $q \cdot k$. Note that for the sentence above we would be calculating the score for query *bumblebee* with each of the values [*bumblebee*, *plays*, *some*, *catchy*, ...]. The score is scaled by dividing each result with a value $\sqrt{d_k}$. A typical value is 8, but others can be used.

Self-attention in a nutshell: Score, scale, soften, mix; then let the network get to work.

3. Ensure that the scores are normalised, positive and add up to 1. This can be done by applying a softmax function.
4. Multiply the value vector v by the normalised score from the previous step.

5. Finally add up all the results into a single vector and create the output of the self-attention. The result is passed to the feedforward neural network.

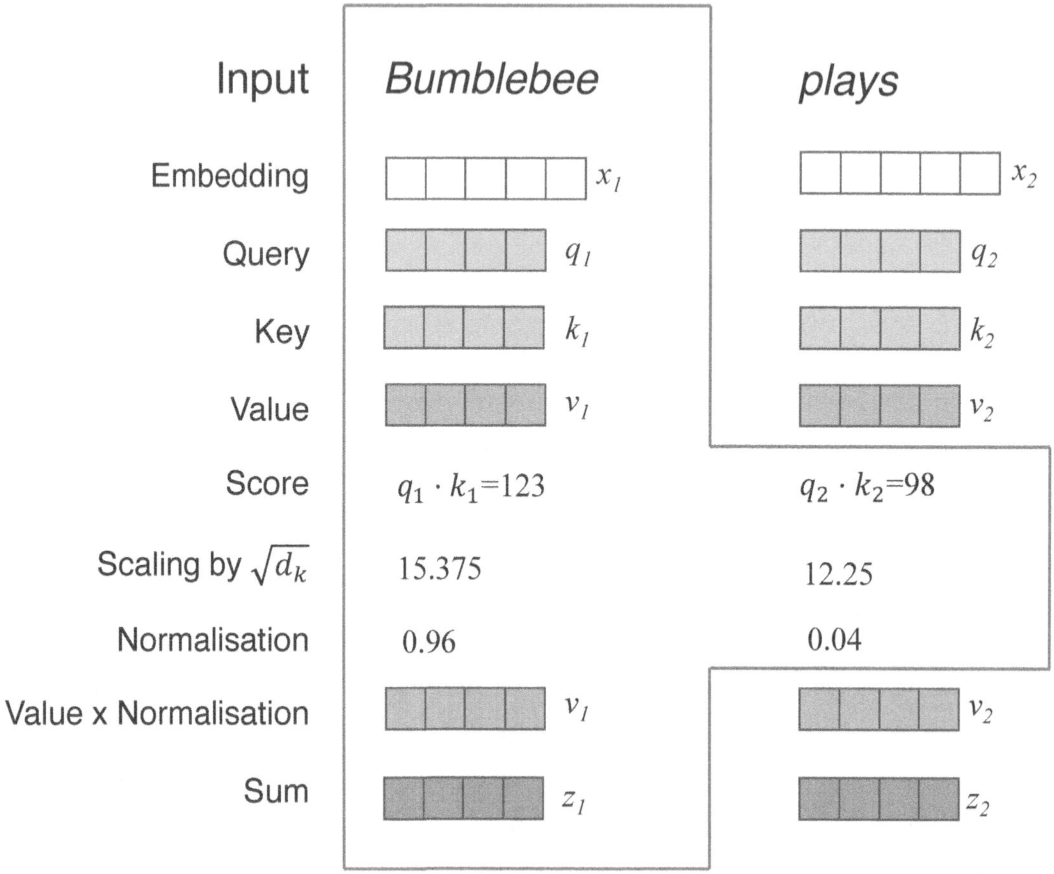

Figure 5.6: Steps of the self-attention process—from embeddings to the final weighted sum—showing how Bumblebee's encoder tunes in to the right "frequencies" to focus on key words in the sequence.

The diagram in Figure 5.6 visualises these steps in action, tracing the journey from input embeddings to the final self-attention output. Starting with the embedded tokens—here represented by $x_!$ and x_2—the model generates the corresponding queries, keys, and values (q_1, k, v_1, etc.), as described in Step 1. The dot product scores between queries and keys illustrate Step 2, followed by the scaling by $\sqrt{d_k}$ to keep the magnitudes stable. The subsequent normalisation through the softmax function (Step 3) transforms these scores into attention weights, which are then multiplied by their respective value vectors (Step 4). Finally, the weighted values are summed to produce the self-attention output z_1 and z_2 (Step 5). Much like Bumblebee tuning into the right radio frequency, the encoder adjusts its focus through these calculations, locking onto the signals, or words, that matter most in the sentence.

A snapshot of self-attention at work, from embeddings to weighted context, all laid out step by step.

Like Bumblebee finding the right station, self-attention locks onto the words that matter.

5.4.3 *Transformers Revealed: From Hidden States to Understanding*

A TRANSFORMER IS A NEURAL network architecture that exploits the concepts of attention and self-attention in a stack of identical layers that combine self-attention and feed-forward neural networks using encoders and decoders; see Figure 5.7.

A layered engine built from self-attention and feedforward blocks, encoders and decoders doing the heavy lifting.

The first encoder takes the input vectors and process them with the self-attention layer before passing them to the feedforward neural net. In a typical architecture each encoder is composed of two parts: Self-attention layer and feedforward neural net, see Figure 5.8. Similarly, each decoder is composed of three parts: Self-attention layer, decoder attention layer and feedforward neural net. Once the work of the first encoder is done, the result is passed to the next encoder and so on until the final encoder sends the

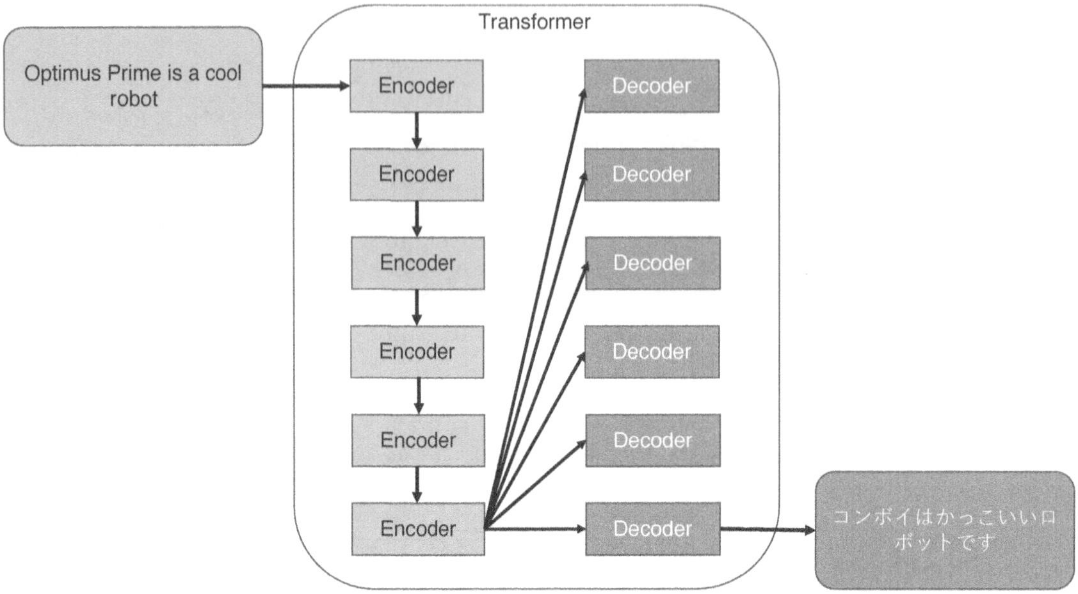

Figure 5.7: The Transformer architecture is made up of a stack of identical layers that comprise self-attention and feedforward networks.

information to the decoders and a similar process ensues.

Multi-head attention allows the model to project queries, keys, and values into multiple subspaces (called *heads*), each learning different types of relationships. The outputs of all heads are concatenated and linearly transformed. This design enables the model to capture syntactic, semantic, and even positional relationships simultaneously.

An important advantage of the transformer architecture over other neural networks, such as RNNs is the presence of context around a token over a longer "distance" and done in a more efficient way. Furthermore, unlike RNNs the input date need not be processed sequentially, enabling for parallelisation. Because Transformers process all tokens in

For example, a word.

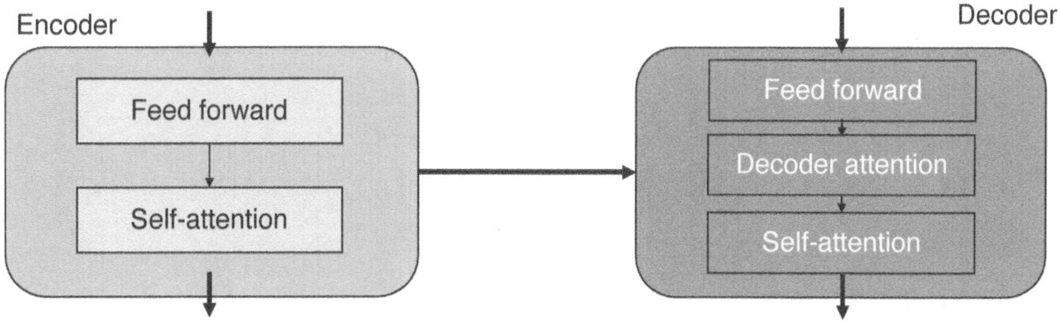

Figure 5.8: Looking inside the encoder and decoder parts in a Transformer stack.

parallel, they make far better use of GPUs and tensor processing units (TPUs) than RNNs, whose sequential nature limits parallelisation. Furthermore, positional encodings (often sinusoidal) are added to the input embeddings to preserve information about word order.

Transformers have rapidly become the tool of choice in natural language processing with some pre-trained models such as Bidirectional Encoder Representations from Transformers (BERT), and Generative Pre-trained Transformer (GPT) architectures that are able to generate new text based on the training data provided, with Generative AI powering over applications such as search, conversation, text completion, and more such as image generation. Other applications are surfacing, for instance the publication of AlphaFold[11] demonstrated the "first computational method that can regularly predict protein structures with atomic accuracy even in cases in which no similar structure is known". The potential provided by transformers has opened up the possibilities for multimodal processing, where applications are able to use multiple

We covered some use cases in the latter part of Chapter 2.

[11] Jumper, J., R. Evans, A. Pritzel, T. Green, M. Figurnov, Ronneberger, et al. (2021). Highly accurate protein structure prediction with AlphaFold. *Nature* 596(7873), 583–589.

types of data, combining media such as images and video, with language.

5.5 *BERT, GPT and beyond: Transformer Models in NLP*

IN THIS SECTION WE ARE going to cover some of the most prominent early Transformer architectures, namely BERT and GPT. The landscape is moving so fast that this is more of a landslide rather than tectonic plate movements. I suggest to you, my Jackalope Data Scientist readers, to look perhaps at this section as an early historical view of the stacks that enable newer and better models available to us by the various providers. Please note that many new models are proprietary, and you will probably need a subscription to be able to use these services. Consider yourself forewarned.

Early Transformer icons on display here; the field has not slowed down since.

BERT is a landmark Transformer-based mode introduced by Devlin et al. at Google[12]. BERT stands for *Bidirectional Encoder Representations from Transformers*, and as the name implies, it uses the encoder half of the Transformer architecture (no decoder). BERT's innovation was leveraging Transformers for language understanding: It was pre-trained on vast amounts of text in a self-supervised fashion to learn deep bidirectional representations of language. Specifically, BERT was trained with a "masked language model" objective and a "next sentence prediction" objective. Through these tasks, BERT learns rich contextual embeddings; essentially, it learns to fill in blanks and gather meaning from both left and right context.

[12] Devlin, J., M.-W. Chang, K. Lee, and K. Toutanova (2018). BERT: Pre-training of Deep Bidirectional Transformers for Language Understanding. *arXiv preprint arXiv:1810.04805*

Masked in the sense of randomly hiding some words in a sentence and training the model to predict them.

Because BERT looks at words in both directions around a mask during training, BERT's attention is truly bidirectional, unlike a "left-to-right" generative model. After pre-training, the BERT model can be fine-tuned to specific NLP tasks like question answering, sentiment analysis, or named entity recognition with remarkable results. BERT-base is a 12-layer Transformer encoder (with 110 million parameters) and BERT-large is a 24-layer encoder (340 million parameters), and these models were released openly, sparking a wave of "BERTology" as researchers probed what linguistic knowledge these attention heads were capturing.

Past and future words for instance.

Huge for their time!

Around the same time, another group of researchers at OpenAI [13] took Transformers in a complementary direction: Generation. Their series of models, called GPT (Generative Pre-Trained Transformer), use only the decoder portion of the Transformer (no encoder stack), focusing on autoregressive language modelling — i.e., predicting the next word in a sequence.

[13] Radford, A., J. Wu, R. Child, D. Luan, D. Amodei, and I. Sutskever (2019). Language models are unsupervised multitask learners. *OpenAI Technical Report*

The first model, GPT-1, was introduced in 2018 as a proof-of-concept of pre-training a Transformer on a large corpus (BooksCorpus, in that case) and then fine-tuning it for specific tasks. This approach was novel because it showed we could achieve great results on language tasks without training on task-specific data from scratch; instead, a generative modelling pre-training could serve as a universal foundation. GPT-1 had on the order of 100 million parameters and already demonstrated the viability of Transformer decoders for language understanding when fine-tuned.

GPT-1: Small by today's standards, but the first clear proof that pre-training plus fine-tuning could rewrite the NLP playbook.

GPT-2, unveiled in early 2019, took the idea and ran with it— in a big way. It was essentially "GPT-1 on steroids": about 10 times larger in terms of parameters and training data. The full GPT-2 model has around 1.5 billion parameters and was trained on an enormous dataset of about 8 million webpages. With this scale, GPT-2 showed astonishing capabilities in generating coherent and sometimes startlingly human-like text.

OpenAI's curated WebText dataset.

Given a prompt, GPT-2 could continue writing a paragraph that stayed on topic surprisingly well, often with correct grammar and sensible (if not always factual) content. This was one of the first times the general public took notice of AI text generation, especially after OpenAI initially withheld the full GPT-2 model out of concern for misuse. Notably, GPT-2 could perform tasks like summarisation or translation in a zero-shot way – meaning, even without being explicitly trained on those tasks, some ability "emerged" from its language modelling prowess. This hinted that scaling up Transformers could unlock even more general intelligence-like behaviour.

They staged a gradual release of GPT-2, releasing smaller versions first.

It is worth emphasising how BERT and GPT embody two sides of the Transformer coin: BERT is bidirectional and great for understanding, whereas GPT is unidirectional (autoregressive) and great for generation. Both leverage self-attention: BERT's attention attends to tokens on both left and right, while GPT's attention is typically masked so that each position can only attend to earlier positions (ensuring the model can't "see the future" when predicting the next word).

BERT looks at an entire sequence and is not tasked with generation.

GPT produces text "left-to-right" so to speak.

These design choices align with their goals; in other words BERT builds an internal representation of text, and GPT produces new text. Importantly, both models are pre-trained on large unlabelled corpora and then fine-tuned, which was a paradigm shift in NLP. Instead of training a small model for each task, the community shifted to pre-training one giant Transformer on generic data and then adapting it to myriad tasks.

A strategy that has proven to yield far better results given enough data and compute.

5.5.1 *Age of Agents and Next Generation of Transformers*

If you thought Transformers were impressive, the story does not stop there. In true cinematic fashion, they have spawned an entire extended universe of cousins, rivals, and spin-offs—each with its own superpowers and (let's be honest) quirks. The modern machine learning landscape at the time of writing feels a bit like the Marvel Cinematic Universe: we have our main hero (currently GPT-5), its earlier incarnations, and an ever-expanding cast of agents, sidekicks, and—occasionally—chaotic neutrals.

And there is no doubt that the saga will continue.

Since the publication of *Attention is All You Need*[14] in 2017, the Transformer architecture has evolved from a promising design into the beating heart of modern AI. OpenAI's GPT line remains the archetypal example. By the time of writing, we have moved through several key evolutionary steps: GPT-4, GPT-4 Turbo, GPT-4.1, and the short-lived GPT-4.5 (*codenamed Orion*) before arriving at the current flagship, GPT-5.[15] Each new model has increased the ability to juggle larger contexts (up to one million tokens), improved

[14] Vaswani, A., N. Shazeer, N. Parmar, et al. (2017). Attention Is All You Need. In *Advances in Neural Information Processing Systems*, pp. 5998–6008. Curran Associates, Inc.

[15] OpenAI (2023b). GPT-4 Technical Report. arXiv preprint arXiv:2303.08774.

reasoning performance, and—perhaps most importantly for those of us who like our results before the heat-death of the universe—reduced latency and cost.

GPT-5 represents a consolidation of the earlier family. It is multimodal, and it merges tasks that were previously handled by separate models: Reasoning, writing, code generation, and data analysis are now integrated into a single architecture. This is not just a bigger model; it is a smarter, more general system designed to act as a true assistant rather than a text parrot. Under the hood, the improvements come from a blend of architectural refinement, scale, and instruction-based fine-tuning. Where GPT-3 showed that large language models could write essays that occasionally fooled your English teacher, GPT-5 is more likely to pass your physics viva, draft your conference slides, and politely suggest that your loss function could be better tuned.

This means that it can handle text, images, and other inputs.

A leap from text mimicry to genuine assistance; scale, tuning, and smarter training make all the difference.

5.5.2 *Rise of Other Agents: A Cast of Many*

OpenAI may have defined the blockbuster format, but it certainly does not hold a monopoly on GenAI. Across the AI ecosystem, a colourful range of agents has appeared, each catering to different needs, budgets, and philosophical leanings. Table 5.1 introduces some of the key players in our expanding cast.

OpenAI set the tone, but the stage is crowded; plenty of capable models now share the spotlight.

Each of these models highlights a different philosophy. Claude emphasises alignment and safety—its creators, Anthropic, even talk about a "constitutional AI" approach to

Agent	Origin	Special Traits and Personality Notes
Claude 3	Anthropic	Built with an emphasis on safety and interpretability. Known for its courteous tone and ethical boundaries—the digital equivalent of that friend who always remembers to recycle.
Mistral 7B / Mixtral	Mistral AI	Compact, efficient open-weight models punching above their size. Ideal for edge devices or cost-sensitive deployments.
Perplexity AI	Independent	A hybrid search-and-generation assistant that cites its sources. Perfect for those who like their facts with footnotes and their opinions with references.
Microsoft Copilot	Microsoft + OpenAI	Deeply embedded across Office, GitHub, and Windows. Think of it as the colleague who never sleeps, never complains, and occasionally refactors your code while you make tea.
Gemini 1.5 Pro	Google DeepMind	Google's entrant into the LLM fray. Multimodal, ambitious, and naturally well-integrated with the Google ecosystem.
LLaMA 3 / Meta AI	Meta	Open-weight Transformer family enabling local deployment and experimentation. Democratises LLM research, sometimes at the cost of computational convenience.

Table 5.1: A brief dramatis personae of modern language agents (as of 2025).

ethics. Mistral's Mixtral models champion efficiency and open access, showing that one does not need a supercomputer to join the conversation. Perplexity AI blends retrieval and generation, producing answers that come with citations—something your undergraduate essays probably lacked. Meanwhile, Microsoft's Copilot integrates GPT models directly into everyday work environments, effectively transforming spreadsheets, presentations, and

Here we are talking about Perplexity AI, not the statistical measure! Read on to learn more about the latter.

even software development into LLM-assisted tasks.

This proliferation of agents signals an important shift: The focus is no longer on training ever-larger single models but on embedding intelligence within applications, workflows, and collaborative ecosystems. Where once we spoke of *a model*, we now speak of *an agent society*. In practice, today's LLMs rarely work alone. They are coupled with retrieval engines, reasoning modules, and external tools. A modern agent may combine a GPT-5 reasoning core with a Perplexity-style retrieval layer, a calendar API, and a vector database, orchestrated by a framework such as LangChain or Semantic Kernel. We are witnessing the birth of the "agent-of-agent" paradigm, where specialised sub-agents collaborate, negotiate, and occasionally argue (politely, one hopes) to solve complex problems.

The age of the lone giant is fading. Intelligence now lives in networks of cooperating agents.

Today's agents are ensembles: LLMs, tools, and retrievers working together in a tidy little hive mind.

The boundary between chatbot and co-worker is rapidly dissolving. We are shifting from chat to capability. Tools like Copilot in Microsoft 365, or Notion AI, are not standalone assistants but integrated co-creators. Their value lies not in conversation alone but in action—summarising documents, generating reports, writing code, and even initiating further queries. In other words, we are moving from *language models* to *action models*.

AI that does not just reply, but gets things done.

5.5.3 *Transformers in Action*

THE ADVENT OF OPEN-SOURCE FRAMEWORKS such as the `transformers` library by Hugging Face has made it remarkably easy to experiment with state-of-the-art models.

Just be ready for new models to appear faster than you can download them.

In this section, we shall see some relatively small and early Transformers in practice. The implementation for larger models follows along the same path, and with the pace of change in the area, I recommend keeping an eye on the availability of new models. It is also important to bear in mind that some models are gated. This means that Hugging Face enables model authors to control access by requiring users to request permission to use their models. Access to gated models does not necessarily require a subscription, but certain features and higher storage capacities may be available through paid plans. In this section we will use open models to show a taste of what you can do.

We will stick to open models here; no gates, no fees, just a taste of what is possible.

BERT for Sentiment Classification

BERT EXCELS AT UNDERSTANDING THE context and meaning of language. In this example, we use a pre-trained BERT model fine-tuned for sentiment analysis. Given a sentence, the model predicts whether the sentiment is positive or negative. Please ensure that you create a Python environment to install the transformers library and activate the environment. For instance:

BERT shines at grasping nuance. Perfect for tasks like sentiment, once you have set up your environment.

```
> conda create -n transformers pytorch transformers
  accelerate torch datasets
```

We are going to use the `pipeline` function from the Transformers library, which allows us to access and use easily pre-trained machine learning models for various tasks like text generation, translation, and sentiment analysis. It provides a simple interface to use complex AI models as we will see.

A pipeline is a quick, one-stop interface for running powerful pre-trained models without the fuss.

```
from transformers import pipeline
```

We are now going to load a sentiment analysis pipeline

```
m='distilbert-base-uncased-finetuned-sst-2-english'
classifier = pipeline('sentiment-analysis',
  model=m
```

We are loading a sentiment analysis pipeline.

In this case we are loading the "DistilBERT" model that can be used for topic classification. We covered some aspects of topic modelling in Section 2.6; in this case we are simply interested in determining if sentences express a positive or a negative sentiment. Let us look at a single sentence to start with:

DistilBERT is a lighter, faster version of BERT that keeps most of its smarts with far less bulk.

```
s = 'Transformers are amazing neural networks'
r = classifier(s)
```

Let us see the result:

```
> print(r)


['label': 'POSITIVE', 'score': 0.9894382357597351]
```

As you can see BERT *thinks* the statement is overwhelmingly positive. What is happening in the background is that the model tokenises the sentence:

Yes, I am anthropomorphising... I should say *scores*!

```
['Transformers', 'are', 'amazing',
'neural', 'networks', '.']
```

and the tokens are mapped to integer IDs known to BERT vocabulary. The tokens are then put through the layers of

Tokens flow through the model with a special one that gathers the whole sentence's meaning.

the Transformer with an added token to capture the overall meaning of the sentence. At the head of the architecture, there is a small layer with a softmax activation function that enables two outputs: Negative and Positive. Let us load some more sentences to play with:

```
sentences = [
  'Transformers are amazing neural networks.',
  'This implementation is quite slow.',
  'I hate debugging CUDA errors.',
  'Optimus Prime is a cool robot!',
  'I love open-source contributions!',
  'I absolutely love the new Transformer ' +
  'architecture!',
  'The results were disappointing and the model '+
  'failed to converge.',
  'Bumblebee plays some catchy music and dances '+
  'along to it.'
```

Some sentences to play with.

We can pass the list of sentences to our classifier directly and look at the results:

```
results = classifier(sentences)
for s, r in zip(sentences, results):
  print(f''{s} -> ''
    f''{r['label']} ({r['score']:.4f})'')
```

We classify the sentences and match them with the result from the algorithm.

The output shows the sentences being scored followed by the binary output, i.e., POSITIVE or NEGATIVE and the numerical score for the sentiment:

```
Transformers are amazing neural networks. ->
  POSITIVE (0.9894)
This implementation is quite slow. ->
  NEGATIVE (0.9815)
I hate debugging CUDA errors  ->
  NEGATIVE (0.9954)
Optimus Prime is a cool robot  ->
  POSITIVE (0.9998)
I love open-source contributions! ->
  POSITIVE (0.9998)
I absolutely love the new Transformer
  architecture!
  ->  POSITIVE (0.9999)
The results were disappointing and the model
  failed to converge.  ->  NEGATIVE (0.9998)
Bumblebee plays some catchy music and dances
  along to it.
  ->  POSITIVE (0.9995)
```

Here are the sentences with their sentiment and corresponding score.

We can use a BERT model intended for use as a sentiment analysis: `bert-base-multilingual-uncased-sentiment`. It is a model for product reviews in any of the six languages it has been trained on, namely, English, Dutch, German, French, Spanish, and Italian.

```
m='nlptown/' + \
  'bert-base-multilingual-uncased-sentiment'

classifier = pipeline('sentiment-analysis',
  model=m)
```

A multilingual BERT tuned to judge sentiment across six major languages. ¡Muy bien!

Let us now see how we can work with a pandas dataframe and some sentences in different languages:

```
import pandas as pd


texts = [
    'The product works as expected.',
    'Estoy muy contento con el resultado.',
    'Absolut fantastische Erfahrung!',
    ''L'interface utilisateur semble lente.'']
```

Working with pandas and different languages. Sehr gut!

Let us create a pandas dataframe out of the list of texts above and apply the classifier to them:

```
df = pd.DataFrame({'text': texts})
df['result'] = df['text'].apply(classifier)
```

Not only does the model provide the score for the classification, but it does return a label in the form of a star scoring. Let us extract the information:

The model provides a star-score as well as a score.

```
df['label'] = df['result'].apply(lambda x: \
  x[0]['label'])
df['score'] = df['result'].apply(lambda x: \
  x[0]['score'])
```

We can create columns for the label and the score.

And now the results:

```
> print(df[['text', 'label', 'score']])
                          text  label   score
0 The product works as expe...  3 stars  0.327469
```

And here are the results!

```
1 Estoy muy contento con el...  5 stars  0.596621
2 Absolut fantastische Erfa...  5 stars  0.940815
3 L'interface utilisateur s...  2 stars  0.506527
```

We can see clearly that the model recognises that the first sentence expresses excitement and assigns it a high positive probability, while the second sentence conveys dissatisfaction and receives a negative classification. We can even look at the two sentences we used in Sections 5.4 and 5.4.2 with Optimus Prime and Bumblebee. I hope you agree that this showcases BERT's ability to estimate sentiment based on context, not just word choice.

A clear reminder that BERT reads tone in context, not just isolated words.

5.5.4 *Using BERT for Masked Word Prediction*

We can use BERT to model masked language or to predict the next word or even the next sentence given some text. Masked language modelling is a technique in NLP in which certain words in a sentence are hidden or replaced with a special token. The model is trained to predict these missing words based on the surrounding context. This approach helps the model learn the relationships between words and improves its understanding of language structure.

Masked language modelling teaches BERT to guess missing words from context.

We will continue using the `pipeline` function from the `transformers` library. In this case, however, we are going to use a `fill-mask` pipeline and use the `bert-base-uncased` model, which is a pre-trained model on English language using a masked language modelling objective.

```
from transformers import pipeline


unmasker = pipeline('fill-mask',
  model='bert-base-uncased')
```

We literally ask the model to fill in the mask.

The model takes a sentence and randomly masks about 15% of its words. It then processes the whole masked sentence at once, learning to predict the missing words. Unlike recurrent neural networks, which read text sequentially, or autoregressive models such as GPT that conceal future tokens, this approach enables the model to capture a truly bidirectional understanding of the sentence.

By masking words and reading both directions, BERT learns a full, bidirectional view of each sentence.

Let us provide a challenge to the model with a sentence containing a masked token:

```
s = 'In machine learning, Transformers
  are [MASK] neural networks.'
```

Notice the `MASK` entry in this sentence.

In this example, the magic lies in the `[MASK]` token itself. When we pass this to the `unmasker`, we are using a model that has been specifically trained to recognise and fill in those placeholders.

When passing the sentence through the unmasker, the model does not just look to the left or to the right like a traditional recurrent network would. Instead, it scans the entire context at once—all the tokens, all the relationships, all the delicious dependencies between words. It builds a bidirectional understanding of the sentence and then

The model scans the tokens in both directions to infer the content of the mask.

decides which word is statistically and semantically most at home in that masked spot.

Under the bonnet, there's a prediction head that outputs a probability distribution across every word in its vocabulary. The model might whisper to itself: "Hmm, 'artificial' has a good ring to it, 'deep' maybe an option, 'advanced' is a good choice, and 'tired' — well, hopefully not." Let us take a look, all we have to do is pass the sentence to our `unmasker` as follows:

I know... anthropomorphising again...

```
results = unmasker(s)
```

And that is it... OK, OK, let us unpack the results. We first split the sentence into two parts, before and after the mask, and look at the proposed tokens to fill in the blank:

```
parts = sentence.split('[MASK]')
print(parts[0] + '\n')
for r in results:
  print(f"-- {r['token_str']} '' +
    ''(score: {r['score']:.4f})'')
print('\n' + parts[1])
```

We split the sentence and look at the proposed tokens together with their scores.

The output will be something similar to the following:

```
In machine learning, Transformers are


-- artificial (score: 0.5856)
-- natural (score: 0.0284)
-- linear (score: 0.0230)
```

The printout may look something like this.

```
-- deep (score: 0.0179)
-- the (score: 0.0081)


 neural networks.
```

The results are actually more complex, let us look at the first one:

```
> print(results[0])


{'score': 0.5855675935745239,
  'token': 7976,
  'token_str': 'artificial',
  'sequence': 'in machine learning,
    transformers are artificial neural networks.'}
```

The `results` object contains more information.

As you can see, it provides the score, the token, and the string corresponding to the token and the actual unmasked utterance. In any case, in short, the model does not have psychic powers, but it has context. The masked token tells it where to guess, and the bidirectional transformer architecture gives it the means to make that guess intelligently. It is neither fortune-telling nor understanding; it is just context turned into probability — but it feels rather like magic all the same.

Not magic, just context turned into smart guesses that feel magical.

5.5.5 GPT for Controlled Text Generation

WE ARE NOW GOING TO look at a Generative Pre-trained Transformer (GPT) model. As the name indicates, these models are all about generation; i.e., cases where we are interested in predicting what comes next, given a starting prompt. By adjusting a few parameters, we can control how creative or deterministic its responses are. We are going to use a decidedly older model, GPT-2, having the advantage of being currently openly available. Once again, we will rely on the `transformers` library and its `pipeline` function. We are now going to use a pipeline for text generation and specify the GPT-2 model:

Now we switch to GPT; models that are built to continue/generate text, not just understand it.

```
from transformers import pipeline
m = 'gpt-2'
generator = pipeline('text-generation', model=m)
```

Continue using `pipeline` in the `transformers` library.

Before we continue, it is useful to talk about some ways in which we are able to control how random or deterministic the text genration of our model is. One parameter at our disposal is the temperature:

- **Low temperature** (< 1): The model becomes *cautious*, choosing only the most likely words.
- **High temperature** (> 1): The model becomes *creative*, taking more risks with less probable words.

Temperature controls how adventurous GPT is, low for predictable replies, high for creative leaps.

You can think of it as tuning between a careful academic and a poet after two espressos.

When generating text, a model predicts a probability distribution over the vocabulary for the next token:

$$P(w_i) = \texttt{softmax}\left(\frac{z_i}{T}\right), \qquad (5.12)$$

where z_i are the model's raw logit, i.e., unnormalised scores, T is the temperature.

- If $T = 1$: you get the normal probabilities.
- If $T < 1$: the logits are divided by a small number, so the distribution becomes sharper and high-probability words dominate.
- If $T > 1$: logits are divided by a large number, so the distribution flattens and the model samples more freely.

Here is how that works for logits.

In order to manage the generation of tokens, we can set the `do_sample` parameter to `True`, in which case the model samples the next token influenced by parameters such as the temperature. If `do_sample=False` the model behaves deterministically, always choosing the top-probability next token and thus giving the same output every time. Let us take a look:

Sampling on means variety; sampling off means the same safe choice every time.

```
prompt = ''Artificial intelligence will''
for t in [0.3, 0.7, 1.2]:
  print(f'\n--- Temperature = {t} ---')
  output = generator(prompt, max_length=40,
    do_sample=True, temperature=t)
  print(output[0]['generated_text'])
```

We are testing three temperatures here: 0.3, 0.7, 1.2.

The result will look similar to the following output:

```
 --- Temperature = 0.3 ---
Artificial intelligence will be a major challenge
for the next five years.
```

And here are some example results.

```
''I think it's going to be a big challenge,''
said Mark Karpeles, a professor of computer
science

--- Temperature = 0.7 ---
Artificial intelligence will help us to understand
the world better, and this will continue in 2020.

''Our future is in human-level computing and AI,
so there is more room for improvement''
--- Temperature = 1.2 ---
Artificial intelligence will have no shortage of
tasks for robots or humans, says David Parnum,
a professor at MIT, who helped develop Google's
software.
But, as AI becomes a
```

We can see the different outcomes in this run. The parameter `max_length` specifies the maximum number of tokens in the entire sequence. Note that it is not the maximum number of words generated, but maximum total token length including the input.

Think words, punctuation, subword fragments, etc.

We can request the model to provide more than one response to our prompt; in the code below we will be requesting two different continuations for a new prompt:

```
prompt = 'Generative AI is fast becoming'
multi_output = generator(prompt, max_length=100,
  num_return_sequences=2, temperature=1.2 )
```

We can request multiple responses with the help of `num_return_sequences`.

We are requesting a maximum of a 100 tokens and are using a higher temperature. Let us see the typical results:

```
> for i, output in enumerate(multi_output):
  print(f'\n--- Output i+1 ---')
  print(output['generated_text'][:250])

  --- Output 1 ---
Generative AI is fast becoming popular. There are
over 400 machine learning products available - one
of them is an AI that allows you to solve abstract
equations in many, many years. In my personal
experience, the amount of data used, the time
requir

--- Output 2 ---
Generative AI is fast becoming more prevalent for
robots, which has created what IBM called a ''smart
machin'' in our society. This isn't an exaggeration
because computers can perform complex tasks much
faster than human computers; in fact, computers
```

Here is the first output.

And the second one.

5.6 *Measures to Evaluate LLMs*

THE EXAMPLES IN THE PREVIOUS Section 5.5.3 illustrate the complementary strengths of Transformer models. We have seen BERT shine in tasks that require deep understanding of context and semantics, while GPT thrives in generative scenarios where coherence and randomness are key.

BERT understands; GPT invents. Together they show how Transformers became universal language engines.

Together, they mark the shift from traditional, task-specific neural networks to universal pre-trained models that can be fine-tuned or prompted for almost any language task.

One of the aspects that Jackalope Data Scientists are interested in is *inference*. Note, however, that in this context the meaning is different from the usage in traditional statistics. The term inference in machine learning comes from Bayesian machine learning, where making a prediction was a kind of inference. As deep learning scaled, the term stuck, even though it now simply means "running the model". Let us explore this a bit more in depth.

Inference is an important task in AI.

Inferring the posterior distribution of model parameters or outputs given data.

In the context of large language models (LLMs), inference refers to the process of using a trained model to generate outputs (predictions) from given inputs.

- During training, the model's parameters (weights) are adjusted by computing gradients and updating the weights via backpropagation to minimise a loss function over the training data.
- During inference, the weights are frozen, and the model is executed forward-only — it takes input tokens, applies its learned transformations, and produces probability distributions over possible next tokens.

Training is when the model learns Inference is when the model "thinks".

Inference is essentially a function of the input tokens for the network:

$$y = f_\theta(x), \qquad (5.13)$$

where f_θ is the trained model (i.e., the network), θ are the frozen weights, and x are the input tokens. During inference, the model embeds input text into vectors and propagates through all Transformer layers. Logits, or scores, are computed for each possible next token and, depending on our sampling strategy, it selects the next token and repeats until a stop condition. No learning happens here—just prediction.

Layers such as attention, feedforward, etc.

Table 5.2: Key Metrics for Evaluating Inference Performance in Large Language Models

Metric	Meaning	Why it matters
Perplexity	How well the model makes predictions	Lower = better language modelling
Latency	Time to complete one response	Lower = faster replies
Throughput	Tokens processed per second	Higher = more efficient
Memory footprint	GPU/CPU RAM required	Affects scalability
Power draw / cost	Energy cost per token	Key for deployment economics

Inference is where all the cost happens after training: Every chat, query, or completion requires a forward pass through billions of parameters. There are several metrics that may help us compare models. We summarise them in Table 5.2 and we explain more about them below. Within that context, you may hear Jackalope Data Scientists talk about optimising inference, and that is because even though training might happen once, inference happens millions of times per day.

Inference is where all the cost happens after training.

Training is a one-off marathon; inference is the daily commute. We optimise the bit that never stops.

Perplexity

WE HAVE ACTUALLY ENCOUNTERED ONE of these metrics before in the context of topic modelling. **Perplexity** is a statistical measure of how well a probabilistic language model predicts a sequence of tokens. Formally, for a test sequence of N tokens $w_1, w_2, \ldots, w_N$, the perplexity P of a model M is defined as:

See Section 2.6.1, page 133 for the use of perplexity in topic modelling.

$$\mathrm{P}(M) = \exp\left(-\frac{1}{N}\sum_{i=1}^{N}\log p_M(w_i \mid w_1, \ldots, w_{i-1})\right), \quad (5.14)$$

or equivalently:

$$\mathrm{P}(M) = \left(\prod_{i=1}^{N}\frac{1}{p_M(w_i \mid w_1, \ldots, w_{i-1})}\right)^{\frac{1}{N}}. \quad (5.15)$$

The inner term $p_M(w_i \mid w_1, \ldots, w_{i-1})$ is the probability the model assigns to the correct next token w_i. Taking the logarithm and averaging gives the average negative log-likelihood. This can be thought of to show how "surprised" the model is, on average, by the true tokens. Exponentiating that value converts the log-space average back into a more interpretable scale.

Perplexity is basically "how surprised the model is" when reading the true tokens.

We can interpret perplexity, in broad terms, as a measure of how many different possibilities the model is effectively unsure between each prediction step. In other words, it reflects the model's average level of uncertainty when selecting the next token. For instance, if the perplexity value is 10, this can be thought of as the model being about as uncertain as if it had to choose uniformly among ten equally

Lower perplexity means a confident model; higher means it is dithering.

likely words at every position in the sequence. A lower perplexity indicates greater confidence and better predictive ability, the model's probability distribution is sharper and more focused on the correct continuation, whereas a higher perplexity suggests that the model's predictions are more diffuse, as though it were hesitating among many plausible options.

Incidentally, perplexity is directly related to cross-entropy loss, which is typically used during training. We can express the cross-entropy loss as follows:

Perplexity is related to cross-entropy loss.

$$H(p,q) = -\frac{1}{N}\sum_{i=1}^{N}\log q(w_i), \tag{5.16}$$

where p is the true distribution, and q is the model's predicted distribution. From that point of view, perplexity is just the exponential of cross-entropy:

I.e., the empirical distribution.

$$\mathrm{P} = \exp(H(p,q)), \tag{5.17}$$

In this manner, a lower cross-entropy results in lower perplexity, and hence the model is more confident and accurate. Let us look at an example.

Consider a model that predicts the following conditional probabilities, $p(w_i \mid \text{context})$, for a 3-token sentence, namely *"The cat sleeps"*: *"The"* $= 0.5$, *"cat"* $= 0.25$ and *"sleeps"* $=$ 10.125. The perplexity is given by:

Nothing like an actual example; perplexity lets us see whether the model is purring with confidence or utterly baffled.

$$\mathrm{P} \quad = \quad \exp\left(-\frac{1}{3}\left(\log 0.5 + \log 0.25 + \log 0.125\right)\right),$$

$$
\begin{aligned}
&= \exp\left(-\frac{1}{3}\log(0.5 \times 0.25 \times 0.125)\right), \\
&= \exp\left(-\frac{1}{3}\log(0.015625)\right) = 4. \qquad (5.18)
\end{aligned}
$$

In this case our model's perplexity of 4 tells us that it is effectively choosing among 4 options.

While being a widely used metric, perplexity, comes with several important caveats. One of the key issues is its scale sensitivity. The value of perplexity depends heavily on the tokeniser used and on the characteristics of the dataset. Different tokenisation schemes can split text into tokens in very different ways. As a result, the same model may report different perplexity scores simply because of how the text is segmented. Similarly, comparing perplexity across languages can be misleading, as languages vary in morphology and structure, influencing how tokens represent meaning and frequency.

Perplexity is useful, but touchy: Change the tokeniser or language and the numbers shift under your feet.

Another limitation is that perplexity is not always aligned with human judgement. A model achieving a lower perplexity merely indicates that it has learned to predict the training distribution more accurately. This does not necessarily mean that the model generates text that is more coherent, creative, or contextually appropriate from a human perspective. In practice, a model could achieve excellent perplexity scores while still producing dull or repetitive language that lacks semantic richness or pragmatic sense. In short, good perplexity can reflect

Perplexity measures prediction, not prose; low scores do not guarantee good storytelling!

statistical skill without guaranteeing anything resembling good writing.

Despite these shortcomings, perplexity remains a gold standard for quantitative evaluation in language modelling research. It offers a mathematically tractable, reproducible measure of how well a model predicts data from a given distribution, which makes it invaluable for benchmarking and comparing model architectures or training regimes.

Flawed but fundamental. Perplexity still anchors most model comparisons.

Latency

IN THE CONTEXT OF LLMs, another useful measure is that of **latency** which is the time delay between sending a request (input text) to the model and receiving the corresponding output, in other words:

Inputs versus output tokens, or response.

$$\text{Latency} = T_{\text{end}} - T_{\text{start}}, \tag{5.19}$$

where T_{start} is the time when inference begins, in other words, just before the forward pass; and T_{end} is the time when the model has generated all output tokens, or the first token, depending on the metric.

In evaluating LLMs, it is essential to distinguish between three related but distinct measures of performance: Total latency, first-token latency, and per-token latency. Each captures a different aspect of how quickly a model responds to input and generates text, and each has its own relevance depending on the application.

Latency comes in flavours—total, first-token, and per-token—each revealing a different speed story.

- **Total latency** refers to the complete time elapsed from the moment an input is submitted until the model has finished producing its full output. This is especially important for user-facing applications such as chatbots, summarisation tools, or document generation, where the user cares primarily about how long it takes to receive a finished response. It includes every stage of processing: Tokenisation of the input text, running the model's forward passes, generating the output tokens, and finally detokenising them back into human-readable form.

Total latency is the whole wait, from input to fully finished output; what users feel most.

- **First-token latency** (FTL) captures how long it takes before the model produces the first token of its response. In interactive systems—like chat interfaces or voice assistants—FTL strongly influences how responsive the model feels. Even if the total generation takes some time, users perceive the system as faster and more engaging when it begins responding almost immediately. In streaming setups, where tokens are displayed as they are generated, first-token latency is a key determinant of the perceived "snappiness" of the system.

First-token latency is all about snappiness: How quickly the model starts talking back.

- **Per-token latency**, on the other hand, measures the average time taken between the generation of successive tokens. It describes the rate at which the model continues producing text once the first token has appeared, and it directly relates to another measure: Throughput, the number of tokens produced per second which we will discuss shortly.

Per-token latency shows how fast the model keeps talking, its steady-state speed.

When measuring latency in practice, Jackalope Data Scientists may take a broad end-to-end approach, timing the entire process including tokenisation and input/output operations, or a model-only approach, isolating the inference time to understand the pure computational cost of the forward pass.

Both can be very informative. On the one hand, end-to-end latency is closer to the user experience; on the other hand, model-only latency gives clearer insight into architectural or hardware performance. Several factors contribute to overall latency. Tokenisation introduces a modest cost when converting text into tokens. The forward pass usually dominates the computation time. Reducing latency has become a central goal in both research and deployment.

End-to-end shows the user's wait; model-only reveals the raw engine speed—both worth knowing.

I.e., the matrix multiplications and attention operations within the Transformer layers.

Let us look at some examples of obtaining latency measures with Python. With end-to-end latency being the most common measure, we can see that it is simple and includes everything in the pipeline. In the example below we will use a GPT-2 model and calculate the time elapsed in the entire text generation for a given prompt such as *"Artificial Intelligence is"*.

A quick timing wrapper: Run a text-generation pipeline, measure start and end, and report total latency.

```
import time
from transformers import pipeline


m = 'gpt'
gen = pipeline('text-generation', model=m)
start = time.time()
out = gen('Artificial intelligence is',
  max_new_tokens=50)
end = time.time()
```

```
latency = end - start
print(f'Total latency: {latency:.3f} s')
```

Let us now look at the model-only latency, excluding tokenisation, I/O, etc. In this case we will use `AutoModelForCausalLM` which is a class in the Transformers library designed for causal language modelling, and `AutoTokenizer` which lets us convert between text and the numerical token IDs used by the model.

For example, predicting the next token in a sequence.

```
from transformers import \
  AutoModelForCausalLM, AutoTokenizer

model_name = 'gpt2'
model = AutoModelForCausalLM.from_pretrained(
  model_name)
tokenizer = AutoTokenizer.from_pretrained(
  model_name)
inputs = tokenizer('Artificial intelligence is',
  return_tensors='pt')
start = time.time()
outputs = model.generate(**inputs,
  max_new_tokens=50)
latency = time.time() - start
```

A quick setup: Tokenise the prompt, run generate, and time the model's forward pass directly.

The argument `return_tensors='pt'` indicates that the output will be a tensor, instead of a NumPy array or plain list. The resulting inputs object contains a dictionary with tensors ready to feed into the model. Let us do just that:

Turning text into PyTorch tensors lets us feed the model exactly what it expects.

```
generated_text = tokenizer.decode(outputs[0], \
  skip_special_tokens=True)
```

The resulting latency value captures the model-only computation time. It does not include overheads such as converting text to tokens, detokenising the output back into words, or transferring data over a network. As such, it provides a clean and practical way to benchmark how efficiently the model performs on the underlying hardware, independent of external factors.

This gives us pure compute latency; a clean measure of how fast the model runs without any extra overhead.

If we now want to undertand the *streaming speed* of the process, we can calculate the per-token latency, which is simply the time taken per generated token:

$$\text{Per-token latency} = \frac{T_{\text{end}} - T_{\text{start}}}{N_{\text{generated tokens}}}. \tag{5.20}$$

Our streaming speed in a single number.

Throughput

At first encounter, throughput feels like one of those quantities that should be trivially obvious. Surely it's just "how fast the model goes", right? Unfortunately, as with many things in machine learning, the devil has not only been in the details but also the stopwatch. Measuring throughput in large language models turns out to be rather more nuanced than simply dividing one big number by another. Let us unpack the idea and pin down the mathematics.

Sounds simple, but measuring "how fast it goes" is trickier than it first appears.

In the context of LLM inference, throughput quantifies the rate at which a model can process or generate tokens and can be expressed as:

$$\text{Throughput} = \frac{N_{\text{tokens}}}{T_{\text{elapsed}}}, \qquad (5.21)$$

where N_{tokens} is the number of tokens processed, generated, or both, and T_{elapsed} is the wall-clock time taken during inference. It is a deeply empirical metric: We count tokens, measure time, and divide—hardly glamorous, but crucial for understanding how a model will behave in the real world. Suppose a benchmark produces 140 tokens in 20 seconds, then we have that:

Depending on your definition.

$$\text{Throughput} = \frac{140}{20} = 7 \text{ tokens/s}. \qquad (5.22)$$

The practical measurement process has three moving parts:

- Counting Tokens: This may be input tokens (prompt), output tokens (generated response), or both (total workload).
- Measuring Time: Use clock time around the inference call. Exclude model loading if you want repeatability.
- Averaging Sensibly: Run several trials. If you are using batches, normalise appropriately to obtain per-instance throughput.

Throughput is simple only when measured carefully—count tokens, time it properly, and average with intention.

It is nothing more mysterious than that but easy to misinterpret if you are not explicit about which components your measurement includes.

A model with high throughput can handle large volumes of tokens per second, making it suitable for real-time streaming, bulk summarisation, or anything else that pours text through the pipeline in industrial quantities. Conversely, low throughput indicates slower processing, often caused by model size, suboptimal kernels, insufficient hardware bandwidth, or simply very long context windows. It is helpful to think of throughput as the effective bandwidth of a language model; in other words, how much linguistic material it can meaningfully move per second.

Throughput is the model's bandwidth: How much text it can push through per second.

Throughput, for all its apparent simplicity, is buffeted by a number of architectural and operational choices. One of the most decisive influences is the model architecture itself. Larger models, with more parameters and more layers, simply have more computational work to do per token. Attention mechanisms also matter; in other words, two models with the same parameter count, but different attention designs may behave very differently once the stopwatch comes out. And when context lengths grow, even efficient architectures can find themselves sweating under the extra quadratic load.

Same size does not mean same speed, attention design and context length can tilt the scales.

A second influence is numerical precision and quantisation. Running a model in full 32-bit floating point is the computational equivalent of wearing heavy hiking boots when all you really need is a brisk walk to the shops. Switching to FP16, INT8, or even INT4 can yield dramatic throughput gains by reducing memory bandwidth requirements and letting hardware vector units actually stretch their legs. Of course, this comes with trade-offs in

Lower precision lightens the load—faster steps with only a tiny wobble in accuracy.

accuracy, but for most modern LLMs the degradation is surprisingly mild — and sometimes invisible.

Then we come to hardware, the silent but decisive partner in this equation. GPUs with wider memory buses and larger caches can push far more tokens per second than CPUs or integrated accelerators, and even between GPUs, differences in VRAM bandwidth or tensor-core layout can produce wildly different performance profiles. On Apple Silicon, the M-series Neural Engine is not used for transformer inference, so throughput ends up limited by the GPU and unified memory bandwidth. In short: what you run on matters just as much as what you run.

Hardware makes or breaks throughput. Our model is only as fast as the silicon beneath it.

Batch size plays its own slightly mischievous role. Increasing batch size can raise aggregate throughput, because parallel work keeps the hardware busy. However, the per-instance latency often increases, so you get more total work done, but each individual user may have to wait slightly longer. Many production systems therefore tune batch size carefully depending on traffic patterns and SLAs.

Tokens per second across all prompts combined

Throughput also depends heavily on sequence length. The longer your input or output sequences, the more work attention layers must do. This is one reason key-value caching is such a gift for autoregressive models: By storing previously computed keys and values, the model avoids re-processing the entire history at every generation step. With caching enabled, long outputs become far more manageable. Taken together, these factors remind us that throughput is not a fixed property of a model, but the emergent result

Longer sequences slow everything down. KV caching keeps the model from rereading its own past like a forgetful time-traveller.

of architecture, hardware, numerical precision, software engineering, and, occasionally, sheer luck.

It is tempting to imagine a clean mathematical relationship between throughput and latency–the sort of equation that would make a physicist smile and an engineer nod approvingly. In the simplest possible framing, you can think of throughput as roughly the inverse of the time it takes to produce each token. Write it on a napkin, and it looks deceptively elegant:

A tidy relationship in theory, but the real world rarely behaves that politely.

$$\text{Throughput} \approx \frac{1}{\text{Latency per token}}. \tag{5.23}$$

As with latency, throughput can have different variations:

- End-to-end throughput: Includes tokenisation, model load, generation, detokenisation, and I/O overhead. It reflects real-world latency
- Model-only throughput: Measures pure forward-pass speed (after warm-up). It is used for hardware or kernel benchmarking

Throughput varies by scope, end-to-end for real workloads, model-only for raw engine speed.

It is important to bear in mind that real systems are rarely so obliging. In practice, latency is a grab-bag of delays: Tokenisation, scheduling overhead, I/O handshakes, memory warm-ups, framework bookkeeping, and the all-important first-token latency—the moment users actually start judging whether your system feels fast or merely "busy thinking". Throughput, meanwhile, averages over the entire stream of tokens once the engine is running at full tilt.

Latency feels messy, throughput only settles once the engine hits cruising speed.

The consequence is that a model may boast superb throughput, happily churning out tokens at a brisk clip, yet still feel sluggish because the time to produce the very first token is high. Conversely, a model with excellent first-token responsiveness may have modest throughput once generation continues. These two metrics rhyme, but they do not march in lockstep. All in all, the dependable definition remains:

Great throughput does not guarantee a snappy start.

$$\text{Throughput} = \frac{\text{Tokens processed}}{\text{Elapsed inference time}}. \tag{5.24}$$

Higher numbers indicate a more efficient system, all else being equal. This efficiency is shaped by model architecture, hardware, quantisation level, sequence length, and any optimisations lurking in the inference stack. Throughput is almost always reported in tokens per second, and despite its apparent simplicity, it is indispensable when planning deployments, especially those that must balance user responsiveness with large-scale workloads. Think of throughput like velocity: Great for describing cruising speed, but useless if you ignore how long it took to get moving in the first place.

Throughput, like velocity, useful once you are moving, blind to the slow start...

Memory Footprint and Power Draw

When evaluating the performance of large language models (LLMs) during inference, two practical considerations often receive less attention than perplexity or latency, yet they fundamentally determine whether a system can be deployed efficiently: The **memory footprint** and the

Memory and power may not be glamorous, but they decide whether your model ships.

power draw. These metrics influence feasibility, cost, and scalability, and thus play a central role in the design of real-world applications. Together they govern the unit economics of every token generated.

The memory footprint of a model refers to the total amount of GPU or CPU memory required to load the network and execute a forward pass. This includes not only the model weights but also:

A model's memory bill covers more than weights; caches, activations, and framework baggage all pile in.

- the key–value (KV) cache used by attention layers during autoregressive generation,
- intermediate activation tensors produced at each layer,
- tokenisation buffers and framework overheads.

In practice, the memory footprint determines whether a model can run on a given device at all. If the total memory requirement exceeds the available VRAM, inference may fall back to CPU execution, leading to dramatic slowdowns, or it may fail outright with an out-of-memory error. Consider, for example, a 7-billion-parameter model. Using FP16 precision, each parameter requires two bytes, giving approximately

Such as Qwen2-7B; see the next section.

$$7 \times 10^9 \times 2 \text{ bytes} \approx 14 \text{ GB}$$

for the weights alone. During generation, the KV cache and activation tensors may require an additional 3–5 GB, leading to a practical requirement of 17–19 GB of VRAM. This fits comfortably on a 24 GB GPU but exceeds the capabilities of most consumer hardware.

By contrast, a 3B-parameter model quantised to 4-bit precision may need as little as 1.5–2 GB of memory in total. This reduction opens the door to laptop or even mobile inference, illustrating how memory footprint directly shapes deployment possibilities.

Trim it, and the model suddenly fits anywhere: Desktop, laptop, even your pocket.

Where memory footprint determines whether a model can be executed, the *power draw* reflects the cost of running it. Power draw measures the amount of electrical power consumed by the hardware during inference, typically expressed in watts (instantaneous usage) or joules per generated token (energy efficiency).

Memory decides if we can run it; power decides what it will cost us.

From an operational perspective, power draw translates directly into financial cost. A single GPU running continuously at 250 W will consume 6 kWh over 24 hours. In a datacentre with hundreds of such devices, this becomes a significant expenditure. As LLMs become increasingly integrated into products and services, understanding energy cost per token is vital for sustainable system design.

At scale, power is not a footnote; energy per token quickly turns into a serious line on the bill.

Inference at scale is not simply a technical problem; it is an economic one. Running a large model continuously—even on a single GPU—can consume hundreds of watts per hour. In a datacentre setting, multiply this by tens or hundreds of servers, and suddenly energy becomes a primary operational cost. From an environmental viewpoint, there is also increasing scrutiny on the carbon intensity of AI systems. Smaller, more efficient models may produce less impressive benchmark scores compared with their larger siblings, but they often win decisively in joules-per-token

Such as SmolLM3-3B, see next section.

metrics.

To illustrate the disparity between models, consider the following comparison. Suppose a 7B-parameter model draws approximately 250 W during inference and achieves a throughput of 0.2 tokens/s. The energy cost per token is therefore:

$$\frac{250\ \text{W}}{0.2\ \text{tokens/s}} = 1250\ \text{J/token}.$$

Nothing like an example to bring the comparison into context.

A smaller, optimised 3B model may draw 110 W while generating 7 tokens/s, yielding

$$\frac{110\ \text{W}}{7\ \text{tokens/s}} \approx 15.7\ \text{J/token}.$$

Although the larger model may deliver lower perplexity and more fluent text, the smaller model is nearly two orders of magnitude more energy efficient.

Memory footprint and power draw highlight an important theme in model selection: Larger models are not always the most practical choice. High-parameter architectures often provide superior generative quality but come with substantial operational overheads. Smaller, well-engineered models—particularly those benefiting from quantisation, architectural efficiency, or extended context capabilities—may offer a far more attractive balance of cost and performance.

Bigger models impress, smaller models are shipped; efficiency often beats sheer parameter pride.

When comparing inference metrics, there is a natural temptation to fixate on perplexity or throughput alone. Yet practical deployment demands a more holistic perspective. Memory footprint determines whether a model fits into

Perplexity and throughput are flashy, but memory and power decide if your hardware actually survives the encounter.

your hardware envelope. Power draw determines whether you can afford to keep it running.

These two metrics, taken together, emphasise a recurring theme in modern model design: Larger is not always better. While 7B–70B parameter models offer remarkable capability, the operational reality often favours smaller, well-optimised models—particularly those benefiting from quantisation, architectural efficiency, or long-context specialisation.

"Bigger is better" fails at the plug socket; lean, tuned models often win in the real world.

Ultimately, choosing the right model requires balancing capability, responsiveness, cost, and infrastructure constraints. Understanding memory footprint and power draw makes these trade-offs explicit, enabling teams to design systems that are not only powerful but sustainable and economically viable. Understanding these metrics enables us Jackalope Data Scientists to make informed decisions about deployment environments, resource planning, and long-term sustainability. As LLMs continue to evolve, balancing accuracy, responsiveness, and efficiency will remain central to system design.

Choosing a model is an engineering trade-off: Speed, cost, power, constraints; no free lunch, just smart design.

5.6.1 Benchmarking LLMs

As we know, there are many models out there and they all come with their advantages and indeed disadvantages. In this section we will run a basic comparison among some models available at the time of writing using the measures described in the previous section. The models chosen are perhaps not the most modern, but the aim is to illustrate

A small, laptop-friendly sampler of models; enough to compare behaviours without needing a datacentre.

ways of comparing outputs by looking at the results of the text generated by different models. Due to restrictions on the length of the book, but also on the availability of some models, we are going to concentrate on a few models that are available via Hugging Face. The models have been chosen, as they are small enough to run on a laptop with enough resources. Larger models will require a more complex architecture. Here are the models we will use:

- **Qwen2-7B**: Part of the Qwen2 series by Alibaba Cloud. The Qwen2 family spans models from $\sim$ 0.5B to 72B parameters. It is a decoder-only Transformer with multilingual capabilities and a large context window. It is, however a big model, and thus it has a higher inference cost (latency).

It supports up to 32,000 tokens

- **SmolLM3-3B**: Developed by Hugging Face's "Smol" family of models: the aim is to push the boundaries of what is possible with smaller parameter counts ($\simeq$ 3B) in an open-source, high-transparency way. It supports long context and is multilingual. Its small size may bring limitations in "depth" of reasoning, domain breadth, or nuance compared to heavier models.

Up to 128,000 tokens via extrapolation.

- **SmolLM3-3B-Base**: This is essentially the un-instructed "base" version of the SmolLM3 model. Because it is the base model, there may be fewer constraints, but it may suffer from extreme latency. A base model may require significant downstream tuning for good results.

Before alignment/instruction tuning.

- **Instella-3B**: Created by AMD as part of the "Instella" family of fully open 3-billion-parameter models.It has 36 decoder layers, 32 attention heads, vocabulary $\sim 50,000$ tokens. It is open-source with full training pipeline disclosed. As with any model, if inference efficiency is not optimal, you may hit practical latency penalties.

Which is still somewhat rare in LLMs.

We are going to continue using the `transformers` library. We will make use of `AutoTokenizer` and `AutoModelForCausalLM`. The former automatically downloads the tokeniser configuration appropriate to a given model. The latter loads the weight files of a model designed for causal text generation. A causal LM is what we normally think of when we say "LLM"—it predicts the next token one step at a time.

I.e., left-to-right text generation

```
from transformers pipeline, \
  AutoTokenizer, AutoModelForCausalLM
import torch
import time
import pandas as pd
```

Imports for the essentials: Models, tokenisers, timing, and a dash of pandas to keep the results civilised.

Let us now create a dictionary with the models we want to benchmark:

```
MODELS = {
   'Qwen2-7B':'Qwen/Qwen2-7B',
   SmolLM3-3B':'HuggingFaceTB/SmolLM3-3B',
  'Instella-3B':'amd/Instella-3B',
  'SmolLM3-3B-Base':'HuggingFaceTB/SmolLM3-3B-Base',
}
```

These are the models we are going to benchmark.

We will be requiring our model to generate text given the same prompt; in this case we are using the following:

```
PROMPT = (
  'Write a short, imaginative paragraph '
  'describing a futuristic London where AI '
  'systems and humans collaborate on '
  'creative projects.'
)
```

A prompt fit for a sci-fi briefing—London in the future, humans and AIs creating side-by-side.

We will request each model to generate a maximum of 120 tokens, and we will save our results in a CSV file:

```
MAX_TOKENS = 120
CSV_OUTPUT = 'benchmark_results.csv'
```

We will now create a few helper functions to call in our benchmarking exercise. First, we will write a function that enables us to load a model and its tokeniser. As an input, it will take the identifier of a model:

```
def load_model(model_id):
  print(f'\nLoading model: model_id')
  tokenizer=AutoTokenizer.from_pretrained(model_id)
  model=AutoModelForCausalLM.from_pretrained(
    model_id,
    device_map='auto',
    dtype=torch.bfloat16,
  )
  return pipeline('text-generation,
    model=model, tokenizer=tokenizer)
```

A helper that loads a model and tokeniser and wraps the whole thing in a text-generation pipeline.

The first stage is to retrieve the model's tokeniser with the `from_pretrained` method of `AutoTokenizer`. Every model

The tokeniser is your Babel Fish turning text into the numbers the model actually speaks.

family has its own tokenisation scheme, vocabulary, and special tokens. The tokeniser abstracts those details and converts raw text into the numerical form required by the model.

Next, the function loads the model weights themselves. This is achieved through a high-level constructor in `AutoModelForCausalLM` instantiates the correct architecture for causal language modelling. In the code above we specify that parameters should be placed automatically across available computing devices. On machines with GPUs, this will result in the model being distributed between GPU and CPU memory according to available resources; on systems with Apple Silicon, layers may be mapped to the mps backend. The precision is explicitly set to a `bfloat16` format, which reduces memory use and speeds up computation while preserving numerical stability for inference workloads. This is a common choice when running large models on modern accelerators. Finally, the function wraps both the model and its tokeniser in a text-generation pipeline. Pipelines provide a unified interface that encapsulates preprocessing, model execution, and decoding of output tokens back into human-readable text.

The function allows the rest of the application to generate text with a simple function call, without needing to manage tokenisation or device placement explicitly.

We are now going to write a function to help us measure perplexity for our models. A Transformer model will typically return logits, i.e., unnormalised values proportional to the likelihood of each possible next token. When training or evaluating a language model, we compare its predicted distribution (the logits) to the actual next token in the text. That actual next token is referred to as the label.

Time to score the models; using logits versus true tokens to compute perplexity.

We will use the logits and labels as input parameters for our function:

This function lets us do just that.

```
def measure_perplexity(logits, labels):
  log_probs = torch.nn.functional.log_softmax(
    logits, dim=-1)
  selected = log_probs.gather(2,
    labels.unsqueeze(-1)).squeeze(-1)
  loss = -selected.mean()
  return torch.exp(loss).item()
```

In the first instance we convert the model's raw output scores into log-probabilities. Applying the log-softmax function produces a stable and numerically robust representation of the log-probability distribution over the vocabulary for every position in the sequence. We then isolate the entries that correspond to the ground-truth tokens (labels). This is accomplished by matching each token in the target sequence with its log-probability at the corresponding timestep. Selecting only these positions allows the function to evaluate how well the model predicted the correct continuation of the text.

Log-softmax help us check how well the model guessed the real next tokens.

Notice that we are taking the negative mean of the selected values which yields the average negative log-likelihood across the sequence. This quantity is a standard loss function in language modelling and provides a direct measure of prediction error: the higher the value, the less confident the model was about the correct next token. Finally, to convert this into the more interpretable perplexity metric, the function exponentiates the average loss. As we

Averaged negative log-likelihood becomes perplexity.

discussed in the previous section, perplexity can be understood as the effective number of equally likely choices the model faces at each step. A model that is very certain about its predictions will have a perplexity close to one, while more uncertain models produce larger values.

We can now start thinking about our benchmarking. We will write a function that provides a complete workflow for evaluating a language model's behaviour: It generates text, measures performance, and derives several metrics used in model benchmarking. Each part of the function corresponds to a specific stage of the evaluation process. Let us take a look:

Time to assemble the full test rig: Generate text, measure speed, and score the model inside one tidy workflow.

```
def benchmark(model_name, model_id):
    generator = load_model(model_id)
    start = time.time()
    result = generator(
      PROMPT,
      max_new_tokens=MAX_TOKENS,
      do_sample=True,
      temperature=0.8,
      top_p=0.9
    )[0]
    end = time.time()

    text = result['generated_text']
    token_count=len(generator.tokenizer.encode(text))
    latency = end - start
    throughput = token_count / latency
```

We instantiate our generator and provide it with our prompt.

Look at our results, count tokens and calculate latency and throughput.

```
inputs = generator.tokenizer(PROMPT,
  return_tensors='pt').to(generator.model.device)
with torch.no_grad():
  outputs = generator.model(**inputs,
  labels=inputs['input_ids'])
  perplexity = torch.exp(outputs.loss).item()

print(f'\n--- model_name ---')
print(text)
print(f'\nTokens: {token_count} \
  | Time: {latency:.2f}s \
  | Throughput: {throughput:.2f} tok/s \
  | Perplexity: {perplexity:.2f}')

return {
  'Model': model_name,
  'Tokens': token_count,
  'Latency (s)': latency,
  'Throughput (tok/s)': throughput,
  'Perplexity': perplexity
  }
```

Then feed the prompt back through the model to estimate perplexity.

Print our measures.

And return the results for comparison.

We start by loading the model through a helper function which produces a text-generation pipeline. Once the generator is ready, the code records a start time. This timestamp will later be compared with a second timestamp, allowing the overall latency of the generation operation to be measured.

The text generation call itself forms the core of the benchmark. The generator receives a prompt and several decoding parameters. The instruction to sample, rather than use greedy decoding, encourages the model to produce more varied output. The temperature and top-p values control the level of randomness during sampling, ensuring that the generation remains creative while still plausible. The call returns a list of results; the function selects the first entry as the generated sample.

A single generation call sets the stage: Sampling, temperature, and top-p shape how adventurous the model becomes.

To calculate throughput, the function encodes the generated text using the tokeniser and divides the resulting token count by the measured latency. We then compute an approximation of perplexity by constructing tokenised inputs from the original prompt and move them to the same device as the model. Running the model in a no-gradient context ensures efficient inference. By passing the input IDs both as input and as labels, the model returns a loss value that corresponds to the negative log-likelihood of the sequence. Exponentiating this loss produces an estimate of perplexity, providing insight into the model's confidence when predicting the next token. Finally, we print a summary of the benchmark results, including the generated text and all computed metrics. The function also returns these measurements packaged in a dictionary, making it straightforward to collect and compare results across multiple models.

Token count, latency, and perplexity give us a quick read on speed and efficiency, all without touching gradients.

We are now ready to run our benchmark on the selected models and save the results:

```
records = []
for name, model_id in MODELS.items():
  try:
    record = benchmark(name, model_id)
    records.append(record)
    except Exception as e:
      print(f'Error with {name}: {e}')
df = pd.DataFrame(records)
df.to_csv(CSV_OUTPUT, index=False)
print(f'\nBenchmark complete! Results saved!')
print(df)
```

A simple benchmarking loop: Run each model, catch any hiccups, and stash the results in a tidy CSV for later inspection.

Let us take a look at one of the outputs:

```
Loading model: amd/Instella-3B


Loading checkpoint shards:   0%|          | 0/2 [00:00<?, ?it/s]
Some parameters are on the meta device because they were offloaded to the disk.
Device set to use mps


--- Instella-3B ---
Write a short, imaginative paragraph describing a futuristic London where AI
systems and humans collaborate on creative projects.


As I walk through the bustling streets of the futuristic London, I am struck
by the seamless integration of artificial intelligence (AI) and human creativity.
The air is filled with the hum of AI systems working in harmony with their human
counterparts, collaborating on creative projects that defy imagination.


The city is home to a network of AI-powered art galleries and museums, where
AI systems generate unique pieces of art that are constantly evolving and
```

```
adapting to the tastes of their human creators. These AI-generated artworks are
displayed alongside the creations of human artists, creating a vibrant and

Tokens: 142 | Time: 79.83s | Throughput: 1.78 tok/s | Perplexity: 47.83
```

The results of the benchmark are shown in Table 5.3, I have used a MacBook Air with the following specifications:

The specs of the machine used for this example.

- Chip: Apple M2
- Memory: 24G
- Number of cores: 8

Model	Tokens	Latency (s)	Throughput (tok/s)	Perplexity
Qwen2-7B	140	824.801692	0.169738	40.386726
SmolLM3-3B	140	19.917259	7.029080	81.636238
Instella-3B	142	79.834915	1.778670	47.826878
SmolLM3-3B-Base	140	6895.904684	0.020302	49.268387

Table 5.3: LLM Benchmark Results

Four small models, same lineage yet wildly different personalities. A perfect snapshot of the trade-offs in play.

The four models under consideration, i.e., Qwen2-7B, SmolLM3-3B, Instella-3B, and the delightfully sluggish SmolLM3-3B-Base, form an illuminating cross-section of LLM behaviour. Despite sharing broadly similar architectural foundations, their performance characteristics could not be more different, and the resulting comparison provides a useful lesson in the perennial trade-offs between speed, accuracy, and engineering pragmatism. I recommend you run your own benchmark.

Let us begin with the heavyweight of the group, Qwen2-7B. With 7 billion parameters, it is unsurprisingly the most capable model in terms of raw language modelling quality; indeed, its perplexity of roughly 40 is the lowest of the set, indicating that it is far more certain about its predictions than its smaller cousins. Unfortunately, this confidence comes at a cost: Its latency surpasses 800 seconds for a 140-token generation. Practically, this means that while the model eventually produces good text, you are advised to put the kettle on while you wait. Its throughput, approximately 0.17 tokens per second, places it firmly in "glacial" territory. As with many large models, Qwen2-7B is best reserved for tasks where quality is a priority and time is a polite suggestion rather than a constraint.

Among those in our benchmarking exercise.

Quality aside, this one writes at glacial speed; plenty of time for a cuppa before the next token arrives.

At the opposite end we find SmolLM3-3B, a compact, efficient model that completes the same task in under 20 seconds. With a throughput of just over 7 tokens per second, it is practically sprinting compared with the aforementioned behemoth. However, this speed comes with noticeably higher perplexity, around 82, which signals that its predictions are more tentative and its generated text more variable. It is the model equivalent of the friend who always answers quickly, sometimes brilliantly, but occasionally with spectacular confidence in the wrong idea. Still, for latency-sensitive applications such as rapid prototyping or interactive systems, SmolLM3-3B's nimbleness makes it an appealing choice.

Fast, lively, and occasionally wrong, SmolLM3-3B is the sprinter you pick when speed matters more than perfect judgement.

Positioned between these extremes is Instella-3B, which strikes a rather respectable balance. Its perplexity of around 48 sits closer to Qwen's performance than to SmolLM's, yet it remains significantly faster than the former, with latency under 80 seconds. While it is neither the fastest nor the most accurate model of the cohort, Instella nevertheless demonstrates solid engineering: Its throughput and quality place it in the "sensible middle", an increasingly rare position in the world of machine learning, where everything tends to gravitate toward extremes.

Instella-3B lives in the sensible middle, neither a rocket nor a sage, but a well-balanced, reliably engineered grown-up.

Finally, we come to SmolLM3-3B-Base, a model that appears to have been constructed primarily as a cautionary tale. Its latency of nearly 7,000 seconds (or close to two hours) suggests that inference was executed without GPU acceleration. Throughput bottoms out at 0.02 tokens per second, making it the only model in this evaluation that one could meaningfully measure in tokens per minute. Curiously, the model's perplexity is not especially poor (just under 50), which indicates that the base architecture retains reasonable modelling capacity. The problem, therefore, is not the model so much as the environment: This is what happens when an LLM is forced to work without the appropriate computational nourishment.

At least it was not on a Victorian abacus!

A decent model starved of compute will still stumble; perplexity survives, performance does not.

Taken together, these results illustrate the fundamental dynamics of LLM performance:

- Large models tend to deliver superior text quality but suffer from increased latency and reduced throughput.
- Smaller models achieve impressive speed but sacrifice some level of linguistic fidelity.
- Well-engineered mid-sized models can provide a useful compromise.

Large models write well, small models run fast, mid-sized models balance the two, and all of them sulk when paired with the wrong hardware.

- And models run on the wrong hardware will, quite understandably, protest.

In practice, the choice between these models depends less on abstract benchmarks and more on operational constraints:

- Do you need high-quality text?
- Do you need it now?
- And, crucially, do you have a GPU handy?

The "best" model is the one your hardware, patience, and ambitions can actually support.

As with most things in life and machine learning, the answer is an exercise in balancing desire, patience, and the limits of one's resources.

5.7 *Large Language Models in the Cloud: OpenAI API*

So far we have focused on running models locally via libraries such as `transformers`. In many practical settings, however, you will be calling a hosted LLM over an API. In this section we are going to use OpenAI to illustrate the general usage. Other providers will have similar ways to expose the latest underlying models available to us.

Accessing more capable, or modern LLMs can be done with APIs from different providers.

We are assuming that you have access to the API platform, but please note that this may require you to have a subscription with OpenAI. You will need to create and export an API key. In MacOS or Linux, export it as an environment variable

You may need a subscription, please ask the bill payer's permission!

```
export OPENAI_API_KEY=''your_api_key_here''
```

In Windows, export it as an environment variable in PowerShell:

```
setx OPENAI_API_KEY ''your_api_key_here''
```

In order to use OpenAI API with Python, we can use the OpenAI Python API Library[16]. Ensure you install it:

[16] OpenAI (2025). OpenAI Python API Library. https://github.com/openai/openai-python. Accessed: 2025-11-08.

```
> pip install openai
```

Let us use the measures we have discussed in the previous section for the same prompt. We start by calling the library and setting the prompt:

We create a client and set up an initial prompt to pass to our OpenAI API.

```
from openai import OpenAI
import time

client = OpenAI()

PROMPT = (
  'Write a short, imaginative paragraph '
  'describing a futuristic London where AI '
  'systems and humans collaborate on creative '
  'projects.'
)
```

We need to define a few parameters such as the model to be used, the maximum number of tokens and the temperature:

```
model = 'gpt-4.1'
max_tokens = 150
temperature = 0.7
```

We define some parameters to pass to the API.

We create a response as follows:

```
start = time.time()
response = client.responses.create(
  model=model,
  input=PROMPT,
  max_output_tokens=max_tokens,
  temperature=temperature,
 )
 end = time.time()
latency = end - start
```

TheOpenAI provides a method to create a response. We simply call it!

Note that we are passing our parameters to the `create` method of `client.responses`. You will notice that we have also recorded the start and end times for the response enabling us to calculate the latency.

We can now extract the generated text:

```
output_text = ''.join(
  part.text
  for item in response.output
  for part in item.content
  if getattr(part, 'type', None) == 'output_text'
 )
```

The generated text is part of the response output. Here we extract it and concatenate it.

In the code above `response.output` is a list where each item represents one segment of the model's response. Each item

Useful when models produce mixed content.

contains a list of parts, each part can be text, commentary, or other structured content. Each part has attributes like `type = 'output_text'` or perhaps `'tool_call'`, `'reasoning'`, etc. We keep only the parts where the type explicitly declares that this is the actual text generated by the model. We join the text for each part and concatenate it. A typical output may look as follows:

```
> print(output_text)

In the neon haze of 2047 London, humans and AI
shared studio lofts above the Thames, sketching
holographic murals that rippled like living fog.
Poets traded verses with language models who could
taste metaphors; architects co-designed bridges
that unfolded like origami at rush hour. Even the
ravens of the Tower had learned to perch on
antennae, offering commentary to passing drones.
Creativity had become a duet, imperfect, electric,
and unmistakably human at its core.
```

Here us a typical response. Your output may be different from this example.

We can now calculate the total number of tokens and throughput:

```
usage = response.usage
total_tokens = usage.total_tokens
throughput = total_tokens / latency \
  if latency > 0 else float("inf")
print(
  f'\nLatency: {latency:.2f}s | '
  f'Total tokens: {total_tokens} | '
```

We obtain the number of tokens generated and calculate the throughput.

```
  f'Throughput: {throughput:.2f} tok/s'
)
```

The OpenAI API returns a usage object that includes detailed token counts. From that `usage.total_tokens` is the combined number of input tokens, output tokens and overhead used for the request. This is useful for cost tracking and performance metrics. That lets us calculate the throughput and in turn print out our benchmarking measures. A response would look something like this:

`usage.total_tokens` does what it says in the tin, i.e., the total number of tokens.

```
Latency: 0.84s | Total tokens: 112 |
  Throughput: 133.45 tok/s
```

5.7.1 *Extending the Input: Adding Instructions or Requesting Images*

When working with the OpenAI API, the structure of the input is entirely under our control. The API treats each message part of the conversational context, which means that altering the instructions is simply a matter of adjusting the content we send. This flexibility allows us to fine-tune behaviour, enforce formatting rules, or shift tasks entirely. We can use this to our advantage, for example by requesting a summary or generating an image.

The structure of the input is under our control.

In the OpenAI API we have two types of messages, system and user. These messages look similar, but they serve very different purposes. The system message shapes the model's identity and constraints. The user message shapes its goal.

They are both pieces of text sent to the model.

Together they give us predictable, controllable behaviour. Let us look at each of them in a bit more detail.

The system message sets the rules of the game. It defines the role, behaviour, tone, and constraints the model must follow throughout the conversation. Think of it as the job description or operating instructions. It tells the model how to think, not what to think about. A strong system message can turn the same model into a tutor, a translator, a safety checker, a minute taker, or a creative assistant simply by redefining expectations.

System = the rules and persona.

The user message provides the actual task or content. This is where the work happens: The question, the text to analyse, the instructions for a summary, the request for an image, and the transcript to process. The user message gives the model something to respond to within the behavioural boundaries set by the system message.

User = the task or payload

5.7.2 *Adding or Changing Instructions*

THE EASIEST WAY TO MODIFY the behaviour of the model is to edit the system message. This message establishes the role, rules, or constraints that the model must follow. For example, we can request the system to act as a senior technical editor whose task (the user message) is to revise a paragraph of text:

We can modify the behaviour of the model by changing the system message.

```
input_messages = [
  {'role': 'system',
    'content': (
```

```
        'Act as a senior technical editor. Your '
        'job is to rewrite the input with '
        'precision and clarity, preserving '
        'meaning while improving structure.')
    },
    {'role': 'user',
      'content'': 'Here is the paragraph I want '
      'you to revise...'}]
```

We provide the API with content for two roles, the system and the user.

Change the system message, and the model changes its entire working style; no code changes required.

We can also combine multiple layers of instruction:

- A system message defining overall behaviour.
- An initial user message describing the task.
- Additional user messages containing constraints, e.g., "use markdown tables only", "do not include equations", "summarise by theme rather than chronology".

This modularity allows us to build templates for different tasks and swap them in as needed.

This dichotomy provides us with enormous flexibility.

5.7.3 *Requesting an Image Output*

OPENAI MODELS THAT SUPPORT IMAGE generation simply require a different API call. To request an image, you modify the input to describe the image you want, and call the image endpoint instead of the text-generation one. Consider the following simple example:

We can do this with the `images.generate` endpoint from the API.

```
response = client.images.generate(
  model='gpt-image-1',
  prompt=('A futuristic London skyline with'
    'AI-assisted architecture, painted in a '
    'cinematic sci-fi style.',
    size='1024x1024')

image_base64 = response.data[0].b64_json
```

We need to use a model that supports image generation and notice that the prompt includes the image size.

We need to ensure that we are using a model that supports image generation. All in all, the only major difference is the prompt style—image models expect purely visual descriptions. No system message is required, but we can emulate one by simply adding constraints into the prompt:

The main constraint here is the use of visual cues.

- "Generate a photorealistic image of..."
- "Create a diagram illustrating..."
- "Produce a black-and-white technical drawing of..."

5.7.4 *Mixing Behavioural Instructions with Image Requests*

WE CAN ALSO PREPARE HYBRID workflow, for instance, summarise a meeting and then request an accompanying diagram. Look at the following example pattern:

```
summary = client.responses.create(
  model='gpt-4.1',
  input=[
```

```
  {'role': 'system',
    'content': 'Summarise the meeting...'},
  {'role': 'user', 'content': transcript} ])

diagram = client.images.generate(
  model='gpt-image-1',
  prompt=f'Create a simple diagram illustrating '+
    'the workflow described here: {summary_text}')
```

This separation of concerns—text first, then image—is typically cleaner and easier to maintain.

In short, changing the behaviour of a model is simply a matter of modifying the system message or expanding the user instructions. The system message sets the tone and role the model should adopt, while additional user guidance can tighten the format, impose constraints, or redirect the task entirely. With just a few adjustments to these inputs, the same underlying model can act as an editor, analyst, tutor, or minute taker.

System sets the role; user sets the task. Tweak both, and the same model becomes anything you need.

If the goal is to obtain a different type of output altogether—such as an image rather than text—the process is just as straightforward. Instead of calling a text-generation endpoint, you simply use the appropriate image-generation endpoint and provide a descriptive prompt. The model then switches from producing language to producing visual artefacts, guided entirely by the detail and clarity of your description.

We can request different output types with the correct endpoints.

More complex workflows emerge naturally when these ideas are combined. You might ask a model to summarise a document, then pass that summary to another call that produces a diagram; or analyse some text before generating a chart, outline, or image based on the findings. By chaining these steps, each model output becomes the input to the next, enabling surprisingly sophisticated pipelines with only a handful of well-orchestrated API calls.

We can chain the steps in our GenAI workflow to create sophisticated pipelines.

This flexibility is one of the major advantages of API-based inference: The model does not change, only the input contract does. For Jackalope Data Scientists eager to explore further, I strongly encourage a visit to the OpenAI API documentation, where you will find a continually updated catalogue of models, code examples, and detailed guides on shaping prompts, handling images, enforcing structure, and integrating the API into real applications. The examples in this section merely scratch the surface: Using models via an API opens the door to far richer capabilities, from automated report generation to multimodal assistants, from background summarisation services to full workflow orchestration. With a few well-crafted instructions and a handful of lines of Python, you can embed state-of-the-art language and vision models anywhere in your software ecosystem.

The model stays the same, your instructions do the shapeshifting. The API is a doorway to far richer capabilities.

A little Python and a clear prompt are all it takes to drop cutting-edge AI straight into your stack.

Give it a try!

5.8 *Into the Modelverse: What Lies Ahead*

Speculating about the future of artificial intelligence is a risky business, but several trends are already visible on the horizon.

Especially when the future keeps arriving early.

- **Unified multimodality.** Future models will handle text, audio, images, video, and perhaps even sensor data in a single framework. Expect models that can read your paper, watch your presentation, and generate a figure to match both.

The future points to all-in-one multimodal models, longer memories, and more local control, smarter, more personal, and harder to forget.

- **Persistent memory.** Long-term memory mechanisms will allow agents to recall prior interactions across sessions, enabling continuity and personality over time. Whether that is comforting or mildly unsettling depends on how much your AI remembers about your deadlines.
- **Federated and local models.** Privacy concerns and regulation will drive growth in on-device and federated learning approaches, letting organisations keep sensitive data within their own walls while benefiting from shared knowledge.
- **Agent orchestration.** Instead of one giant model doing everything, future systems will use networks of smaller, specialised models cooperating in real time—think less monolith, more jazz ensemble.

Expect coordinated teams of specialist agents—and far tougher questions about who's in charge, and why.

- **Transparency and alignment.** As models become more powerful, questions of ethics, bias, and interpretability will move from conference panels to boardroom agendas. The conversation will shift from "Can it be done?" to "Should it be done, and by whom?"

We can reasonably expect future iterations to focus less on raw size and more on adaptability, memory, and verifiability. There is also a growing interest in *open-weight* or partially open models, such as OpenAI's own GPT-OSS initiative,

The next gains will not come from sheer size, but from smarter, more transparent, and more adaptable models.

aiming to bridge the gap between proprietary performance and community transparency.

The world of Transformers has expanded from a single architecture into an entire ecosystem of intelligent agents. From OpenAI's flagship GPT-5 to Anthropic's Claude, from the lean efficiency of Mistral to the retrieval-powered Perplexity, and the office-bound industriousness of Microsoft Copilot, we now have a pantheon of digital colleagues. Each represents a different answer to the same question: *how should artificial intelligence interact with us?*

From lone architectures to a full ecosystem; today's models are a diverse workforce, not a single machine.

As we look forward, the line between model, agent, and collaborator continues to blur. If the early neural networks were inspired by neurons, today's systems seem inspired by *teams*. The next leap may not come from a single Transformer but from how they all work together—perhaps the real attention mechanism was the collaboration we built along the way.

Transformers have transformed (pun fully intended) the landscape of machine learning. By replacing recurrence with attention, they have unlocked massive improvements in both performance and efficiency. Models such as BERT and GPT exemplify how this architecture can excel in understanding and generating language, respectively. The continuing evolution of Transformer-based architectures—from GPT-2 to GPT-4 and beyond—suggests that *attention truly is all we need.*

By ditching recurrence for attention, Transformers rewrote the rules.

5.9 *Summary*

If this chapter has done its job properly, the evolution of language models should now feel less like a parade of acronyms and more like a slow, sometimes clumsy, but ultimately ingenious attempt to teach machines how to remember, pay attention, and mean something—in roughly that order.

We began in the age of Recurrent Neural Networks, the computational equivalent of trying to understand a novel by reading it one word at a time while suffering from mild amnesia. RNNs were a bold first step: They acknowledged that language is sequential and that yesterday's word might matter today. Unfortunately, their memory was fragile, their gradients temperamental, and their ability to remember anything beyond the recent past about as reliable as a goldfish with a PhD. These limitations were not bugs so much as consequences of architectural design; a recurring theme that will haunt us (productively) throughout modern AI.

Enter LSTMs, which introduced gates, memory cells, and the radical idea that forgetting should be a learned skill. By explicitly managing what information to keep, discard, or update, LSTMs stabilised training and extended the temporal horizon of neural memory. For a while, they were the undisputed workhorse of sequence modelling. But even LSTMs, impressive as they were, still processed language like a queue at airport security: strictly ordered, frustratingly slow, and impossible to parallelise at scale.

The real plot twist arrived with the Transformer—a model that asked a heretical question: *What if order is not the point?* By replacing recurrence with attention, Transformers reframed language understanding as a problem of relational context rather than temporal bookkeeping. Words no longer waited their turn; they simply looked at one another and decided what mattered. Meaning, in this view, emerges not from position alone but from patterns of relevance. This single architectural move unlocked massive parallelism, long-range dependency modelling, and, incidentally, the current AI arms race.

From this foundation emerged two philosophical siblings with very different personalities: BERT and GPT. BERT reads like a careful academic, absorbing text from all directions and inferring meaning by filling in blanks. GPT, by contrast, is a storyteller, trained to predict the next word and then the next, and then, if left unsupervised, the heat death of the universe. The distinction is more than stylistic: It illustrates how training objectives sculpt cognition. Architecture sets the stage, but the loss function writes the script.

As models grew larger and more capable, our old ways of judging them began to look increasingly inadequate. Usual scores could not tell us whether a model understood, reasoned, or merely hallucinated confidently. Evaluation, we saw, is no longer a single number but a portfolio: benchmarks, task-specific probes, human judgement, and an ever-present dose of scepticism. In short, if you would not assess a human with one exam, do not do it to a trillion-parameter model either.

The chapter then shifted from laboratories to production systems, where large language models now live as cloud-hosted cognitive services. Through APIs such as OpenAI's, LLMs have become less like artefacts to be trained and more like infrastructure to be orchestrated. Prompting, retrieval, fine-tuning, latency, cost, and governance now matter as much as gradients ever did. The centre of gravity has moved: Intelligence is no longer just built, it is deployed.

Looking forward, we glimpsed the expanding modelverse: Multimodal systems that see and hear, agentic models that act, retrieval-augmented systems that remember facts instead of inventing them, and hybrids that borrow ideas from symbolic reasoning while retaining neural flexibility. The future does not point toward a single omniscient model, but toward ecosystems of specialised intelligences; less HAL 9000, more Federation of Planets.

The deeper lesson of this chapter is that progress in language AI is not a straight line toward "understanding", whatever that may mean. It is a series of conceptual reframings: From sequence to context, from memory as state to memory as attention, from models as artefacts to models as services. Each shift changes not only what machines can do, but how we, as Jackalope Data Scientists, designers, scientists, and users, think about intelligence itself.

And if that feels slightly unsettling—good. That is usually a sign that something genuinely interesting is happening.

6

Here Is One I Made Earlier: Machine Learning Deployment

WE HAVE COVERED A LOT of ground in this and its companion book *Data Science and Analytics with Python*[1]. We have discussed the trials and tribulations of Jackalope Data Scientists, seen the differences between supervised and unsupervised learning, and talked about models such as regression, decision trees, time series, neural networks, logistic regression and natural language processing techniques, not to mention convolutional and recurrent neural networks, deep learning, large language models and more. It is a large landscape, and there are many areas into which we could delve much deeper, or indeed some others we have not even touched.

[1] Rogel-Salazar, J. (2025). *Data Science and Analytics with Python*. Chapman & Hall/CRC Data Mining and Knowledge Discovery Series. CRC Press.

Of all those areas, in this chapter we will discuss some aspects that we need to take into account in order to not only build a powerful model, but also make it part of a data product that can be used by its intended users and

We can build powerful models, but who will use them?

consumers. Not only does this require the close collaboration of the triumvirate formed by a Jackalope Data Scientist, project manager and data architect, but also the support of a product owner and subject matter experts.

We will first talk about data products, the requirement to build pipelines and processes and the need for creating machine learning and artificial intelligence models able to perform scoring and inference on device. We will then provide an example for deploying a simple machine learning model in a mobile device such as an Apple iPhone. We will then look at Foundation Models Framework which provides access to the $\sim$ 3 billion parameter on-device language model powering Apple Intelligence. To that end, we will use some of the capabilities that the ecosystem for these devices offers, including the use of Xcode and the Swift programming language.

We will build a couple of iOS apps!

6.1 *The Devil in the Detail: Data Products*

NOTHING IS AS PERVASIVE AS a product. We all recognise them, buy them, sell them and/or use them. Let us consider here a product to be a method, a good idea, information, object or service that has been created as a result of a determined process in order to satisfy a need or want. Typically we think of products as tangible objects. With that being the case, it could be surprising to us when we first hear about a data product. We should think of a data product as any other product, but one whose existence

Products are not exclusively tangible objects!

meets the need or want we mentioned above through the employment of data.

That definition is still quite broad and wide-encompassing; after all, a number of digital products out there use data. Things such as apps or websites/portals for example. In our case we would like to concentrate on those data products whose main *raison d'être* is centred around data. You may think that we are splitting hairs here, but hear me out. A data product is still a product, and thus the standard considerations of developing a product do apply: Meet a customer need, improvement through feedback, competition, prioritisation, etc. You name it. That is true even for those super expensive products in fictional planet *Algon*, the fifth world in the system of Aldebaran, the Red Giant in the constellation of Sagittarius.

Ok, read me out... This is not a podcast after all!

No bananas on Algon though!

Nonetheless, a data product distinguishes itself for the development considerations we need to make around the availability, processing and meaning of data. No wonder that the powers of a Jackalope Data Scientist are in high demand around the creation of data products. The main consideration is therefore the incorporation of data, data science, machine learning and artificial intelligence techniques while going beyond data analysis, to the provision of value for the customer. The idea behind a data product is to put data understanding into production.

Or indeed of a rangale of Jackalope data scientists.

Let me be clear, a data product is not "some data in a database", nor is it a chart that happens to look persuasive on a slide. A data product is something deliberately built so that data does useful work for someone else. In other words, a data product is an engineered artefact that uses data, models, or algorithms to deliver a repeatable outcome to a user. That outcome might be insight, a recommendation, a prediction, or an automated decision. The key word is outcome. If nobody can act on it, it is not a product, it is just data having a quiet lie-down. Also, please note that repeatable does not necessarily mean deterministic. Remember that machine learning systems rarely offer a deterministic guarantee, and pretending they should is how disappointment enters the room. If your model gives exactly the same answer every time, you may not have built intelligence, you may have built a lookup table with a confidence problem.

If nobody can act on it, it is not a product, it is just data having a quiet lie-down.

At the product level, what matters is that the decision quality is repeatable, even if individual predictions are not. What this means may vary; for example we may need fewer breakdowns over time, faster response times, better triage outcomes, more efficient utilisation. The model may roll a different number each time, but the system consistently produces better outcomes than the alternative. That is repeatability a board can understand. Repeatability in machine learning systems is not about getting the same answer twice, but about getting answers you can rely on behaving sensibly over time.

Deterministic systems repeat answers. Intelligent systems repeat outcomes.

We can think of different categories of data products including:

- Raw data — Making data available through appropriate pipelines.

A categorisation of data products in increasing order of complexity.

- Derived data — Processing and calculating fields that can be used later in the funnel.

- Algorithms — This has been the main topic of our discussions. We pass some (raw/derived) data through an algorithm to obtain understanding useful to the users.

- Decision support — Enabling the user to make a decision based on better information. The aim is to provide the information in an easy way to be consumed. These are the products we will talk about in this chapter.

Humans decide; machines advise.

- Automated decision-making — This is closer to the overall goal of artificial intelligence where the process of making a decision is delegated to the machine without user intervention.

As we move from raw data into automated decisions, not only do we move in an increasing scale of complexity, requiring different skills in the development of the product, but also the products have different intended audiences. For raw and derived data products, as well as algorithms, the audience tends to be technical. However, for the decision support and automated decision-making, the end users will tend to be more specialised and perhaps not even technical at all.

The different data product categories above have very different intended audiences.

We have been considering the usage of algorithms as data products to be consumed by technical users to understand the patterns available in our data. However, models are not data products on their own. A trained model sitting on disk is like a brain in a jar. Technically impressive, but not terribly helpful. It becomes a data product only when it is

That's right, us, Jackalope Data Scientists.

fed with fresh, well-defined inputs so as to produce outputs in a form someone can use. It should be integrated into a wider system or workflow, and evaluated, monitored, and occasionally told off. This is why deployment, interfaces, and governance matter just as much as clever modelling. Users do not care how elegant your loss function is; they care whether the answer will be available before their meeting
starts.

Not just data in isolation.

In this chapter we are concerned with that next level in the scale described above, where the available data is provided to a suitable algorithm to extract an insight and we are then interested in providing this power to our users or customers, particularly non-technical ones. In short, data products are where data science grows up. They are not about exploring data for its own sake, but about embedding intelligence into systems that people actually use, sometimes knowingly, sometimes blissfully unaware that a Jackalope Data Scientist is working behind the scenes.

Turning maths into buttons.

As it is the case with many other products, they do not simply arise fully formed, like Venus from the sea-foam. Instead, we need to apply investigation, feedback and expertise to hone in on the problem we are trying to solve. A methodology that comes to mind in these situations is Agile[2], which gives us the opportunity of exploring and understanding our problem, while being flexible providing us with an opportunity to learn, evolve, pivot and create better products. With that in mind, the concept of a unicorn data scientist is not the ideal in an agile development cycle.

[2] Stellman, A. and J. Greene (2014). *Learning Agile: Understanding Scrum, XP, Lean, and Kanban.* O'Reilly Media.

Instead we need a team of shrewd Jackalope Data Scientists to enable the wider team working in the development of a data product to be nimble and multi-functional.

The multi-functional team we refer to is not just made out of data scientists. In general we require data architects, engineers, product managers and subject matter experts in order to create a successful data product. Data scientists need to liaise with engineers to obtain a reliable dataset; subject matter experts need to provide their know-how at crucial development stages and verify how useful results may be, while informing product managers about the direction of development that the product is taking. Communication among all these agents is therefore paramount, and Agile may be able to facilitate this as part of the ceremonies that form part of a good implementation of the methodology.

Working in a multi-functional team under a methodology such as Agile enables the successful creation of good products.

Simply having daily standups does not mean you are already applying Agile.

There is no magic number for the amount and number of data sources or indeed data observations required by a data product. Data science is a hungry, even greedy, affair: The more data available, the better. Having said that, it is important to bear in mind that the quality of the data is of great importance too. Actually, the V's of (big) data[3] come to mind: Volume, Velocity, Variety, Veracity as well as Visibility and Value.

[3] Rogel-Salazar, J. (2023). *Statistics and Data Visualisation with Python*. Chapman & Hall/CRC The Python Series. CRC Press

The assessment that the team will need to make is not only about the data quantity and quality, but also about the timeliness of data availability, as well as the data combinations that can be pursued in order to create models that benefit/improve the product. Furthermore, depending on the type of algorithms employed in the data product, it may be possible to make indirect observations of signals in the data to predict useful information.

All in all, as any data product is still a product, it will need to meet the needs or solve the problems that real users/customers/people have. The important thing therefore is to start with the problem statement and iterate it. There is no doubt that technology is an important factor in the successful development of a data product, but it is not a panacea. Starting up with the technology and finding a problem to solve is the equivalent of using a hammer to tighten a screw. In some cases it may work, but it would be better to find technology that helps solve the problem at hand.

Starting with the problem statement is paramount.

Or any product actually!

The success of a good data product relies on the collaboration and effort of the team behind it and, to a larger extent, on the users whose pain points the product helps mitigate. As such, our task as Jackalope Data Scientists is to use the most appropriate data to employ in our development, make use of suitable algorithms and collaborate with data engineers, architects, product and project managers, and yes, even users. We can then let our tools, languages and platforms deliver a solution to the problem statement.

After all, if the users do not see the value in the product, they will not use it.

This may take many forms, and one way to tackle this challenge is through the creation of user-friendly interfaces. These applications let users consume the results of the data

The creation of a user-friendly interface may help in serving the need of our customers better than handing them a Python script.

product. For instance, consider a product that applies a multivariate regression algorithm to predict house prices. It supports users that are interested in climbing the property ladder, and they can be better served with the help of a purpose-built application that makes the prediction easier to compute. Compare this to handing them a programming script or a table with numbers.

We will build a similar solution later on; stay tuned!

The deployment of machine learning algorithms as part of a data product can be achieved in various ways. Depending on the ultimate goal of the product and its intended audience, this may range from programmatic authoring, scheduling and monitoring of data pipelines with tools such as Apache Airflow[4] or Luigi[5]; within platforms such as Dataiku, Sage or Databricks; or in device, where processing happens directly in a smart phone for example. The extension to this is the concept of machine learning at the edge, where computing power is distributed across a network of devices, making use of the Internet of Things, instead of a centralised system in the cloud. We may not cover here computing at the edge, but let us take a look at deployment on a single device.

[4] Apache Airflow (2014). Apache Airflow Documentation. https://airflow.apache.org. Accessed: 2019-09-30.
[5] Spotify (2014). Luigi. https://github.com/spotify/luigi. Accessed: 2019-09-30.

IoT for short.

6.2 *Apples and Snakes: Core ML + Python*

WITH THE HIGH AVAILABILITY OF a large number of connected devices, the computing power that can be harnessed for the application of machine learning is huge. A lot of these devices are small enough to be carried around with us and are part of our daily lives. Furthermore, they

Here, we are interested in harnessing the power of mobile devices.

come with a variety of sensors and monitors that can gather data, which in turn can be used by the data products we build for the benefit of our users.

It is possible to implement our data products to be deployed in a mobile device, enabling the machine learning algorithms to process and execute directly there, without the need of sending data or information to a server and coming back to the user. This has advantages for data privacy, as the information never leaves the user's device and reduces friction in terms of latency for the user, for example. As you can see, this offers a number of advantages, as the machine learning models we develop are delivered into the hands of users, quite literally.

The processing happens directly in the device!

We want to deliver our models into the hands of our users.

There are some tools that enable the deployment of machine learning models into a device, taking a trained model and encapsulating it in a format that is compatible with the ecosystem of the device in question. In this case we are going to concentrate on some of the tools that Apple has made available to developers in order to integrate machine learning workflows into applications, aka, apps. One such tool is Core ML which is a computer framework, in other words a software abstraction that enables generic functionality to be modified as required by the developer to transform it into software for specific purposes. This enables us to develop complex projects or simple apps.

Although we are concentrating our discussion in the Apple ecosystem, there are other solutions out there!

Our aim is to deploy a machine learning model into an app.

Core ML is a framework created and provided by Apple to speed up the development of apps that use *trained* machine learning models. Notice that word we wrote in italics in the description of the framework: Trained. This means that the model has to be developed externally with appropriate training data for the specific project in mind. For instance if you are interested in building a classifier that distinguishes Jackalopes from hares, and horses from unicorns, then you need to train the model with lots of images of Jackalopes and hares, horses and unicorns first. Then you can apply the Core ML framework to integrate the model within an app.

Core ML takes pre-trained machine learning models and makes them available within an app.

Core ML supports a variety of machine learning models, from generalised linear models (GLMs) to neural networks. A summary of the models that can be used with Core ML is shown in Table 6.1. It is possible for you to develop your own custom conversion tool in case your model is currently not supported. Core ML also helps with the task of adding the trained machine learning model to your application by automatically creating a custom programmatic interface that supplies an API to your model. All this is within the comfort of Apple's own IDE: Xcode.

Check the Apple Developer documentation for further models supported in the future.

API stands for Application Programming Interface.

There is an important point to remember. The model has to be developed externally from Core ML; in other words you may want to use your favourite machine learning framework, computer language and environment to cover the different aspects of the data science workflow. You can read more about this in chapter 3 of *Data Science and Analytics with Python* book[6]. In any case, whether you use scikit-learn, Keras or another supported framework, the model you develop has to be trained (tested and evaluated) beforehand. Once you are ready, Core ML will support you in bringing it to the masses via your app.

That word again; in this case think Python libraries such as scikit-learn for instance.

[6] Rogel-Salazar, J. (2025). *Data Science and Analytics with Python*. Chapman & Hall/CRC Data Mining and Knowledge Discovery Series. CRC Press.

Model Category	Supported Model Types	Source Frameworks
Linear and Generalised Models	Linear regression, logistic regression, ridge, lasso, elastic net	Scikit-learn, Create ML
Tree Ensembles	Decision trees, random forests, gradient boosted trees	Scikit-learn, XGBoost, LightGBM, CatBoost
Neural Networks	Feedforward, convolutional (CNN), recurrent (RNN/LSTM), transformers	PyTorch, TensorFlow/Keras
Support Vector Machines	Regression and classification	Scikit-learn, LIBSVM
Feature Engineering	Normalisation, scaling, categorical encoding, vectorisation	Scikit-learn, Create ML
Pipeline Models	Chained preprocessing + model inference	Scikit-learn Pipelines
On-device Learning (limited)	Personalisation layers, parameter updates	Create ML, Core ML APIs

Table 6.1: Machine learning models and source frameworks supported by Core ML (modern Core ML 5+ ecosystem).

You can find more about integrating machine learning into your app with Core ML in the Apple Developers' Documentation pages[7]. Since its original release, Core ML has evolved from a model conversion utility into a fully-fledged on-device machine learning runtime. Modern versions of Core ML take advantage of Apple Silicon by automatically dispatching computation across the CPU, GPU, and Neural Engine, optimising for latency, energy consumption, and privacy. In practice, this means that a

[7] Apple Inc. (2017b). Core ML — integrate machine learning models into your app. Accessed: 2025-12-21.

single `.mlmodel` can be deployed unchanged across iOS, iPadOS, macOS, watchOS, and visionOS devices.

Further to that, in 2019 Apple announced the release of an application called Create ML, bundled within the set of tools they make available to developers. Create ML enables the training and deployment of machine learning models directly on macOS, with the output produced natively in the Core ML format. As a result, no explicit model conversion step is required.

You can use Create ML to create a model natively into the Apple ecosystem.

We will not cover Create ML in detail here, as it is outside the remit of this book. Interested Jackalope Data Scientists are encouraged to consult the Apple Developers' documentation[8] for further information. Since its introduction, Create ML has expanded its support for tabular data, computer vision, natural language processing, sound classification, and activity recognition based on sensor data. It offers both a graphical interface and Swift-based workflows, making it particularly suitable for rapid prototyping, smaller datasets, and teams with limited exposure to Python-based machine learning stacks.

[8] Apple Inc. (2019b). Create ML — train machine learning models. Accessed: 2025-12-21.

As for the advantages of Core ML, Apple[9] mentions that it is optimised for on-device performance. This minimises the memory footprint and power consumption of the app. Also, the fact that the model runs strictly on the device ensures the privacy of user data and guarantees that the app remains functional and responsive when a network connection is unavailable. In order to use our model within

[9] Apple Inc. (2017b). Core ML — integrate machine learning models into your app. Accessed: 2025-12-21.

our app, we need to translate our implementation into a `.mlmodel` format. Let us find out more about how we can do that by building our own app.

6.3 *Machine Learning at the Core: Apps and ML*

IN THIS SECTION WE WILL cover the end-to-end creation of a simple app with machine learning at its core. Starting with the creation of a suitable Python environment for the creation of the model and its translation to Core ML format, all the way to running it in your iPhone. We are largely following the workflow depicted schematically in Figure 6.1, starting with the development in Python using libraries such as scikit-learn and Keras. We then will convert our Python model into Core ML using Core ML Tools. We then integrate the translated model into our app development and finally deploy the app to our users.

Yes, at its (Apple) Core (ML)!

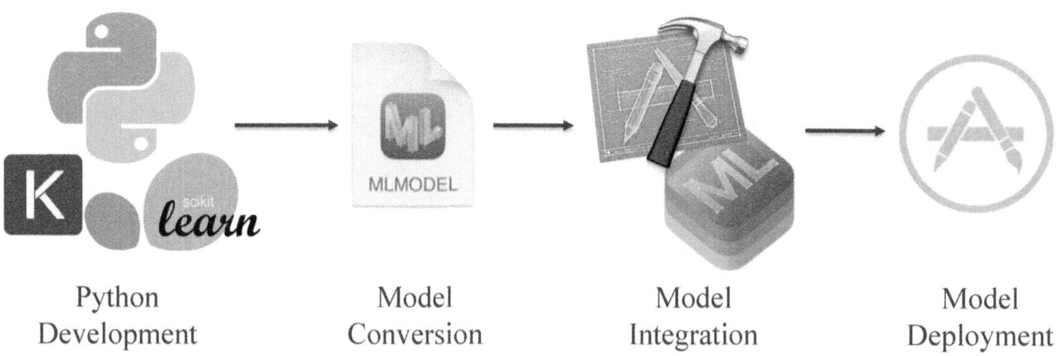

Figure 6.1: We follow this workflow to deploy our machine learning models to our app.

6.3.1 *Environment Creation*

IN PREPARATION TO TRAINING A model which will be converted into Core ML so as to be integrated within our application, it is best practice to make sure we have a suitable environment to work on. When Core ML first came to light, the Core ML module only supported Python 2! Fortunately, things have moved on since then and now Python 3.x is also supported.

Creating an environment for Core ML is best practice.

In order to ensure reproducibility of the stack, we will create an environment with the appropriate modules. In this case we are using Anaconda and will create a conda environment called `coreml` with Python 3.7; it will include some of the libraries we may be using such as scikit-learn, pandas, Matplotlib, etc.

You may use your favourite Python distribution.

At the time of writing, Core ML supports up to version 1.5.1 of scikit-learn.

```
> conda create --name coreml jupyter
  scikit-learn=1.5.1 pandas matplotlib
```

We need to install the Core ML Tools module[10], and the easiest way to do this is to use `pip install`:

[10] Apple Inc. (2017a). Core ML tools. https://github.com/apple/coremltools. Accessed: 2025-12-21.

```
> conda activate coreml


(coreml)
> pip install coremltools
```

Do not forget to activate your environment to use the libraries. You may need to deactivate it too.

6.3.2 *Eeny, Meeny, Miny, Moe: Model Selection*

NOW THAT WE HAVE A suitable environment to carry out our development, we need to get to the ever so difficult task of choosing a model. This is not as simple as picking up one of the many algorithms available to us, and the decision depends to a large extent on the use case at hand. The main recommendation is therefore to consider the problem statement that we are trying to address, obtain the appropriate data to help with answering the problem and brainstorm with the rest of the team to assess best actions.

Remember to use the data science workflow. Start with the problem statement and use appropriate data.

Model selection will also be dictated by the metrics of your algorithm and indeed the application of best practices in terms of data splitting, feature engineering, cross-validation, etc. We will not cover these steps here, as they have been addressed in Chapters 1 and 3 of *Data Science and Analytics with Python*[11]. Instead, we are interested in the steps that follow the successful selection of the model. Let us consider for the sake of argument and without loss of generality that we are relying on our good old friend, the dependable linear regression model.

[11] Rogel-Salazar, J. (2025). *Data Science and Analytics with Python*. Chapman & Hall/CRC Data Mining and Knowledge Discovery Series. CRC Press.

We are indeed all familiar with a line of best fit, and surely many of us remember doing some of it by hand! Also, who has not played with Excel's capabilities to perform a linear regression? Let us remind ourselves of some of the basics behind this modelling technique: A linear regression is a model that relates a variable y to one or more explanatory (or independent) variables x_i.

You know who you are!

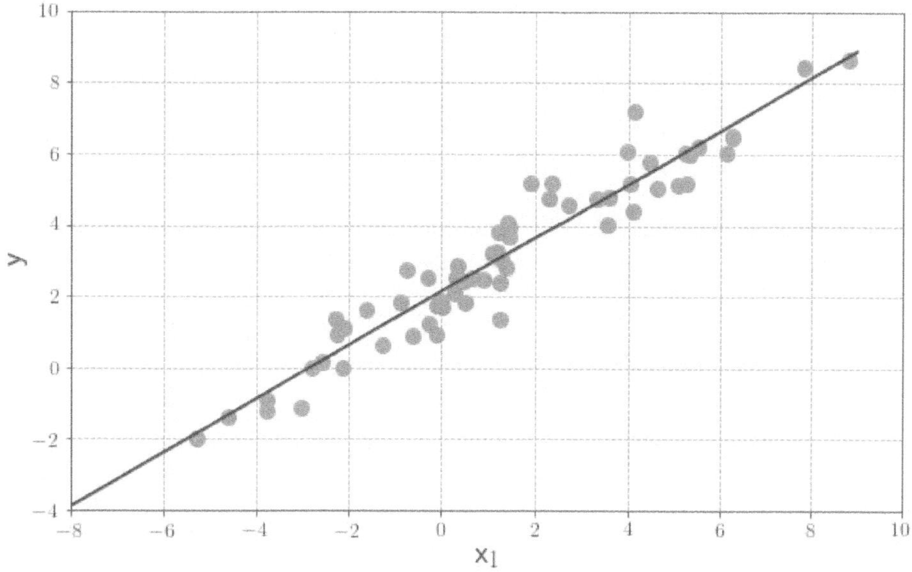

Figure 6.2: A line of best bit for the observations y dependent of features x_1.

The parameters that define the model are estimated from the available data relevant to the problem. Remember that there are a number of assumptions about the explanatory variables. You can find more information in Chapter 4 of the companion book mentioned above. We can think of the goal of a linear regression model to draw a line through the data as exemplified in Figure 6.2. In such a case, data for the independent variable x_1 is used to determine the value of y.

We can think of the goal of linear regression as finding a line of best fit.

Let us take the case of two independent variables x_1 and x_2. The linear regression model to predict our target variable y is given by:

$$y = \alpha + \beta_1 x_1 + \beta_2 x_2 + \epsilon, \tag{6.1}$$

where α and β_i are the parameters to be estimated. Once the estimation is obtained, we use these parameters to generate predictions. With the aid of techniques such as least squares, it is possible to estimate the parameters α, β_1 and β_2 by minimising the sum of the squares of the residuals, i.e., the difference between an observed value, and the fitted value provided by a model. Once we have determined the parameters, we are able to score new (unseen) data for x_1 and x_2 to predict the value of y. For more information on linear regression, I recommend you check chapter 4 of *Data Science and Analytics with Python*[12].

Once we have estimations for α, β_1 and β_2, we can use the model to score new, unseen data points.

[12] Rogel-Salazar, J. (2025). *Data Science and Analytics with Python*. Chapman & Hall/CRC Data Mining and Knowledge Discovery Series. CRC Press.

In this updated example we will use the "California Housing" dataset, which contains information collected during the 1990 U.S. Census. Our aim is to predict the median house value in a district based on a small number of numerical attributes. This dataset is widely used for regression problems and is readily available through scikit-learn.

We will use the "California Housing " dataset for our example.

6.3.3 *Location, Location, Location: Exploring the Data*

We consider that our problem statement is the challenge of predicting the price of properties is a given. What about concentrating in California? It seems like a great location to explore. There is a bit of a caveat in this case; we will transport ourselves with our TARDIS to the 1990s, as the dataset we will use comes from that time.

Other time-travelling methods may be available... at some time or other...

The dataset in question has information collected by the U.S. Census Service concerning housing in California, and published by Kelley Pace and Barry[13]. It is structured using census block groups as its fundamental unit of observation. Census block groups are the smallest geographical entities for which the U.S. Census Bureau releases sample data, generally encompassing populations between 600 and 3,000 individuals. The original aim for this dataset was to illustrate the power of sparse spatial weight matrices in computing autoregressions.

[13] Kelley Pace, R. and R. Barry (1997). Sparse spatial autoregressions. *Statistics & Probability Letters* 33(3), 291–297.

To make our discussion more manageable, we will use our knowledge of one of the most well-known models in statistics and, yes, machine learning: Linear regression. We know that we can relate the values of input parameters x_i to the target variable y to be predicted. Let us however do some basic exploration of our dataset.

Other machine learning models are available!

The dataset contains 20,640 data points with 8 features:

- MedInc — median income in block group (in tens of thousands of dollars)
- HouseAge — median house age in block group (in years)
- AveRooms — average number of rooms per household
- AveBedrms — average number of bedrooms per household
- Population — block group population (count of people)
- AveOccup — average number of household members
- Latitude — block group latitude

The features of the California Housing dataset.

- Longitude — block group longitude

The target variable is the median house value for California districts, expressed in hundreds of thousands of dollars ($\$100,000$).

We are going to use scikit-learn, and fortunately the dataset comes with the module. The input variables are included in the data method and the price is given by the target. We are going to load the input variables in the dataframe `housing_df` and the prices in the array `y`:

That is awesome, right?

```
from sklearn.datasets import \
  fetch_california_housing
import pandas as pd


housing = fetch_california_housing(as_frame=True)
X_full = housing.data
y = housing.target


housing_df = pd.concat([X_full, y], axis=1)
```

We retrieve the dataset directly from scikit-learn!

To build our model for this example, we deliberately restrict the number of features used. In a real application, asking users to provide a large number of inputs is rarely practical. Furthermore, in this case it also enables us to fit our discussion. We therefore focus on two intuitive attributes for our model, namely:

We need to keep our users in mind!

- `MedInc`: Median income in the district
- `AveRooms`: Average number of rooms per household

As mentioned before, the decision to limit the number of features may provide a more straightforward user experience: We are asking our users to focus on aspects that are of importance to them and have an impact in the prediction they are seeking. In that way, we are making a friendlier version of the app, rather than creating a bloated one that no one would like to use. In a more realistic situation, these are decisions that would need to be carefully considered as part of the product development and testing sprints.

For ease of discussion, we will only use two variables in our model: Median income and average number of rooms.

Fewer dials, clearer answers; because usability beats feature hoarding every time.

In any event, let us concentrate on the features we mentioned above. To make things a bit more human-readable, we are going to rename the features as `Income` and `Rooms`:

```
X = housing_df[['MedInc', 'AveRooms']]
X.columns = ['Income', 'Rooms']
```

We select the variables of interest.

The descriptive statistics for the selected variables provide useful insight into the scale and distribution of the data. It will also let us define suitable values to show to our users. We can use pandas to our advantage and get a description of these two attributes with the help of the `describe()` method. Let us take a look at the statistics:

```
> X.describe()


              Income         Rooms
count   20640.000000  20640.000000
mean        3.870671      5.429000
```

```
std        1.899822     2.474173
min        0.499900     0.846154
25%        2.563400     4.440716
50%        3.534800     5.229129
75%        4.743250     6.052381
max       15.000100   141.909091
```

We can see the descriptive statistics for our variables of interest.

The median income variable exhibits a right-skewed distribution, with a median value of approximately 3.53 and an upper bound capped at 15, reflecting the normalisation applied to the original census data. Most observations lie between the first and third quartiles, indicating a relatively compact central distribution. The average number of rooms per household has a mean of 5.43 and a median of 5.23, suggesting a fairly symmetric distribution for typical housing units. However, the maximum value is unusually large, pointing to the presence of outliers that represent districts with exceptionally high average room counts. These summary statistics are informative not only for understanding the data, but also for guiding sensible parameter ranges when exposing model inputs to end users through an application interface. We can see the relationships of these two features versus the house price values in Figure 6.3.

The data behave nicely in the middle... then do something weird at the edges. You know data!

Summary stats are not just for admiration. They will help us stop users from dialling inputs into fantasy land.

6.3.4 *Modelling and Core ML: A Crucial Step*

In the last section we have taken a look at the California Housing dataset, loaded it directly from scikit-learn and

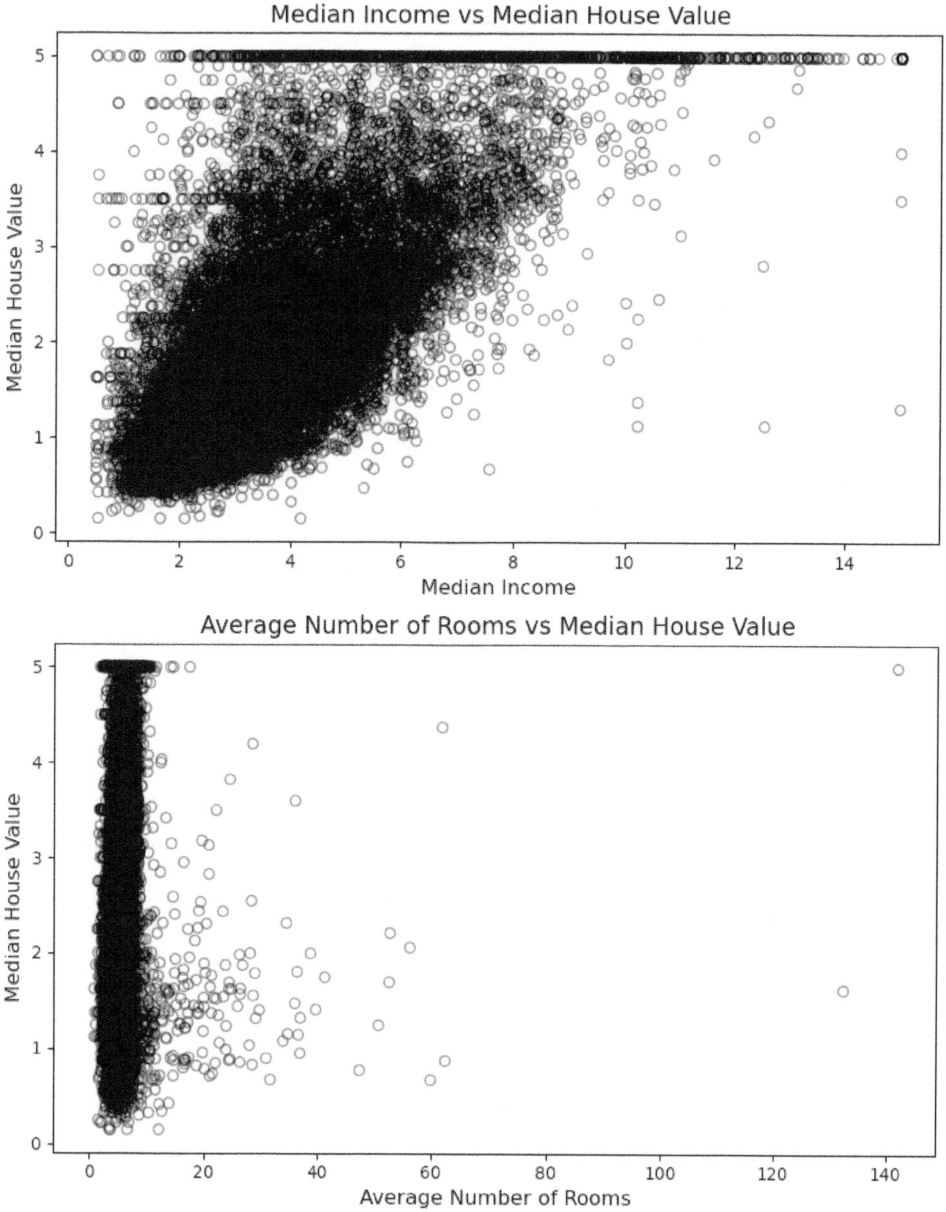

Figure 6.3: Median income (top) and average number of rooms (bottom) versus median house value in the California Housing dataset.

looked at some of the features of interest for our predictive model. It is now time to build the linear regression model we talked about earlier. Then we will convert it to a `.mlmodel` to be used in an iOS app. As usual, we are going to need some modules:

We will build a linear regression model for this dataset.

```
import coremltools
import pandas as pd
from sklearn import linear_model
from sklearn.model_selection \
  import train_test_split
from sklearn import metrics
import numpy as np
```

Importing modules is second nature to us!

We are familiar with the modules and methods mentioned above. The newcomer in this case is `coremltools` which will enable the conversion of our model to be used in iOS.

We have already loaded our data in the previous section and created a subset of features including the crime rate score and the number of rooms in the property, as well as our target variable. Although this dataset is not too big, we are going to follow best practices and split the data into training and testing sets:

Remember best practices always!

```
X_train, X_test, y_train, y_test=train_test_split(
  X, y, test_size=0.2, random_state=7)
```

We split our data into training and testing.

In this case we are reserving 20% of the dataset for testing, and the split is initialised with a random seed equal to 7. Remember that the idea is to use the training set only in the creation of the model. We then test with the remaining data points.

Let us now create a self-contained function to build a generalised linear model:

```
def glm_housing(X, y):
  print('Implementing a simple linear regression.')
  lm = linear_model.LinearRegression()
  gml = lm.fit(X, y)
  return gml
```

This function implements and fits a linear regression model from scikit-learn.

This creates an instance of the `LinearRegression` algorithm in scikit-learn and fits it with the data in X to predict the target y. Let us use this function with our training data:

```
my_model = glm_boston(X_train, y_train)
```

The linear regression model we are implementing is of the form:

$$y = \alpha + \beta_1 x_1 + \beta_2 x_2 + \epsilon, \tag{6.2}$$

Here, we refer to α as the intercept and β_i as the coefficients.

and the fitting of the model we just performed will let us extract the fitted parameters α and β_i that will enable us to make predictions. Let us see our coefficients:

We can see the estimated value of our coefficients with the aid of the properties `.intercept` and `.coeff_` of our model.

```
coefs = [my_model.intercept_, my_model.coef_]
```

We can check what the values are:

```
> print('The intercept is {0}'.format(coefs[0]))

The intercept is 0.5808599461504964.

> print('The coefficients are {0}'.\
    format(coefs[1]))

The coefficients are [ 0.43282143 -0.03511876].
```

Our equation is $y = 0.058 + 0.4328x_1 - 0.035x_2$.

The model is ready to be tested against the test data:

```
y_pred = my_model.predict(X_test)
```

The `.predict` method of the model lets us score unseen data and make predictions.

We can take a look at some metrics that let us evaluate our model against the test data:

```
> print('The mean absolute error is {0}'.format(\
    metrics.mean_absolute_error(y_test, y_pred)))

The mean absolute error is 0.631231475332099.

> print('The mean squared error is {0}'.format(\
    metrics.mean_squared_error(y_test, y_pred)))

The mean squared error is 0.7142486136975783.
```

It is important to look at evaluation metrics for our model.

Another important metric we would like to take a look at is the R-squared:

```
> print('The r-squared is {0}'.format(\
    metrics.r2_score(y_test, y_pred)))

The r-squared is 0.4689666500816947.
```

R-squared is a typical metric used in linear regression.

We know that a value of 1 means that we have a perfect prediction. In other words, the variance of the data will be explained fully by the model. In this case we have a bit more than 45% of the variance explained... Not bad, not great... not bad at all for a simple initial model. Let us continue with this model. Remember that our aim here is to look at the deployment of the model rather than the accuracy we achieve with it.

Remember that our aim here is to look at the deployment of a model. You can spend more time finding a better model than this good enough one (for our purposes!)

Let us take a look at one of the test samples and its prediction. We will set up a dictionary for the input features and see the prediction that the model makes:

A dictionary will be used in passing values to the Core ML model!

```
sample = { 'income': X_test.iloc[0]['Income'],
    'rooms': X_test.iloc[0]['Rooms'] }
ypred_sample = y_pred[0]
```

Making a prediction with a pair of values for our chosen attributes.

In this case we are extracting the first set of values in the testing dataset. The prediction for this set of values is stored in the first element of the array `y_pred` we calculated before:

```
> print('A property with {0} is valued \
  ${1:,.2f}'.format(sample, \
  ypred_sample*100000))
```

We can easily check the predicted value for the chosen parameters.

```
A property with {'income': np.float64(2.0278),
'rooms': np.float64(2.8469284994964754)}
is valued $135,855.46
```

A property with an average number of rooms equal to 2.84 in a location with a median income of $20,278 is predicted to be valued as $135,855.46.

If we imagine that this is the model that we are interested in deploying to our users, then we are ready for the big moment: Converting our model to an `.mlmodel` object!! Ready?

In reality, you will probably have to spend more time pondering this.

```
coreml_model = coremltools.converters.\
  sklearn.convert(my_model,\
  input_features=[income, 'rooms'],
  output_feature_names='price')
```

The named parameters in the translation will be used in the app implementation later on.

Since we are using scikit-learn to develop our model, we need to employ the `sklearn.convert` method of `coremltools.converters` to convert the model into Core ML format. Remember that currently you can also convert models developed with PyTorch, Keras, TensorFlow, XGBoost, LightGBM, CatBoost, LIBSVM, etc. In the code above we are passing the name of our model from scikit-learn, together with the names we would like to use for our input features, i.e., `income` and `rooms`; we also provide a name for the output, in this case `price`.

We are using `sklearn.convert`, as our model is originally developed with scikit-learn. Core ML supports other frameworks too.

Now that we have a Core ML object, we can edit some of the metadata attached to it. This will make it easier to be integrated to the rest of the deployment stack via XCode. For instance, information about the author, licensing and others can be consumed by Xcode UI.

Adding metadata to our Core ML model is easy.

```
coreml_model.author = 'JRogel
coreml_model.license = 'BSD'
```

We are adding metadata about the author and the licensing.

We are also able to provide other metadata such as a description for the model, as well as for the inputs and output.

```
coreml_model.short_description = ('Predicts median'
  'house prices in California based on median'
  'income and average number of rooms (1990s)')
coreml_model.input_description['income'] = (
  'Median income in the district (tens of'
  ' thousands of USD per year)')
coreml_model.input_description['rooms'] = (
  'Average number of rooms per household')
coreml_model.output_description['price'] = (
  'Predicted median house value (in thousands'
  'of USD)')
```

We are adding some useful descriptions to our model.

Including descriptions for the inputs and output.

Finally, we can save the model for later use. We will import the saved model in our app later on, but for now we store it in a file with the name `'CaliforniaHousePricer.mlmodel`.

```
coreml_model.save('CaliforniaHousePricer.mlmodel')
```

We can save our model with the `save` method.

Earlier versions of Core ML Tools provided limited visualisation capabilities directly from Python. In modern

Core ML workflows, model inspection and visualisation are instead handled within Xcode. Opening a `.mlmodel` file in Xcode provides an interactive view of the model structure, inputs, outputs, and metadata, and it is the recommended approach for understanding and validating converted models prior to deployment. An example of the information shown by Xcode can be seen in Figure 6.4.

Xcode provides some interactive views to explore a Core ML model.

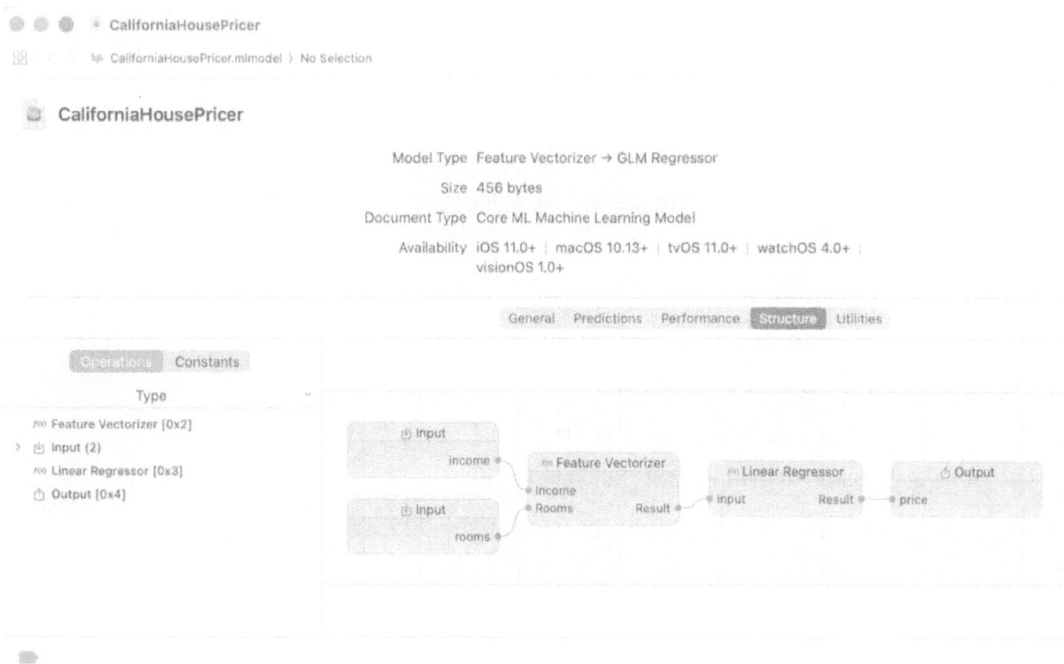

Figure 6.4: Xcode interactive view of our Core ML for the California Housing dataset.

Let us check that the converted model returns the same predictions as the scikit-learn model. All we need to do is pass to the Core ML model a dictionary with the features defined in the conversion, in this case `income` and `rooms`. This can be for instance the dictionary called `sample` we defined above:

We can check the predictions by passing a dictionary with the predictor values.

```
cml_pred = coreml_model.predict(sample)
```

Let us print the result:

```
> print(cml_pred)


{'price': 1.3585546351167848}
```

We can check that the prediction of the Core ML model matches that of the original scikit-learn one.

and as we can see, the result is a dictionary with `price` as a key and its value matches the prediction obtained with our linear model defined in scikit-learn. We are ready for the next step, and that is to deploy our model in an app. We will be using Xcode for that purpose.

6.3.5 *Model Properties in Core ML*

We have created our Core ML model out of a linear regression algorithm developed with scikit-learn. The model predicts prices for properties in the California area based on two predictors, namely median income in the district in tens of thousands of dollars and average number of rooms. It is by no means the best model out there, and our aim is to explore the creation of a model (in this case with Python) and convert it to a Core ML model that can be deployed in an iOS app.

Our aim here is to demonstrate the use of Core ML.

Before we move on to the development of the app, it would be good to take a look at the properties of the converted model. If we open the `CaliforniaHousePricer.mlmodel` we saved in the previous section, we will see the information shown in Figure 6.5. We can see the name of the model

Opening it in Xcode of course!

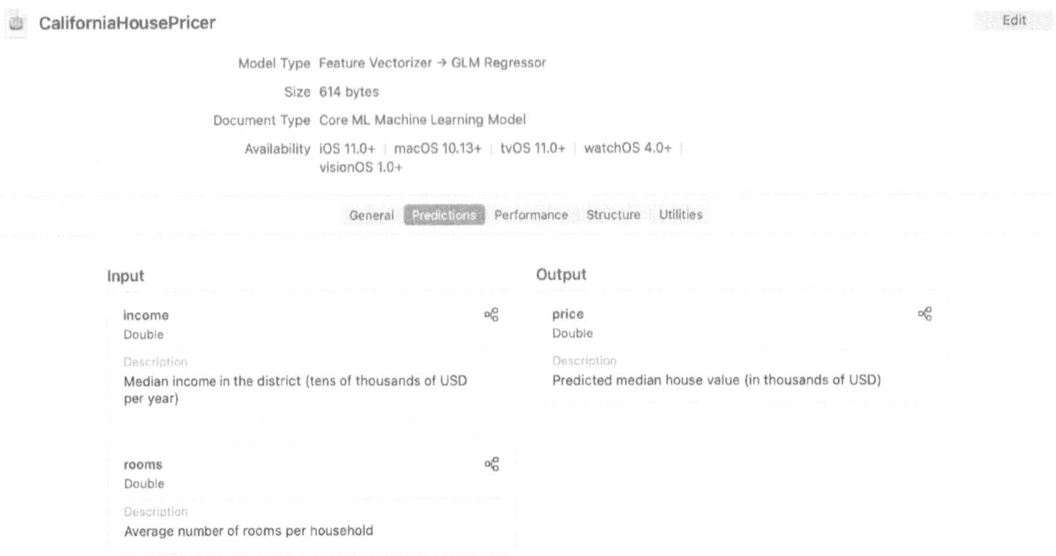

Figure 6.5: Properties of the California Housing Pricer Core ML model created from scikit-learn.

(`CaliforniaHousePricer`) and the fact that it is a "GML Regressor". We saw that the model can be given various metadata attributes such as Author, License and various Descriptions. We can also see the listing of the Prediction parameters in the form of Inputs (median income and number of rooms) and Outputs (price).

We can see the metadata we added to the model.

```
Input                   Output
==================      ========================
  income                price
  Double                Double


  rooms
  Double
================================================
```

Note that the inputs and outputs are expected to be doubles. We will come back to this point later on.

Once we integrate the model into our app, the autogenerated Swift code will define the input variables and feature names as well as a way to extract values out of the input strings. It will set up the model output and other components such as defining the class for model loading and prediction. All this is taken care of by Xcode in one go, making it very easy for us to use the model in our app. We will start building that app in the next section.

Once we add our model to a project, Xcode will autogenerate the target class for us.

6.4 *Surprise and Delight: Build an iOS App*

We have come a long, way and we are now ready to unleash our California Housing Pricer algorithm to the World! An implementation in scikit-learn will be useful for a number of cases. In many others, we need to take into account the shocking fact that not everyone is interested in openning a Jupyter Notebook to run a prediction. Instead, if we are interested in deploying our algorithm to, say, non-technical users, we will have to surprise and delight them with a well-built app.

If only everyone could use Jupyter notebooks, or, even better, Python scripts in the terminal... not!

In this section we will cover the overall steps that will get our algorithm encapsulated into a very simple iOS app. The intention is to provide a flavour of the steps that need to be covered, and I would encourage you to spend more time thinking about the functionality of the app, the interactions that your users will need to go through, the flow of the application, the look and feel, the design, logos and images. And perhaps more importantly user testing and acceptance. With that warning, let us get started.

The app will be very simple, and I hope you take some time to improve it!

6.4.1 *New Project: Xcode*

LET US START BUILDING AN iOS app that will use the model we created above and enable our users to generate a prediction for the price of a property based on input values for the parameters used in the model, namely, average number of rooms and crime rate score. Our aim is to build a simple interface where the user enters the values of the chosen features, and the predicted price is shown in the device. Make sure you have access to Xcode and the Core ML model we created earlier on. Ready?

An estimate? A valuation?

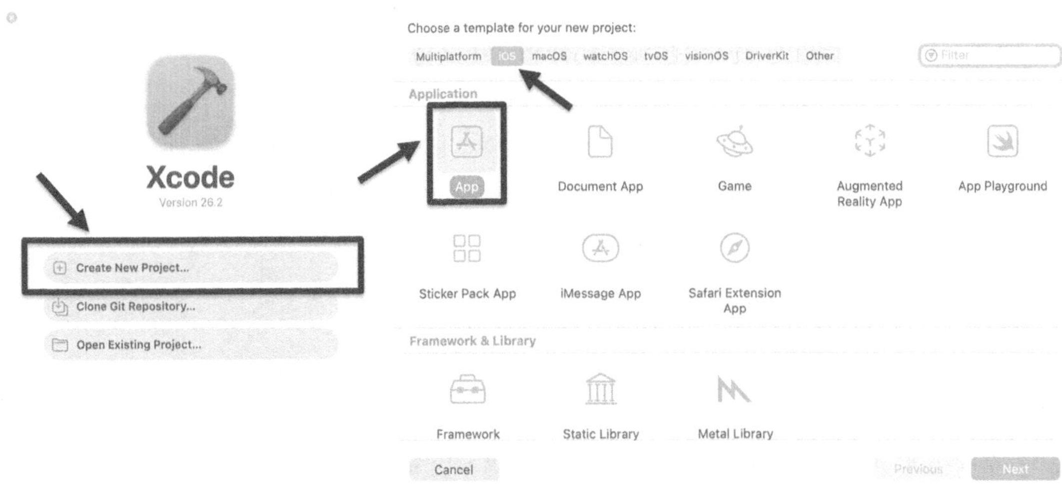

Figure 6.6: Creating a new Xcode project for a Single View App.

Open up Xcode and select "Create a New Project...", which will open up a new dialogue box; from the menu at the top make sure you select "iOS" from the top menu and from the options shown under "Application" please select the "App" option and then click the "Next" button. See Figure

6.6 where the options mentioned above are highlighted with black squares.

We are building an "App"! Yay!

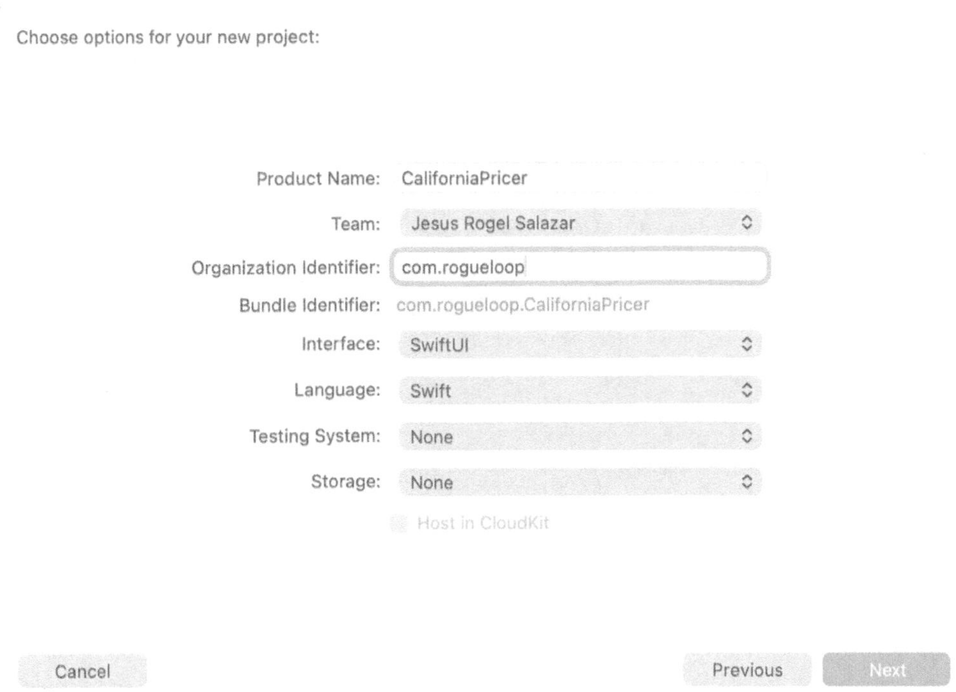

Figure 6.7: We need to provide some metadata for the project we are creating.

The steps above will let us create an iOS app with a single page. If you need more pages or views, this is still a good place to start, as you can add further "Content Views" while you develop the app. In the next dialogue box, shown in Figure 6.7, Xcode will be asking for options to create the new project. Give your project a name, something that makes it easier to elucidate what your project is about. In this case, let us call the project "CaliforniaPricer". You will also need to provide the name of a team (team of developers contributing to your app, for instance) as well as an organisation name and identifier. Please note that entering

You can add more views to your project, if needed.

Go team!

Figure 6.8: A very simple "Hello World" app built in a couple of clicks.

suitable information about this is important in case you are planning to send your app for approval to Apple. Make sure that you select "SwiftUI" as the Interface, and "Swift" as the programming language, and we are leaving Testing System and Storage dropdown menus as "None".

We are using SwiftUI to build our user interface.

After clicking "Next", Xcode will ask for a location to save your project and will ask to confirm whether you want to create a Git repository. Best practice suggests you definitely should do that. After you click on the "Create" button, Xcode will automatically open a new editor, and you will see some autogenerated code. On the left-hand side you will see the Project Navigator; look for and click on the "ContentView.swift" element as shown in Figure 6.8. This is

How cool is that!

the main view that our users will see when the application is launched. A View Controller lets us decide what appears on the screen and how the app responds when you tap, swipe, or type, acting like a manager between the visuals and the app's logic. Depending on the target device we choose, the View Controller responds as required. In this case, we are targeting an iPhone.

A View Controller manages what appears on the screen and how the app responds.

You can now marvel at running your first iOS app. Actually, you do not have to do anything, as Xcode will run the code in the Preview Pane as shown in Figure 6.8. You can also click on the play button on the top left-hand side of the Xcode window, launching an iPhone simulator. Once the app starts, you will see the message "Hello World" in the best style of first programmes in any programming language.

Clicking on the play button in Xcode will launch an iPhone simulator where our app will run!

With the advent of SwiftUI, building apps is much easier than ever. In the past you may have to deal with the so-called *Interface Builder*, where we had to drag and drop windows, buttons, labels, etc. Dragging and dropping was great, but the functionality for each of these objects needed to be developed independently using the Model-View-Controller pattern. However, with *SwiftUI* we can build our apps in a declarative manner. We can also drag-and-drop components, and the framework supports previews of our design without having to launch the simulator. Furthermore, the declarative nature of the framework means that we do let the operating system take care of the state of the objects and even their location in the canvas.

Uugghh!

SwiftUI will actually make a lot of us Pythonistas feel more at home.

We mentioned at the beginning of this section that some autogenerated code is shown when creating our project. This code is responsible for displaying the "Hello World" message as seen on the right-hand side of Figure 6.8. We can see this code by clicking on the `ContentView.Swift` file on the Project Navigator on left-hand side of our screen. You will see an editor similar to the one shown in Figure 6.9. If you cannot see a preview of the app, make sure you click on the Resume button on the canvas view.

The autogenerated code we mentioned before is responsible for the "Hello World" message.

Figure 6.9: The autogenerated code that prints "Hello World" to the screen can be found in the ContentView.Swift file.

Let us change the text of the autogenerated code from "Hello World" to "California Pricer". We can also add some formatting to the label by making the font title size:

```
struct ContentView: View {
    var body: some View {
    Text(''California Pricer'').font(.largeTitle)
    }
}
```

For the rest of the code in this section, the boxes contain Swift code.

We need to ensure that the different objects we add to our interface are part of a navigation view. Also, since we are letting the operating system organise these objects, we need to ensure they are contained in either horizontal or vertical stacks. For that, SwiftUI lets us create `VStack` and `HStack` objects, respectively. We can create a `NavigationView` with a vertical stack, or `VStack`, containing our text label:

```
struct ContentView: View {
  var body: some View {
  VStack {
    Text(''California Pricer'').font(.largeTitle)
    }
    .padding()}
}
```

A VStack enables us to place objects in a vertical stack. Hence the name! You can imagine what an HStack does, right?

Note the use of `.padding()` after the VStack, adds some space to ensure correct alignment in the target screen.

We will start placing a few other objects in our app. Some of these objects will be used simply to display text (labels and information), whereas others will be used to create interactions. In particular, we are interested in letting our users select input values and generate a prediction. In

We are adding objects in a horizontal stack, or `HStack`.

this case we will start by adding a couple of labels in a horizontal stack (`HStack`) and a button. After the line of code starting with `.padding()`, type the following code:

```
HStack {
  Text(''Median Income (USD)'')
    .padding(.trailing, 10)
  Text(''No. of  Rooms'').padding(.leading, 10)
  }
  .padding(.vertical, 40)
  Button(action: {}) {
    Text(''Get Prediction'')
}
```

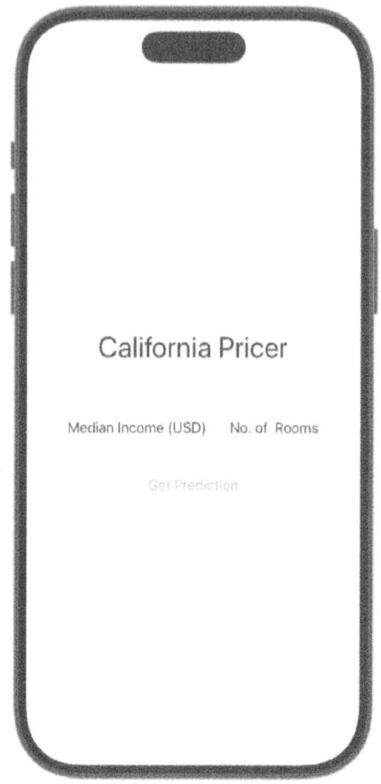

Figure 6.10: The app layout is automatically handled with SwiftUI.

The horizontal stack creates two labels side-by-side, one with the text "Median Income (USD)" and the other one with "No. Rooms". The button has the label "Get Prediction", and thanks to the use of `padding(.vertical, 40)` we request some padding of 40 points above and below the HStack. The layout of the app looks great in any screen size required. See Figure 6.10.

6.4.2 *Push My Buttons: Adding Functionality*

We now have a nice looking app. If we were to run the simulator with the code we have, things will work. However, nothing will happen. We need to add functionality to our objects. In this case we only expect the user to tap on the button to trigger an action. This eventually will show the prediction for the property price with the attributes selected. First, let us make sure that we can add an action to the

We need to add functionality to our app.

button such that when it is tapped it displays a suitable and informative message.

Before we delve into the code, let us talk about states. Consider a real object such as a lightswitch that is used to turn the lights on and off in a room. The switch may have an indicator for on and off. The *state* of the room is such that it is illuminated when the switch is in the on position, and it is plunged into darkness when the switch is in the off position. The actions of the person in the room can change the state of the room by changing the position of the switch. Furthermore, the state of the room can also be changed by other circumstances such as the time of day, the number of people in the room, the temperature of the room, etc. We refer to these variables as *state variables*, and all possible combinations of every possible value for the state variables referred to as the *state space*.

Bear with me... we will get there.

The state of illumination in a room is controlled by a variable state that takes the values *on* or *off*.

The state space of our current app is the equivalent of the on and off switch. There are two states:

Our app also has two states: Before and after pressing the button.

1. The screen shown before the user presses the button. This is shown in Figure 6.10.
2. A pop-up message after the user hits the button. When the user dismisses the message, we revert back to state 1 above.

We need a state variable to keep track of the two states we have described. In this case a Boolean will suffice. We declare a state variable in SwiftUI with `@State`. At the top of the code in the content view, make the following modifications:

A state variable is declared with `@State` in Swift.

```
struct ContentView: View {
    @State var popUpVisible: Bool = false
    var body: some View {
    ...
```

The popUpVisible will let us toggle a pop-up with information about the property price prediction. I love some alliteration!

We are declaring a Boolean state variable called popUpVisible and assign it the value of false. We can now tell our app to change its state when the user presses the button. To that end, let us make the following changes to the button we implemented before:

```
Button(action: {
  self.popUpVisible.toggle()
}) {
  Text(''Get Prediction'')
}
.alert(isPresented: self.$popUpVisible) {
  Alert(title: Text(''Prediction''),
    message: Text(''Prediction will be
      shown here.''),
  dismissButton: .default(Text(''Cool!'')))
}
```

An alert takes a title, a message and an action for when the alert is dismissed.

The first thing to note is the addition of a line in the action for the button. In this case we toggle the value of the state variable with .toggle() when the user presses the button. After the label of the button, we are also adding a few lines of code. The alert() method of the button will present a popup alert to the user. The title is the bold title of the window; the message displayed is handled by message, and importantly the `dismissButton` is a button that dismisses the window when the user is done. The result of pressing the button can be seen in Figure 6.11.

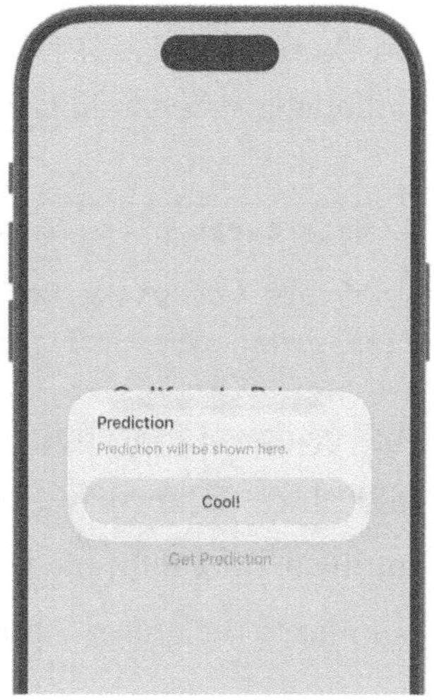

Figure 6.11: The app state after pressing the button.

6.4.3 *Being Picky: The Picker View*

WE NEED TO PROVIDE OUR users with an easy way to pick the attributes of the property they need to value. Currently our app contains three labels and one button. We need to add a couple of pickers, one for the crime rate score and another one for the number of rooms.

Let us start creating constants to hold the potential values for the input variables. At the top of the `ContentView` struct, make the following changes:

The modifier `let` declares constants in Swift.

```
struct ContentView: View {
  @State var popUpVisible: Bool = false
  let incomeData = Array(stride(from:0.05,
    through: 14, by: 0.5))
  let roomData = Array(2...10)
  ...
```

These values are informed by the data exploration we carried out in Section 6.3.3 earlier on. In fact we could have done a much better job with this. You may remember for example that the average number of rooms had some really high values, which perhaps in practice no user will ever need. In any event, we are going to use the arrays defined above to populate the values that will be shown in our pickers. For this we need to define a data source for each

Median Income from 0.05 to 14 in steps of 0.5, and Rooms from 4 to 10.

picker as well as a state variable. Right below the definition of the constants incomeData and roomData, let us add the following state variables:

```
@State var pickerIncome = 0
@State var pickerRoom = 0
```

We need some state variables for each of the pickers.

Let us now add a couple of pickers. In the ContentView, after the "California Pricer" label, let us change the content of the HStack with the following code. The result will be similar to the one in Figure 6.12.

Figure 6.12: Adding a couple of pickers to our app.

```
HStack(spacing: 40) {
  VStack(alignment: .leading) {
    Text(''Income ($10k USD)'')
      .font(.caption)
    Picker('''', selection: .constant(1)) {
      Text(''1'').tag(1)
      Text(''2'').tag(2)
    }
  }

  VStack(alignment: .leading) {
    Text(''No. Rooms'').font(.caption)
    Picker('''', selection: .constant(1)) {
      Text(''1'').tag(1)
      Text(''2'').tag(2)
    }
  }
}
```

We are combining HStacks and VStacks to improve the layout of our app.

In the code above we are specifying the horizontal stack to have a spacing of 40 points between objects. Inside the HStack we have two VStacks aligned to their left edge, each with a label and a picker. The labels have a font attribute equal to `.caption`, and currently the pickers have values 1 and 2 only. However, what we really want is to show the values from the constants we defined above. Let us look at the Income picker first:

Done with `HStack(spacing: 40)` and `VStack(alignment: .leading)`.

```
Picker(selection: $pickerIncome,
  label: Text(''Income'')) {
    ForEach(incomeData.indices, id: \.self) { ix
      in Text(''\(incomeData[ix],
        specifier: ''%.2f")").tag(ix)
    }
}
```

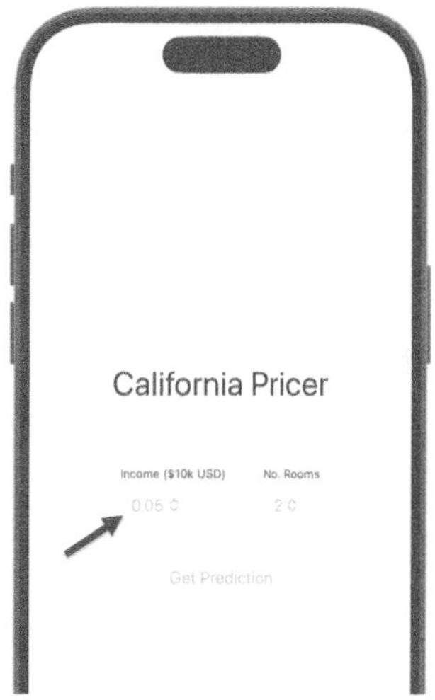

Figure 6.13: The pickers are now showing the correct values we specified.

We are first specifying that the variable state `pickerIncome` is used in this picker's selection. Note the use of `$` as a suffix to the variable name to indicate we are using a state variable. The content of the picker is then given by each of the indexed entries in the `incomeData` array. We need to convert the doubles into text. We do this by string interpolation by enclosing the name of the variable between "`\( ...)`". Think of this operation as a substitution of the variable value. Finally, we specify that we only require two decimal points with the formatter "`%.2f`".

String interpolation is a fancy name for substituting the value of a variable in a string.

Let us now change the second picker to show valid values for the number of rooms:

```
Picker(selection: $pickerRoom,
  label: Text(''Rooms'')) {
    ForEach(roomData.indices, id: \.self) { ix in
      Text(''\(roomData[ix])'').tag(ix)
  }
}
```

In this case there is no need to format the numbers, we simply interpolate the array values.

In this case we simply convert the integers into text, as there is no need to specify a format for these strings. The result of the code above can be seen in Figure 6.13.

We can check that the state variables are indeed capturing the state of the app. Let us change the alert shown by the button so that it shows the values picked by the user. At this stage, we are not going to worry about formatting the value of our double array `incomeData`. Modify the button implementation as follows:

Let us check that we can capture the current state of the app.

```
Button(action: {
  self.popUpVisible = true
}) {
  Text("Get Prediction")
}
.alert(isPresented: self.$popUpVisible) {
  Alert(title: Text(''Prediction''),
    message: Text(''The values picked are\n
      Median Income: \(incomeData[pickerIncome])\n
      Avg No. Rooms: \(roomData[pickerRoom])''),
    dismissButton: .default(Text(''Cool!'')))
}
```

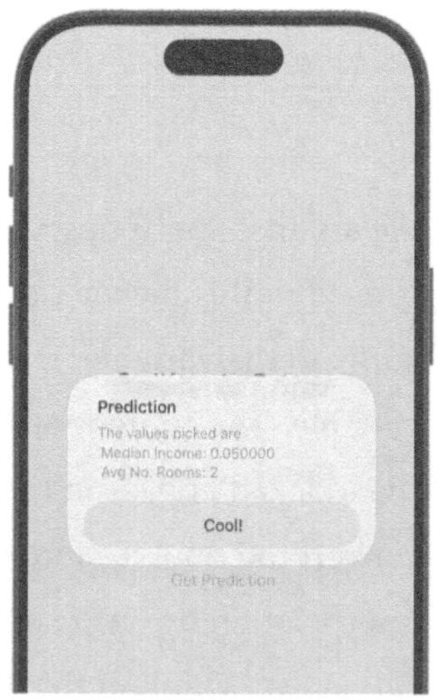

Figure 6.14: We can see that the app is capturing the correct state for the pickers.

The result can be seen in Figure 6.14. It is now time to bring the model into our app. Ready?

6.4.4 *Model Behaviour: Core ML + SwiftUI*

LOOK HOW FAR WE HAVE come... We started this chapter looking at what Core ML does and how we can use the tools provided by Apple to translate our Python models. In this case we decided to use linear regression as our model, and chose to use the California Housing dataset in our exploration for this implementation. We built our model using Python and created our `.mlmodel` object. We have put together an app that can be run in an iPhone, and we are ready to include our Core ML model in our Xcode project. The aim is to use the inputs selected from our pickers and calculate a prediction based on our model and display the result to our users.

Perhaps we may want to refer to our prediction as a valuation?

Let us start by adding the `.mlmodel` we created earlier on so that it is an available resource in our project. In the Xcode project navigator, select the "CaliforniaPricer" project. At the bottom of the window you will see a plus (+) sign, click on it and select "New Group" (see Figure 6.15). This will create a sub-folder within "BostonPricer". Select the new folder and hit the return key, this will let you rename the folder to something more useful. In this case we are going to call this folder "Resources".

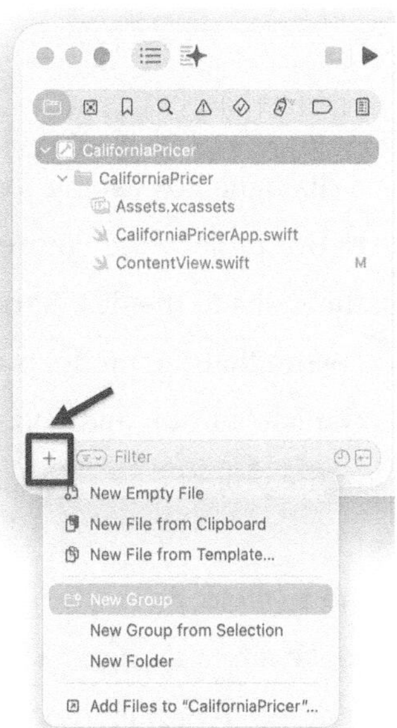

Figure 6.15: Adding a New Group to our project.

In your Mac, open Finder, and navigate to the location of the `CaliforniaHousePricer.mlmodel` we created earlier on. Drag the file inside the "Resources" folder. This will open

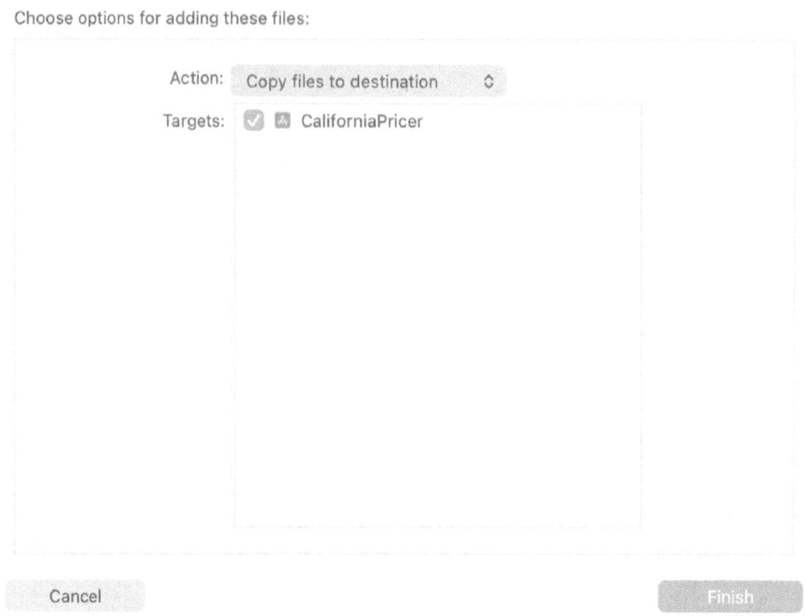

Figure 6.16: Adding resources to our Xcode project.

a dialogue box asking for some options for adding this file to our project (see Figure 6.16). Make sure that you copy the items to the destination as needed. Tick the Targets to ensure that the model is used by the app and click on the "Finish" button and you will see the model now being part of the project.

It is a good idea to keep our Xcode project tidy with the help of groups.

Go to the code in the Content View where we are going to make a few changes. The first change is to tell our project that we are going to need the powers of the Core ML framework. At the top of the file, locate a line of code that imports SwiftUI; right below it type the following:

```
import SwiftUI
import CoreML
```

We are importing CoreML, easy!

In what follows we will need to write some Swift code. Sadly, covering the usage of Swift is out of the scope of this book; you can find some excellent resources[14] out there. Ready?

[14] Hudson, P. (2015). *Hacking with Swift*. HackingWithSwift.com. Online tutorial/book.

Inside the definition of the `ContentView` struct, let us define a constant to reference the model. Look for the declarations of the state variables and the `incomeData` and `roomData` constants. Make sure that you use the name of the Core ML model you added as a resource earlier on. For reference, I put the definition of the `ContentView` struct in the code below:

We need to instantiate a our model, just like we do in Python.

```
struct ContentView: View {
  let model: CaliforniaHousePricer = {
    do {
      let config = MLModelConfiguration()
        return try CaliforniaHousePricer(
          configuration: config)
    } catch {
      print(error)
      fatalError(''Couldn't create
        CaliforniaHousePricer'')
    }
  }()
  ...
```

We are creating an instance of our model. Since we imported our CoreML model, Xcode now knows about its class and autocomplete is available for it.

You will see that when you start typing the name of the model, Xcode will suggest the right name, as it knows about the existence of the model as part of its resources, neat! The code defines and immediately initialises a machine-learning model object in a safe, controlled way. The model variable is declared as a constant of type `CaliforniaHousePricer` and is assigned using an anonymous closure that runs once at initialisation time. Inside the closure, a configuration object (`MLModelConfiguration`) is created and passed into the model's constructor, which can throw an error if loading fails. The do–try–catch block handles this possibility explicitly: If the model creation succeeds, the fully initialised model is returned and stored in the model; if it fails, the error is printed for debugging, and the app terminates immediately with a clear message. This pattern is commonly used in Swift to initialise complex or fallible resources while keeping the calling code clean and guaranteeing that model is always valid once created.

A closure is a self-contained block of code.

For example, if the compiled model file is missing or incompatible.

This is a typical pattern in Swift.

We will create a method that is able to read the values selected by the user for the crime rate and number of room pickers. These values will be used to calculate a valuation. Our method will return a string containing the predicted price. Look for the `View` code that reads as follows:

```
var body: some View {
  NavigationView{...}
}
```

Look for this snippet of code in your project.

Make sure you write the following code below the snippet shown above and still within the `ContentView` struct.

```
func predictionMsg() -> String {
  let income = incomeData[pickerIncome]
  let rooms = Double(roomData[pickerRoom])
```

```
guard let priceCalifornia = try?
  model.prediction(income: income,
    rooms: rooms) else {
      fatalError(''Unexpected runtime error.'')
    }

let number = NSNumber(value:
    priceCalifornia.price * 100000)

let formatter = NumberFormatter()
formatter.numberStyle = .decimal
formatter.usesGroupingSeparator = true
formatter.minimumFractionDigits = 2
formatter.maximumFractionDigits = 2

let price = formatter.string(from: number) ??
  String( format: ''%.2f'', number.doubleValue)

let Msg = ''Your property value is\n $\(price)"

return Msg
}
```

The model has a `.prediction` method to calculate our prediction.

We format our result to be ready for display.

Finally, we get the message that we want to display.

Our method is called `predictionMsg`, and it returns a string contained in the variable `Msg`. First it reads the values of the pickers and assigns them to two constants: `income` and `rooms`. These are the input names expected by our model, remember?

Notice that we have cast the `rooms` constant as a double, as the model expects this type for this variable.

Note how we are formatting numerical model output into a human-readable dollar amount suitable for display in our UI. First, we multiply the predicted house price by $100,000$ to convert it from a scaled model value into actual currency units. We then wrap the result in an `NSNumber`, which is required by Apple's formatting APIs. A `NumberFormatter` is configured to format numbers in standard decimal style, enabling separators for thousands and forcing exactly two decimal places to match conventional currency formatting. The formatter then attempts to convert the number into a formatted string; if that conversion unexpectedly fails, the code falls back to a manual two-decimal formatting approach to ensure a valid string is always produced. Finally, the formatted value is interpolated into a user-facing message string that displays the estimated property value in dollars.

We require to build a formatter to display the prediction in a human-readable way.

For example, 123,456.

In Section 6.4.4 we saw that our `CaliforniaHousePricer` model has a method for predictions given the inputs `{income, rooms}`. The result of this method is assigned in the code above to a `priceCalifornia` output instance. The `price` property of this instance is used to get the prediction. We know that the values are in hundreds of thousands of dollars, and that is why we are multiplying the predicted value by $100,000$ before using it in a string to be returned by the function.

That is the line starting with `guard`.

We are finally ready to call our Core ML model with the values that the user selects in the UI from the pickers. We simply need to make a small change in the code for the button as follows:

```
Button(action: {
  self.popUpVisible.toggle()
}) {
  Text(''Get Prediction'')
}
.alert(isPresented: self.$popUpVisible) {
  Alert(title: Text(''Property Valuation''),
  message: Text(predictionMsg()),
    dismissButton: .default(Text(''OK''))
  )
}
```

This is the whole code for the button, but we only need to change the content of the `Alert`.

When the user clicks on the button, we are calling our `predictionMsg` method, which in turn calls the prediction method of our Core ML model and formats the prediction for output.

We can now run our app with the simulator, and the result will be a fully functional model, first developed in Python, producing predictions in the hands of our users through an iOS app. See Figure 6.17 to get an idea of what to expect, and the final version of the app is available in GitHub[15]. There are many more things that we can do to improve the app. For instance, we can test that the layout works for a variety of screen sizes. Also, having a picker may be a bit cumbersome for some of the inputs, perhaps a stepper would be more appropriate. We may also want to enable the users to enter values and ensure they fall within range. Another important aspect in the experience that we want to give to our users is the overall look-and-feel and usability

[15] Rogel-Salazar, J (2025). CoreML—California Housing Pricer. https://github.com/rogelj/coreml_california_housing. Accessed: 2025-12-26.

Figure 6.17: The final app producing predictions for our users out of a linear regression model first developed with Python.

for the app. This includes the design of appropriate icons in various sizes. You can now enroll a test device to run your application and use the app as intended, in a mobile device. You can find more information about that in the Apple Developer
site[16].

[16] Apple Inc. (2019a). Apple Developer. https://developer.apple.com. Accessed: 2025-12-26.

6.5 *A Firm Basis: Apple's Foundation Models*

UNTIL NOW, MOST OF THE models we have discussed in this chapter have been narrow in scope and purpose-built: regressors that predict prices, classifiers that label images, or models trained to solve a specific task well. These models are effective, interpretable, and relatively easy to deploy. However, they are not particularly flexible. They do one thing, and they do it repeatedly. We can indeed look at the plethora of models that we have covered in this book and its companion *Data Science and Analytics with Python*[17] and find ways to deploy them in a suitable setting. Let us stay for a moment within the Apple ecosystem and see what else we are able to do.

[17] Rogel-Salazar, J. (2025). *Data Science and Analytics with Python*. Chapman & Hall/CRC Data Mining and Knowledge Discovery Series. CRC Press.

Apple has made it possible to use existing models that developers can easily implement within their apps. Enter the era of *foundation models*. These are large, general-purpose models trained on vast and diverse datasets, capable of performing a wide range of tasks without being explicitly retrained for each one. Instead of learning a single mapping from inputs to outputs, foundation models learn representations of language, images, audio, or multimodal data that can be adapted to many downstream
uses.

Cue the dramatic music. Possibly a low-frequency hum.

If traditional machine learning models are specialised tools, foundation models are closer to the Swiss Army knife of modern AI. They can summarise text, answer questions, extract information, classify content, generate responses, and reason across inputs in ways that would previously have required multiple bespoke models.

Still no lightsabers. I checked. But perhaps a step closer to Protocol Droids!

6.5.1 *Apple's Take on Foundation Models*

APPLE'S APPROACH TO FOUNDATION MODELS is characteristically opinionated. Rather than exposing a single monolithic model and leaving developers to fend for themselves, Apple integrates foundation-model capabilities deeply into the operating system and developer tooling, with a strong emphasis on privacy, efficiency, and on-device execution. They are called foundation models because they sit at the bottom of the AI stack, not the top. Everything else is built on them. Think of them as reinforced concrete rather than interior décor.

Not surprising to see an opinionated integration from Apple, right?

A foundation model is:

The characteristics of foundation models.

- Trained once, at scale, on vast and diverse data
- General-purpose, not task-specific
- Adaptable via fine-tuning, prompting, or lightweight heads
- Reusable across many applications without retraining from scratch

As such, with foundation models, we do not train one model for email classification or image tagging. We train one to understand language, images, audio, or behaviour, and then specialise later. At the platform level, Apple provides foundation-model capabilities through what is now marketed as *Apple Intelligence*, spanning iOS, iPadOS, and macOS. These models power system-level features such as text summarisation, rewriting, semantic search, and image

In other words, R2 with a natural language synthesiser.

understanding. Foundation models are called that because they are shared, general-purpose cognitive infrastructure—not products, not features, but the bedrock everything else stands on.

They are the part we really do not want cracking later.

From a developer perspective, these capabilities are surfaced through high-level APIs rather than raw model weights. Where possible, inference is performed on-device using Apple Silicon, leveraging the CPU, GPU, and Neural Engine via Core ML. When tasks exceed on-device capabilities, Apple adopts a hybrid approach, carefully managing what data—if any—leaves the device.

HAL 9000 would not approve, but your DPO probably will.

In parallel, Apple has also released *MLX*, a research-oriented framework optimised for Apple Silicon, enabling developers and researchers to experiment with large language models locally. MLX is Apple's low-level, Apple-Silicon-native machine-learning framework designed to make serious ML workloads run efficiently on device rather than in the cloud. It provides a single unified array abstraction that transparently spans CPU, GPU, and Neural Engine using Apple's unified memory, avoids costly data copies, and uses lazy execution to fuse operations and optimise performance per watt, making it particularly well suited to local inference for transformer-based models, embeddings, speech, and vision.

MLX is not an app framework, not a Core ML replacement, and definitely not "PyTorch but with a fruit logo".

While MLX sits somewhat outside the Core ML deployment story, it signals Apple's longer-term intent: foundation models that are efficient, local-first, and deeply integrated with the hardware. Foundation models shift the role of the Jackalope Data Scientist. Instead of training a model to perform a single task, we increasingly design *interactions* with a general-purpose model. This has important implications for data products. Much of the complexity moves away from feature engineering and model selection, and towards the following:

You are no longer training the alien; you are negotiating with it.

- Framing effective prompts and instructions
- Managing context and user intent
- Ensuring outputs are safe, reliable, and interpretable
- Integrating results into user workflows

The new workflows open up by foundation models.

In other words, deployment becomes less about shipping a model and more about orchestrating behaviour.

Let us look at some of the principal capabilities exposed by foundation models within the Apple ecosystem[18]. Table 6.2 summarises them with some typical use cases.

[18] Apple Inc. (2025). Apple Developer—Foundation Models. https://developer.apple.com/documentation/foundationmodels. Accessed: 2025-12-26.

- **Natural Language Understanding**: Intent detection, multi-turn dialogue management, and grounding in on-screen context are performed on-device to enable low-latency interaction. For queries requiring broader world knowledge or long-context reasoning, processing may be extended to privacy-hardened cloud execution.
- **Natural Language Generation**: Text summarisation, rewriting, proofreading, and smart reply generation are executed on-device by default, enabling offline use. Cloud-based generation is used selectively for longer or more computationally intensive outputs when required.

We can perform natural language understanding and generation, as well as context aware requests.

Capability	Typical Use Cases
Text summarisation	Concise summaries of documents, meeting notes, reports, and email threads
Text rewriting and transformation	Simplification, proofreading, tone adjustment, and clarity improvement
Information extraction	Extracting tasks, decisions, entities, and dates from unstructured text
Question answering	Answering user questions from provided text or contextual information
Semantic understanding	Intent-based search, content classification, and recommendation
Multimodal reasoning	Interpreting documents that combine text with images or other media
On-device inference	Low-latency, privacy-sensitive, and offline-capable applications
Instruction-driven behaviour	Natural-language control of workflows and rapid feature prototyping

Table 6.2: High-level capabilities of foundation models available within the Apple ecosystem.

- **Personal Context Awareness**: Reasoning over personal data such as messages, contacts, calendar entries, and reminders is performed entirely on-device, allowing highly personalised assistance without exposing private user information beyond the device.

- **Image Processing and Generation**: Visual recognition, object identification, image clean-up, and stylised image generation are handled on-device using Apple's vision and generative models. Optional cloud-assisted image generation is available for advanced styles when explicitly enabled by the user.

- **On-Device Inference**: Foundation models are optimised for local inference across CPU, GPU, and Neural Engine, delivering low-latency responses with no network dependency. Cloud resources are invoked only to extend capabilities beyond local compute constraints.
- **Multimodal Input Handling**: Voice, text, and on-screen content are fused on-device into a unified contextual representation, enabling seamless transitions between interaction modes. Cloud processing is used selectively for complex document or image interpretation.
- **Privacy-Preserving AI**: All capabilities default to on-device execution. When cloud processing is required, requests are routed through privacy-hardened infrastructure with explicit user consent and no data retention.

As well as image generation, on-device inference, handling multimodal input and all with preservation of privacy!

Apple's stance on foundation models is unapologetically *local-first*. Instead of casting the device as a glorified remote control for some omniscient model in the cloud, Apple assumes that intelligence should live where the user lives, i.e., on the device itself. Language understanding, text generation, vision, and personal-context reasoning are therefore executed on-device by default, taking full advantage of the intimate coupling between software and Apple Silicon. The payoff is immediate: Low latency, offline capability, and the welcome reassurance that your data is

No wizard behind the curtain.

Hardware and software, finally on speaking terms.

not being quietly uploaded to a digital Death Star for later analysis. The cloud still exists, of course, but only as a supporting character rather than the main protagonist, called upon sparingly, for tasks that genuinely exceed local compute limits, and wrapped in privacy-hardened infrastructure with explicit user consent. The resulting system feels less like an all-seeing oracle hovering overhead and more like a well-trained companion, helpful, discreet, and notably uninterested in sharing your information.

Your secrets remain planet-side.

Think *Star Trek*'s computer, not HAL 9000.

Equally important is that these models are not built as single-purpose contraptions, but as general linguistic and semantic engines that can be steered through instruction. Summarisation, information extraction, rewriting, and question answering are not separate models in different costumes, but different behaviours of the same underlying system. With a change of prompt rather than a retrain, the model swaps roles with ease, like a particularly competent character actor. Because many of these capabilities run on-device, they deliver immediate responses while preserving user privacy; a combination that would have seemed optimistic in earlier, cloud-bound deployment patterns. The emphasis thus shifts away from endlessly building new models and towards the more interesting problem of designing interactions and orchestrating behaviour. Less *Frankenstein's lab*, more *Mission Control*.

One model, many tricks.

Method acting, but for tensors.

Once upon a time, everything phoned home.

6.5.2 A Small App with a Big Brain: On-Device Text Insight

LET US CONCLUDE WITH A small, deliberately modest example. Imagine a simple iOS app that helps users make sense of text they are already working with from meeting notes, emails, or reports. The app will provide a text input area and a buttons to summarise the information entered by the user in a concise manner. No model training is required. Instead, the app invokes an Apple-provided foundation-model API, passing the user's text and a short instruction describing the desired behaviour.

Yes, we will help our fellow human being read. Hurrah!

This is not fine-tuning. This is persuasion.

From a deployment perspective, this app is almost trivial: There is no dataset to curate, no regression coefficients to interpret, and no model file to convert. The intellectual effort lies in deciding *what* the model should do and *how* its output is presented to the user. In many real-world products, this is precisely where the value lies.

As before, I encourage you to explore areas where you can improve this app.

We will start in a similar fashion to the app we developed in Section 6.4. Open Xcode, create a new project and select the template to be an iOS App. Give the project a suitable name, select the iterface to be SwiftUI, the language to be Swift and provide your team and organisation identifier. Get rid of the autogenerated "Hello, world!" code in the app and replace it with a `NavigationView` as follows:

Take a look at Section 6.4 for the steps to follow.

```
struct ContentView: View {
    var body: some View {
        NavigationView {
        ...
        }
    }
}
```

Again, the code in this section is mostly Swift.

A navigation view is a container that manages a stack-based interface, allowing users to move between views with a navigation bar and back controls. Let us create a suitable VStack and handle any errors with the help of two state variables called `showError` and `errorMessage`:

```
struct ContentView: View {
  @State private var showError: Bool = false
  @State private var errorMessage: String  = ''''

  var body: some View {
    NavigationView {
      VStack(spacing: 20) {
      }
      .padding()
      .NavigationTitle(''Text Summariser'')
      .navigationBarTitleDisplayMode(.inline)
      .alert(''Error'', isPresented: $showError) {
        Button(''OK'', role: .cancel) { }
      } message: { Text(errorMessage) }
    }
  }
...
```

Figure 6.18: Our initial view with a navigation bar. Stay tuned!

We are creating a VStack with objects spaced 20 points from each other. The title of the navigation view is "Text Summariser", and it is displayed in line. If the view fails to load, we handle this error gracefully. See Figure 6.18.

We are building our user interface first; bear with me!

We are now familiar with the idea of state variables. In this case we require to keep track of the input text, the output text returned by the app and a flag one to keep track of the processing. At the top of the content view, declare the following variables:

```
@State private var inputText: String = ''''
@State private var summaryText: String = ''''
@State private var isProcessing: Bool = false
...
```

We are keeping track of the input and output text as well as the status of the processing.

Inside the navigation view, we are now going to create our input text area which will include a label and a text editor.

```
VStack(alignment: .leading, spacing: 8) {
  Text(''Input Text'')
    .font(.headline)

  TextEditor(text: $inputText)
    .frame(minHeight: 150)
    .padding(8)
    .overlay(
      RoundedRectangle(cornerRadius: 8)
        .stroke(Color(.systemGray4), lineWidth: 1)
    )
}
```

Figure 6.19: Our initial view with three buttons ready to help us.

As you can see in Figure 6.19, we can tap on the text editor and enter some text. In this case a famous "Hello world!!".

We are now going to create a button to start the text processing. The button takes an action, which in our case will be the text summarisation with Apple Intelligence. For the time being, we will leave the action empty. Our button will only be available when there is text in the editor or when the action is not running. We are also going to change the label in the button depending on whether the action is running or not. We can do this by looking at the state variable `isProcessing` we defined earlier on. The result is shown in Figure 6.20.

```
Button(action: { }) {
  Text(isProcessing ? ''Summarising...''
    : ''Summarise'')
      .font(.headline)
    .padding()
}
.disabled(inputText.isEmpty || isProcessing )
.buttonStyle(.glass)
```

Figure 6.20: We are adding a text editor to our app.

We need an object to present the summary text. We will only show this if there is a summary to show. We know if that is the case with the help of the `summaryText` state variable. We will show a label and the text inside a suitable frame. Below the button definition, type the following:

```
if !summaryText.isEmpty {
  VStack(alignment: .leading, spacing: 8) {
    Text(''Summary'')
      .font(.headline)
    Text(summaryText)
    .padding()
    .frame(maxWidth: .infinity,
      alignment: .leading)
```

We will only show the summary text when it is available. SwiftUI is a very versatile framework!

```
    }
}
```

Figure 6.21: We now have an area where our summary will appear.

I have tricked the preview panel by changing the value of the `summaryText` state variable to show you what the result of the code above is in Figure 6.21.

It is good practice to check that the model we are going to apply is available in the devices of our users. If so, great; however, if not, we should politely let them know about this. To do this, we are going to write a function to check the availability of the model. First at the top of our Swift code, let us import the foundation models framework as follows:

```
import FoundationModels
```

We also need a new state variable to keep track of the model availability. Type the following near the other state variables we have declared before.

```
@State private var modelAvailable: Bool = false
```

We can now write the function we mentioned above. Inside the content view and after the view declaration, type the following:

This simple function lets us check that the language model is available to use! This *is* the language model we were looking for!

```
var body: some View {
    ...
    }
```

```
func checkModelAvailability() {
  modelAvailable =
  SystemLanguageModel.default.isAvailable
}
```

All we are doing with this function is check whether the system language model is available, and if so toggling the value of the `modelAvailable` state variable. That is all good, but we have not called the function when the view appears. In order to do just that, we add a task to our navigation view. At the bottom of the `NavigationView`, look for the place where we define the title display mode and before the alert type the following:

We request to check the availability of our language model asynchronously.

```
...
.navigationBarTitleDisplayMode(...
 .task {
  checkModelAvailability()
}
 .alert(...
```

We are showing the code lines just before and after the place where we insert our task.

What this means is that when this view appears, we run this asynchronous task. What `.task {}` does is it attaches an asynchronous task to the view's lifecycle. It starts when the view appears, and it is automatically cancelled if the view disappears. The task runs on Swift's structured concurrency system, and it makes our life much easier.

And whenever SwiftUI decides it needs to re-run the task.

Now that we have checked the availability of our language model, we can make some changes to our view. For example, we can make the summarisation button only available not only when there is input text or when the model is not processing text, but also when the model is available. In the button definition, look for the `.disabled` method and modify it as follows:

```
.disabled(inputText.isEmpty || isProcessing
  || !modelAvailable )
```

Furthermore, if the user device does not support the use of Foundation Models, we need to tell the user about this. In this case, if the model is not available, we will add a stack with a notification in an orange colour letting the user know that Apple Intelligence is not available. We do this by adding the following code in our content view after the area where the summary text is shown.

Figure 6.22: If Foundation Models are not available in the device, the user will be informed in this way.

```
if !modelAvailable {
  HStack {
    Image(systemName:
    ''exclamationmark.triangle.fill'')
      .foregroundColor(.orange)
    Text(''Apple Intelligence not available
      on this device'')
  }
  .padding()
  .background(Color.orange.opacity(0.1))
}
 Spacer()
```

We are using the exclamation mark triangle SF Symbol, and we provide sufficient spacing for the notification to be shown. The view can be seen in Figure 6.22 where we have forced the `modelAvailable` state variable to be false.

We are now going to concentrate on writing the function to call the Foundation Models framework to carry out the summarisation task. After the declaration of the `checkModelAvailability` function, type the following swift code:

```
func summariseText() {
  guard modelAvailable else {
    errorMessage = ''Apple Intelligence is not
      available.''
    showError = true
    return
  }
  isProcessing = true
  summaryText = ''''

  Task {
    do {
      let session = LanguageModelSession()

      let prompt = """
        Summarise the following text concisely,
        capturing the main points in 2-3 sentences:

        \(inputText)

        Provide only the summary, no additional
        explanation.
```

We first check that the model is available.

Toggle the flag to indicate that the processing is taking place and reset the summary text string.

Start a task by initialising our `LanguageModelSession`.

Set up a suitable prompt.

Wait for a response.

```
        """

        let response = try await session.respond(
          to: prompt)

        await MainActor.run {
          summaryText = response.content
          isProcessing = false
        }
    } catch {
      await MainActor.run {
        errorMessage = error.localizedDescription
        showError = true
        isProcessing = false
      }
    }
  }
}
```

Capture the content of the response.

In case there is an error, we catch it and show a suitable message.

The function above is where the app stops being polite and starts being intelligent. We begin defensively by checking that Apple Intelligence is actually available on the device. Once availability is confirmed, we flip the processing flag and clear any previous output so the UI can signal that something clever is about to happen. The real work then takes place inside an asynchronous task, where we initialise a `LanguageModelSession` and construct a prompt that is deliberately opinionated: Concise, focused, and strictly no waffle. The session call waits patiently for the model to

There is little point asking a model to summarise anything if it does not exist.

respond, after which we hop back onto the main thread to update the interface with the generated summary. Finally, because reality has a habit of intervening, we wrap the whole affair in error handling, ensuring that if anything goes wrong, the user is informed politely rather than being left staring at a spinning wheel and questioning their life choices.

We are almost there. The last thing we need to do is to call the summarising function when the button is tapped. Look for the button declaration in the navigation view and add the function name to the action as follows:

```
...
Button(action: { summariseText() }) {
...
```

We simply call our function as an action for our button and we are done!

And that is it! You can now launch your app, enter some text and request your summary. A typical view would look similar to that in Figure 6.23. We launch our app, and at the click of a button we get our summarised text. Such an app would have been science fiction a decade ago. Today, it is a few views, a button, and a call to a foundation model running on a device that fits in your pocket.

Somewhere, a Starfleet engineer is quietly nodding in approval.

Foundation models do not replace the techniques we have discussed earlier in this book and its companion *Data Science and Analytics with Python*[19]. Linear models, decision trees, classifiers, graphs and bespoke pipelines remain essential tools. What foundation models offer is a new layer of abstraction, one that allows us to build data products that feel less like algorithms and more like collaborators.

[19] Rogel-Salazar, J. (2025). *Data Science and Analytics with Python*. Chapman & Hall/CRC Data Mining and Knowledge Discovery Series. CRC Press.

Just do not feed them after midnight!

Figure 6.23: The final Text Summariser app. We enter some text, tap the Summarise button and get our summary. All is done with the power of Foundation Models.

6.6 *Summary*

As WE SAID AT THE beginning of this chapter, we have indeed covered a lot of ground. And yet, there are still quite a few areas that we can explore in a deeper way. There are also many more subjects we have not touched on at all. In this last chapter we have looked into the perennial issue of bringing our models, predictions and solutions to our customers, users and stakeholders.

We provided a working definition for a data product as one that meets the needs, wants and/or requirements of our users through the use of data. We saw that it is of particular importance to take into account any development considerations around data. This may include things such as its availability, processing, meaning and understanding, to name a few. We also need to include in our development cycles the usage of data science techniques, going beyond data analysis.

We have also explored the complexity of data products: Ranging from raw data and algorithms through to automated decision-making. The vast majority of our discussions before this chapter have been centred around the usage of data, and data science techniques, by Jackalope data scientists. In this chapter we were actually interested in bringing the fruit of our efforts to a non-technical audience too. To that end, we explored the requirements of a multi-functional team including the need, not just for data scientists, but also data architects, engineers, product managers and subject matter experts.

As a way to bring our trained models to our potential users, in this chapter we looked at building a couple of applications that can be deployed in a mobile device. In this case we have chosen to explore the Apple ecosystem including Xcode, Swift, SwiftUI, Core ML and Foundation Models. We saw how Core ML offers us, Pythonistas, a way to convert our trained models into a format that can be integrated within an app, and be brought to the hands of our users. Core ML tools enable us to translate a scikit-learn model into the `.mlmodel` format used by the iOS, iPadOS and MacOS applications we intend to develop, closing the development cycle.

We used a dataset to make predictions of the value of a property in the California area (in the 1990s). In order to keep our discussion manageable for the scope of the chapter, we used a linear regression model, covering the different stages of the data science workflow: From data understanding to exploration, model training and testing and finally deployment.

Also, we used Apple's Foundation Models framework to demonstrate how existing frameworks enable us to create data product, using large language models directly in users' devices. We developed a Swift application that summarises text provided by the user. Although technically this is not Python, I believe that it demonstrates the evolution that a Jackalope Data Scientist needs to experience when bringing machine learning and artificial intelligence workflows to life in the form of data products.

As we noted in the companion volume of this book, *there is no such a thing as a perfect model, only good enough ones*, and thus the model we present to our users may not be the one and only model we develop, tweak, improve and supersede. We can continue using anthropomorphic language to refer to models that *learn*, *see*, *understand* and *recognise*, but we will not be able to disguise the fact that mathematics, statistics and software development sit at the heart of our efforts. Enabling those efforts has been the intention of this, and its companion, book. Enjoy!

A

Information Criteria

IN OUR TIME SERIES DISCUSSION in Chapter 1, we mentioned our interest in determining the current value of a series based on the past observations. We saw a few models that can be used, and in many cases it involves how many lag terms we need to include. The coefficients of these terms provide us with information about the effects of the past in predicting future values.

When adding more terms we are effectively gaining information, but inevitably at the same time we make our model more complex. In order to balance this dichotomy, in many other cases we use regularisation. Various information criteria help us with this regularisation task by balancing the information gained by including additional lag terms versus increasing the complexity of our model.

Some of the most frequently used information criteria include the Akaike information criterion (AIC)[1], the Bayesian—sometimes referred to as Schwarz—information

[1] Akaike, H. (1969). Fitting autoregressive models for prediction. *Annals of the Institute of Statistical Mathematics* 2(1), 243–247.

criterion (BIC)[2], or the Hannan-Quinn information criterion (HQIC)[3].

[2] Schwarz, G. (1978). Estimating the dimension of a model. *The Annals of Statistics* 6(2), 461–464.
[3] Hannan, E.J. and Quinn, B. G. (1979). The determination of the order of an autoregression. *Journal of the Royal Statistical Society, Series B* 41, 190–195.

In general, the information criteria mentioned above have the form:

$$IC_k = \log \hat{\sigma}_k^2 + \frac{kp_n}{n}, \tag{A.1}$$

where $\hat{\sigma}_k$ is the standard deviation to be estimated when k parameters are to be determined, and n is the number of observations. The first term in the expression above is the goodness-of-fit, which is to be balanced with the second term which effectively measures the complexity of the model. For each of the information criteria, the coefficient in this penalty term takes the form:

$$p_n = \begin{cases} 2, & \text{for AIC.} \\ \log n, & \text{for BIC.} \\ 2\log\log n, & \text{for HQIC.} \end{cases} \tag{A.2}$$

In each case, the aim is to find the model with the lowest value of the selected information criterion.

B

Power Iteration

Let A be an $n \times n$ matrix. We start with an arbitrary initial vector $\mathbf{x}^{(0)}$, and we form the vector sequence $\left\{\mathbf{x}^{(k)}\right\}_{k=0}^{\infty}$ by defining:

$$\mathbf{x}^{(k)} = A\mathbf{x}^{(k-1)}, \quad k = 1, 2, \ldots \tag{B.1}$$

It is clear from the expression above that:

$$\mathbf{x}^{(k)} = A^k \mathbf{x}^{(0)}. \tag{B.2}$$

The main idea behind power iteration is that $\mathbf{x}^{(k)}$ will converge to an eigenvector associated with the eigenvalue of the largest magnitude.

In general, we are interested only in the direction, not necessarily in the length, of the eigenvector. In practical terms, it is best practice to include a normalisation step to Equation (B.1). This leads us to the power iteration algorithm as follows:

1. Start with a vector $\mathbf{x}^{(0)}$ with $||\mathbf{x}^{(0)}|| = 1$

2. $k = 0$

3. Repeat

4. $\quad k = k + 1$

5. $\quad \mathbf{y}^{(k)} = A\mathbf{x}^{(k-1)}$

6. $\quad \mu_k = \|\mathbf{y}^{(k)}\|$

7. $\quad \mathbf{x}^{(k)} = \mathbf{y}^{(k)} / \mu_k$

8. Until a convergence criterion is satisfied.

All the vectors $\mathbf{x}^{(k)}$ generated by the algorithm have a norm equal to one. In other words, $\left\{\mathbf{x}^{(k)}\right\}_{k=0}^{\infty}$ is a sequence on the unit sphere in n dimensions.

C

The Softmax Function and Its Derivative

WE HAVE ENCOUNTERED THE SOFTMAX function in Chapter 4 and given its importance in the context of activation functions for neural networks; we would like to cover some information related to its characteristics, including its derivative.

The softmax function is a generalisation of the sigmoid function. It takes real values as input and maps them to a probability distribution where entry is in the range $(0, 1]$. Furthermore, all the entries add up to 1. We know from Chapter 4 that the function is given by:

$$\text{softmax}(z_i) = \sigma(z_i) = \frac{\exp(z_i)}{\sum_{k=1}^{N} \exp(z_k)}, \text{ for } i = 1, \ldots, k. \quad \text{(C.1)}$$

We can see that $\sigma(z_i)$ is always positive and is bounded between 0 and 1. If we were to evaluate the function for the elements $[0, 1, 2, 3, 4]$ we have that the function will return the values $[0.0116562, 0.0316849, 0.0861285, 0.2341216, 0.6364086]$ which add up to 1. In other words, with this function we find a "soft" version of the maximum, where the maximal input gets a proportionally large contribution compared to the other elements, but all getting part of it.

The characteristics of the function are such that it is suitable to be used for probabilistic interpretation. In cases where we have multiple classes, we can use the function to assign probabilities for an input to belong to each of the classes.

It is bounded between 0 and 1 and the values add up to 1.

In the context of activation functions in neural networks, the softmax function plays an important role, particularly in the output layer, and as such we require its derivative so that we can perform backpropagation. The derivative of the softmax function is therefore expressed as:

$$\frac{\partial\sigma(z_i)}{\partial z_j} = \frac{\partial \frac{e^{z_i}}{\sum_{k=1}^{N} e^{a_k}}}{\partial z_j}. \tag{C.2}$$

We can apply the quotient rule to the expression above such that $g = e^{z_i}$ and $h = \sum_{k=1}^{N} e^{z_k}$ and thus:

$$\begin{aligned}
\frac{\partial\sigma(z_i)}{\partial z_j} &= \frac{\frac{\partial e^{z_i}}{\partial z_j}\sum_{k=1}^{N} e^{z_k} - e^{z_i}\frac{\partial}{\partial z_j}\left(\sum_{k=1}^{N} e^{z_k}\right)}{\left(\sum_{k=1}^{N} e^{z_k}\right)^2} \\
&= \frac{\frac{\partial e^{z_i}}{\partial z_j}}{\sum_{k=1}^{N} e^{z_k}} - \frac{e^{z_i}\sum_{k=1}^{N}\frac{\partial}{\partial z_j}e^{z_k}}{\left(\sum_{k=1}^{N} e^{z_k}\right)^2} \\
&= \delta_{ij}\frac{e^{z_i}}{\sum_{k=1}^{N} e^{z_k}} - \frac{e^{z_i}}{\sum_{k=1}^{N} e^{z_k}}\frac{e^{z_j}}{\sum_{k=1}^{N} e^{z_k}} \qquad \text{(C.3)} \\
&= \sigma(z_i)\left(\delta_{ij} - \sigma(z_j)\right) \qquad \text{(C.4)}
\end{aligned}$$

where δ_{ij} is the Kronecker delta function.

C.1 Numerical Stability

WHEN IMPLEMENTING COMPUTATION FOR THE softmax function, we need to take into account the presence of numerical instability for large input values. This is related to the calculation of exponential functions involved in the definition of softmax.

Normalisation of the inputs can be achieved with the introduction of an arbitrary constant C as follows:

$$\sigma(z_i) = \frac{\exp(z_i)}{\sum_{k=1}^{N} \exp(z_k)} = \frac{C\exp(z_i)}{\sum_{k=1}^{N} C\exp(z_k)} \tag{C.5}$$

Using the properties of the exponential function, we are able to write the expression above as:

$$\sigma(z_i) = \frac{\exp(z_i + \log C)}{\sum_{k=1}^{N} \exp(z_k + \log C)} \tag{C.6}$$

where $\log C$ is still an arbitrary constant we can choose. One option is $-\max[z_1, z_2, \ldots, z_i]$ which has the effect of shifting the inputs to a range close to zero.

D

The Derivative of the Cross-Entropy Loss Function

GIVEN THE CROSS-ENTROPY LOSS function:

$$L = -\sum_i y_i \log \hat{y}_i = -\sum y_i \log \sigma(z_i), \qquad \text{(D.1)}$$

where $\sigma(z_i)$ is the softmax function, we want to obtain the derivative with respect to the parameter z_j.

$$\begin{aligned} \frac{\partial L}{\partial z_j} &= -\sum_i y_i \frac{\partial \log \sigma(z_i)}{\partial z_j}, \\ &= \\ &= -\sum_i y_i \frac{1}{\sigma(z_i)} \frac{\partial \sigma(z_i)}{\partial z_j}. \end{aligned} \qquad \text{(D.2)}$$

We need to calculate the derivative of the softmax function, and information about this can be seen in Appendix C.

There are two cases, one for $i = j$ and the other for $i \neq j$:

$$\frac{\partial L}{\partial z_j} = -y_i(1 - \sigma(z_i)) - \sum_{i \neq j} y_i \frac{-\sigma(z_i)\sigma(z_j)}{\sigma(z_i)},$$

$$= -y_i + y_i\sigma(z_i) + \sum_{i \neq j} y_i\sigma(z_j),$$

$$= \sigma(z_i)\sum_i y_i - y_i = \sigma(z_i) - y_i, \qquad \text{(D.3)}$$

as $\sum_i y_i = 1$.

Bibliography

ACE 2004 Multilingual Training Corpus. https://catalog.ldc.upenn.edu/ LDC2005T09.

Address Before a Joint Session of the Congress. Barack Obama. 44th President of the United States: 2009-2017. https://www.presidency.ucsb.edu/ node/286218.

Beautiful Soup. https://www.crummy.com/ software/BeautifulSoup/.

Chardet. https://chardet.readthedocs.io.

Cursive Re. https://github.com/Bogdanp/ cursive_re.

re - Regular expression operations. https://docs.python.org/3.6/ library/re.html.

Scrapy. https://scrapy.org.

spaCy. https://spacy.io.

Unicode 16.0. http://www.unicode.org/ versions/Unicode16.0.0/.

Abadi, M. et al. (2015). TensorFlow: Large-scale machine learning on heterogeneous systems. http://tensorflow.org/. Software available from tensorflow.org.

Akaike, H. (1969). Fitting autoregressive models for prediction. *Annals of the Institute of Statistical Mathematics* 2(1), 243–247.

Anaconda (2025). Anaconda Distribution. `https://www.anaconda.com/download/`.

Apache Airflow (2014). Apache Airflow Documentation. https://airflow.apache.org. Accessed: 2019-09-30.

Apple Inc. (2014). Swift programming language. `https://swift.org`.

Apple Inc. (2017a). Core ML tools. https://github.com/apple/coremltools. Accessed: 2025-12-21.

Apple Inc. (2017b). Core ML — integrate machine learning models into your app. Accessed: 2025-12-21.

Apple Inc. (2019a). Apple Developer. https://developer.apple.com. Accessed: 2025-12-26.

Apple Inc. (2019b). Create ML — train machine learning models. Accessed: 2025-12-21.

Apple Inc. (2025). Apple Developer—Foundation Models. https://developer.apple.com/documentation/foundationmodels. Accessed: 2025-12-26.

Archer, S. (2017). Apple hits a record high after crushing earnings (AAPL). http://markets.businessinsider.com/news/stocks/apple-stock-price- record-high-after-crushing-earnings -2017-8-100222647. Accessed: 2018-05-01.

Ball, W.W.R. and Coxeter, H.S.M. (1987). *Mathematical Recreations and Essays*. Dover Recreational Math Series. Dover Publications.

Bapat, R., T. Raghavan, C. U. Press, T. S, G. Rota, B. Doran, P. Flajolet, M. Ismail, T. Lam, et al. (1997). *Nonnegative Matrices and Applications*. Encyclopedia of Mathematics and its Applications. Cambridge University Press.

Barto, A. G., R. S. Sutton, and C. W. Anderson (1983). Neuronlike adaptive elements that can solve difficult learning control problems. *IEEE Transactions on Systems, Man, and Cybernetics SMC-13*(5), 834–846.

Bengio, Y. and Ducharme, R. and Vincent, P. and Jauvin, C. (2003). A neural probabilistic language model. *Journal of Machine Learning Research 3*, 1137–1155.

Blei, D. M., Ng, A. Y., and Jordan, M. I. (2003). Latent Dirichlet Allocation. *Journal of Machine Learning Research 3*, 993–1022.

Box, G. and G. Jenkins (1976). *Time series analysis: forecasting and control*. Holden-Day series in time series analysis and digital processing. Holden-Day.

Brown, T., F. Mann, N. Ryder, M. Subbiah, et al. (2020). Language models are few-shot learners. In H. Larochelle, M. Ranzato, R. Hadsell, M. Balcan, and H. Lin (Eds.), *Advances in Neural Information Processing Systems*, Volume 33, pp. 1877–1901. Curran Associates, Inc.

Brownlee, J (2018). Airline passengers. https://github.com/jbrownlee/

Datasets/blob/master/airline-passengers.csv. Accessed: 2025-07-18.

Butler, S. (1999). Erewhon; Or, Over the Range. Project Gutenberg https://www.gutenberg.org/ebooks/1906. Accessed: 2025-10-10.

Carroll, L. and J. Tenniel (1897). *Through the Looking Glass: And what Alice Found There*. Altemus' illustrated young people's library. Henry Altemus Company.

Cho, K., B. van Merrienboer, et al. (2014). Learning phrase representations using RNN encoder-decoder for statistical machine translation. *CoRR abs/1406.1078.*

Chollet, F. et al. (2015). Keras. `https://github.com/fchollet/keras`.

Data61, C. (2018). Stellargraph machine learning library. `https://github.com/stellargraph/stellargraph`.

Deerwester, S. and Dumais, S.T. and Furnas, G.W. and Landauer, T.K. and Harshman, R. (1990). Indexing by latent semantic analysis. *Journal of the American Society for Information Science 41*(6), 391–407.

Devlin, J., M.-W. Chang, K. Lee, and K. Toutanova (2018). BERT: Pre-training of Deep Bidirectional Transformers for Language Understanding. *arXiv preprint arXiv:1810.04805*.

Euler, L. (1736). Solutio problematis ad geometriam situs pertinentis. *Comment. Acad. Sci. U. Petrop. 8*, 128–140.

Fagles, R. (1997). *The Odyssey*. A Penguin Book. Penguin Books.

Firth, J.R. (1957). A synopsis of linguistic theory 1930–1955. In *Studies in Linguistic Analysis*. Philological Society.

Fortunato, S. (2010). Community detection in graphs. *Phys. Rep. 486*(3-5), 75–174.

Gabasova, E. (2016). *Star Wars* social network. https://doi.org/10.5281/ zenodo.1411479.

Girvan, M. and Newman, M.E.J (2002). Community structure in social and biological networks. *Proc. Natl. Acad. Sci. USA 99*, 7821–7826.

Glenberg, A.M. (1997). What memory is for. *Behav. Brain Sci. 20*, 1–55.

Goodfellow, I., J. Pouget-Abadie, M. Mirza, B. Xu, D. Warde-Farley, S. Ozair, A. Courville, and Y. Bengio (2014). Generative Adversarial Nets. In *Advances in Neural Information Processing Systems (NIPS)*, pp. 2672–2680.

Grandjean, M. (2016). A social network analysis of Twitter: Mapping the digital humanities community. *Cogent Arts and Humanities 3*, 1–14.

Greff, K., Srivastava, R. K., Koutník, J., et al. (2017). LSTM: A Search Space Odyssey. *IEEE Trans. Neural Netw. and Learning Sys. 28*(10), 2222–2232.

Hannan, E.J. and Quinn, B. G. (1979). The determination of the order of an autoregression. *Journal of the Royal Statistical Society, Series B 41*, 190–195.

Hinton, G. E. and R. Salakhutdinov (2006). Reducing the dimensionality of data with neural networks. *Science 313* 5786, 504–7.

Hinton, G. E., Osindero, S., and Teh, Y.-W. (2006). A Fast Learning Algorithm for Deep Belief Nets. *Neural Computation 18*, 1527–1554.

Hochreiter, S. and Schmidhuber, J. (1997). Long short-term memory. *Neural. Comput.* 9(8), 1735–1780.

Hudson, P. (2015). *Hacking with Swift*. HackingWithSwift.com. Online tutorial/book.

Hugging Face. (2019). Sentence-transformer all-MiniLM-L6-V2. https://huggingface.co/sentence-transformers/all-MiniLM-L6-v2. Accessed: 2025-08-07.

Intel OpenVINO Team (2025). OpenVINO Documentation. `https://docs.openvino.ai/`. Accessed: 2025-09-22.

Ioffe, S. and C. Szegedy (2015). Batch normalization: Accelerating deep network training by reducing internal covariate shift. *CoRR abs/1502.03167*.

JAX Authors (2024). JAX: High Performance Array Computing. `https://docs.jax.dev/en/latest/`. Accessed: 2025-09-22.

Jumper, J., R. Evans, A. Pritzel, T. Green, M. Figurnov, Ronneberger, et al. (2021). Highly accurate protein structure prediction with AlphaFold. *Nature 596*(7873), 583–589.

Karinthy, F. (1929). Chains in Everything is Different. Online at http://bit.ly/karinthy_chains. Translated from Hungarian and annotated by Adam Makkai. Edited by E Jankó.

Karpathy, A. (2015). The Unreasonable Effectiveness of Recurrent Neural Networks. https://karpathy.github.io/2015/05/21/rnn-effectiveness/. Accessed: 2025-10-05.

Kelley Pace, R. and R. Barry (1997). Sparse spatial autoregressions. *Statistics & Probability Letters 33*(3), 291–297.

Kingma, D. P. and J. Ba (2014). Adam: A method for stochastic optimization. arxXiv:1412.6980. Comment: Published as a conference paper at the 3rd International Conference for Learning Representations, San Diego, 2015.

Krizhevsky, A. (2009). Learning multiple layers of features from tiny images. Technical Report TR-2009, University of Toronto, Toronto.

LeCun, Y., L. Bottou, Y. Bengio, and P. Haffner (1998). Gradient-based learning applied to document recognition. *Proceedings of the IEEE 86*(11), 2278–2324.

LeCun, Y., Boser, B., Denker, J. S., et al. (1989). Backpropagation applied to handwritten zip code recognition. *Neural Computation 1*(4), 541–551.

Masters, D. and C. Luschi (2018). Revisiting Small Batch Training for Deep Neural Networks. *Computing Research Repository http://arxiv.org/abs/1804.07612.*

McCulloch, W. S. and Pitts, W. (1943). A logical calculus of the ideas immanent in nervous activity. *Bull. of Math. Biophysics 5*(4), 115–133.

McKinney, W. (2012). *Python for Data Analysis: Data Wrangling with Pandas, NumPy, and IPython*. O'Reilly Media.

McKinney, W. (2011). pandas: a foundational python library for data analysis and statistics. Python for High Performance and Scientific Computing: O'Reilly Media, Inc.

Microsoft DeepSpeed Team (2025). Deepspeed documentation. `https://deepspeed.readthedocs.io/en/latest/`. Accessed: 2025-09-22.

Mikolov, T., K. Chen, G. Corrado, and J. Dean (2013). Efficient estimation of word representations in vector space. *CoRR abs/1301.3781*.

Mikolov, T., I. Sutskever, et al. (2013). Distributed Representations of Words and Phrases and Their Compositionality. In *Proceedings of the 26th International Conference on Neural Information Processing Systems - Volume 2*, NIPS'13, USA, pp. 3111–3119. Curran Associates Inc.

Milgram, S. (1967). The small world problem. *Psych. Today 1*(1), 60–67.

Minsky, M., S. Papert, and L. Bottou (2017). *Perceptrons: An Introduction to Computational Geometry*. The MIT Press. MIT Press.

Moody, J. and White, D. (2003). Social cohesion and embeddedness: A hierarchical conception of social groups. *Am. Soc. Rev. 68*(1), 103–128.

Noichl, M. (2017). Relationships between Philosophers, 600 b.c - 160 b.c. https://homepage.univie.ac.at/noichlm94/full/Greeks/index.html. Accessed: 2019-02-18.

OpenAI (2023a). ChatGPT (Mar 14 version) Large Language Model. `https://chat.openai.com/chat`.

OpenAI (2023b). GPT-4 Technical Report. arXiv preprint arXiv:2303.08774.

OpenAI (2025). OpenAI Python API Library. https://github.com/openai/openai-python. Accessed: 2025-11-08.

Papachristou, N. et al. (2019). Network Analysis of the Multidimensional Symptom Experience of Oncology. *Scientific Reports* 9(1), 2258.

Pedregosa, F., G. Varoquaux, A. Gramfort, V. Michel, et al. (2011). Scikit-learn: Machine learning in Python. *Journal of Machine Learning Research 12*, 2825–2830.

Pennington, J., R. Socher, and C. Manning (2014, October). GloVe: Global vectors for word representation. In A. Moschitti, B. Pang, and W. Daelemans (Eds.), *Proceedings of the 2014 Conference on Empirical Methods in Natural Language Processing (EMNLP)*, Doha, Qatar, pp. 1532–1543. Association for Computational Linguistics.

Press, W., S. Teukolsky, W. Vetterling, and B. Flannery (2007). *Numerical Recipes 3rd Edition: The Art of Scientific Computing*. Cambridge University Press.

Pritchard, J. K., Stephens, M., and Donnelly, P. (2000). Inference of population structure using multilocus genotype data. *Genetics 155*(2), 945–956.

Puterman, M. L. (1994). *Markov Decision Processes: Discrete Stochastic Dynamic Programming*. John Wiley & Sons.

Python Software Foundation (1995). Python reference manual. `http://www.python.org`.

Radford, A., L. Metz, and S. Chintala (2016). Unsupervised Representation Learning with Deep Convolutional Generative Adversarial Networks. *arXiv preprint arXiv:1511.06434*.

Radford, A., J. Wu, R. Child, D. Luan, D. Amodei, and I. Sutskever (2019). Language models are unsupervised multitask learners. *OpenAI Technical Report*.

Řehůřek, R. and P. Sojka (2010, May). Software Framework for Topic Modelling with Large Corpora. In *Proceedings of the LREC 2010 Workshop on New Challenges for NLP Frameworks*, Valletta, Malta, pp. 45–50. ELRA. `http://is.muni.cz/publication/884893/en`.

Reimers, Nils and Gurevych, Iryna (2019, 11). Sentence-BERT: Sentence Embeddings using Siamese BERT-Networks. In *Proceedings of the 2019 Conference on Empirical Methods in Natural Language Processing*. Association for Computational Linguistics.

Reitz, K. Requests - http for humans. http://docs.python-requests.org/en/master/.

Rogel-Salazar, J. (2016, Jan). Data Science Tweets. https://doi.org/10.6084/ m9.figshare.2062551.v1.

Rogel-Salazar, J. (2018a, May). Apple Inc. Prices Apr 2017 - Apr 2018. https://doi.org /10.6084/m9.figshare.6339830.v1.

Rogel-Salazar, J. (2018b, Jun). Bitcoin/USD exchange rate Mar 31-Apr 3, 2016. https://doi.org /10.6084/m9.figshare.6452831.v1.

Rogel-Salazar, J. (2018c, Sep). Iris Webpage. https://doi.org /10.6084/m9.figshare.7053392.v4.

Rogel-Salazar, J. (2018d, Jul). Sunspots - Monthly Activity since 1749. https://doi.org /10.6084/m9.figshare.6728255.v1.

Rogel-Salazar, J. (2019a, Apr). *Star Wars* Network. https://doi.org/10.6084/ m9.figshare.7993292.v1.

Rogel-Salazar, J. (2019b, Aug). Neural Network - Observation dataset. https://doi.org/10.6084/ m9.figshare.9249074.v1.

Rogel-Salazar, J. (2019c, Apr). Zachary's karate club. https://doi.org/10.6084/ m9.figshare.7985174.v1.

Rogel-Salazar, J. (2023). *Statistics and Data Visualisation with Python*. Chapman & Hall/CRC The Python Series. CRC Press.

Rogel-Salazar, J. (2017). *Data Science and Analytics with Python*. Chapman & Hall/CRC Data Mining and Knowledge Discovery Series. CRC Press.

Rogel-Salazar, J (2025). CoreML—California Housing Pricer. https://github.com/rogelj/coreml_california_housing. Accessed: 2025-12-26.

Rogel-Salazar, J. (2025). *Data Science and Analytics with Python*. Chapman & Hall/CRC Data Mining and Knowledge Discovery Series. CRC Press.

Rosenblatt, F. (1962). *Principles of neurodynamics: perceptrons and the theory of brain mechanisms*. Report (Cornell Aeronautical Laboratory). Spartan Books.

Rumelhart, D. E., G. E. Hinton, and R. J. Williams (1986). Learning representations by back-propagating errors. *Nature 323*(6088), 533–536.

Russell, A. (2014). *Open Standards and the Digital Age*. Cambridge Studies in the Emerg. Cambridge University Press.

Said, S. E. and Dickey, D. A (1984). Testing for unit roots in autoregressive-moving average models of unknown order. *Biometrika 71(3)*, 599–607.

Salton, G., A. Wong, and Yang, C.S. (1975). A vector space model for automatic indexing. *Communications of the ACM 18*(11), 613–620.

Sanchez-Lengeling, B., C. Outeiral, G. Guimaraes, and A. Aspuru-Guzik (2017). Optimizing Distributions over Molecular Space with Deep Generative Models. ChemRxiv preprint, doi:10.26434/chemrxiv.5309668.v3.

Schrödinger, E. (1935). Die gegenwärtige Situation in der Quantenmechanik. *Naturwissenschaften* 23(48), 807–812.

Schuster, A. (1906). II. On the periodicities of sunspots. *Philosophical Transactions of the Royal Society of London A: Mathematical, Physical and Engineering Sciences 206*(402-412), 69–100.

Schwarz, G. (1978). Estimating the dimension of a model. *The Annals of Statistics 6*(2), 461–464.

Scientific Computing Tools for Python (2013). NumPy. `http://www.numpy.org`.

Simas, T. et al. (2017). Food-Bridging: A new network construction to unveil the principles of cooking. *Frontiers in ICT 4*, 14.

Spärck Jones K (1972). A statistical interpretation of term specificity and its application in retrieval. *Journal of Documentation 28*, 11–21.

Spotify (2014). Luigi. https://github.com/spotify/luigi. Accessed: 2019-09-30.

Stellman, A. and J. Greene (2014). *Learning Agile: Understanding Scrum, XP, Lean, and Kanban*. O'Reilly Media.

Sutskever, I., J. Martens, G. Dahl, and G. Hinton (2013, 17–19 Jun). On the importance of initialization and momentum in deep learning. In S. Dasgupta and D. McAllester (Eds.), *Proceedings of the 30th International Conference on Machine Learning*, Volume 28 of *Proceedings of Machine Learning Research*, Atlanta, Georgia, USA, pp. 1139–1147. PMLR.

Sutton, R. S., D. McAllester, S. Singh, and Y. Mansour (2000). Policy gradient methods for reinforcement learning with function approximation. In *Advances in Neural Information Processing Systems*, pp. 1057–1063.

van Rossum, G. (2009). Text Vs. Data Instead of Unicode Vs. 8-bit. https://docs.python.org/release/3.0.1/whatsnew/3.0.html.

Vaswani, A., N. Shazeer, N. Parmar, et al. (2017). Attention Is All You Need. In *Advances in Neural Information Processing Systems*, pp. 5998–6008. Curran Associates, Inc.

Vincent D. Blondel, Guillaume, J.-L., Lambiotte, R., and Lefebvre, E. (2008, Oct.). Fast unfolding of communities in large networks. *J. Stat. Mech-Theory E 2008*(10), P10008.

Watts, D. and Strogatz, S. (1998). Collective dynamics of small-world networks. *Nature* 393(1), 440–442.

Weir, A. (2022). *Project Hail Mary: A Novel.* Random House Publishing Group.

Werbos, P. (1994). *The Roots of Backpropagation: From Ordered Derivatives to Neural Networks and Political Forecasting.* Adaptive and Cognitive Dynamic Systems: Signal Processing, Learning, Communications and Control. Wiley.

Wolf, T., L. Début, V. Sanh, J. Chaumond, C. Delangue, et al. (2020, October). Transformers: State-of-the-art natural language processing. In *Proceedings of the 2020 Conference on Empirical Methods in Natural Language Processing: System Demonstrations*, Online, pp. 38–45. Association for Computational Linguistics.

Yu, L., W. Zhang, J. Wang, and Y. Yu (2017). SeqGAN: Sequence Generative Adversarial Nets with Policy Gradient. In *AAAI Conference on Artificial Intelligence*, pp. 2852–2858.

Zachary, W. W. (1977). An information flow model for conflict and fission in small groups. *J. Anthropol. Res.* 33(4), 452–473.

Index

For Product Safety Concerns and Information please contact our EU representative GPSR@taylorandfrancis.com Taylor & Francis Verlag GmbH, Kaufingerstraße 24, 80331 München, Germany

Batch number: 10732716

Printed by Printforce, the Netherlands